Satya Chandra Mukerji

Indian history of our own times

Satya Chandra Mukerji

Indian history of our own times

ISBN/EAN: 9783337305772

Printed in Europe, USA, Canada, Australia, Japan

Cover: Foto ©ninafisch / pixelio.de

More available books at **www.hansebooks.com**

INDIAN HISTORY

OF OUR OWN TIMES.

PART I, 1859-68.

BY

SATYA CHANDRA MUKERJI, M.A., B.L.

Vakil, High Court, N. W. Provinces.

OTHER TWO PARTS TO FOLLOW.

CALCUTTA:

PUBLISHED BY S. K. LAHIRI & CO.,
54, COLLEGE STREET.

1891.

[*All Rights Reserved.*]

CONTENTS.

	Pages.
INTRODUCTORY	1—7
CHAPTER I (1859)	9—19
CHAPTER II (1860)	20—29
CHAPTER III (1861)	30—38
CHAPTER IV (1862)	39—50
CHAPTER V (1863)	51—60
CHAPTER VI (1864)	61—73
CHAPTER VII (1865)	74—84
CHAPTER VIII (1866)	85—94
CHAPTER IX (1867)	95—106
CHAPTER X (1868)	107—120
CHAPTER XI (THE FIRST DECADE UNDER THE CROWN)	121—145

INDIAN HISTORY OF OUR OWN TIMES.

INTRODUCTORY.

Since some years past I have conceived a strong desire to bring out such a work as the one, now before the public. There is nothing which is so entertaining and intensely interesting as a faithful narration of the various phases of social and political history of one's own times, and of the times immediately preceding them, which helps the thoughtful mind in fully grasping and at times anticipating the phenomena in the various spheres of life around him. To the average mind, the history of the past is comparatively dull reading, but the history of those times wherein we live, affording a clear and penetrative insight into the great social and political landmarks visible all round us, is considered to be a thing which every man of culture ought, above all things, to care about. This is a sentiment not only accidentally prevailing among the majority of the public who can read and write, in the greater part of the civilized world, but is founded upon deep-rooted tendencies of human nature. The abstruser branches of human learning must always remain the monopoly of the gifted few, but history if written in a popular style and contain graphic illustrations of the men, the manners, the social and political phenomena actually observed or observable, either in remote times or in our own generation, has instructed and delighted the reading public in every age and country, and has profitably occupied leisure hours otherwise spent too often in moral or intellectual dissipation. The taste for newspaper—reading which in the most civilised countries has grown to be a passion and has been turned to be almost one of the necessaries of life among the cultured classes is but one patent illustration of the truth, stated above. But newspapers contain only the news of the day or the hour, ordinarily read but once and soon forgotten. No one except the intending historian or the professed scholar ever cares to busy himself with the files of old newspapers. At the end of each generation in uneventful times, and at the end of every eventful period, it is highly necessary that a connected account in a narrative form of the men and measures of the time that has gone by should be available to the enquiring public. Those who have already reached the middle age of life will find in such a work the recapitulation of that period they have lived, and will be able to reflect by the calm light of their maturer years, events which once aroused their interest and curiosity in younger days, and the men just beginning their lives in the world will find in it those materials which are absolutely necessary to a proper understanding of the current literature of their society. In England and other countries of civilised Europe contemporary history is so fashionable a study, and so necessary to the young politician or the young journalist, that books on that subject are available by scores, but in India it is unfortunately quite otherwise.

All the histories of India that are now available to the literary public end with the Indian Mutiny,—that terrible catastrophe which shifted the administration of the land from the hands of the East Indian Company to those of the Crown. Prior to that exciting period many capable historians have written delightful works on many of the particular periods of Indian history, which mostly are the product of personal observation, and rare literary gifts,—works widely read not only in India but wherever the English language is known. But all such works terminate with Kaye and Malleson's splendid volumes on the Indian Mutiny. The grand evolution of Indian social and political life, during the first thirty years of administration under the Crown, a period which is characterized by steady and rapid progress, and reconstruction on a sure and improved basis on the ruins of a fallen administration, has not yet been put before the public in a readable shape by any writer whatever. Those who have lived through the past thirty years will readily admit that it was a most interesting period of peaceful reconstruction in every department of administration, in which work the experiences of the past hundred years of British rule had been wisely utilized. Some official writers and some casual travellers have occasionally, dealt with certain detached portions of this period in works that acquired a contemporaneous celebrity, but a connected picture of the whole period has not yet been forthcoming. It is universally admitted however, that travellers from foreign lands reproduce but hastily conceived impressions, without any thorough mastery of the Indian sociology and polity, and their works though constituting charming reading in newspapers and periodicals can hardly be transferred to the sober realms of history. Official writers on Indian affairs again labor under great disadvantage owing to the extreme reserve of oriental character. The growing taste for reading and writing for newspapers among the educated men in every part of India and the increased political activities manifest everywhere, render it imperatively necessary that this period of the history of India (from 1859-1889) wherein lie the germs of every institution of progress that seem flourishing round us, should be thoroughly and carefully studied. Those, whose duty or privilege it will be to aid in the advancement of Indian administration or civilization in any of its aspects, in the next generation should, above all things, take into consideration the history of the generation that is just gone by. Just after leaving the University of Calcutta, where I was fortunately the recipient of the best training in History and political economy available in the Presidency of Bengal, I cast about on all sides for any one book whence I could learn all about the political measures and the social life of the first generation of direct Indian administration by Her Gracious Imperial Majesty, but to my deep regret, I found that I shall have to go to the files of newspapers for any such entertaining and profitable study. I do not unfortunately belong to the leisured classes and being under the necessity of following a profession I could with much difficulty spare the time that this process of study implied. I have therefore made up my mind to do what I can to remove all such difficulties from the path of the future student of Indian contemporaneous history. In attempting to write the following pages, I am but too conscious of my own imperfections for the momentous task that I have undertaken. How much I wish this duty to our country had been taken up by some one of that long array of able men whom our country has produced, and who would unite to natural abilities and acquired culture, the most unlimited leisure and opportunities for threading out this subject in all its variety of details. But there is yet in our country such splendid careers open to every man of real abilities whether natural or acquired, that I am afraid they will not find time for that amount of miscellaneous drudgery which a work like this implies, and I thought, and perhaps rightly that I might with my limited culture, rush into a region where better men would fear to tread and should I prove a failure here, there would be no harm caused, as I am sure to be followed by abler men in the work of writing on this portion of Indian history, among my own countrymen. In the mere mechanical work of piling up facts on facts, one man has not much superiority over another, but my work will probably be without those acute and philosophic reflections that in the hands of the really finished scholar, enliven the narration of the driest details, and intersperse with attractive and central truths of life, any subject, however dull it may be to the average mind.

After having decided on undertaking this work, there still remained to me the difficult task of accurately settling its plan. I thought I might take each year by itself and availing myself of the learned retrospects of each year that appear in the columns of some Indian newspapers, I might give its history concisely. But this plan I decided, was hardly suited to a work which pretends to be a regular history of the period it treats of as its adoption would lead to frequent interruption in the chain of naration of any one or any connected set of historic phenomena. Nor did I think it wise to make the work merely a series of essays on detached subjects, which form the heads of discussion. After mature consideration I thought of adopting the plan that I have seen adopted by some of the greatest historians of the modern age of keeping intact the thread of narration of the main events and devote separate chapters to the discussion of those items that require a separate treatment. The fact, that I am a professional man, and that I can attend to this business, which has been lying nearest to my heart for some years, only in the intervals of professional labour, again compels me to place this book before the public in three parts. I shall take up a decade in each of the parts and deal with it as thoroughly as I can with reference to all the phases of activities visible through it. Should no unlucky interruptions intervene, I hope to place before the public, the completed work within a measurable distance of time.

I have also thought it proper to avoid long strings of names and places in describing a military campaign and while omitting no material details have confined myself to a general outline of every event in each year. The admonitions in their annual addresses of every vice-chancellor of that university where I laid the foundations of every thing I strive after now, to those situated like myself, with reference to employing their spare hours to those pursuits that were the delights of their academic days had a good deal to do towards my undertaking this work of patient and arduous labour. I shall feel very thankful if my work is at all deemed to be useful to that vast class of the educated Indian public for whom it has been mainly intended, and should any errors or defects meet the kind eye of any of my readers, or any suggestions of improvement occur to them, I shall respectfully solicit them to communicate the same to me. With many apologies for my shortcomings, and with the earnest hope that my work would be judged indulgently, I respectfully place this book in the hands of the educated Indian public.

SATYA CHANDRA MUKERJI.

INDIAN HISTORY OF OUR OWN TIMES.

PART THE FIRST.

CHAPTER I.

1859.

THE CLOSING SCENES OF THE MUTINY—The point from which we intend to take up the history of our own times, will be the year 1859. A vast catastrophe had just swept over the land, whose causes, many fertile brains were left to speculate upon. The old order of things gave place to the direct control of the British cabinet on Indian affairs. The local officials, no less than the British public, took notice of every circumstance that might in any way have contributed to the sharp malady of the body politic. The necessity of a centralized administration, of a due proportion in the numbers of the European and the native army, and of the use of every legitimate means for reconciling the vast body of alien population to British rule, became every day more and more apparent. The work of destruction had been going on for a tolerably long period of sharp disorder, the work of reconstruction was now to begin. The mutiny, it was readily perceived, was a mere military revolt. The vast mass of the Indian population had absolutely nothing to do with it. Some writers who lost their balance of mind on hearing the sad stories of the cruelties practised on English men and women by the mutineers in many of the great cities of the N. W. Provinces, indulged for a time in a sweeping denunciation of the native races of India and cried bitterly for their utter annihilation. But with the lapse of time and the soothing of angry and excited feelings it became clearly apparent that the native subjects of the East India Company had little or nothing to do with the rebellion. They had in most cases suffered as much from the rebellion as the English residents themselves, and many English officers, who have lived to tell the story of the rebellion to a later generation have borne testimony to the unflinching devotion with which many native gentlemen of rank and respectability did not hesitate, even at the peril of their own position, to shelter the English officers and their families wherever possible, even in the most excited districts. Before the beginning of 1859, the rebellion had been crushed out in the most important centres. Delhi, Agra and Lucknow had all passed again from the complete or the partial grasp of the mutineers, to the possession of the British. In all these great towns and many places elsewhere the mutineers gathered in large numbers and turned against the English Government all those appliances of civilized warfare and all that knowledge of military tactics that it had derived in the quarters and under the officers of the same government, and a race of valiant captains whom the times called forth had after many gallant deeds and much heroic struggle, succeeded during the troubled years of 1857 and 1858, in stamping out the flame of rebellion in the most populous provinces of India. The story of those heroic deeds and sufferings have been told to the world by men who could set off to the best advantage the tragic interest of that dark page of Indian History, and it would be idle to attempt to do anything more than incidentally to allude to them in this place. When the year 1859 opened, the last traces of the rebellion could only be found among the arid tracts, the dense jungles and the deep ravines of Central India. On the 18th of January 1859, Lord Canning from his Allahabad camp proclaimed in a state paper that the rebellion should be taken to have completely ended as far as Oudh and the North Western Provinces were concerned and gave the due meed of thanks to the army, through whose exertions this desirable result had been brought about, mentioning prominently its accomplished chief. But still the attention of the Governor-General had soon to be directed to the detached bands of rebels who still frequented parts south of Rajputana and the whole of Central India. In these regions, which are still in the possession of those who are known as the feudatory chiefs, the same system of strict surveillance does not exist as in British India, and the natural features of the country present many wooded hills, with steep and precipitious ascents, and many deep ravines, which easily harbour those who are at war with society and government. The mutineers, were condemend to the gallows wherover caught but a great number of them managed to escape in these disordered times and knowing that their discovery meant sure death, they preferred to die the death of soldiers to the ignoble one of criminals. Bands of such desperadoes, whom no motive on earth could again incline to lay aside their savage course, mustered sometimes in hundreds and thousands and took up their position either in the natural fastnesses of India, or in cities or villages which were too weak to offer them any resistance. They carried fire and sword in calm and peaceful villages and lived on plunder and rapine. The Governor-General rightly felt that these stray bands of marauders should be vigorously pursued and their career checked and the character of the military operations now undertaken, underwent a considerable change with the altered state of things. Numerous battalions were ordered to rove through the length and breadth of the disturbed tract of land and effectively crush the scattered bands, that still bade defiance to established authority. It would be tedious and positively distasteful to the general reader, were we to give a detailed account of the many skirmishes and encounters, that took place between the remnant bands of the mutineers and the British soldiery. They all resemble one another in their description, of which the official papers of the period are full, and they are not without those touches which human nature is always apt to display, when in interesting and critical situations. The only leader of note whom the British soldiery in work in Central India was most anxious to secure was, Tantia Topee. This intrepid Maharatta, had shown a rude genius for command and a dashing courage and in the closing scenes of the rebellion had taken as prominent a part as Nana Saheb himself. He was still wandering with a large following in the regions between the Chambal and the Nerbudda when he reached the territories of a chief, who was in his confidence and in the jungles of whose dominions he felt himself quite secure. This chief had a prominent trait of rude Asiatic character in him, that of playing a double game and it was through the information he supplied the British contingent with, as to the exact whereabouts of Tantia Topee that that dashing but cruel soldier was captured when fast asleep, and found himself in the hands of the countrymen of those whom he had assisted in butchering at Cawnpur. The fate that awaited him was too well known to him, and with the summary forms of a court martial he was sent on to eternity. The military operations in Central India were carried on under the directions of Sir Hugh Rose, an officer about whose merits many conflicting opinions have been pronounced in high quarters, but the ability and discretion he brought to bear on this occasion in the difficult task of completely subduing a wild tract of country, with chiefs on all sides who, to say the least required a careful management, will probably be universally admitted. The military operations in this direction were completely successful and soon brought all Central India to a state of peace and order. Some operations on a slight scale were also found necessary in Oudh where Sir Hope Grant pushed on detachments, to the north of the Goomtee and the Gogra and drove a large force of rebels to those jungles which extend for many miles together at the foot of the Himalayas, sheltering wild beasts and wilder men. Scattered troops drove every considerable band of rebels out of the limits of the province of Oudh, and when they sought protection in the Nepal territories the enlightened minister of that state Sir Jung Bahadur captured them and sent them on to receive the punishment for their past wrongs to the British Government. The Nana with a few followers managed to escape, nor has any authentic information been received of him ever afterwards. He was probably living in the disguise of an ascetic in the many inaccessible places to the north of India and the utmost efforts of the British Government failed either to capture him or to get the certain news of his death.

THE DUMPY MUTINY AND ARMY AMALGAMATION—Just after the closing scenes of the Indian rebellion have been recorded, we must notice the open manifestation of insubordinate spirit, by a section of the European army which event is sometimes called by the rather exaggerated title of the mutiny of the Dumpies. The news of the mutiny of the native troops and the cruel scenes enacted by them, had reached England in due course and spread there a good deal of alarm. It was thought fit by the authorities in England to send as many available regiments, as possible to aid the local Indian force and many of the irregular regiments of horse that had been raised for the closing operations of the Crimean War, were shipped off to this country along with some regular regiments. These irregular regiments of horse on arrival at the Indian Presidency towns were constituted into regular regiments of cavalry and on the transfer of the Government from the Company to the Crown were ordered to bear their allegiance to the English sovereign power. Unfortunately many of the privates in these irregular regiments were either raw recruits who did not care to stop in the country or men who in their own cities were out of all employment or the rejected of all professions. Finding the Government in a rather embarassed condition and depending solely on British bayonets after the recent volcanic eruption in the native army, these regiments, which unfortunately were full of unprincipled men, determined to squeeze what they could, out of the then unfortunate situation. They openly demanded that they should get a second bounty for being transferred to the service of the Crown and being primarily enlisted to bear allegiance to the Company and that Company having ceased to exist they claimed to be entitled to their discharge and free passage home. It is said that these malcontents in the European army found some lawyers to back up their pretensions and they asserted their claim with all the show of a legal right. The legal question was never formally raised nor was it of such a nature that it could have been formally raised, with success. But the European malcontents showed a passive disobedience to authority, in many large cantonments, such as Meerut, Allahabad and Berhampur. The experience of the past three years in dealing with a refractory spirit among the troops had evidently borne fruit and the tactics that had been so successfully used by the Punjab Government, in nipping the rebellion everywhere within its jurisdiction in the bud, began to be used. At every place where there was the slightest show of insubordination, the officers exhibited great firmness, insisted on an immediate compliance with the orders issued, seized the ringleaders and effectually punished them. These measures were sufficient to quell the disturbances in the bud, and it was only at Berhampur that any active preparations for hostilities had to be made, which fortunately enough did not come on. Some of the organs of public opinion remarked at the time that the European army had some real cause of grievance in as much as their services had not at all been taken notice of in the Queen's proclamation, but it was evident that the army wanted not an empty compliment but a substantial amount of money, and men in the search of solid gold can scarcely be pacified by any other thing. The Government at home granted discharge to all such as wanted it, some they transferred to the regiments then on active service in the Eastern waters against China, and others, who could not be identified with any recent manifestations they re-enlisted by the offer of a bounty. It is said that many of the discharged soldiers were again taken into the service in England. The European army in India which had become a huge and unwieldy body and grown out of all proportions to the need for it, owing to the feverish excitement in England, was considerably relieved by this process of pruning. With the armies of England and India owing allegiance to the same supreme power the scheme was set on foot of the amalgamation of both the armies into one homogenous whole. During the days of the East India Company the Company enlisted its own soldiers and settled the terms with the recruits, the European force in India constituting a purely local force. It was now proposed to place both the Indian and English army under the control of the English War Office and Lord Canning's government was asked to suggest a practical scheme for this object. The amalgamation was effected and India is now a partner with England with regard to the European portion of her army. Whether this arrangement has been one to the advantage of India is a question that has frequently been considered in later times, both in the despatches of the Government of India and the ablest organs of the native press. We shall have to refer again and again to the subject of military expenditure in the later portions of this work and we shall not anticipate the discussion at this place. Together with army amalgamation a good many changes were effected in army organization, which are scarcely intelligible to those who are unfamiliar with the details of regimental rank and allowances, and which changes did not come in force until they were repeatedly reconsidered by able committees in England. It was an open secret at the time and has been since affirmed emphatically by Mr. Henry Fawcett in his work on Indian Finance that the amalgamation of the Indian army took place against the express desire of Lord Canning's government. Whether it has been advantageous to India or not, is one of the most interesting questions of modern politics on which we shall dwell in its proper place.

LORD CANNING'S DURBAR AT AGRA AND TOUR IN UPPER INDIA.—After peace was entirely restored in every part of British India, the Governor-General issued a peace proclamation and appointed the 28th of July 1859 at the day for public thanksgiving. At the end of the monsoons His Excellency left for a tour in the Upper Provinces of India. We, who are accustomed to see our Viceroys and provincial governors move about in all parts of the extensive territories in their charge, would find it difficult to realise that in pre-railway days our rulers could scarcely move beyond a narrow circle from Calcutta. Few governors general previous to Lord Canning had undertaken any extensive tours, and those only when the state of public affairs urgently required them, to see any province with their own eyes. Lord Canning at the close of the mutiny was very unpopular with the local European community. The great danger to which the Empire in India lay exposed in 1859, placed Lord Canning, who had at his disposal but inadequate resources for such a heavy emergency, in a most critical position. The falling of town after town in the Upper Provinces in the hands of the mutineers, and the occurrence of many butcheries of the European residents, were popularly attributed to the want of decisive measures at the head of the government. Men in times of great personal danger and trouble or when strongly in sympathy with the unmerited fate of others, are but too often apt to attribute all the misfortunes to the weakness of the government. Lord Canning who was in the midst of a hurricane that he was powerless to check, came unfortunately to be regarded, by a large section of the local European community as wanting even in the resolution, the decisive firmness and capacity for action that were necessary at such a time.

Personal acquaintance with him during his tour in Upper India in a great measure modified those opinions, if not altogether removed them. Lord Canning also held a large Durbar at Agra where he paid a deserved tribute to the loyal services of the Maharajas of Gwalior and Jeypur and rewarded them by some grants of territory. In his elegant and spirited address to the Maharaja of Gwalior, Lord Canning publicly recognized the right of the Indian chiefs to adopt, on failure of natural heirs,—a declaration that set at rest the minds of many Indian chiefs, who looked with alarm and suspicion to the policy pursued during the previous regime of absorbing state after state on the failure of natural issue.

GENERAL EVENTS.—The Lieutenant-Governorship of the North-Western Provinces which had remained vacant since the lamented death, within the Agra Fort of Mr. Colvin was filled in January this year by Mr. Edmonstone of the Civil Service, who had his training under Sir John Lawrence in the Punjab and in the Foreign Office. It is beyond our scope to enter into a detailed description of the trying scenes, amidst which Mr. Colvin passed his last days but his tomb within the Agra Fort is a touching record of his unswerving duty to his country and fidelity to his countrymen. Sir John Lawrence who at this period was the most favored official and whose efforts in checking the mutiny were singularly successful retired in February 1859, being succeeded in the government of the Punjab by Sir Robert Montgomery. The troubles caused by wild races on the western border caused the despatch of a force under Sir Neville Chamberlain, known as the Koorum Field Force which succeeded in keeping these tribes in check for the time. Nor should any writer on 1859, omit to record, the splendid services during these troubled times to his country and to the government of the first great Indian journalist, Babu Hurrish Chandra Mookerji, the first editor of the *Hindu Patriot*, whose writings were conceived with singular breadth of views, force and elegance of expression and an accurate grasp of the situation. His able defence of the policy of Lord Canning when it was vigorously assailed has been since pronounced to be a specimen of true statesmanly production.

LAND QUESTION IN OUDH—The land question in India has always been a vexed problem for our rulers. When the Permanent Settlement of 1793 was entered into by the government of Lord Cornwallis with the Bengal zamindars, the theory adopted was that the state, the absolute master of the soil had granted to the zamindars the entire proprietorship. How far this theory represented the actual state of things in Bengal will be considered when we come to speak of the Acts passed from time to time to place on a satisfactory basis the relation between the landlords and tenants in Bengal. On the annexation of Oudh, the English found nearly two thirds of the province in the hands of a body of men known as the Talookdars, who, as Sir John Strachey declared from his place in the Council on the 17th July 1867, had undoubted rights of property in the soil. By some misconceptions on the part of the local officials, this class of men had been very unfairly dealt with in the land settlement of Oudh of 1856. The greater part of the landed aristocracy were ousted as interlopers, and in some cases princely revenues were cut down to a mere pittance. This treatment of the rights of the Talookdars was based on the view of Talookdari tenure derived from the experience of the province of Bengal where the best revenue authorities had declared the system to be one of but little consequence. The Talookder of Oudh was a very different personage from the Talookdar of Bengal and as the course of subsequent events showed, the Government had committed a great mistake in the view it adopted of the Talookdar's Tenures in 1856. This unfortunate state of things made the Talookdars in many cases justify to their own minds their secret aid and in some cases overt assistance to the mutineers, before the province was again completely held at bay by British troops. Lord Canning issued a proclamation which was dated March 1858, in which the noble Lord totally uproots the settlement of 1856-57, confiscates the entire proprietory rights in the soil and then proceeds to re-grant these rights to all such as could prove valid claims to them under the native Government, provided they are acquitted of all complicity in the recent revolts. The terms in which this proclamation was couched called forth a severe criticism from the Home authorities in their despatch of the 19th of April 1858, but the speech in which Lord Canning addressed the assembled Talookdars when he made the first state entry into Lucknow after the disturbances, in October 1859, completely settled the policy of the Government towards the ancient landed aristocracy in Oudh. Lord Canning there said "you, all of you who are here present received yesterday the grants of those estates which the Government has restored to you; you will have seen by the terms of those grants, that the ancient Talookdari system of Oudh is revived and perpetuated." This speech and the state documents where its substance is embodied have always been relied on as the great Charter of their rights by the Oudh Talookdars.

We now pass on to the history of the next year. Legislation, education and social progress, cannot be presented piecemeal and will be treated of in the general chapter with which the history of this decade will end. It was not till the close of the year that the able financier Mr. Wilson assumed the portfolio of Indian Finance but his reforms during his short career in India, brought to an end by premature death, did not engage public attention till the next year.

3—2

CHAPTER II.
1860.

THE INDIGO CRISIS IN BENGAL.—The province of Bengal proper was this year deeply agitated by what is known as the Indigo Crisis. The feelings of the natives of Bengal were excited to the highest pitch, though the actual number of disturbances within the cognizance of the Criminal Law, were few. The representatives of the planting interest and the representatives of the Native Press, then but a new-born institution, carried on the Indigo controversy with bitter acrimony and the real facts at issue were. almost lost sight of in showers of abuse. The planters who were scattered over every portion of the province used to make advances to the cultivators, and bound them down by a special form of contract, to deliver a certain ascertained quantity of indigo, the consequences of the land producing a lesser quantity being to make the obligation shift on the produce of the succeeding years. The cultivators in the majority of instances, were far from being moneyed men and they, in the course of years went on applying for fresh advances to the planters and in many cases became hopelessly involved. As years went on, the yoke of the planters became more and more heavy and the factory people, not unoften, used their authority over poor cultivators in a most oppressive manner. These debts of the cultivators descended from father to son, till the best lands of the debtors had always to be sowed with indigo and in case of refusal, the servants of the factory, it was broadly stated, kidnapped, placed in wrongful confinement and otherwise behaved brutally with the poor cultivators. The evil was a severe and wide-spread one and despair chiefly drove the cultivators in many instances openly to defy the planters, refuse to fulfil the contracts, and in some cases, even to resort to open violence. The loss of life and property, considering the excited state of feelings, was marvellously small. In the districts around the metropolis, as well as in Furreedpur and Pabna, the cultivators entered into a strike not to fulfil their contracts. This strike placed also the cultivators in a miserable plight by depriving them of the large amount that circulated among their number in the shape of wages. The Government found it high time to interfere, and by passing a short Act on the 9th of April, by whose provisions all breaches of contract in this respect, were made criminal, sought to prevent, the immediate and inevitable ruin of the planting interest. At the same time, the authorities at the head of affairs found that the grievances of the cultivators were too well-founded, and appointed a Commission to enquire into and report on the whole affair. The Commission was composed of Mr. Seton-Karr, Mr. Temple, Rev. Mr. J. Sale, Mr. W. Fergusson and Babu Chandra Mohun Chatterji. The missionaries, were openly charged with having incited the cultivators by their preachings to a state of active resistance to the planters and thus, they came to be represented on the Indigo Commission. The Commission held a most exhaustive inquiry, not only into the broad facts of the case, but into all the side-issues raised more especially into the conduct of the police and the authorities, during the recent disturbances, which had been openly and repeatedly assailed. The planters urged before the Commission that the cultivators under them were in reality better off, than under any previous system as they were not subjected to any irregular exactions, and the planters on the whole were humane and strove to extend to them the blessings of civilization. But the findings of the Commission were against the planters. The Commission found that the ryots were most inadequately remunerated for all they did, that the planters often compelled them if not by actual violence, at least by strong pressure to plough up and sow the best land with indigo. In some instances, some individual planters might have been humane and might have established dispensaries and schools, but this fact did not affect at all the general unsoundness of the system. The charges of actual and brutal violence against the planters fell through, in most cases, for want of evidence. The report also finds "the assertion, that the refusal of the ryots to sow indigo has been produced by the preaching of the missionaries is one entirely without foundation in truth." The Commission recommended the abolition of the system of advances, the planters being left to purchase indigo from the cultivators. The representative of the planting interest did not concur in the conclusions arrived at by his colleagues, adding that the language and tone of the report tended to give a coloring and to lead to conclusions not proved. The report of the Commission, will be found at this distance of time to have taken a calm and dispassionate view of the situation, in an unusually excited period when party feeling ran high. As a result of the findings of the Commission more Subordinate Courts were established and the reform of the police was attended to. During the whole period of these disturbances Babu Hurrish Chandra Mookerji championed the cause of the voiceless cultivators of Bengal in a series of articles which will remain to posterity in India, as models of journalistic composition. To his articles on the subject in the columns of the *Hindu Patriot*, the country is mainly indebted, for the prompt, the vigorous and the beneficent action of the Government.

SCARCITY IN UPPER INDIA AND GENERAL EVENTS.—A terrible famine raged this year in Upper India, due to the total failure of the rains. Those precautions that have been since taken to minimise the horrors of famine did not then exist, and the rise in prices of the necessaries of life was sudden and unexpected, and pressed severely on a population the greater part of which is always on the margin of subsistence. The last severe famine was in 1833, and the Upper Provinces had during twenty-seven years enjoyed a fair measure of prosperity. But the horrors of the year 1860, made many parents leave their children on the road-side that they might attract the notice of the charitably disposed. The missionaries collected many of these children at a place opposite the great Emperor Akber's tomb near Agra and established an orphanage there, which is still in a flourishing condition and which is the only institution of its kind through a vast territorial area. Relief works were opened by the Government, and the amounts raised by public subscriptions both here and in England served to mitigate the horrors of starvation. A measure which greatly enhanced the unpopularity of Lord Canning among his fellow-countrymen in India was the Disarming Act (Act 31 of 1860) which made it penal for all subjects of Her Majesty to have any arms, in their possession without express permission. The Europeans and the natives were put exactly on the same footing as regards this Act and the commotion in the European community every where was manifest in public meetings and petitions. Subsequently the the provisions of the Act were modified, by exempting all who would enlist as volunteers from its operation, but this concession which the European community thought came too late, failed to satisfy them, and the privilege of volunteering was availed of, in only a few instances, at first. Some detachments under Colonel Lumsden were sent into the Derajat, the country to the west of the Indus, and succeeded in punishing the wild tribes who were making raids and harbouring offenders. Similar smaller operations were undertaken from Pegu and Assam on the eastern frontier. The Raja of Sikkim had offered an unprovoked insult to the British power by imprisoning Dr. Hooker, who was continuing his botanical researches in the Himalayas, and Dr. Campbell the presiding officer over Darjiling, who had accompained him. A small force under Col. Gawler, occupied the Sikkimese capital on the 9th of March 1861, when a treaty was concluded which provided for the residence of a British representative in the capital of the state.

THE FINANCES—The year 1859 was the first one, when a regular budget was issued by the Imperial Government of India. It was in the same year that Mr. Wilson was appointed Finance Minister and his principal duty was to effect economical reforms and to reduce the expenditure without weakening the efficiency of the administration, that the enormous deficit which had become chronic might not absorb the resources of the empire. The mutiny had brought about a lavish expenditure of public money. The new regiments, whose numbers were very large, caused an immense increase under the heading of military charges and public works of utility whose want was first felt during the dark days of 1857-58, had to be undertaken on a large scale. The enormous naval establishment of India had also become a source of great increase in the expenditure of the empire. The need of retrenchment was sensibly felt both by the authorities here and in England and retrenchment, in every department of administration was resolved upon. A financier was sent, straight from England to whom was entrusted the difficult and disagreeable task, of prudently applying the shears, so that the efficiency and vigor of the administration might remain unimpaired and great vested interests be reconciled to a state of greatly decreased emoluments. It was rightly thought that for this task, a financier from England would have the advantage to even the best trained mind in the official circles of India. Some of the greatest writers on political philosophy have ventured to pin their faith on the theory that long training in official routine in any particular department, while it makes the excellent man of business often impairs, that vigor and originality of mind which can introduce reforms in that department and that for this purpose, a man new to the subject, who had evinced previously a capacious and well-trained mind, and who is wedded, as far as that particular topic is concerned, to no long-established system, is best fitted. Mr. Walter Bagehot one of the most powerful writers of this century vigorously enunciates this truth when he defends the system of government in England by a cabinet, that system which often places men with little or no training in the particular branch of state affairs he is called upon to administer, at the head of a great department. Mr. Bagehot says that by this system of choosing the head of the department, vitality and vigor are preserved in the department which otherwise is but too prone to degenerate into official red-tape. Just after his arrival in the country Mr. Wilson took a rapid tour through the N. W. P. and the Punjab and he had previously conferred on the subject of the impending reforms with Sir Charles Trevelyan, his old associate, who was then governor of Madras. Mr. Wilson at once appointed a Military Finance Commission whose duty it was to cut down the weeds that had fastened themselves on the overgrown tree of the Indian army, in the first instance and then to bring the tree to its normal dimensions. Mr. Wilson died an untimely death and he did not live to see the completion of the labours of that commission which he had inaugurated but his successor Mr. Laing alluded to the work of the commission in the most flattering terms. He prominently mentions in his budget speech of 1861-62, the names of Mr. R. Temple, Colonel Simpson, Captain Rennie and of Colonel Balfour, without a mention of whose names, he emphatically declares, the future history of India will remain but imperfect. The army charges which in 1857, were in round numbers, £11,500,000 a year in India and £1,250,000 in England, had swelled in 1859 to £21,000,000 in India and £3,750,000 in England. Lord Canning had to meet the crisis, raised enormous levies, and the guerilla warfare that was necessary to extinguish the dying embers of the rebellion, had caused every officer of importance to raise up bands of troops for the safety of his own district and these irregular levies which had done great and meritorious services, were still kept in the pay of the State. Not only were these overgrown charges to be found in Bengal but the panic had spread so wide that Mr. Wilson declared speaking in February 1860, that the increase of military charges, in Madras was fifty per cent. and in Bombay, thirty per cent. and that even these returns did not include the military police, the civil corps, and the new levies in Bengal or the new levies in Madras, the statement being confined to the troops under the Commander-in-Chief of each of the three presidencies. Enormous reductions were at once effected till we find from the State papers of the period, the military expenditure was in 1859-60 brought down to £2,750,000 in England and £17,750,000 in India making as compared with the figures already given an enormous saving of £4,250,000. In 1860-61 the same plan was continued and a further reduction of £2,500,000 was effected and in the following year, the reduction under this head amounted to £3,220,000. On the 1st of August 1859, the Secretary of State for India had made in the House of Commons the alarming statement that the deficit in the annual budget for the official year 1859 would amount to ten millions sterling, in round numbers. In the following year the deficit was brought down to six millions and a half sterling, according to a statement drawn up in India but which seeming improvement vanishes in the thin air by the light of Mr. Wilson's comments. Mr. Wilson also clearly exposed the ruinous system of borrowing in times of peace, which had in 1860 burdened the country with a debt of £97,851,807, whose interest of about five millions was regularly charged on the annual revenues of India, forcibly remarking that the normal condition of Indian Finance may be said to be one of chronic deficit and addition to debt. State loans in India were defended at the time and since as a very politic measure as by investing largely in Government Securities, the wealthier classes among the natives of India, become anxious for the stability of the British Government. But Mr. Wilson entered at the same time into a vigorous defence of that statesman, to whom the country was entrusted during the crisis of the mutiny and who had even in those troubled times scrupulously fulfilled every contract, and acted on the best principles of honesty and integrity. Mr. Wilson had to look about him for increased sources of revenue, as further reduction in expenditure could scarcely be made. The exports of India showed an increase of twenty-five millions sterling when the figures of 1859 and those of twenty-five years previous, were compared. Just before Mr. Wilson's arrival in the country the duty on exports had been raised from five to twenty-five per cent, this causing a vast loss in the proceeds of that impost. Mr. Wilson reduced, this duty to ten per cent, and with the view of encouraging trade, he remitted the export and import duty on certain goods altogether. The railway receipts continually expanded with the return of the times of peace. Mr. Wilson also proposed to levy an income tax which would extend to all incomes of 200 rupees a year. Incomes from 200 rupees to 500 rupees to be taxed at the rate of two per cent and incomes above 500 at the rate of four per cent. The zamindars, he proposed to assess on half of the amount of their rent to the estate, as representing a fair estimate of their profits. The income-tax was first levied in India by Mr. Wilson and has been subsequently resorted to by other financiers, in times of pressure but uniform experience shows, that while in theory nothing could be more just, than a tax to which every man is liable according to the measure of his income, in practice the income tax has always been in India an unsuccessful and unpopular tax. This opinion is not only confined to the ruled classes in India, but the officers entrusted with its administration have all borne testimony to the fact that it is not only an odious impost, as being inquisitorial in its nature, and pressing most heavily on the most conscientious, but that it even fails to bring a large amount of money into the coffers of the State. The relative merits and advantages of direct and indirect taxation had long been debated among the first minds of the civilized world, and Adam Smith, whose work on political economy effected a great change in the policy of nations, was the first practical writer who had brought to bear the powers of one of the finest and most powerful of human intellects, to the discussion of this problem. John Stuart Mill has in our own generation, devoted many pages to a discussion of the relative merits of direct and indirect taxation and even that first-rate writer has found so many difficulties in the way of an equitable working of the income tax that at the end of an elaborate discussion through many chapters he is inclined to concur in the opinion, which had generally prevailed in England through many years, that direct taxes on income should be reserved as an extraordinary resource for great national emergencies in which the necessity of a large additional revenue overrules all objections. Not to speak of the cost of collection, the income tax, can hardly be fairly worked in practice, without a conscientious co-operation on the part of the tax-payer, and it has been unfortunately found by experience even in the most advanced parts of the civilized world, that few even among the educated and the well-to-do classes would scruple to play false with an impersonal body—such as a Government or a Corporation. Mr. Fawcett has given in one of his economic productions a striking illustration of this truth which is familiar to the educated Indian public. In India the difficulties in the way of the income tax being successful are immense. Mr. Wilson's measure proved a failure as might have been expected. The tax, it was estimated by its able author, would realize a sum of nearly 30 lakhs of rupees, but the actual result proved that it yielded not more than half the amount. In India the difficulties in the way of a proper assessment were enhanced by the admittedly inferior honesty of the subordinate staff available, as well as, the long established character of the population who regarded with anything but a favourable eye, the direct payments peremptorily demanded by the tax Collector, of the state. Sir Charles Trevelyan and the Madras council vigorously protested against this measure and Sir Charles took the unusual step of publishing his protest in the newspapers of the Madras Presidency, a step which fixed the attention of all India to this gross breach of official discipline and open manifestation of an insubordinate spirit, and which made Lord Canning comment severely on his conduct in a despatch that led to the early recall of that great but impulsive statesman. We shall not anticipate the chronological order of things but leave for the next chapter, our narration of the financial measures of Mr. Samuel Laing, who succeeded Mr. Wilson as Finance Minister.

We should not close the history of the year 1860 without a notice of that accomplished Commander who retired this year from the head of the Indian army. Lord Clyde must be admitted to be a successful commander. He came to India to quell the military rebellion of 1857, and he remained at his post till the last embers had been trodden out. But even his best admirers will be constrained to find fault with him for the unnecessary dilatoriness of his operations, which though proceeding from a cautious temperament was certainly carried to excess, and occasioned a great loss of human lives by the effects of the irregularities and exposure of a protracted camp life. The historian of India will naturally hesitate to accord to a commander whose military feats, though never unsuccessful, were neither brilliant nor decisive, a place among the foremost generals of this country.

CHAPTER III.

1861.

NATURAL VISITATIONS.—When the year opened the famine in the N. W. Provinces and the Punjab to which we have alluded in our last chapter, was showing signs of abatement. As is apparent from the statements in Colonel Baird Smith's report, the tract of country affected by the famine was a large one, but the sufferings of the starving population had been considerably relieved, by the liberal contributions in aid of those suffering from all classes of the population. Bengal was visited this year by a flood of unusual severity. Her rivers become very powerful during the rains, when the hill-torrents from Upper India send in large volumes of water. Many Bengal rivers, have usually in the rains to be restrained from leaving their beds by powerful embankments, but should unfortunately these embankments give way, as they often do, when the rains are excessive throughout the vast regions of Upper India and Bengal, all of which are, in the last resort, drained by the rivers of Bengal, the loss of human lives and property in many instances become appalling. The waters retiring, after the cessation of the rains gave birth to a terrible epidemic of malarious fever which decimated every village throughout the inundated area.

THE COTTON TRADE.—The hostilities about the Slave Trade between the Northern and the Southern portions of the American United States produced a remarkable influx of wealth into India by the sale of her cotton. The great mills at Manchester and other towns of England, were supplied by the raw American cotton, but the breaking out of a Civil War totally checked this article of import and threw hundreds of operatives of the cotton mills out of work. The costly machinery had also to be maintained while there were no raw materials to keep it engaged to the immense loss of the capitalists. Every effort was made by English manufacturers to make Indian cotton supply the gap that had been caused by American cotton. The demand for raw cotton greatly exceeded the supply of it and thus the prices rose considerably. But the cotton of India was principally grown in places which were not readily accessible in those times for want of good roads and other facilities of communication, and there could be the rapid accumulation of an unusually large stock of cotton in the cotton marts of India with great difficulty. Therefore India could not to the full extent avail herself of the opportunity given to her by the American difficulties. The Indian staple was again found to be inferior to the American. Every effort was made to introduce improvements in the production of cotton, and the best seeds were imported from all parts of the world. Still when the cotton fever raged high, the speculators all over the country, especially in Bombay found it easy to realize enormous fortunes. The cotton trade in India thus received an unusual stimulus and exports of raw cotton began to increase steadily in subsequent years.

GENERAL EVENTS.—It was in this year that two important acts were passed relating to the constitution of the Legislative Councils and the High Courts. The changes consequent on the passing of those acts, did not come into operation in India till the next year, and the important subjects embraced by them will be considered fully in the next chapter. The Indian Civil Service was thrown open to competition, thus introducing a method of recruitment far different from that which prevailed during the old days of the Haileybury College, when the appointments in the East went exclusively through the patronage of the Court of Directors. The system of competitive examinations in the Civil Service owes its birth like the system of high education through the medium of the English tongue in this country, to one of the brilliant minutes of Lord Macaulay, full of glowing periods and antithetical sentences. The system of recruitment by a competitive examination to which every one can present himself without any reference to any considerations of parentage or social position, has been attacked from various quarters. A full discussion of this subject does appropriately belong to a much later period when the system might be considered to have had its full trials. It was also during this year that currency notes were introduced on an extensive scale and began to substitute the place of gold and silver in the relations of life. The Banks of Bengal, Bombay and Madras date their foundation in 1861 and by affording great facilities to the transmission of specie and thus facilitating commerce, conferred great benefit on the Indian public. The Government was anxious to attract European capital to this country, which it was rather difficult to do after the partial ruin of and the rude shock to the indigo interests in 1859-60. A bill was introduced into the Supreme Council known as the Contract bill which made the breach of Contract in India a criminal offence. The bill was regarded by the native population with great aversion and it was stigmatized in the organs of native public opinion as the "Slavery Bill." The Act would have given rise to considerable unpleasantness and friction in its practical working but the bill came to be dropped by Sir Charles Wood's intimating that he would veto it, if it passed the Council. It was in this year that the exalted order of the Star of India was first founded and the new members' of the order were invested with the badge and the color with great ceremony. The idea of founding this exalted order was a happy one. It shone with singular lustre on the breasts of those who after a long and meritorious career had nothing more in fortune, position or reputation still to win, while the young official or non-official might well fix their eyes on it, which will be an additional incentive for the display of rare qualities of the head or the hand, that inspire public confidence and win public esteem. The Government while providing for the reward of singularly brilliant merits in arts or arms, politics or diplomacy in the order of the star of India, created the new office of Honorary Magistrates by which lesser local merit might be rewarded and the people of the country might be gradually trained, to administer their own affairs. The dispensation of justice, in however petty cases often requires a degree of ability, and the men of local influence might, when in these offices, do much, to improve their own selves and purify the administration of justice by keeping a strict eye on all oppression by whomsoever committed. Many who had been invested with Magisterial authorities under this system had failed to exercise them with credit either to the Government or to themselves, but this was owing rather to the selection of the wrong men, than to any inherent defect in the system itself. The indigo disturbances in Bengal, again took a head this year, and a commission had to be appointed consisting of Mr. Morris and Mr. Montressor. The ryots refused on principle to sow their lands with indigo and they secured a victory which was however dearly purchased by their sufferings through the long struggles. The Small Cause Courts were established in Bengal as an experimental measure to afford a speedy remedy in the case of small debts. These Courts, if they simplify the procedure, unless presided over by exceptionally able men whose number is limited, do not inspire the same confidence as the ordinary tribunals whose discretion and ability in weighing evidence are capable of being corrected by a Court of Appeal and some cumbrousness was again sought to be introduced into its procedure, when provision was made for reference and revision of the judgments of the Small Cause Courts in a great many cases. Attention was paid to the means existing for education of Anglo-Indian boys and girls and it was through the efforts of the Bishop of Calcutta, Dr. Cotton, that special schools were established all over the country in healthy localities and some schools were also located in the sanitariums of the Himalayas. The Raichori Doab, the Dharased and Shoraporo districts of the Berars, were restored to the Nizam under the provisions of a new treaty concluded with him this year. Lord Canning also promulgated an order with a view to the reclamation of the waste lands in India and developing the material resources of the country. He proposed to sell waste lands, at the rate of two rupees and a half per acre in the jungly tracts and five rupees per acre in the cleared tracts, the maximum allotted to each individual being three thousand acres. The order of Lord Canning was welcomed by English capitalists and soon arrangements were in progress for taking up large tracts of culturable waste lands. But Sir Charles Wood, the then Secretary of State, by a resolution of the 9th June 1862, totally upset this state of things and allowed the local officials under the modified orders, to fix prohibitory prices on pieces of land if they so pleased. We lost this year Lady Canning, by a jungle fever and she was interred in a beautiful spot on the banks of the Ganges at the Viceregal garden at Barrakpur, a few miles north of Calcutta. Those who have visited her chaste mausoleum with its feeling inscription from the pen of her lord, on a site which nature and the highest art have combined to make singularly charming, will think it a fitting resting-place for a high-minded and well-bred lady like the consort of Lord Canning. The Viceroy survived her but seven months, and four months after her death left the shores of India to succumb to the effects of those unparalleled labors, that had signalized his vice-royalty.

THE FINANCES.—Mr. Samuel Laing's budget was published on the 27th April 1861. The budget showed a deficit of nearly seven millions sterling in round numbers, which was met by taking the amount from the proceeds of the recent loans. Mr. Laing then proceeded to increase the duty on cotton yarn and the tax on salt. At the end of the financial year the large deficit entirely disappeared, the improved receipts from salt duty, the income tax and the stamp duty and the cutting down of allotments to provincial governments for the much-needed public works produced a financial equilibrium on paper. To these causes must be added the receipts of the Government from the great expansion of the Indian opium trade, and the savings effected by reductions to the extent of £3,590,750. The finances began to improve after this period, and the Indian Finance Minister had not up to 1868-69, to struggle with any serious difficulties. The Indian revenues, in the hands of any finance minister, can be made to expand considerably, if need be. The constitution of the Indian Government is such that there are not the same difficulties in the way of increased taxation, as exist in other countries. When the resources of the state fall inadequate to meet the expenditure, the Finance minister thinks more of making the revenues elastic than of effecting any reductions in expenditure. The only thing he has gravely to consider, is the shape which the new taxation will take, and when he has made up his mind there is no difficulty in the way of his thoughts being embodied in an act of the council. His brother-officials in the council are certain to ratify his measures and such public opinion as exists in the country finds no vent in the constitution of the state and is an element that it is not necessary to influence. Whether India is a heavily-taxed country is a question that receives from time to time a great measure of public attention, but that the taxation of the country is gradually on the increase is fully proved by the official records of the period embraced by this book. The Indian Finance Minister has not the same sort of rough work that an English Chancellor of the Exchequer has, who every time that a new tax has to be imposed, has to offer a lucid statement of the situation under the most searching scrutiny and has to appease the powerful opinion of the House of Representatives of the people.

We have already adverted to the fact that the Indian revenue is indebted for a large slice of it to the proceeds of the impost on opium which is exported in large quantities from this country to be consumed by the many millions of subjects in the Celestial Empire. Whether a Christian government is at all justified in raising a large part of its revenues from a trade whose direct effect is the spread of intemperate habits among a considerable portion of the human race is an interesting problem of political casuistry. The policy of the government of India in this respect had been repeatedly and vigorously assailed, and Mr. Laing and Sir Charles Trevelyan entered into a vigorous defence of the governmental policy from their place in the Supreme Council.

Opium.—Opium-smoking and opium-eating are practices to which the Chinese are very largely addicted. This habit has been much condemned as physically and morally injurious in the highest degree, but the Chinese regard it as a drug which has stimulating effect at times, and at other times a soothing and soporific influence. We do not see that this habit is to be more condemned than the free use of spirituous and alcoholic liquor, which is the pratice in many civilized countries. Mr. Laing truly remarked in his budget-speech of 1862-63 that the cold climate of Northern Europe makes some nervous stimulant peculiarly necessary which is resorted to, in the shape of alcohol by the Saxon races, so the Chinese whose greatest deficiency, as shown by the whole history, religion and literature of the race, is in the imaginative faculties, resorts to that which stimulates his imagination and makes his sluggish brain see visions and dream dreams. He continues " An English Chancellor of the Exchequer goes on with equanimity, relying on a taxation of 400 or 500 per cent *ad valorem* on spirits and tobacco for twenty millions sterling of his revenue, and while this is the case I can see nothing in any general consideration as to opium to prevent us from doing the same."

The second objection against the revenue derived from opium is that is a most precarious source of revenue and that the moment a cheaper and better article will be substituted for it in the Chinese market, the revenue from opium will begin to fall considerably till it might almost vanish altogether. The other side of the question has been very eloquently stated by Sir Charles Trevelyan who says "that we have gone on calling the opium revenue precarious long after the contrary has been demonstrated by actual experience. It is anomalous but it is not precarious. It rests upon precisely the same basis as the excise upon spirits in England with this difference that the spirits are consumed by Her Majesty's subjects while the opium is consumed by the subjects of the Emperor of China. But the Chinese will no more go without opium than, it is feared, certain classes of our fellow subjects will forego the use of spirits." It has been pointed out by an acute and eloquent writer on this subject that both Mr. Laing and Sir Charles Trevelyan commit a mistake when they broadly assert that the opium revenue in India is based on the same basis as the excise upon spirits in England. "There is a sort of resemblance between the two, in as much as both are derived from deep-rooted instincts of human nature, but the English excise revenue is a tax upon spirits and the Indian opium revenue is a profit that accrues from the sale of an article of common use and consumption in a country." The writer whose opinions are above given, draws an analogy between the position of the Indian opium in the Chinese market and the position of the American cotton in the European market. "The moment a cheaper or a better article would come into competition, the sale would fall off." "It was obvious that if the Chinese could get their opium cheaper and better elsewhere than from India, they would do so, and in that case the Indian revenue might be the loser to the extent of seven or eight millions per annum." But there is no reasonable foundation for the anticipation that the Chinese would abandon the use of opium any more than that the greater portion of the Anglo-Saxon stock would abandon the use of alcoholic spirits. Sir Charles Trevelyan also scouts the idea that the Chinese will ever be independent of the Indian opium. He says that the quality of certain articles of Indian produce has never yet been excelled, such as indigo and opium and the free cultivation of opium in China, will not only increase the status and the price of the

Indian opium as an article of luxury, but in that case as the experience of the past few years showed, the demand upon India for opium will be continually increasing. The analogy between the Indian opium revenue and the English excise revenue fails in another point, as the tax on opium which is a Government monopoly in India is an open encouragement to its production, while the English tax on liquors considerably lessens its consumption by making the article dearer. The future of the opium revenue does not come within the purview of this chapter. We shall see later on, how far the confident anticipations about the gradual expansion of the opium revenue were destined to be realized in our review of the later years.

CHAPTER IV.

1862.

THE LEGISLATIVE COUNCILS.—The Indian Councils Act was passed in 1861 but the first meeting of the Legislative Council according to the provisions of the said act, assembled in the Council Chamber of the Government House at Calcutta on Saturday the 18th of January, 1862. The Indian Councils Act established Legislative Councils on a model that exist to this day. The Mutiny had evidently made apparent to the public mind both here and in England, the danger that might occasionally befall the Empire by neglecting the non-official opinions on all subjects, and provision was made for the due vent of these opinions even in the council chamber by representatives both of the European non-official and the native public. This was the first step towards popularizing an administration which had hitherto remained exclusively official and the concession to the non-official public was hailed with great joy. The warmest opponents of the present constitution of the Legislative Councils in our own days, would readily admit that a greater concession was not possible in the year 1861. The native public with the amount of education and enlightenment, it then possessed had no claim to be allowed to choose their own representatives in the Council. The Universities had but just been founded and it was with the establishment of these examining bodies, and of first-grade colleges and high schools, whether directly by the Government, or under the grant-in-aid system formulated by Sir Charles Wood in his Education Despatch of 1854, that high education became extremely popular, till only a few years later, the Vice-Chanceller of the Calcutta University proudly declared that no institution in the country excites so deep an interest among the native population from Calcutta to Lahore, as do the examinations of the University. The freedom of the press so wisely conferred by Sir Charles Metcalfe, though abused in certain cases, began from this period to give an unusual impetus to freedom of thought and writing. The country has admittedly made great and rapid strides since the Indian Councils Act was passed, which is expressed in the oft-quoted sentence "the England of Queen Anne was hardly more different from the England of to-day than the India of Lord Ellenborough from the India of Lord Ripon." This admitted advancement in Indian political and educational life, has made the reform of the Legislative Councils on a popular basis a burning question of these days. That some reform is necessary in the direction of giving a wider recognition to native political thought as an element to guide the Councils of the Empire has been admitted by a cautious and astute statesman like Lord Dufferin, and that accomplished statesman and eminent scholar Sir A. Colvin, who now presides over the N. W. P. administration, has also approved of some gradual and moderate reforms in the same direction. Whether the country is yet ripe for representative institutions, whether the elective system should be introduced in the constitution of the local and supreme councils, what the electorate will be, if the elective principle is at all recognized in the constitution, are questions that are now exciting a good deal of attention both here and in England and are being discussed sometimes with good sense and sometimes with violence of language and invectives. The Indian Law Commissioners had been for several years labouring to bring about a systematic compendium of the unwritten laws of the land and to engraft them with such modifications as the English Government introduced into regular codes of laws. The Indian courts, under the Mahomedan rule and under the English rule, till the laws were systematised, used to act on well-known customs and usages applied with discretion to the circumstances of the case, but the law is now a rigid system capable of expansion either under new enactments of the Legislative Councils or the principles of equity that are always introduced by Judge-made law. A systematic and centralized administration must have a rigid code of laws, but it has often been said by even high authorities that India, with her wild ways of the past was better governed, under the loose system prevailing in other days. Sir Erskine Perry's remark is too well-known, that the History of British India is full of examples of the great mischief done by clothing imperfect theories in the rigid garb of law. Before the renewal of the Charter to the East India Company in 1853, the report of the Indian Law Commissioners on many of the subjects entrusted to them and the drafts of many proposed measures had been received in England and the Charter of that year, introduced several improvements in the constitution of the Imperial Legislative Council. The Legislative Councillors, acquired by the Charter of that year, the power which the Law Commissioners had not, of proposing any law they considered necessary or opposing any law which they deemed unnecessary or injurious, and the Chief Justice and Judges of the Supreme Court were appointed members of the Imperial Legislative Council. The measures of the Legislative Council could not be transferred into laws unless assented to by the Governor-General, who had full power to ratify or to annul the proceedings of the Council, and representative members from the official circles of the sister presidencies, were also introduced. After the Mutiny, Lord Canning pointed out in his memorable despatch of the 9th December 1859, that the Legislative Councils should be further improved. He pointed out that there were 136 standing orders to regulate the proceedings of the Council, and that the absence of representatives of the non-official community, of local legislatures to deal with local wants, were great inconveniences. He proposed that local legislatures be established as a part of the regular machinery of the local administrations, and all measures affecting the local administrations and not affecting the revenue should fall within the competency of the local councils. Lord Canning's proposals were accepted by Sir Charles Wood and the Indian Councils Act embodied most of the former's recommendations. It was provided by the Councils Act of 1861, that the sanction of the Governor-General will be necessary to introduce all measures affecting the public debt or revenue, or the religion or religious rites of any part of Her Majesty's subjects, or the discipline or maintainance of any part of Her Majesty's military or naval forces, or any matter relating to the foreign affairs of the State. Local Legislatures were bound to transmit authenticated copies of every measure which they have passed for the assent of His Excellency the Viceroy. The procedure in the Viceregal Council was as follows ; whenever, any member of the council makes up his mind to bring in any particular measure embodying either the suggestions of some local administration, or some individual in high official station, or his own idea, he gives notice to the secretary at least three days before the next meeting of the council, of his intention to bring in a bill. He then asks permission, of his fellow-councillors to bring in the bill and if the permission is granted he submits to the secretary the draft bill with a full statement of the objects and reasons and any other papers, the member might consider necessary to bring to the notice of the council. These papers are then printed and circulated in English and in the vernacular of those members who may not know English. After two weeks have elapsed the draft bill may be introduced at the next meeting of the council. The council then settles its main underlying principle and the more important provisions, the rest being left to the consideration of the select committee to whom the bill, if the council so please, is referred. When a bill is referred to a select committee, the draft bill together with a statement of the object and reasons and all other papers, is published in English and vernacular in the various official gazettes, and a time is also fixed, to be extended by the council if necessary, within which the select committee is to submit its report. The council may consider the bill any time after a week has elapsed from the date when the members have been furnished with the report of the select committee. Should any Hon'ble member propose to bring in any amendment, he should send at least three day's notice of it to the secretary. If any amendments are proposed, the council may dispose of them either at the same or the next sitting, and finally the bill has to be assented to by the Viceroy, to be transformed into a part and parcel of the laws of the land.

The Legislative Council was to consist of the members of the Supreme Executive and such non-official members as the Viceroy may appoint, the whole number of councillors, not exceeding the limits of a manageable body. The presidencies of Bombay and Madras were to be represented by official or non-official members as the Viceroy might consider necessary. The council as thus constituted launched forth into a bold course of legislation and filled the statute book of the land with innumerable acts whose number and variety make it an exceedingly difficult task for the professional lawyer to be well-acquainted with the laws of the land, that he might be fitted for the task of advising others about it. The legislative enactments, their scope and provisions will be considered in the general review of the ten years from 1859 to 1868, with which the present part comes to an end.

THE HIGH COURTS—Another important change in the constitution of the highest courts of the land which came into operation at the commencement of this year deserves more than a passing notice. Under the regime of the East India Company the highest Appellate Courts were the Sudder Diwany Adalut and the Sudder Nizamat Adalut, which were presided over by the Company's civilians and side by side with these courts, were the Supreme Courts at the Presidency towns, which administered English Law and were presided over by judges, trained and appointed in England. This year first saw the modern High Courts which grew out of the amalgamation of the two systems of Courts. The High Courts were established by Royal Charter in the presidency towns of Calcutta, Bombay and Madras and the High Court of the North-Western Provinces was created three years subsequently. By the provisions of the Royal Charter, one third of the judges must be members of the Civil Service who had been zillah judges for at least three years, one third must be selected from barristers of at least five year's standing and the other third not from any specific body. The High Court at Calcutta saw among its first body of judges, a native of India. The first native of India selected for this exalted and responsible appointment was the Hon'ble Ramaprosad Ray, the ablest native practitioner in the bar of those times but unfortunately his last illness had set in before his elevation to the bench, and he did not live actually to put on the ermine. He was the son of the first great native reformer, Rajah Rammohun Ray, whose memory is still venerated in native society. After his death his place on the bench was filled by that eminent Cashmiri pandit, whose ability and integrity first justified the appointment of natives of India to the highest judicial offices of the land, the Hon'ble Justice Shumboo Nath Pandit. He came from a noble family that had long settled in Oudh and by dint of ability and industry, rose to the front rank of the legal profession and when he came to be selected as a judge of the High Court of Bengal, his appointment diffused universal satisfaction. The appointment of natives of India to high judicial offices, was hailed with a sentiment of gratitude by the educated public in every part of India, and it is but just to mention, that with the exception of a black sheep here or there, the native members of the judicial service, when properly selected, have maintained the same high standard of ability, tact, and integrity, that are so conspicuous in the best men among their European compeers. With the establishment of the High Courts, the procedure of all the Indian Courts including those high tribunals, was made uniform, much to the disgust of the English bar. The High Courts, ever since their establishment, have been gradually shutting out by its bye-laws, from the ranks of the legal practitioners, either before itself or before its subordinate courts, all but the English-educated members of the native community and have thus been giving silently but very effectively the highest impetus to the progress of high education. In the more advanced provinces, the High Courts at once set about effecting reforms in the method of the selection of the legal practitioners all over the country and a high standard of ability and education has since been rigidly exacted of all, who aspired either to be members of the bar or of that branch of the public service which is recruited from the bar. In the N. W. Provinces, where education was in a very backward state the same salutary measures could not at once be enforced, and are now gradually being introduced till a sufficiently high standard has been secured. No one can doubt that the High Courts by rigidly insisting on a high English education as an absolute qualification either for the bar or the judicial service, had done as much in spreading enlightenment and civilization in the more important centres of population as by its impartial administration of justice it has brought about, the most unbounded faith in security of person and property under British rule. The bar in every country is in constant contact with the people, and much more so in India, where the only profession outside of Government service to which educated young men of the country most largely resort to, is the bar. Sir Henry Maine makes the interesting observation in one of his Convocation addresses that in every country which is just awakening from the torpor of ages to the light of civilization, the bar must be the profession most largely resorted to, as it is a profession which is money-making and study at the same time. He instances the case of other countries as exactly in point—of Rome when she was first ennobled by the poetry, the philosophy, the arts and arms of Greece, and of other European countries when first revivified after the middle ages during the period of the renaissance. To the High Courts the country is also indebted for many improvements in the enactments, that suited them to the wants of the people and for many sound maxims of law and principles of jurisprudence which it has unconsciously introduced.

THE MYSORE PRINCE'S APPEAL TO ENGLAND.—The Indian Government was rather tickled by the success of Prince Golam Mahomed's appeal to England on the question of what is known as the Mysore Grants. Since the absorption of Mysore into British territory, the numerous descendants of Hyder Ali and Tippu were taken down to Calcutta and made to live there on pensions. Gradually the number of the persons claiming the blood of the Mysore sovereigns increased and the stipends allotted cost the state a considerable sum. Lord Dalhousie had proposed that the pension should be stopped to all who were in more than the fifth degree of descent from Tippu Sultan but the Court of Directors, did not entertain Lord Dalhousie's recommendation. Lord Canning was for diminishing the amount of these pensions though he opposed doing away with them altogether. Prince Golam Mahomed seeing the pension of his family members to be in peril, sailed for England and without revealing his object to any one in India intended to lay his grievances before and to appeal to Sir Charles Wood. The appeal was allowed and Sir Charles ordered that a net sum of £520,000 sterling be paid to the pensioners that it might serve partly for the expenses of buying residences, and all the heads of families might have their separate allotments in full. The Government of Lord Canning strongly protested against the order of Sir Charles Wood, which, at a time of great financial pressure imposed a serious burden on the Indian exchequer, and which would teach influential natives of India to look to the mysterious power beyond the sea, for the final decision of all their grievances, thus considerably weakening the prestige and authority of the Viceroy. Sir Charles Wood on the contrary in his despatch dated February 4th, 1861, defended his action on the clearest grounds of justice and expediency. This action of Sir Charles Wood greatly enhanced his popularity with the native community of India while with the European residents he became proportionately unpopular.

GENERAL EVENTS.—Lord Canning this year extended a

privilege to the landowners all over India, of redeeming the annual payments of land revenue by paying down twenty year's revenue at once—a privilege which was availed of by but few. During this year a sudden mania arose for the cultivation of tea and numerous tea companies were formed, many of which unfortunately ended in complete collapse, and ruined many helpless persons. India it was thought, afforded immense facilities for tea-planting, and enormous profits realized by some individual planters, who had some plantations worked under their own eyes in the regions just below the Himalayas, confirmed this impression. Every day, in the great money-markets of India, immense amounts of capital were subscribed for the tea-companies, but it was soon found unfortunately that though some regions in the Kumaon and Garhwal districts, or near Dera Dun, Muree, and Assam or the Kangra and other valleys, afforded natural advantages for the tea industry yet the cost of transport of the produce of large plantations, the comparative mismanagement that is an inevitable incident of all joint-stock companies, and the want of labor in Assam and the want of water in the drier tracts, made plantations on a large scale almost sure failures. It was however discovered that tea grown on some of the hill-tracts of India was the best of its kind and could be compared as far as refreshing power and aromatic flavor went, with the tea grown on the best plateaus of China. It was with much diplomacy that a treaty was obtained by Sir Arthur Phayre, from the Chief of Burmah formally ceding the districts that Lord Dalhousie had annexed after the second Burmese War and which also provided for the residence of a British representative at the Court of Mandalay and afforded some facilities to British traders. The expenses of maintaining the police being considered a too heavy charge on the State, a Commission was appointed to effect reforms in the Police department. The Commission recommended the allotment of one constable to every square mile or every thousand inhabitants and adopted the principle of organization introduced by Sir

Charles Napier in Sindh of drilling the police in a regular way and render that body effective in suppressing all local outbreaks. The Police charges, were considerably cut down in the case of every province, a saving of a million sterling being alone effected under the heading of expenditure, in the case of the N. W. Provinces Government. The Commission which had been appointed by Mr. Wilson to inquire into the working of the military department of the state with a view to effect reductions continued under Col. Browne to overhaul all the other departments of the state. Its labours were still unfinished when the year closed. A small detachment had to be sent to suppress a rising of wild tribes near the Jyntea hills in Assam, and Brigadier General Showers, and the Lieutenant-Governor of Bengal, Mr. Beadon tried to conciliate the rebels who had been exasperated by the attempt to levy a house-tax on them, and the malcontents again returned to their allegiance.

CHANGES IN THE PERSONAL OF THE GOVERNMENT.—Lord Canning made over charge of his high office to Lord Elgin on the 12th of March this year and sailed for his native land. He left India among the universal praise of the native population of India and of somewhat mingled feelings on the part of his own countrymen. Even his greatest detractors have drawn a line between Lord Canning's official policy after the rebellion had been suppressed and his policy previous to that period. The latter, has often been condemned in the most unmeasured terms but the former has been pronounced to be a success by writers whose views on all topics of public interest differ almost diametrically. Like all viceroys Lord Canning was a learner in Indian affairs for sometime after his arrival in this country and the policy of the first years of his administration, was more in the hands of his advisers than it was the product of his own unassisted judgment. After the suppression of the rebellion Lord Canning directed the affairs of the state, with a less reliance on his advisers and his administration was marked by vigor and foresight. But, he had a reserved and icy temperament. Every one of his steps he took with the utmost possible deliberation, with caution and prudence, and it was not easy to warm him into enthusiasm. Lord Canning however will be credited by posterity, with having been a wise, just, and impartial ruler and his uniform calmness of judgment was as far removed from mere impulse as from lofty enthusiasm. He was rather unfortunate in some of his advisers and he had but few men of commanding ability to serve him. The judgments formed of him immediately after he left for England were obscured by passions and sentiments, but at this distance of time, the historian of India, will find in his career, nothing of that weakness indecision and pusillanimity the alleged existence of which was signified by the nickname, applied to him, with questionable taste, of Clemency Canning. He landed at Marsailles in good health but soon after his arrival at London became indisposed and breathed his last on the 17th June 1862 being buried at the Westminister Abbey on the 21st June 1862, Lord Palmerston, Lord Clyde and Sir James Outram being among the pallbearers.

Sir John Peter Grant, the Lieutenant-Governor of Bengal, made over charge of his office to Sir Cecil Beadon on the 23rd of April. Sir John Peter Grant was, on his retirement from India, immediately selected to fill the important position of Governor of Jamaica, which island was then in great commotion owing to the rising of the black population against their white masters. Sir John Peter Grant was universally unpopular with the European community in Bengal. He had put down with a firm hand what he considered to be the wrongs to the agrarian population of Bengal, suffered at the hands of the European planters. The great demonstration of the ryots weeping and begging submissively for help that met the Lieutenant-Governor's eye for seventy miles together, on both the banks of the river Jamoona, on his return by river from Dacca, made such a tremendous effect on his mind that he took up the question of the ryot's wrongs without a moment's delay. But there was a certain want of tact and discretion in managing the then situation and the indigo interests in Bengal have since received a blow from which they have not yet recovered. Sir John Peter Grant's son was many years the Judge of Hooghly and officiated twice on the High Court bench. He was a very popular judge, and was liked both by the profession and the public.

Another office which also changed hands during the year was the Bombay Governorship by the retirement of Sir George Clerk. Sir George was attached to the Punjab as a political officer during a part of Ranjit Singh's reign and he displayed much quickness and tact during the troubled times through which the province passed after the death of Ranjit Singh. He was not however in the good graces of the Secretary of State and he laid down his office at the beginning of the year. His abilities and energy found a fresh field in Africa, where he was deputed to assist in the Orange River Settlement. He also undeniably claims, the merit at the hands of the historian of having early perceived the abilities of the brother Lawrences and having brought them prominently to the notice of the Government.

CHAPTER V.

1863.

LORD ELGIN—Lord Canning had been succeeded in the Viceroyalty of India by Lord Elgin whose Indian career was too short and the only event of importance which he was called upon to deal with, was what is known as the Wahabee conspiracy. He left on the 5th February for a tour in the upper provinces, from which alas! he was never destined to return. Lord Elgin belonged to a noble family of Scotch peers, and having been trained from his earliest years in politics had rendered conspicuous services to his country in the counsels of the House of Lords and in diplomacy, and the success he achieved as Governor-General of Canada led mainly to his being selected for the Viceroyalty of India. Lord Elgin on setting out on his tour held durbars at many places, the most imposing being those at Patna and Agra. The durbar at Agra was one of the largest ever held. It was here that Lord Elgin met all the principal chiefs and nobles of Rajputana, and Central India besides the influential personages of Agra and the surrounding districts. Lord Elgin proceeded to Simla from Agra and remained there for some months when he set out on his travels amidst the gorges of the Himalayas, and breathed his last in the small hill-station of Dharmsala, on the 20th of November 1863. The charge of the office of the Viceroy was held according to official rules by Sir William Denison then governor of Madras who was the senior in Indian service of his brother-governor of Bombay. The news of Lord Elgin's death reached England simultaneously with that of the Wahabee conspiracy and the troubles created not only on the western borders but in many peaceful Indian cities by the preachings and secret movements of bands of fanatical Mahomedans from beyond the confines of India; and all eyes in England were at once turned towards that man whose vigor and administrative ability had nipped the Mutiny in the Punjab in the bud and who was popularly known as the saviour of the Punjab. Sir John Lawrence was selected to be the Viceroy and entrusted with the task of saving India from the machinations of the fanatical Mahomedans. He landed in Calcutta on January 12th, 1864.

THE INDIAN MUSSULMANS.—The fanatical spirit of the Mahomedans has been a source of great political trouble in the old world even since Mahomet propagated his famous religion. And while to all external appearance the surface of the Indian political society was tranquil and calm, there was discovered a conspiracy with many ramifications, which was fortunately nipped in the bud when it was of the size of a cloud no bigger that a man's hand, before the whole scheme had time to mature. The Mahomedans under British rule have not evinced the same amount of contentment at their present position as have the Hindus, but it must be borne in mind that the better classes of Mahomedans in every part of India are perfectly appreciative of the great blessings of British rule, and are free from every taint of disaffecton. But the problem of the situation of the Indian Mussulmans has been presented to the notice of the public during the thirty years from 1859—1889 by many able writers. Sir William Hunter's fascinating book on Indian Mussulmans has achieved a permanent fame. The heads of large Mahomedan seminaries have frequently drawn public attention to the subject ; and two of the Lieutenant-Governors of the North Western Provinces whose reputation as men of letters equals their high position as officials, Sir William Muir and Sir Alfred Lyall have written on the subject with their wonted vigor and practical wisdom.* But the problem has not advanced much beyond its original stage thirty years ago. It is but natural that those who were the masters of India before

---

* A few passages here are taken from a paper on Indian Mussulmans contributed by me to a leading Indian periodical.

the commencement of British rule and whose religious faith
is perhaps the most intolerant in the world should feel a little
uneasy under an administration dispensing just and equal
laws, and enforcing a religious policy, which though it leaves
to the Mussulmans the free enjoyment of their own religion,
yet takes away from it its aggressive spirit and restrains them
from asserting their tenets by force. The many pretenders
and usurpers who flourished towards the close of the Mogul
Empire also made large demands of rent-free lands for endowments under imperfect and at times forged documents and the
scrutiny with which British officers examined all these claims and
disallowed a large number gave facilities to the malcontents to
raise a hue and cry that funds Sacred to religious purposes were
being sequestrated. This fancied grievance which had been ventilated from time to time in the public press acquired some
weight by the diversion for a time of the splendid endowment
of Mahomed Mohsin to secular English education—an acknowledged mistake on the part of the government which
was set right by the enlightened action of Sir George Campbell. But the head and front of the grievances thirty years
ago was, and still continues to be, that the administration of
the country being carried on mostly through the medium of
the English tongue shut out the Mahomedans from active
participation on a large scale, because they have, by reason
of their religious sentiments, hitherto availed themselves but
little of the opportunities for a training in western literature
and science. The Mahomedans, it is urged, consequently
occupy but a numerically small fraction of the public offices
in India. Whether Lord Macaulay committed a mistake or
not, when he de-orientalized the system of higher education in
this country and subsidized the acquisition of that species of
knowledge which makes fifty years of Europe better than a
cycle of Cathay is a question that admits of but one answer.
But owing to the sentiments of the proud followers of Mahomet, who were at once called upon to accept a position far

lower than that which it was their privilege to occupy, in the days immediately preceding the British rule, and the natural disappointment of those, the majority of whom entered India as soldiers of fortune and retaining to the end that character, found that with the advent of universal peace within the borders of India their occupation was gone and the traditions of a religion whose texts until modified by ingenius interpretations, raised an important question as to the obligation laid on a faithful Moslem to rise in arms against the British Government, being bound to do so by conscience, and whose avowed principles made a thoroughly completed religious education, an essential condition before the beginning of secular learning—the Mahomedans until very recently resolutely refused to accept the new order of things and were left behind in the race of progress. When on the establishment of the Indian High Courts, English was substituted for Urdu, as the language of the Courts universally in Bengal and to a less extent elsewhere, the Mahomedans were gradually displaced by the Hindus considerably in the public service of Bengal and in a smaller degree in other places. In the N. W. Provinces where many departments of public business are still conducted in Urdu which is more the vernacular of the Mahomedans than of the Hindus the grievance as to the exclusion of the Mahomedans from clerical service does not to the same extent exist. But the remedy for such grievances as the Mahomedans may feel, as the ablest among them have long since perceived and as they have been repeatedly told by many of those who are their sincerest well-wishers, lies in their own hands. The British Government in the case of all its subject races adopted the sound administrative principle of fair play and no favor in the selection of the members of the public services. It is hopeless to expect that the British Government will modify this broad rule of justice and practical expediency in favor of the angular sentiments or prejudices or the immoveable supineness of any particular individual or set of individuals. The only way to official preferment and to the enjoyment of life in all its aspects in Modern India, lies through the gate of that higher education which first saw its inception in Lord Macaulay's famous minute. The Mahomedans should provide as many as possible of their own educational seminaries, where secular and religious instruction may be combined and the Government will certainly afford every aid to them under the grants-in-aid system. The Mahomedan intellect is presumably not inferior to that of the Hindu. The Moslems have inherited the noblest traditions and carried both the arts of war and peace to perfection when Europe was still the land of painted savages. Within the last thirty years many of their race have achieved distinctions in the liberal culture and the cultivated arts of the West, and there is no reason why if they look to the situation fully in the face and display one-tenth of that noble energy that their forefathers have enshrined in the pages of the world's history their grievances will readily disappear. By this means and by none other can the Indian Mussulmans become as favored and contented a race as any other enthological division of Her Majesty's Indian subjects.

THE WAHABEE CONSPIRACY.—The Mahomedans in every part of the world firmly believe that a second prophet of the name of Imam-Mahdi will appear, at some future date, and it has been a common trick with clever imposters ever since the Mahomedan religion was founded to pretend to be this expected prophet and thus lay claim to spiritual and temporal greatness. It was industriously propagated as a piece of stirring news in all the Indian bazaars that the expected Islamic prophet has appeared far beyond the western borders of India at a place named Sittana, and aggression and propagation of the true creed by the bayonet and the sword being the most favorite dogmas of the Mahomedan faith, it was naturally expected that the so-called prophet will wage a holy war with the British Government and secret emissaries and preachers were sent to all the great towns of the Presidency of Bengal as far east as Dacca to collect men and supplies and excite secret disaffection. The designing men at Sittana found a willing ally in Mahomed Shuffee of the Punjab who held extensive contracts for the supply of meat to all the European regiments in the province and had many agents and servants travelling constantly from place to place. Captain Parsons through some of his Afghan policemen got scent of this wide-spread disaffection and ceaseless activity amongst those who in conjuction with the rude tribes on the west of the India meditated an united rising against the British Government. A native editor also published an inflammatory pamphlet that was being then circulated by the emissaries and gave a distinct warning as to the existence of other similar pamphlets and agencies for exciting disaffection. Mr. William Tayler the Commissioner of Patna also found that the plot had spread a complicated network in his division and he promptly seized all the suspected persons—a measure which was deemed by the head of his government to have been quite useless and for which Mr. Tayler suffered severely. The Panjab conspirators headed by Mahomed Shuffee and Juffir Ally, were also tried and found guilty of treason, though the extreme penalty of the law was modified in certain cases by the executive government. The conspiracy which had spread far and wide was effectually suppressed, an expedition had also to be sent against the mountaineers beyond the Indus, which terminated next year and will be dealt with in the next chapter. In this connection it is due to the better classes of Mahomedans in all parts of India to say, that though they might ventilate their grievances in a perfectly legitimate and constitutional way, they held themselves quite aloof from this conspiracy whose main object was secretly to undermine the British Government.

GENERAL EVENTS.—Lord Elgin started at the end of autumn for a tour in the Himalayas and his route lay through the Kangra Valley. This beautiful vale of nature is known to the

Indian public chiefly on account of that superior sort of tea that bears its name. It has however one of the lovliest sites of the Himalayas, which, as all the civilized world knows, abound in lovely, and sublime sceneries, and is ranked only inferior to the valley of Cashmere, that romantic land of India, which had evoked the grandest flights of many of India's greatest writers, and which holds in popular fancy, the place of a land full of all that is lovely and delightful. The Kangra Valley is also rich in the grandest panoramas of majestic beauty, and is surrounded on all sides by lofty ranges with Kooloo, Ladak and Spiti on one side and Chineba and Cashmere on the other. It was, when amidst these mountain scenes, which in the graphic style of a Ruskin or any other æsthetic writer would call forth the deepest feelings of the human heart, that Lord Elgin had his constitution deranged by an unusual amount of nervous exertion on these giddy heights. The shock his system suffered from the consequent nervous exhaustion was too much for his over-worked frame and he had to lie down on that bed from which his soul quickly took its flight with the cheering confidence that illumines the path of the virtuous to heaven. He was interred in a beautiful spot which Lady Elgin selected for his tomb in the village of Dhurmsalla. It is idle to speculate whether Lord Elgin would have fulfilled in the Indian Viceroyalty, the high expectations formed of him. His career was too short and he had time but barely to master the details of this vast and complicated mechanism of Indian administration. His policy was eminently conciliatory but but no one can now speculate as to the later developments it might have assumed. He died regretted by all, the first Viceroy who could not return to his native land.

Sir Charles Trevelyan who had been recently recalled from the Governorship of Madras came back to India as the Finance Minister. His reappointment removed the cloud under which his reputation rested and the Home Government thus dealt to him a measure of tardy justice. His budget statements are remarkably clear expositions of the situation and he rendered himself popular with all classes by trying to remove the abnoxious income-tax from the statute-book and eventually succeeding in doing so two years hence. The government of the North-West Provinces changed hands during the year by the retirement of Mr. Edmonstone and he was succeeded by the Hon'ble E. Drummond of the Bengal Civil Service who had acquired the reputation of being an able financier. The task entrusted to Mr. Edmonstone was a very difficult one. He had to heal the effects of the terrible wound caused by the Mutiny which was still gaping in the provinces under his sway, when he took charge. By assiduous vigor and industry he succeeded in putting the machine again in right order. Though trained in the school of Lawrence and Montgomery, he had not the striking originality of either though in the ordinary duties of provincial administration he always evinced a fair degree of ability. The administration of his successor the Hon'ble E. Drummond was marked by some attempts to establish provincial exhibitions. Soon after his retirement Mr. Edmonstone breathed his last in his native land. A distinguished writer refers in connection with Mr. Edmonstone's death, to the fact that a good many Anglo-Indian officers of distinction died almost immediately after their retirement and arrival in England. The effects of the Indian climate were popularly ascribed as the chief cause of these lamentable occurrences but the writer above alluded to has very pertinently shown that the sudden relaxation from all labour, and the sudden change from the habits of years had as much to do with the dissolution of Anglo-Indian constitutions as the ravages of the Indian climate. The only event of importance during Sir William Denison's short tenure of the Indian Viceroyalty was in connection with the Umbeyla Campaign and will find a more appropriate place in the next chapter. He was called upon to face a situation to deal with which decision of character and a broad grasp of affairs were essential.

This year was remarkable for some fluctuations in the money-market, which might be briefly noticed here. The exchange question had assumed, in our own days a serious and threatening aspect in the case of India which had by time-honored arrangements to make large annual payments in England in gold. This question and the solutions of it proposed and the labours of the Currency Commission which tended to relieve the situation, will be dealt with in their proper place. The abnormal profits realized by the cotton trade during the period of the American War, as well as the rage for speculation which runs high in some particular periods, led to the formation of Joint Stock Companies in the presidency towns, in large numbers, and which proposed to lay out capital and labour on every conceivable article of human use and comfort. Many of these Companies or rather the greater part of them entirely collapsed, and the losses inflicted on individual families were immense. The *Friend of India* estimated the losses in the case of Calcutta alone at nearly 15 lacs of rupees. Sir Charles Trevelyan in his budget speech for the next year also dwells on the fact that the piece goods trade underwent great fluctuations. The native dealers at Calcutta and Bombay did not readily accept the high prices of manufactured cotton-goods of the English exporters but changed their minds on finding that the prices would not fall thus bringing a sudden re-action and enormous profits to certain traders. The question of India's export and import trade engaged the attention of the Government during the year, and several schemes for introducing a gold currency were submitted to it. Mr. Fawcett's opinion as to the introduction of a gold currency in India, as being totally unsuitable to a country which has to make the majority of its payments in small sums had the upper hand in the counsels of the government. The creation of a greater demand for the improved productions of England, will, it was hoped, equalize the exports and imports and save the necessity of exporting bullion in this country. How far these hopes were realized and how far the figures of export and import trade support the inferences drawn from them by the contending schools of Indian politicians, will be fully discussed much later on.

CHAPTER VI.

1864.

THE CENTRAL PROVINCES.—The vast tract of country which is known in Indian geography and politics as the Central Provinces is bordered by Bengal and Orissa on the East, by Central India and other hilly tracts on the North and West and by Berar and the Nizam's dominions on the South. This immense extent of territory had been acquired by the British Government at different times by wars and treaties but they were first organized into a Chief Commissionership by Lord Canning. The first Chief Commissioner appointed was Colonel Elliot, whose administration was of the average and ordinary run of mediocre officers but it is due chiefly to Sir Richard Temple's enthusiasm and extraordinary abilities that the vast mass of chaos existing there was reduced to order and the province first came under a regular and systematized administration. Sir Richard was Chief Commissioner of the province for nearly 4 years having got a transfer in 1866 to the Residentship of Hyderabad. To the lot of those historians who have dealt with the earlier periods of British rule in India has fallen the noble task of recording the grandest feats of Anglo-Saxon energy and ability in constructing a systematized administration out of a heterogeneous and disordered organism and no more pleasing duty can fall to the lot of the modern historian. After 1859, the great feat of introducing every one of the methods and appliances of civilized life into a vast territorial area still in a primitive condition first fell to the indomitable energy and organizing ability of Sir Richard Temple. When Sir Richard took charge of the province, one could have easily seen that he will have to perform a mission similar to that undertaken by white men in the west with the exception that he was never to injure them in the slightest degree nor use any means of compulsion. The province contained large tracts covered with dense jungles and although, by the greatest difficulty traces were found of some centres of population, no regular roads existed by which they could be brought into communication with one central station. Sir Richard Temple's labors in first visiting every part of his dominions at every season of the year through pathless forests and deep and noble rivers, can not be too highly praised. He resolved upon visiting every centre of interest and importance at whatever risk and cost and before he could introduce a systematic and centralized government into such an unwieldy mass, it was absolutely requisite for him, to make himself acquainted personally with every detail and nature of the workable schemes, for securing the uniformity he so much disired. One can not however appreciate the full extent of Sir Richard Temple's difficulties without knowing the fact that the jungles which spread for many miles round on every side in these territories were very unhealthy and the absence of roads and travelling stages made even the Chief Commissioner travel on foot or on horse-back and depend at times upon the coarsest fare. Sir Richard Temple went first to Mundla on the Nerbudda and thence to Seonee and Nagpur, whence he turned southwards visiting Chindwarra, the Berars and Omrawatee, in his first tour. In the second tour, he went down the Godavery, to Coconda on the coast of the Bay of Bengal, and thence through Sumbulpur and Chhatisgarh back to Nagpur. In his third tour he struck towards the Panchmari Hills, and came back through the Chundla and Seonee districts. In the course of these tours Sir Richard Temple, had taken care to collect every information regarding the land tenure, the systems of civil and criminal justice in vogue and the customs and usages of a rude people and then laid all his views in a masterly document before the Supreme Government, along with other particulars of his information gleaned during the travels. In his own eloquent words, "Nature and circumstance, with a severe impartiality have distributed the points of interest and importance over the whole 'length and breadth of the land. In one distant direction it will be local political affairs that claim attention; in another the land tenures, in another the navigable rivers, in another the arrangements for defence and protection, in another the forests and in another, the communication through the passes." Sir Richard Temple first set himself after collecting this information, about completing the land settlement. He fixed the revenue for thirty or twenty years as the case might have been, had all the rights in the land recorded, and had all absolute and relative obligations fixed, so as to avoid future uncertainties. He then began to effect reforms in the Police and magisterial departments and gave commissions as magistrates, to a good many native gentlemen, who assisted the regular establishment by disposing of nearly one-fifth of the cases with credit and ability. He undertook the construction of good metalled roads, which in the absence of better means are the broad highways of commerce. There was also a great deal of progress in the sanitary and hygienic condition of the province, and the climate was sought to be improved by the clearing off, of dense forests. The increase of litigation surely be-tokened the advent of a peaceful administration and a settled society. The Central Provinces did thus under the simple machinery of the non-regulation system and with the assistance of the administrative genius of Sir Richard Temple took a great leap towards civilization. The area known as Central Provinces has a great future before it ; its noble rivers, its fertile soil, its salubrious climate, and its unbounded capacity for natural products afford the highest scope for true statesmanship and forms a field of work worth the ambition of the most gifted specimens of Anglo-Saxon energy. In our own days, Mr. Alexander Mackenzie followed in the foot steps of Sir Richard Temple. The latter's successor Mr. Morris pays a graceful tribute to his indefatigable efforts and unique success as an administrator in his official report for 1866-67.

THE UMBEYLA CAMPAIGN—The country was threatened with a grave disaster from the fanaticism and the political combination of the Moslems on the west. The widespread Mahomedan conspiracy discovered during Lord Elgin's reign, was supported by the Sittana fanatics beyond the frontiers of India and the government in 1863 determined upon sending a military force to coerce them to submission. The hardy and uncivilized races on the western borders of India had always been a source of grave political danger and their occasional raids and forays, have from time immemorial disturbed the peace of the cultivated frontier districts. To carry on a war with them is at the same time the most difficult of all military operations. They were secure in their own mountain fastnesses and while the natural situation of their country, affords them the greatest facilities, for offensive operations, it serves at the same time as a perpetual barrier against any sort of organized military tactics and allows only a desultory guerilla warfare. Even the vetern Lion of the Punjab Ranjit Singh could hardly bring them to anything like complete subjection and the best-disciplined troops of Great Britain suffered at their hands an unprecedented and unmerited fate in that campaign of 1842, which cost England so dear both in men and the prestige of her arms. On the morning of the 20th of October 1863, Sir Neville Chamberlain with a small force entered the Umbeyla pass, and had a difficult march through precipitious roads and watercourses. The enemy sent stray shots from the heights on both sides, and the arrangement was adopted of crowning the heights on either side with flanking parties of guide Infantry. One evening the British troops came across the enemy who were occupying Umbeyla, and the mountaineers rushed upon the disciplined regiments with hideous enthusiasm and in great disorder. Scuffles ensued and after some losses the enemy was for the time held in check by a regiment of the Muzbee Sikhs and the 20th Panjab Infantry. The British troops then made a halt for the night but the Bonairs rushed upon them with shouts and yells, and there was desultory firing on both sides. The terrible difficulty through which this mountain campaign will have to be conducted now became apparent on all sides. Sir Neville Chamberlain saw that he would have to advance by fighting every inch, that it would be extremely difficult to keep communications open, with the headquarters on the frontier, and to get supplies, while it was almost impracticable to inflict deadly losses on any large body of the enemy by organized military action. The Bonairs did actually block up Sir Neville Chamberlain's rear and that gallant General saw that his only means lay in maintaining his position. The ranks of the enemy on the 26th October received accessions from the Swatees and the Moslems from Mulka, on the northern side of the Mahaban range, and by keeping up a stray firing gave the British troops absolutely no rest. The British troops formed a small body and to advance at each step was so difficult that the commander had to think of making a prolonged stay where he was, as long as sufficient reinforcements did not arrive. On Friday the 6th of November 1863, the enemy gathered in great numbers and attacked the advanced guards of the British troops under Ensign Marry, Captain Rogers, and Major Hardinge. The British troops were effectually protected for a time by a low ridge of hills which admirably served as a breastwork, but the overwhelming numbers of the enemy had the advantage, and the small party after waiting for reinforcements which did not arrive, had to retire carrying the dead and wounded as best they might. This small measure of success spread like wildfire among the mountain-tribes and their ranks received again an accession of over 3000 men and on the night of the 12th November, they vigorously attacked the picket thrown on the right of the little camp on a high craggy peak which was known as the Craig picket. They captured this picket and slaughtered to a man Lieutenant Davidson and his small band of soldiers. On the news of this fresh success of the enemy reaching Sir Neville, who was encamped in the pass below, Colonel Salisbury, was immediatly ordered to proceed and retake the defensive position at any cost. Colonel Salisbury with Major Ross and Lieutenant Inglis bravely ascended the precipitous rocks and rushed on the enemy with great fury, scattering them for the time and recovering the lost picket. Another skirmish took place on the 19th November between Captain Smith's party and the Bonairs in which several officers were killed. On the 20th, the enemy made again a desperate attack on the Craig picket and though it was vigorously defended by Major DeLafosse succeeded in again capturing it. The position had to be retaken by a dreadful fight, and at a great sacrifice by Colonel Hope and the Highlanders. Major James the Commissioner of Peshawar who had an intimate knowledge of the country and the habits of the mountaineers joined the force as political officer on the 19th November, and through his diplomatic efforts, the less zealous members of the enemy's camp abandoned the sacred Moslem cause. Sir Neville Chamberlain was himself laid up with a severe wound and the command of the force devolved upon Major-General Garvock, who had distinguished himself in the African campaigns. The situation was now perilous in the extreme and the authorities at the head quarters were seriously called upon to consider whether the campaign should be a protracted one or the force should be ordered to retire. Lord Elgin was then on his death-bed and the council was mostly in favor of a retirement on the part of the force sent through the Umbeyla pass. Sir Robert Montgomery, the Lieutenant-Governor of the Panjab was himself vacillating but Sir Hugh Rose stoutly opposed all thoughts of our troops being ordered to fall back, and Sir William Denison who had taken charge of the Viceroyalty, strongly seconded Sir Hugh Rose's opinions. Sir William Denison rightly thought, that a policy of falling back was liable to be misconstrued by the mountaineers and it might add fresh and ever recurring troubles to the Panjab districts on the western border. It was therefore resolved that the campaign should be a protracted and extended one and for this decisive and beneficial policy posterity will ever remain indebted to Sir William Denison who, overruled the halting counsels of those around him. A campaign on a large scale was organized and the brigade was ordered to assemble at Hati Mardan near Peshawar, and the first operations of the new detachments were against the village Laloo, which stronghold was completely destroyed by Colonel Turner's brigade. The heights leading up to the Garoo mountain and the Bonair pass were next swept of their armed men, and the Chumla valley occupied. After a series of rapid and brilliant successes the enemy was considerably weakened by the desertion of their allies, and the original object of this war, the destruction of Mulka was accomplished on the 22nd of December without much trouble. The disasters that occurred during this campaign were due to the simple fact that the strength of the enemy had been too much under-rated and a sufficient number of regiments was not sent in the first instance, and but for the subsequent prudent counsels that prevailed the British troops would have been in a serious predicament. The frontier question in India is always a knotty question. The wild tribes will never come under any settled system of government nor will they betake themselves within even a long period to peaceful and industrious habits. Whenever any operations are undertaken to punish them, it must be remembered that the campaign is of the most difficult sort of all Indian campaigns, and it will be found that in subsequent years the lessons learnt in 1863-64 were not thrown away.

SIR JOHN LAWRENCE.—The advent of a Civilian Governor-General for the first time in the History of India was hailed with great delight by those who had previously any knowledge of the Viceroy—elect. The people in the Panjab who had been familiar with Sir John and his brother Sir Henry Lawrence, also a towering figure in Indian History, for many years now saw in the Viceroy the same officer whom they beloved and respected as commissioner and provincial governor, and the enthusiasm of the people in that part of the country was unbounded. In other parts of the Indian continent the same enthusiasm was felt for a name that had become a household word since the dark days of the Mutiny for having so successfully resisted the tide of aggression when ever it came in contact with the Lahore Government. With the Umbeyla complications on the western frontier, and Bhotan complications on the eastern border, with the exaggerated importance that popular fancy and the rumours spread by designing men, attributed to the conspiracy among the Mahomedans that had been discovered it was universally felt that India required at her helm a ruler whose very name would be a tower of strength to the British Government, and whose past career was associated with grand and unvarying success in the cabinet and the field. Among the members of his own service the feeling was of a mixed character. Such is human nature unfortunately in the planet where we live, that any one is hardly free from the jealousies and evil designs of his fellow-men. The most scrupulous honesty and the most brilliant abilities are often depreciated and underrated by those whose innate badness of heart or personal pique is excited, and there is hardly a man to-day in any sphere of life whatever, who is not spoken ill of, whose motives and actions are not misconstrued, by those whose interests clash with his, or who, incapable of those steady efforts and that unerring faculty of seizing opportunities, that distinguish the really able man from one of mediocre and average abilities are deservedly left behind in the race of life. By many members of his service, it was broadly hinted that Sir John Lawrence had been much overrated, and while the majority rejoiced at finding a member of their own service, raised to such an exalted and dignified position, there were not wanting discordant notes, expressing open disapproval at the selection made for the Viceregal office. We shall not anticipate here whether the expectations entertained of him were fulfilled by Sir John Lawrence. Among the military classes his advent was hailed with unmixed delight, and all watched with interest and curiosity the career in the most exalted appointment in the British Empire outside England, of one who was not a stranger to the country, who had risen from the lowest step of the official ladder, to the highest-paid post in the world. But his presence in India at this crisis was a distinct gain, it was worth the presence of an army and confidence on all sides was restored, when it was found that the Lion of the Panjab was once more in the land to quell rebellion and sweep away disaffection with an iron hand, whereover they might appear. It is interesting to read in the papers of those times the account of the feeling welcome which the new Governor-General received in the Panjab, or that feeling address in which Sir John welcomed his friends and associates in his old province speaking in a majestic voice and for the first time for a Viceroy, in the language of the province. Sir John landed in Calcutta on the 12th January 1864, and was heartily welcomed in his new office.

GENERAL EVENTS—Sir John Lawrence spent the summer in the cool heights of the Himalays, and held a large durbar at Lahore in the end of autumn. The durbar was attended by the chiefs of the Panjab, and the Viceroy addressed them in their own language. Sir John Lawrence's address was not that piece of rhetorical effort and string of rounded and well-turned sentences that we always read with so much pleasure from the literary point of view, in our own days. His address proceeded from the depths of his heart and it was a feeling welcome and admonition to those among whom he had lived for thirteen years, and with whom he had been associated most intimately. He impressed them with the solid advantages of British rule, and referred with pride to the loyalty the Panjabee soldiers and Panjabee chiefs had shown during the disasters of 1857 and the following year. He took occasion to mention the names of those distinguished officers who had co-operated with him in the government of the Panjab and the Maharajas of Cashmere and Patiallah, the Sikh chiefs of

Malwah and the Manjha, the Rajput chiefs of the hills, the Mahomedan Mullies of Peshawar and Kohat, the Sirdars of Derajat, Hazara, and Delhi, received the address with deep emotions, as they beheld the officer so well-known to them speaking with the inmost feelings of his heart. Calcutta and Lahore were also prominently before the public this year, by reason of the Exhibition of Arts, Manufactures and Produce in those cities. The Calcutta Exhibition also included agricultural machinery and at the opening of the exhibition much enthusiasm was displayed, even the Viceroy being present. The Lahore Exhibition collected together the produce and the curiosities, the minerals and the handicrafts from every remote corner of the province. As Sir Robert Montgomery observed in his opening address "But God has richly blessed these provinces with natural gifts ; with mountains abounding in forest timber ; with plains needing nothing but artificial irrigation to produce the finest crops ; with rivers capable of watering the whole soil. But to render them increasingly serviceable to human sustenance and comfort, they must be brought under more complete subjection by human labour." Thus the Panjab exhibition was a grand affair and was an humble attempt to imitate on a small scale those splendid and inimitable shows in Great Britain and Ireland with which the name of the late Prince Consort will for ever remain associated. It was evident that the Panjab within a short period of British rule had made much more progress, than any other province, and this was due equally to the noble character of the races that inhabit the province and the exceptionally able men who under the loose system of the non-regulation provinces could do their best to bring their ability and energy into full play. The metropolis of India, Calcutta was visited this year with a terrible cyclone which did considerable damage to life and property. The wind became violent at about four-o'clock on the 5th October 1864, and lasted till about a quarter to ten. The violence of the wind again increased considerably after nearly an hour and the winds continued to rage till nearly two in the morning. The river on the western side of Calcutta which in ordinary times, is calm and placid like an artificial lake, was raging and foaming and vast extent of black water swept through a greater part of its course from the sea, deluging hundreds of miles, sweeping away homesteads and cornfields and irreparably ruining the great vessels, whose masts and riggings in ordinary times form such a beautiful and imposing spectacle on the Hoogly. Trees were torn up by their roots, and thrown about by the force of wind, and a great number of houses constantly fell down with terrible noise and crushed hundreds of human victims. As the Calcutta *Englishman* described at the time " carriages and palkees were upset and strewed the roads, mingled with the debris of roofs verandahs, gates, and fallen trees. Corrugated iron roofings were torn doubled up and blown away like sheets of paper. By two-o'clock the Eastern and Southern Suburbs of the city, and those parts of it to the westward, which from their proximity to the plain and the river were the most exposed were more or less a wreck. Except the cocoa-nut and other palms scarcely a tree was anywhere to be found standing. The beautiful avenues in Fort William were entirely destroyed ; the Eden Gardens were turned into a wilderness ; the Tank Square, the trees and shrubs were blown away and in many parts the iron railing torn up and over-thrown. In Garden Reach the roads were blocked up and rendered impassable from the trees that fell across them. The damage done to buildings was considerable. Among these we notice the roof of the Free School was blown away ; the upper part of the Roman Catholic Church at the upper end of Bowbazar road entirely destroyed, and the steeple of the Free Church of Scotland, the minarets of the Mosque in Dhurmtollah were all blown away ; St. Jame's Theatre was unroofed and nearly destroyed ; the roof of the Cathedral was much damaged ; the sheds of the East India Railway Company were unroofed and Messrs Thacker Spink and Co's premises seriously damaged. In fact scarcely a pucca house in Calcutta has escaped without injury while the native huts, especially in the Suburbs were almost all blown down. The Telegraph Lines are interrupted: all is confusion, and it is scarcely known, what ships have been entirely lost, what are immediately damaged and are safe. With few exceptions, the shipping were driven from their moorings, and cast ashore or jammed together on the opposite side of the river, while several were sunk in mid channel and others stranded by the storm wave high up on the Calcutta shore." There are no precise data, as to the exact amount of the loss of lives but the loss to life and property was considerable. This year saw the birth of three Commissions—the Sanitary Commission, the Commissariat Commission and the Cholera Commission. The Sanitary Commission continued its labours from year to year. The Commissariat Commission was appointed at the instance of Sir Hugh Rose and effected several important reductions in the ruinous Commissariat charges. The Cholera Commission had at its head, Sir John Strachey, who with his colleagues, a military and a medical officer visited all the places where the Cholera of 1861 had broken out in a rather severe form and collected all the items of information, with reference to the origin and the suppression of the disease. It was found that the most culpable neglect prevailed with reference to the health of the British troops and it was discovered with amazement that at the Meean Mir hospital near Lahore, the latrines contained the accumlated filth of ten years, though for the circuitous proceedings prevailing in all departments of admistration in every civilized country it was not easy to fix the responsibility of this dreadful state of things on any one individual. Considerable improvements also took place in the general modes of life of the European soldiers. The dwellings allotted to the British soldiers in the Cantonments were bad enough and the first grants of the funds of the country were spent in constructing barracks for the British troops. The British soldier had under the system of barracks inaugurated in this year, large and well-ventilated rooms, with a place attached in each range of buildings where he might be engaged in reading or devout meditation if he so pleased. The mortality among the European troops which always involved heavy losses to the state was also engaging the attention of the government. By the building of double-storied barracks preventing the soldiers to sleep on the ground-floor in hot and unhealthy seasons of the year, it was sought to keep them beyond the attacks of malaria. And the expedient was also seriously thought of *viz.*, utilizing the large and healthy hill-stations of India for large cantonments and locating the greater part of the European soldiers, permanently in a climate which compares not unfavorably, with that of the regions of Northern Europe. The plan it was thought, could be safely adopted when the hill stations would be linked by extensive lines of railway, with every part of the Indian continent. Some complications took place on the Bhotan frontier which along with the war that ensued are detailed in the next chapter. The temperance movement was prominently before the Indian public in the course of this year and temperance associations were organized in large centres of European army. The finances were in equilibrium and Sir Charles Trevelyan, who continued as Finance minister introduced strict economy and went on curtailing useless expenditure.

CHAPTER VII.
1865.

THE BHOTAN WAR.—One of the troubles bequeathed to Sir John Lawrence by the previous administration was with reference to Bhotan affairs. Bhotan is one of the three semi-independent native states, which lie between Thibet and the British Indian dominions. To its north and east lies Thibet, to the west the territories of Nepal and Sikkim and to the south Bengal Proper and Assam. This mountainous tract of land forms a small kingdom that owns the overlordship of Thibet. It is inhabited by a hardy race who depend more on hunting than on agriculture for their daily food and are not unoften accustomed to make raids and forays into the neighbouring territories, where a peaceful population can ill afford to withstand effectively their savage attacks at all times. The difficulties with reference to the frontier tribes have always been a source of standing trouble and difficulty to the British Government. The warfare with them, is always something in which the superior discipline of the British Indian army gives but little advantage, and the only effective way of checking their depredations and holding them at bay, is to blockade the mountain passes through which alone the mountain tribes can get their supplies. The state of Bhotan always laid claim to the valleys, at the foot of the Bhotan mountains bordering on Bengal and Assam known as the "Dooars." There are passes from these valleys leading to the interior of the hills, of which five are well-known, Dhalimkote Chamoorcha, Balla, Baxa or Pusakha and Bishensing each defended by a fort and presided over by a Bhotanese officer known as Jungpen. To the east of Bishensing is another pass known as the Dewangiri pass and fort. The Dooars bordering on Assam belonged in the days of the native kings of the province to the

Bhotanese on condition of their paying a stipulated tribute in kind. When the British Government took possession of Assam, it demanded of the Bhotanese government the arrears of revenue due, but the Bhotanese raised various objections. At length a mission was sent in 1837 under Colonel Pemberton, and it was arranged that the British Government should have the possession of the Dooars bordering on Assam on condition of paying a revenue of ten thousand rupees annually. From 1841, this arrangement had been in force, and the British Government always fulfilling its obligations, the raids of the Bhotanese on the Dooars were discontinued. In 1842 a similar arrangement was made with reference to a tract of country known as Ambaree Fallacottah. But with reference to the "Dooars" bordering on Bengal the occasional outrages continued and the period of 1828 to 1863, was always marked by some violation or other of the treaty obligations of the Bhotanese government. It was thought in 1861, that some pressure should be brought on a government which was quite heedless of the principles of international law, by stopping to pay the Ambaree rents from that year, intimating at the same time that payment would be resumed as soon as the British property and subjects that had been carried away, had been restored and the Bhotanese government made satisfactory arrangements for the discontinuance of the raids on the part of its subjects. Bhotan had always two rulers, like some other countries of Asia, one the head of spiritual affairs and the other, the head of temporal affairs—known respectively as the Dhurm Raja and the Deb Raja. Under the Bhotanese constitution the Deb Raja's authority was merely nominal, the Dhurm Raja being the sole ruler of the state. The country was also parcelled out into three governorships—known as Western, Eastern and Central Bhotan, whose viceroys were respectively known as the Paro, the Tongso and Daka Penlows. In 1862 a native messenger was sent to the Deb Raja, who went with a letter offering to send an accredited embassy of the British Government for the sake of settling all disputes then pending and asking for arrangements to be made for the safe journey of the Ambassador and his escort. The reply was that the complaints received by the British Government were of too trivial a nature to be referred to the Dhurm Raja, that no mission was necessary but that a few officers of the Bhotanese government known as Zinkaffs would proceed to settle all disputes. But the Government did send the mission in November 1863, the accredited envoy being the Hon'ble Ashley Eden who was accompanied by Captains Austin and Lance, Dr. Simson and Cheboo Lama who was the interpreter. When the mission started there were internal disturbances at Bhotan and the Deb Raja had been expelled, the governor of Eastern Bhotan heading the rebellion. Mr. Eden on the 10th November addressed the Chief at Dhalimkote asking what arrangements had been made about his mission. The Jungpem of Dhalimkote was the follower of one of the members of the council who had taken part in the rebellion but being subject to the governor of Western Bhotan he was in danger of losing his appointment. He therefore thought to make his own position strong by befriending Mr. Eden's mission and without any authority from the central government he sent friendly messages to Mr. Eden, and had a long interview with Cheboo Lama, the Thibetan interpreter with the mission. Sir William Denison, who was then holding the office of Viceroy, was telegraphed to by Mr. Eden for orders, whether to proceed when the country and the seat of government was in a disorganized state. Sir William Denison thinking that the Deb Raja might take the advantage of an alliance with the British Government against the rebels, ordered Mr. Eden to proceed straight to the capital. Mr. Eden's difficulties lay principally in his not being able to secure a sufficient number of coolies and the continued desertion of those whom he had secured. On reaching Dhalimkote, the chief openly received the mission and paid the envoy a visit in his tents, drinking the whole day in the tents of Mr. Eden and Cheboo Lama. He, while about to depart, found some coolies being flogged for desertion, within the British encampment and demanded their immediate release, and on its being refused, he threatened to cut down the officer in attendance. Mr. Eden remonstrated with him about his conduct and refused to see him until he had sent in a written apology, which he did the next day. Mr. Eden halted for several days at Dhalimkote but as no stock of supplies was to be had there except at an enormous price, Captain Austin was sent to purchase supplies at Jalpigoorie. While at Dhalimkote Mr. Eden received a message from the Deb Raja enquiring the object of his mission and asking him to refer it to the Chief of Dhalimkote. Mr. Eden wrote back to say that the object was such that it must be referred to the head of the state. The Deb Raja evidently thought it politic, to coquet with the British mission seeking to make some political capital out of it in his then insecure position in the state. On the 29th November Mr. Eden found that he could not by any possibility get a sufficient number of coolies to convey all his escort and luggage and he determined to leave behind a considerable part of his tents, baggage, stores and escort. This was a political blunder as it considerably depreciated the mission in the estimation of the Bhotanese people, who have not yet learnt to adopt the European simplicity in all political matters. From Dhalimkote Mr. Eden proceeded to Sipchoo, where he was again in great difficulties owing to the want of coolies, and here he left behind every one of his escort who could be spared. He received no assistance from the Bhotanese officials on the way, who pleaded that they had received no order with reference to the mission from the central government. On the 7th December the mission reached a place known as Tsanglee, and he sent orders, to his officers and men at Sipchoo and Dhalimkote, to return to Darjiling. Mr. Eden also committed a mistake in asking the petty officials for permission to proceed, saying that if they wished him to return he would do so but they must answer to their own government for the consequences. The council at Bhotan afterwards took hold of this little circumstance to say, that they could scarcely believe that an officer who consented to such sacrifice of dignity was in reality accredited by the Viceroy. At Paro, the envoy was subjected to a series of studied insults and in each little matter he was put to affront by the petty officials. The officers, all along the way, neither asked him to proceed nor communicated any definite orders to fall back and Mr. Eden, for the first time in the history of British India, in his capacity as the Viceregal envoy proceeded into a country where he was distinctly given to understand that he was not wanted. Mr. Eden reached the capital on the 15th of March 1864. The capital city was Poonakha, and two days after Mr. Eden's arrival he was summoned to attend the council. As neither party could understand a word of what the other spoke, it was suggested by the council that the negotiations might be left with Cheboo Lama. On the 20th March the envoy was summoned to meet the Rajas, and here more affronts were in store for him. The council assured the envoy that the matters of complaint were altogether on the side of the Bhotan government, and renewed the demands for the arrears of rent and the cession of the Assam Dooars, and the chief Tongso Penlow was unusually vehement in his expressions saying openly that they would have war, and they doubted exceedingly whether Mr. Eden had any authority from the Viceroy. On return to his own camp Mr. Eden sent for permission to depart but on the council's sending excuses for the affronts and the behaviour of Tongso Penlow, he consented to attend the council again. A draft treaty was agreed upon, on Mr. Eden's withdrawing his demands for the residence of a British representative and for the privileges to British traders, but the question of the Assam Dooars was not so much as even discussed at this interview. On the 24th March the envoy was summoned to attend the council and the demands for the cession of the Assam Dooars were renewed. The discussion was warm and the envoy's person was also insulted by some gross breaches of propriety. On his return to the camp on the 24th the mission was threatened with seizure and imprisonment in case Mr. Eden refused to sign a paper ceding the Assam Dooars. In vain Mr. Eden protested that he had no authority and he was compelled to secure his own safety and that of the mission by signing a paper which purported to be the treaty but he took care to write under his own signature the words "under compulsion". Whether these two words had been conscientiously interpreted by Cheboo Lama, and whether the Bhotanese council ever came to know at the time what these words exactly meant, do not clearly appear. Mr. Eden was then given permission to depart, and on the 31st reached the Paro Fort and had no further difficulties on the way back to the British territory.

That the Bhotan mission was a grave political blunder few at this distant date will deny. The initial mistake was the determination to send a mission in a country about the nature of whose government, the authorities in British India had no precise information, and who, it might have been presumed, would not recognize those obligations of international law which in the more civilized parts of the world would make the person and dignity of an envoy sacred. The prestige of the British name did not escape insult, when the spectacle was presented of an envoy accredited by the Governor-General, subjected to a series of affronts, which when taken in the aggregate, meant a good deal, and then denied even the ordinary courtesy of civilized intercourse. When it was known again that the Hon'ble Ashley Eden had signed a paper ceding to the Bhotanese the Assam Dooars, the news was received by the Europeans and Indians alike with vehement expressions of disapprobation. The Government at once repudiated the treaty and a peremptory demand was sent to the Bhotanese government for the restitution of all British subjects held in captivity at Bhotan, the alternative being the annexation of the Bengal Dooars. The demand, it is needless to say, was not complied with and a proclamation of war was issued in November 1864. The action of the Government in repudiating a treaty signed by its envoy was severely criticised at the time. Whether the words " under compulsion" below Mr. Eden's signature, justify such a course it is useless to discuss, as it does not appear, that the Bhutanese council knew what those words meant and accepted a treaty on the face of it invalid. The action of Mr. Eden had seriously compromised the Government, and whether the conduct of the British Government in disregarding treaty obligations though with a power, that did not observe the first principles of international law in their dealings with it, can be properly defended is a complicated question of political casuistry, upon which it is not easy to offer a decided opinion. To the ordinary mind, it would seem that the British Government had in this instance been guilty of a non-observance of those principles of eternal justice and integrity which it professes, and of which it had given several sterling proofs in its relations with the subject-races of India. But the sound principles of international law, it was argued, had no application to a state of things in which one of the high contracting powers were absolutely devoid of all integrity and observance of treaty obligations in their own transactions. The relations of civilized nations with uncivilized ones, in other parts of the world had been marked by a breach of faith much more culpable than the one attributed to the British Government, but whether the resort to an ingenious subterfuge, for repudiating the envoy's action, became a government, founded on the same noble principles as the British, is much to be doubted, and the historian cannot but wish that Mr. Eden had not purchased the safety of his mission by pretended cession of the Assam Dooars and by seriously compromising the government.

The Bhotan War was a short one. The campaign opened by two columns being sent under Brigadier-General Mulcaster and Brigadier-General Dunsford to capture the forts nearest to the British territories. This was done without much difficulty, the greatest resistance offered was at Dhalimkote, which stoutly held out for a day and fell into the hands of the British in the evening. Brigadier-General Dunsford on the 19th of December marched towards the fort known as Chamoorcha. The garrison fled as the British troops approached and the fort was captured with but little fighting. The forts at Buxa and Balla were also similarly captured almost without opposition. Captain Macdonald, captured the Dewangiri Fort with a small escort and the Bishensing fort was also taken possession of, without firing a single shot. The British army then occupied all the forts. The Bhotanese governor Tongso Penlow now made a serious effort to recover these forts and sent a warning letter to the officer commanding the British troops, which unfortunately could not be read there and had to be sent two hundred miles to Darjiling to be translated. The Bhotanese governor surprized the garrison of the Dewangiri Fort on the morning of the 29th January 1865 and by cutting off the sources of water-supply, and blocking up all passes through which all ammunition and reinforcements could reach the fort, forced Colonel Campbell and his troops at Dewangiri to retreat. The wounded and others who fell into Tongso Penlow's hands were treated by him exceedingly well. This serious loss brought about the best exertions on the part of the British Government, to recapture the fort, and one of the best Brigadiers-General was placed in command of the troops on active service at Bhotan and Dewangiri was re-captured by the overwhelming British army now directed against it. The victory was however tarnished by the cold-blooded murder by the British troops of 120 Bhotanese found within the Dewangiri Fort.

Thus closed the Bhotan war a dark chapter of Indian history which it might be said was a series of mistakes throughout. A treaty was concluded in 1866 by which the British Government was to pay Rs. 25,000 as tribute for the Bengal Dooars, and all aggressions on British Frontier were to cease, the tribute to be doubled in case this stipulation was observed by the Bhotanese Government. The responsibility of the Bhotan war must rest with the Imperial Government who had directed every step down to the treaty of 1866.

GENERAL EVENTS.—This year's budget (1865-66) proposed a loan for public works of nearly 13 lacs and an increase in the export duties. But as the measure affected the large and powerful interests of the Manchester and the Liverpool merchants, Sir John Lawrence and Sir Charles Wood looked upon the measure with disfavor. Sir Charles Trevelyan had however the satisfaction, of abolishing that tax against which he had vehemently fought while at Madras and he 'laid up' the income tax for the time, which in his own words was "a potent and but imperfect fiscal machine upon the shelf complete in all its gear ready to be re-imposed in case of any new emergency." This year witnessed the retirement from Indian Service of Sir Hugh Rose and Sir Herbert Edwardes. Sir Herbert Edwardes was a distinguished statesman of the Lawrence School. As Commissioner of Peshawar and Umballa he had displayed qualities that established his claims to a higher act in preferment, which unfortunately was denied to him. His last act in India was the trial of the Wahabee conspirators. Sir Hugh Rose was succeeded in his important appointment by Sir William Mansfield, who was then the head of the Bombay army. The Bombay Command devolved on Sir Robert Napier and the Madras Command on Sir Gasper Le Marchant on the retirement of Sir Hope Grant. A good deal of excitement was created by some assassinations on the Peshawar border. Major Adam the Deputy Commissioner of Peshawar and Lieutenant Ommaney of the guide Corps were rudely attacked and cut down, and the expedient had to be resorted to, as the only means of preventing these constant assassinations, of burning the bodies of the Mahomedan assassins—a process which in popular fancy was associated with a denial of those privileges in heaven which a Moslem earns by slaying an infidel. The terrible epidemic that broke out in the ranks of an European regiment who had been ordered to march a long distance under the greatest heat of an Indian sun brought down a severe reprimand on General Green who was responsible for the orders concerned. Nagpur was the seat of an Exhibition held on the lines of those at Calcutta and Lahore. An Engineering College was established at Roorkee near the foot of the Himalayas and in the vicinity of that place where the Ganges Canal takes its rise from the main stream. The College has been the means of training natives of India in the higher branches of engineering, and the country is much indebted to this college for the diffusion of that high class of scientific knowledge applied to the practical arts of life, and that familiarity with the skilled mechanism of the West which this College affords. The Governor of Bombay Sir Bartle Frere devoted great attention to the improvement of the Maharatta race. He met the assembled sirdars twice in durbar and delivered to them spirited addresses exhorting them to display in these times of peace the same energy that had made the names of their ancestors respected in other days. The inconveniences of Calcutta as a port had been long felt and a serious attempt was made this year to convert a place near the mouth of the Hoogly known now as Port Canning, as the port of Calcutta. Enormous capital was subscribed and spent for the purpose but the Port never became a popular one. The greatest disadvantage of Calcutta as a trading-port arises from the fact that navigation on the Hoogly is extremely difficult and the treacherous sandbanks which are to be found all along the length of the Hoogly seriously impede navigation and make it almost impossible for any vessel to go out or come in without the aid of experienced pilots. With the organised pilot service and with light-houses and buoys, this inconvenience has been much diminished. Bombay witnessed a wild commercial speculation and the consequent excitement. The cotton trade and the land reclamation schemes, had realized enormous profits, and the speculative mania, as usual in cases when certain trades are found to bring enormous profits knew no bounds. House accomodation always dear in the capital of western India began to realize fabulous rents. Shares in projected companies and in companies which already carrying on business, extended to undue proportions, rose to ten or twelve times the par value. The Directors of the Bank of Bombay, shared in the general excitement and began to to make enormous advances on the security of the bubble shares. The Bombay market was again flooded with that sort of share speculations which is known as time-bargains, that is the purchaser buying at the market value on some particular date promised to pay at a long future date and in the interim hoped to realize a large profit by the rise of the market value of shares. But when many of the companies failed one after another the crash came all at once on thousands of households. The general failures to meet engagements resulted in a petition to the Legislature, for amending the Insolvent Act in such a way as to hasten the procedure. Mr. Justice Anstey dealt severely with those who had speculated in time-bargains and had been ruined thereby. We should not close this chapter without mentioning Mr. Crawford's efforts to improve the sanitary condition of Bombay, which notwithstanding its beautiful site and its enormous wealth, had been terribly neglected as regards its municipal business. Bombay, the focus of Indian trade, and with its picturesque islets and its rich tropical verdure, the lovliest city in India, began from this year to make that steady improvement in municipal matters, which had been so complimentarily referred to by many an Indian Viceroy as they landed on Indian shores.

CHAPTER VIII.

1866.

THE ORISSA FAMINE—The most important event during this year and the first half of the next was the Orissa famine, which caused a large number of deaths from sheer starvation or from the consequent effects of constant under-feeding. The total failure of crops in the three most important districts of Orissa in 1865, followed by a scanty harvest in the early part of 1866 and by inundations on a large and extensive scale later on in the year, produced a widespread scarcity and the food in the province was not sufficient for the number of its inhabitants. Unfortunately it was not until the state of things had reached a crisis and many thousands had perished for want of food that government efforts were directed towards this serious state of things and the sufferings of the survivors of the greatest natural calamity that has befallen Orissa, were considerably mitigated. Early in the year 1867, there was a public meeting in Calcutta where the Viceroy and the leading officials asked the co-operation of private charity on the part of the non-official and native community of the province of Bengal, to relieve the famine-stricken people of Orissa. Orissa is naturally a fertile tract of country watered by the Mahanady and other rivers. But the failure of the usual rains in an Indian province was always attended with the most disastrous consequences. The system of artificial irrigation now so widely resorted to, in the more thickly-populated provinces of India, was hardly in vogue in 1866, and the old Moghul canals and aqueducts which brought water to the great centres of population and commerce and in the case of the city of Delhi, to every door in every quarter of the city had been allowed to fall in a condition of sad neglect. Added to the failure of rains in 1865, there was again a partial failure of rains in the early part of 1866, and later on in the year, the rainfall in the rocky regions where the Orissa rivers take their rise being rather heavy, the calm channels assumed a formidable shape and flooded an extensive tract of land then full of standing crops. The historian of India has unfortunately to record that much valuable time was thrown away in dealing with the Orissa famine of 1866, and that the same timely measures were not taken to prevent the severity of the calamity that was so conspicuous in the case of the Behar famine of 1873-74. The East Indian Irrigation Company which was then engaged in large and extensive operations in the province anticipated a scarcity of food and began to import food grains for its numerous staff. But the local officials made light of the situation and did not unfortunately take the same timely steps in imitation of the laudable conduct of Colonel Rundall, engineer of the above company. The non-official gentlemen who resided in the province and the native press which had already grown to be a powerful institution sounded the note of warning in no uncertain terms but the Board of Revenue, and the Local and Supreme governments gave no heed to these representations. As usual in such cases the miserable people of Orissa, who were proverbially simpletons and exceedingly poor could hardly buy the food-grains whose prices had risen considerably and began to die by thousands. In the early part of 1866, the loss of lives was appalling. People were seen leaving their villages with their starving family and famished cattle, and proceeding they knew not whither, leaving women and children by the roadside when they could no longer walk. The scene as described in the official papers and by the press at the time was the most distressing spectacle ever seen in Bengal. Half-starved people crowded to Calcutta by hundreds and strove in every way they could to get a subsistence. The official apathy at this crisis was remarkable and the Supreme Government thought the apathy so culpable that it appointed a commission to enquire into the causes of the failure to take proper and timely action and when the report of the commission was submitted, the Viceroy in a minute dated the 20th April 1866 concurred in the opinion of the commission that due precautions for the mitigation of the natural visitation had not been taken and that valid reasons were not adduced for this neglect. An excuse was put forward by the commission on behalf of the Bengal officers, in the fact that they had no previous experience of the character of Indian famines, but the Viceroy did not think this a sufficient excuse and emphatically remarked that there was a want of foresight, perception, and precaution regarding the impending calamity which was quite unaccountable. The Supreme Government, had not however taken any action of its own motion by the light of the indignant remonstrances of the press which brought the true condition of Orissa to light long before its condition was represented to be serious, through the usual official channels. Considerable excitement prevailed at the time over a minute of Mr. Grote the senior member of the Board of Revenue in Bengal, who excused the conduct of the said Board in this crisis on the general principle that state interference in such a crisis deemed inexpedient and had been condemned by many high authorities. He instanced the conduct the ministry in England in 1846, who on the occasion of the Irish potatoe famine reduced their interference to a minimum and quoted largely in support of his views, from an article of Sir Charles Trevelyan published in the Edinburgh Review of 1848, in which an account of the Irish crisis of 1846, and the measure of state interference in that crisis were given in detail. The adjacent Madras districts which were similarly afflicted fared better under the rule of Lord Napier, who personally visited the places, in the greatest distress in the Indian heat of the month of May, and organized and superintended the relief operations in person. The Viceroy in his speech at the public meeting in Calcutta stated that it was necessary to import 12 lacs of maunds of rice before the year was half-advanced, to give an appreciable measure of relief, and 10 lacs of rupees would be necessary for the support and maintainance of the orphan children who had been left totally destitute. The Viceroy also begged the assistance of the Secretary of State, Lord Cranborne in the matter of raising subscriptions in aid of the sufferers of the Orissa famine, in England, but Lord Cranborne after consulting the Lord Mayor of London thought that no subscriptions could be raised in aid of the above object. In India the subscriptions went on well. The Indian public well recognized the fact that, in the annals of India there was not another instance in which distress was so prolonged for so long a period and over so large an area as in the case of Orissa. The foremost journalist of the present generation, the late Hon'ble Kristodas Pal delivered one of the earliest of his speeches at this meeting and in exhorting his countrymen to supplement state efforts by private benevolence pointed out that India had contributed over six lacs to the fund raised on the occasion of the terrible and indeed unprecedented calamity that lately swept over the Bengal provinces, and further added that Lord Cranborne's disheartening message to the Viceroy should teach us still more to rely upon ourselves. The Viceroy himself headed the donations of the relief fund by a contribution of Rs. 10,000 and eight subscriptions of Rupees 2,500 each were forthcoming on the spot. The native princes and the wealthy men in every part of India were appealed to, not in vain, and soon relief came to the sufferers in a tangible shape.

Famine making frequent appearance in the land, the question of the prevention of the occurrance of those terrible visitations came to occupy the attention of the rulers of the land. The Orissa famine had carried off an immense number of human beings and had reduced the population in the villages of the most afflicted tracts to a mere handful. It was therefore thought proper to bring back into a condition fit for use, the old canals constructed by the Moghul Government and to construct new canals wherever practicable. The important question arose as to whether the construction of canals should be by State funds solely or be left to private enterprize. There were eminent men advocating both sides of this question. Lord Canning had sanctioned the undertaking of irrigation works in Orissa by the East India Irrigation Company and Lord Stanley also favored the policy of private enterprise by giving the Madras Irrigation Company a guarantee of five per cent on 10 lacs for 25 years. Sir Charles Wood and Sir John Lawrence with Mr. Maine were against the policy of private enterprize in the construction of irrigation works on the ground that water should never become private property, and that the people who would avail themselves of such works should not be put into the hands of a Joint Stock Company. Mr. Massey, the new Finance minister was of opinion that Government and private enterprize should co-operate. There was an equally vehement controversy between the Madras and the Bengal schools of engineers about the proper method of the construction of canals. After the controversy had raged for some time it was decided that the Government might borrow for the purpose of such necessary and reproductive public works as canals though more such works should not be taken in hand than are almost certain to repay the interest on capital and the working expenses if not a surplus, to liquidate the amount of borrowed capital. Colonel Strachey who was appointed Superintendent of Irrigation also succeeded in getting over the professional controversy. An extensive system of canals was now projected, a full enumeration of which is given in the speech of Sir John Lawrence to the Council on the 31st March 1868. It would be improper to anticipate here the financial aspect of the canals, how far they were reproductive, and whether they were attended by any consequent disadvantages. Among the irrigation works projected, Sir John Lawrence enumerated the Sutlej canals and the improving of Bari Doab Canal and the Western Jumna Canal, in the Punjab, the Canal leaving the Jumna below Delhi and irrigating the districts of Agra and Muttra, and the remodelling of the Ganges Canal and utilizing the chief rivers of Bundelkhand and Oudh, for canals in the N. W. Provinces and Oudh, and went on to indicate extensive surveys for canals undertaken in other provinces *viz.*, Central Provinces, Madras, Bombay, Gujrat, Khandesh, Deccan, Mysore and Travancore. The Governor-General further added that to cope with this vast increase of work the Secretary of State had sent out thirty Civil Engineers, and the number will be increased in coming years. The Government of India also established at the head quarters of every province a separate head to the Irrigation branch of the Public Works Department. In the course of the next few years these canals were constructed. They have no doubt minimised the chances of famines occurring occasionally, but it had been asserted by high authorities that artificial irrigation seriously diminishes the productive powers of the Indian soil. We shall have occasion to recur to this subject again in the history of the next decade, and we reserve till then a discussion of the irrigation question in India in all its details and the consideration of the problem as to whether the system has been, on the whole, beneficial.

GENERAL EVENTS.—Almost at the end of the year, the Governor of Bombay Sir Bartle Frere retired from the service and was succeeded by the Right Hon. Seymour Fitzgerald. Sir Bartle Frere was one of the most prominent of the officials of his time. He was possessed of great natural ability and energy and capacity to adapt himself to circumstances and in the non-regulation province of Sindh where he was the Chief Commissioner he managed to effect great improvements in the system of administration and every department received a vigorous impetus under his able sway. As Governor of Bombay he became unpopular with the native community for his support of the action of Mr. Justice Anstey, a judge who combined with much innate goodness of heart and rare abilities natural and acquired, a singular eccentricity of manners and an unique vehemence in expression and whose severe dealing with the speculators in the flood-tide of the share mania, caused him to be thoroughly unpopular with the native community. Some Bombay citizens at an enthusiastic public meeting adopted a petition for his immediate recall which however produced no result. With the military officers in staff employ against the reduction of whose emoluments he resolutely stood, and with the European community in general he was thoroughly popular. He showed the versatility of his talents by being equally successful as an administrator under the loose system of Sindh and the hard-and-fast system of Bombay. The established Church in India sustained a great loss by the death, from an accident in missing his footstep while getting into a vessel at Koostea, of Dr. Cotton, the Lord Bishop of Calcutta. It is always a pleasure to bear testimony to the worth of a man, from whom though one might differ in religious views, who conspicuously embodies in his own character the highest ideals of love of duty, charity, sincerity and humility. The educated natives of India at the present day will acknowledge the debt of endless gratitude which they, as a body, owe to the first missionary settlers in the land. The missionaries, it must be admitted did their best to spread education and enlightenment through the land. They started the first Indian newspaper and they first strove unceasingly to create a vernacular prose. The names of the Serampur missionaries Carey, Ward and Marshman excite as much reverence in the circles of educated natives of India, now as they did two generations back among their ancestors. But the paid clergy of the Anglican Church had done but little to establish a brilliant reputation for energy, literary abilities or piety. The vices of the clergy in England which had been depicted so well in the pages of Fielding had their counterpart in India and with but little effective supervision from the head quarters the indolence and apathy of the paid Christian clergy were daily increasing. What an immense amount of leisure and freedom from the cares of the world are afforded to the clergy who have a decent competence from state coffers, for religious and literary culture, and how easily can that body become, if it only will, the most learned and polished community in all India. But unfortunately the clergy in India does not afford us many notable names in literature or science. The writings of. Bishop Heber, which first served to diffuse into the west, a knowledge of the social structure, and the beauties of the east form a remarkable exception. Under these circumstances, the historian of India cannot but record with interest the lively energy displayed by Dr. Cotton, in the improvement of his immense diocese, in the strict supervision over his subordinate clergy which made that body, industrious and active and in the education of a native pastorate. The Bishop's College owes its foundation to Dr. Cotton and the pastoral tours he used to undertake were so frequent that everywhere the clergy and the laity were kept wide awake of their duties to their Creator. Dr. Cotton was prematurely cut off, and the Church in India could ill afford to lose a man, whom even those who did not share his faith respected for his many sterling qualities.

In the beginning of the year a Chief Court was established for the Punjab and somewhat later on the High Court for the N. W. Provinces. The High Court N. W. Provinces was established by Royal Charter and had its seat at Agra till it was removed to Allahabad. The question of making gold a standard currency in India had been repeatedly mooted. Mr. Wilson soon after his arrival in India found that gold coins were not a legal tender of the Government revenue in India since 1852 and there was a small amount of bank notes in circulation, and in the banks the Government held shares. He proposed to withdraw the paper in circulation and to substitute for it Government notes in the three Presidency cities and to retain one-third of the amount of bullion represented by the notes always in hand and to reconcile the banks to this state of things, it was proposed that they should have the management of the Government debt. The main objections against adopting gold as a standard in addition to silver were that fluctuations in the values of the two metals would introduce a variable quantity in the money market and that the obligations of India being contracted in silver an additional weight might be put on the country by being called upon to discharge them in gold. But the commercial community was strongly in favor of a gold currency and the Chambers of Commerce of the three Presidency cities urged the adoption of a gold currency. After much discussion it was notified on the 13th November 1854, that English and Australian sovereigns and half-sovereigns would be a legal tender at the Government treasuries at par value. This notification was modified in October 1868. In 1866, a Currency Commission was appointed with the special object of expressing an opinion as to whether the gold currency standard was suitable to India and should be adopted. The Commission recommended that gold was much sought for by merchants and bankers, that the demand for a gold currency was unanimous throughout the country, that gold coins of the value of 15, 10, and 5 rupees would find more favor than notes of the same value, and that the opinion seemed general through the country that the currency should consist of gold, silver and paper. The Commission strongly recommended that the Government should continue in the policy of making gold a legal tender in the country which it recommended to the Secretary of State two years ago. The Commission found that the result of the experiment in paper currency initiated in 1861 was rather unfavorable but attributed the result to the conservative habits of the native Indian population, who could not be induced to take to new methods all at once. Sir William Denison was succeeded at Madras by Lord Napier. Sir William Denison strove hard though unsuccessfully to introduce improved agricultural implements among the agricultural classes in his territories but although he had a successful career in Australia his career at Madras was characterized by a routine administration, and by what was called at the time, a policy of masterly inactivity. Posterity should however acknowledge that his firmness at a critical moment had saved the prestige of British arms.

CHAPTER IX.

1867.

POLITICAL ASPECTS OF THE COUNTRY.—This year was marked by an unusual activity of the Russians in Central Asia. The Cossack armies had long been active in Central Asia and the dominions of the Czar were constantly developing beyond the southern boundary of Siberia. This year witnessed the absorption by Russia of the Khanate of Bokhara. The proximity of Russia to Afghanistan made that estate, with a very weak central authority, constantly the dupe of Russian intrigues and from this period dates the never ceasing complications of the relations of the British Government in India and the ruler of Afghanistan. Sir John Lawrence simply watched and informed himself about the position of Russia in Central Asia. He sent an embassy consisting of Pandit Manphool and some others to procure intelligence. The western frontier of India contained a series of the most difficult passes, and should any civilized power attack the British empire on the western border, the most impenetrable defence would consist in those difficult mountain situations, peopled by a race of dashing soldiers. Russia has ultimate designs towards British India and in the conflict between England and Russia, which might one day take place in Asia, that power would be most at a disadvantage who would be drawn away the farthest from its own borders. The policy of the Government of India, during the last generation with reference to its military affairs and Afghanistan had been shaped by a sideglance to the fact that, effective preparations should be made for the crisis of a Russian war, should any such unfortunately come and that Cossack influence must be kept out of the Afghan territories. We shall see later on the future developments of the policy of our Government in this respect and it shall be our duty to record how often the Government of India had to be engaged in negotiations, military demonstrations and strengthening the frontier, in the course of the succeeding viceroyalties. It was brought to the notice of the Government this year by a Talookdar in Oudh that there have been widespread rumours in that province to the effect that the people of Oudh had been corrupted by Russian gold. The rumours, on closer scrutiny were found to be without foundation, but that they were deemed worthy of the notice of the Government clearly shows how watchful and sensitive the ruling body had been since the Sepoy Mutiny and how morbidly acute its impressibility was in the decade immediately succeeding the rebellion. There is scarcely any doubt of the fact that the people of India do not in the least want a change of masters. They know full well that they have everything to lose and nothing to gain by such a change. The English Government is not a perfect institution, and no human Government can be so, but who would not say that it is as good Government as under the circumstances the ruled classes can expect. The more education is being spread on all sides of the country, the greater is the diffusion of the appreciation of the manifold blessings of British rule, and the stronger is the bulwark erected against the weakening of the authority of the English Government. The State of Hyderabad in the Deccan seemed to be, at one time, a source of political trouble but this has ceased to be the case ever since Sir Salar Jung had the control of its affairs. The State of Hyderabad was full of Arab and Afghan mercenaries, and enterprizing Mahomedan adventurers from all parts of Central and Western Asia and India. But against all these causes of disaffection there was a sufficient guarantee in the fact that Sir Salar Jung had the upper hand in the control of its affairs. The Nizam twice dismissed Sir Salar Jung, in 1861 and again in 1867, accusing him of subservience to the British Government at the expense of his estate, but a regard for his own true interests again compelled him to take the sagacious minister back. Sir

Salar Jung introduced great improvements in the Hyderabad administration. He filled the important offices of the state by able and cultured Mahomedans from upper India and for many years the official classes in Hyderabad were a purely exclusive body and extremely disliked by the native aristocracy of that independent state. It was not until the last ten years, that the natives of Hyderabad itself are being raised to high offices and it must be noted too, that the jealousy felt for the officials from northern India, caused the Hyderabadis to exert themselves to an extent, which they would never otherwise do, to qualify their more prominent members by high intellectual culture and practical experience, for the duties of office. It was under Sir Salar Jung's administration, too that that taste for manly sports developed itself among upper-classes of Hyderabad society which make them almost a match for the Englishmen in the sporting-field. Any one visiting Hyderabad now-a-days, would come with the best impressions about the constitutional character of the administration and the noble and manly qualities of those who have leisure for their cultivation, but it must be recorded that Hyderabad owes this prosperous state of things to the inspiring influence and the prudent statesmanship of Sir Salar Jung. There were internal disturbances at Bhotan owing to the discontent arising from the distribution of the British tribute among the principal chiefs. Tongso Penlow who had shown both valour and ability, in dealing with the British demanded the largest share. The British Government allowed the several parties to fight out their own quarrels and did not interfere with them. Emboldened by the fact that the British Government had conceded to the demand of a perpetual tribute by the Bhotanese, the Sikkim durbar filed a humble petition to receive a share of the prosperity of Darjiling which the Government had leased from that estate on a perpetual tenure. The Viceroy granted an annual increment of Rs. 3,000 to the original tribute in reply to this petition. Nepal was occupied by a race whose hardy habits and whose capacities for the field had been tested in many a hotly contested campaign, and with such martial subjects, one need not wonder at the fact of Nepal's making some raids towards the regions of Thibet and Tartary. She was cramped southwards by a power whom she dared not defy but with the Chinese durbar in a state of internal dissension she was free to develop northwards and this she did by encroaching on some patches of territory beyond her original northern borders. The Viceroy's attention was also directed towards Cashmere both with reference to her internal and external policy. That fine valley, to which the crown among the Himalayan valleys had been given by the pen and the imagination of many a poet both Eastern and Western will occupy our attention more than once in the succeeding pages. Cashmere was rebuked by the Viceroy for forming small Central Asian alliances, a course which she could hardly adopt under the provisions of that treaty into which she had entered with the British Government. Her internal policy also underwent much criticism at the hands of the paramount power. Complaints reached the Supreme Government of no end of exactions on the part of the revenue authorities of the Maharajah. A British spy was located at Leh to collect information and at length matters came to a satisfactory settlement by the Cashmere durbar expressing an adhesion to the principles of free trade and making large reductions in the tariffs and giving up the State monopolies. Captain Sladen and another official succeeded in concluding an advantageous treaty with Burmah. Burmah also expressed a reluctant adoption of the principles of political economy with reference to her commercial policy. Lord Cranborne, who had succeeded to the office of the Secretary of the State recognized the independence of Mysore against the decisions of successive Viceroys. The Nawab of Tonk was deposed for his barborous murder aggravated by the deepest treachery of the uncle of his feudatory the young chief of Lawa. His brother was raised to the *musnud*. The Maharajah of Jeypur Sewai Ram Singh, improved considerably the administration of that naturally-fortified and fertile state, and introduced that constitutional method of disposing of business which can compare not unfavourably with that in use in the neighbouring British districts. But Sir T. Madhava Rao's successful administration of Travancore brought the highest credit on that acute thinker and accomplished statesman. That Travancore now rejoices in a government, well-calculated to diffuse effective protection in every part of the kingdom and to afford encouragement for the cultivation of the habits of industry is principally due to the constitutionalization of the administration under the influence of that distinguished minister. The uniform and rapid justice that the Travancore subject can always get, the means for the diffusion of mass and high education, to be found in that state and the excellent fiscal arrangements make Travancore a model kingdom. The historian should advert to the Abyssinian war which though by no means an Indian war, had still cost India a large sum of money. The war was begun in the London Foreign Office, but it was decided by the British Cabinet, that a portion of the expenses should be paid by India. The Viceroy, ably seconded by Sir William Muir who was then a member of the Supreme Council, protested against the injustice of throwing a portion of the burdens of this war on the Indian taxpayer. But Sir Strafford Northcote who was then in charge of the India Office defended the policy of the Cabinet on the ground, ingenious enough, that the Mahomedan pilgrims to Mecca would have returned with tales of the disgrace of their Sovereign in Africa, had not the war been undertaken to maintain British prestige and that the possession of India made it absolutely necessary that the African relations of Her Gracious Majesty should be always of an advantageous character. India occupied also a prominent share in the Parliamentary debates, on the Mysore and Orrissa famine questions, the Indian administrative reform, the Jervis Court Martial, the foreign service of native Indian troops and the entertainment of the Sultan of Turkey at India's expense. During the year there was a Durbar at Lucknow, where all the grandees of Oudh assembled in their splendid and flowing robes. The Lieutenant-Governor of Bengal Sir Cecil Beadon retired with a broken reputation, and was succeeded by Sir William Grey. Dr. Milman who was appointed to succeed Dr. Cotton in the Calcutta bishopric was installed in the Cathedral on the 2nd April.

GENERAL EVENTS.—This year was marked by the introduction by Mr. Massey of what is known as the License tax. The Secretary of State found out errors in Mr. Massey's budget. Mr. Massey also committed the error of under-estimating the opium revenue and not charging reproductive public works to loans. The License tax or as it was called the Certificate tax was a tax on trades and professions and though a public meeting was held in Calcutta to protest against the tax still the country was thankful, that it had been spared an income-tax. The opposition outside the Council against this measure was not so much against the tax itself as against the procedure of the Council on the day the bill became law. The bill was proposed for the first time on the 8th of March and the bill was formally brought before the Council and became law on the same day. The complaint on this head was thus expressed in the memorial on the subject to the Secretary of State. "That a measure of such grave public importance should not have been laid before the Council for final decision without due notice being given to allow of some expression of opinion upon it on the part of the public and the haste with which the bill was hurried through the usual stages and passed was as unseemly as it was unnecessary." The License tax again was not charged on incomes above Rs. 25,000 a year, for the excess after deducting 25,000 rupees, and between certain long limits the tax paid was the same. This scheme of taxation therefore was also open to the charge, that it pressed heavily on those whose incomes were the smallest and practically exempted the wealthier classes. In its operation the financial results of the tax were inconsiderable. The Viceroy was obliged to give class after class the benefit of the exemption classes and had to sustain two defeats in working the tax, the one legal and the other from public opinion. The memorialists to the Secretary of State asserted that they were not opposed to fresh burden of taxation. They saw, they stated, that a permanent addition to the resources of the country had become inevitable and they strongly protested against a tax which took the same amount from the man with a lac a year, as from him who lived upon two thousand a month. The memorial was rejected by the Secretary of State but so many difficulties were experienced in working the tax that the original law was repealed and a fresh bill in a modified form was passed. Lord Lawrence in the course of the year adopted the system of exempting natives of high rank from compulsory attendance in the Civil Courts. There is a morbid sentiment in the oriental mind against being compelled to attend courts of justice. To the European, who has no objection whatever on account of his high rank or exalted position in society, to appear whenever called upon, before the constituted courts of the land, this sentiment of the oriental mind may appear totally unreasonable yet it is well-known to those who have lived long enough in the country, that no privilege seems more dear to the wealthy native, and none whose loss will be more deeply felt, than the one which allows him, as a matter of right to be examined by commission at his own place whenever for the purposes of justice his evidence need be recorded. Cases have been known in which the wealthier classes of natives have rather given up large claims to be spared the indignity, as they thought it to be, of being compelled to attend court either as suitors or witnesses.

This privilege of exemption from the ordinary Civil Courts of the land embodied in a section of the Civil Procedure Code was very sparingly granted during previous years, but Sir John, took a distinct step in advance in this direction by increasing the number of those admittted to the enjoyment of this privilege. The Bengal Government, curiously enough granted the exemption to seven persons, on the ground that they were or had been members of the Legislative Council and thus we had the interesting spectacle of persons, who had played the role of legislators and had assisted in making the laws of the land, being allowed to be exempt from personal appearance at the courts of law because of their connection past or present with the Local Legislative Council. The Chamber of Commerce for Bengal, pointed out that this privilege in itself was a most unreasonable one that instead of a foolish sentiment like this, being humoured it should be knocked on the head, and a privilege of this nature did not exist, and was not recognized in any other part of Her Majesty's dominions but the Chamber got gently snubbed by the Lieutenant-Governor of Bengal for addressing the Government on a matter which had no apparent connection with the commercial interests of Bengal. During the year the Census of two large political divisions of India was taken—that of the North-West and the Central Provinces. The Census of the north-west, whose results were very lucidly stated by Mr. Plowden, brought out the fact that the Hindus bore to the Mahomedans the proportion of six to one. In the Central Provinces, the aboriginal tribes were found to number two millions. The whole population of the North-West was found to be 3,011,615 and the Central Provinces 9,104,511, of which nearly five millions were Mahomedans.

The Indian community suffered great loss by the death during the year of Sir Raja Radha Kant Deb Bahadoor K.C.S.I. and the Hon'ble Justice Shumbhoo Nath Pundit. Sir Radha Kant was the head of the leading aristocratic family of Calcutta and called by nature to an exalted position, had fully made use of the splendid opportunities given to him of acquiring a ripe scholarship and taking a deep and active interest in the regeneration of his countrymen. His merits were rewarded by the Government repeatedly and in his death at a temple in the holy city of Brindaban, the Hindu community in India lost its acknowledged leader and its foremost patron of learning. In Justice Shumbhoo Nath Pundit passed away the first of those great luminaries in the legal line, who had been elevated to the highest position, that a native of India can up to the present day aspire to, and who was fully equal to the heavy duties and responsibilities of the highest judicial tribunal of the land. His tact, ability and legal acumen had fully vindicated the claims of his countrymen to the most exalted offices under the Government. He was succeeded on the bench by Mr. Justice Dwarka Nath Mitter, an educated native of India who though prematurely cut off in the height of his fame and the full vigour of his intellect, had shown in the discharge of his duties, the most brilliant abilities and the keenest tact and discernment. The career of Dwarka Nath Mitter will ever stand forth to the younger generation in British India, as an illustrious example of a self-made man, whose literary talents illumined his legal judgments and whose juristic acquirements elicited the highest praise from the veteran Lords of the Privy Council. His talents and independence which had shone conspicuously in the bar, were transferred during the course of the year to the bench. Miss Mary Carpenter visited India this year, and she took great interest in the progress of female education in India. She founded Social Science Associations, for the promotion of a healthy intercourse between the rulers and the ruled. Her unselfish labours earned for her the lasting gratitude of the native community. The year was also marked by a great gathering of human beings from all parts of India at the "Coombh mela" at Hurdwar. This celebrated mela takes place at the interval of every twelve years, and the Hindu ascetics from all parts of India congregate at the large cities where this mela is held. The sacredness of the river Ganges, it was said, would pass away in another twelve years and the mela this year at Hurdwar was held on an unprecedentedly large scale. Those who have seen any fair of this sort will readily admit that it is a most interesting assemblage, where all the phases of Indian asceticism, can be seen to their fullest advantage. The pilgrims poured in, from every part of India and special arrangements had to be made for preventing an epidemic. Arrangements were most successful till the last day when some how or other probably by the drinking of water polluted by the bathing of many thousands, Cholera made its appearance among the pilgrims and soon spread to many parts of the country. The pilgrims after the great purification ceremony of the 12th April began to leave and by the 15th they had nearly all left. It was generally thought, the pilgrims on their way back, had spread the seeds of disease in many places. Dr. Brydon who was an especial authority on Cholera, had however, from his knowledge of the general physical conditions which regulate the appearance of Cholera, had predicted as early as 25th February this year, a general epidemic in the Terai Districts. Calcutta was visited this year by another cyclone which though not half so damaging as that of three years ago, was still very destructive in its course. The ships on the river had a timely warning from the meteorological department of the Government but the native huts suffered most severely. The great railway lines were planned out and partly taken up. Up to this time the East India Railway Company had constructed a broad gauge line from Calcutta to Delhi, and the Madras and Beypur line had also been constructed. It was now proposed to construct lines from Delhi through the Punjab, through Umballa, Amritsar and Lahore to Multan, and from Multan to Kotra, opposite Hyderabad in Sind, the line from Kotra to Kurachee being already complete. Lines had been constructed from Bombay to Ahmedabad and Bombay to Nagpur. It was proposed to construct a line from Agra to Ahmedabad and make that line the highway of commerce between Northern and Western India. This was a part of Lord Dalhousie's original plan but Lord Lawrence decided upon making Allahabad the point of junction whence the route from Upper India would diverge towards Bombay. In his despatch of the 7th March 1867 the Secretary of State at once ordered that the complete surveys for the extension of the Bombay-Baroda line through Rajputana to Agra should be at once taken up. But political considerations, led to the modification of of this plan. It was also suggested to construct a line west of the Aravalli hills between Ajmere and Delhi. The route had to be very carefully selected as the soil was for the most part a rocky and sandy one and the ever-shifting sands of the desert was a formidable enemy of the architect or the engineer. The traveller to Bikaneer must, it had been beautifully said, be content to journey by the old-fashioned ship of the desert, whose domains would not be invaded by the iron horse for many years yet. The closing of the Bank of Bombay led Mr. Dickson of the Bank of Bengal to contemplate the establishment of a general State bank to be located in Calcutta with branches in Bombay and Madras, and also at other stations. He had succeeded in prevailing upon the directors of the Bank of Bengal to adopt this plan, and it was generally thought that he had also the support of the Government of India. But the opposition to this scheme was great in Bombay and a strong party was formed there to resuscitate the old Bombay Bank on improved principles and to oppose the amalgamation scheme, head and heart. The Bombay party found an able advocate in the press in the *Times of India*. The original scheme of Mr. Dickson was abandoned because of the opposition and only an agency of the Bank of Bengal in Bombay for the transaction of its own business was established. The Bombay Banks Commission was appointed and brought out many startling revelations. The commission had not closed its labours till the expiration of the tenure of office of Sir John Lawrence. Mr. Monteath in his note on the state of education 1865-66 instituted a comparison between the universities in the three Presidency cities. Sir A. Grant, took Mr. Monteath's remarks greatly to heart and addressed an elaborate defence of his own university. It was the general opinion at the time among those versed in the subject that the Calcutta University had been worked by Cambridge men, and in its system there was a preponderance of science and mathematics, while the University of Bombay having been moulded by Oxford men, literature and philosophy had the preference. A party in the North West advocated the establishment of a vernacular University for Upper India overlooking the fact that the vernacular of Upper India could scarcely satisfy the wants of the times, as it was a most inefficient instrument for that regeneration that was going on everywhere. This idea was effectually combated by Sir Charles Aitchison, than whom a more enlightened ruler never ruled the Punjab, fifteen years later and was almost abandoned when the plan of a separate university for the N. W. Provinces was broached by Sir A. Lyall.

CHAPTER X.

1868.

SIR JOHN LAWRENCE'S ADMINISTRATION.—Before the year expired Sir John Lawrence had laid down the helm of Indian administration and his successor had arrived in India. Sir John Lawrence is the first Viceroy whose entire administration, the historian of India of the present generation is called upon to undertake to review. By the scope of our work we are precluded from taking into consideration the greater part of the administration of Lord Canning, indeed we cannot review his policy with reference to that event which has called forth quite a library of books, viz. the Sepoy war. Lord Elgin's administration was too short to admit the historian's entering into an elaborate review, but Sir John Lawrence's administration which was much discussed at the time both here and in England, imperatively demands the judicial summing-up of the historian. Sir John is the first member of Civil Service who had been raised to the Viceroyalty. His knowledge of the character, the language and the institutions of the people saved him the preliminary training which a Viceroy fresh from English politics has to undergo in India. Sir John had retired from India with a brilliant reputation and on his return home in 1859, had been received with open arms. He was especially fortunate in dealing with the Sepoy Mutiny whenever it came in contact with his Government and he was also lucky in his subordinate officials. It was however hinted in some quarters that the Punjab system of administration bred the habit of mind of looking at every thing from the point of view of the executive officer, and that however suited that system might be for a backward and disorganized province, it was a system for the repression of all individuality on the part of the subjects. Misgivings were expressed that one who had been accustomed to such a system would scarcely be able to take that broad and statesmanlike view of things, that is necessary for the Viceregal office. The impartial historian who had carefully and conscientiously studied the leading organs of Indian public opinion existing at the time, cannot but perceive that Sir John Lawrence left as an unpopular man, among those of the ruled classes who had received an education, to understand his actions and comprehend his measures. His administration began by estranging the natives of the soil on two principal counts. He issued orders for the exclusion of the native gentry from Viceregal balls and entertainments. His notification on the burning-ghat question gave great offence by placing obstacles to the cremation of the bodies of the dead Hindus on the banks of the sacred river Ganges. The action of Sir John Lawrence in this respect was dictated purely on grounds of sanitation and convenience, but it was unfortunately susceptible of misconstruction as an undue interference with the cherished religious feelings of the people. It is rather strange that a notification like the one on the burning-ghat question, which was condemned by the by the leading organs of public opinion in England, should emanate, from one who had emphatically placed on record his conviction that the Mutiny owed its origin solely to the alarm of the native Sepoys for their religion. But towards the close of his administration, the Viceroy had made himself much less unpopular with the Indians. He paid great attention to every thing that appeared in the columns of the Anglo-Native press and he had ordered a special summary to be made weekly of the contents of the vernacular press thus immensely increasing the importance of that particular section. He pointed out firmly the iniquity of the contract clauses. The third-class native passengers by the railway lines owe a debt of endless gratitude to him for the interest that he took in their condition, and for the many improvements that were made at his instance. He appointed a Sanitary Commission which might collect information about the epidemic diseases and make suggestions for their prevention. The vexed question known as the shoe question was solved by him entirely to the satisfaction of the natives of India. These measures met with the unanimous approval of the native press and it was admitted on all sides that the case of the Indian taxpayer in the matter of the Abyssinian War could not be advocated with greater ability than was done by Sir John. His relations with the feudatory chiefs were of a satisfactory nature but this was due to the fact that he kept himself entirely aloof from their affairs and allowed things, almost always to go on as they were. His action in the case of the Tonk Nawabs deserves all praises, but he deeply grieved Scindia by interesting himself in the case of Sir Raja Dinker Rao, and retaining the Gwalior Fort, of which His Highness was fond to madness. He was opposed to the restoration of Mysore but he was overruled by the Secretary of State Lord Cranborne who nobly vindicated his own policy in Parliament. With reference to the foreign relations of India he was singularly unfortunate. As the head of the Government, the whole responsibility of the Bhotan imbroglio rests upon him and British prestige also suffered by the Hazara Campaign. There was was also a want of diplomatic tact in his relations with Cabul. It was generally remarked at the time that he had thrown away a golden opportunity of turning the tide of Cabul affairs in our favor. He left behind him three unpopular imposts—the police tax, the licence tax and the increased stamp duty. The opponents of the system of the Government of India's and the Provincial Government's migrating to the hills, for nearly two thirds of the year with the heads of departments and a great portion of the office staff, have poured their anathemas, in later days on Sir John Lawrence, as the author of what is in their opinion an expensive and obstructive precedent. During his administration there were some of the severest of natural visitations and the indifference for a considerable period of time of the Government to the sufferings of the people in one notable instance threw a cloud on Sir John's reputation. Sir John while a member of the India Council had written able minutes advocating the extension of the Permanent Settlement. He contended that the periodical settlements if they increase the acquisitions of the estate from one source, cut off the other indirect sources of revenue which the estate can avail itself of, under a permanent limitation of the demand of the state on the soil, which result in a general increase of prosperity. Sir John pointed out that periodical settlement entails a considerable expenditure in surveys and assessments and the Indian cultivators at the time of settlement throw much land out of cultivation a practice damaging to the state though more injurious to them. The Permanent Settlement, he added, would considerably improve the general condition of the poorer and the middle classes of the community without appreciably diminishing the receipts of the state, taken together from all sources. During the first year of his Viceroyalty Sir John did some efforts towards introducing permanent settlement over a wide area, but the opposition of the N. W. Province officials headed by Sir William Muir together with the adverse mandates of Earl De Gray and Ripon made him abstain from all such efforts during the succeeding years of his tenure of the Indian Viceroyalty. The establishment of State scholarship for enabling the natives of India to proceed to England, for purposes of study and the appointment by the Viceroy of a a commission to enquire into the relations of the planters and the coolies were measures that met with the unanimous approval of the Indians.

His administration has been criticized in the following sentences by one of the foremost Indian writers of the day. " He was every inch a routine governor. He originated nothing important, carried out nothing grand. He has followed and not led his councillors. His whole 'adminitration is characterized by masterly inactivity. His past experience, his knowledge of the Indian character and acquaintance with the details of Indian Government have conferred no special benefit on the people. Of course the country has progressed during the five years that he has ruled over us, but nothing can stay its progress. The tide is rolling on and no Caunte can command it back. The genius of the English Government and of the English institutions which have been introduced here, and of English civilization will not permit retrogresssion. It would have been a merit in Sir John if he as the head of the Government, taking advantage of the onward march of time, had given it a great impetus. But his whole administration had been unhappily characterized by what is called masterly inactivity. It is said Sir John has not at any rate done any positive mischief but that is a negative merit and we have yet to know that for that a ruler deserves a statue. We can believe that Sir John meant well but it is only the Almighty that can dive into the heart." We have not hesitated to quote Kristodas Pal's estimate of Sir John Lawrence's administration at length. The passage here given expresses pithily the standard by which all administrations whether of the Viceroy or of provincial governors, have been judged by the educated classes. The system of high education in existence in the country for many years have produced, a class of men who are thoroughly imbued with the spirit of European literature and institutions. Many of them are familiar with those great works that ennoble the English language or record the matchless annals of England's fame and some of them correspond on equal terms with the great scholars of Europe on topics of literary, scientific and antiquarian interest. But the number of such men as compared to the total number of the Indian population, is infinitely small. When Sir John Lawrence laid down his exalted office, education had touched but the outer fringe of Indian society and the statesman who guided the affairs of the country, had to consider the interests not only of the advanced portions of the ruled classes, who might be fit for a system of administration giving much freeer scope to the people, but the general condition of the country at large and its adaptibility to liberal institutions, some of which, it is universally admitted, England had conferred unsought on this land in the earlier days of her rule. But an Indian Viceroy has to go through so much routine business, has to think of so many conflicting and far-reaching interests, and has to deal with such a complex and delicate administrative mechanism, that it is only statesmen of the highest rank with uncommon foresight and grasp of mind, who can cautiously introduce any administrative experiments in a system of Government unique in history. The ordinary run of Indian Governors, must be content to watch over every department of administration and keep the machinery in proper order. That Sir John Lawrence, did not as Viceroy exhibit that enlargement of mind that was expected as the result of his intercourse with the best minds of England on his return from the Punjab, is a fact which admits but of little doubt. That India was quite free from any political troubles and that the complications on the frontier ceased to appear in a threatening aspect the moment he landed, are due to the weight and prestige of his name. With the European soldiers, whose interests he had always at heart, and for whose accomodation he had sanctioned extensive barracks in the large contonments, he was decidedly popular. By many of his own service he was undisguisedly and undeservedly disliked. With the landed aristocracy with whose best interests he was thought to have waged war, he was an object of open denunciation, and by the non-official European community he was regarded with the same feelings with which the Civilian of a generation back, who was generally represented as opposed to the settlement of non-official Europeans in the land, was looked upon. Sir John Lawrence declared in his farewell speech that he had striven before God and man to do his duty. He lived in England to a good old age and died in 1879.

THE HAZARA CAMPAIGN AND OTHER MILITARY EVENTS.— The Huzaraines, who lived on the Black Mountain to the west of the Indus had been, as usual with mountain tribes committing depredations on the plains. In 1868, a party of that tribe assaulted the police station of Leghee in the Agror Valley, and though they were instantly driven back, an expedition was fitted out under the directions of General Wylde, to enter the country of the offending mountain tribes and exact reparation for the injuries they had done from time to time. Twenty thousand troops were collected from the garrison in Upper India and two columns under the command of Brigadiers-general Bright and Vaughan advanced from Abbotabad into the Agror Valley on the 26th of September. On the 3rd October, Oghee was reached, and an attack was decided on Koon Gullee a village on one of the spurs of the Black mountain. The village was carried after a slight skirmish and the enemy having evacuated it, the force had to be moved to a height known as Munna-ka-Dunna and entrenchments were thrown up. This was a strategic move in the right direction, and the advantage the mountaineers always have of firing on the British troops from the heights, was taken away from them by the advanced posts of the British army who established pickets on the more prominent heights and spurs. On the morning of the 4th of October the Chutturbul peak of the Black mountain was in the hands of the British, and on the 5th, the Muchai peak was carried. On the 7th operations were directed successfully against the Pararee Synds, and the British officers received on the same date offers of submission from some of the mountain clans. The British troops then marched triumphantly through several villages, and on the 10th a formal peace was concluded with the chief Pathan clans, and on the 11th, the force was on the return journey. The campaign was a very successful one and the military experiences gleaned from the Umbeyla campaign, had been wisely utilized. But the public in India was dissatisfied with the fact that an enormous force had been got up at a great expense and dismissed after only a few shots. The Government was right however, in only punishing the mountain tribes, without trying to repress them. The prudent policy with reference to these tribes would be to make them friends and utilize their rude vigour in shutting the western gates of India, while at the same time they must be impressed with the belief that the British Government is too powerful to be awed by them. The sacred shrine at Dwarka, was up to 1815, in the possession of the Waghurs of Kattywar, when it was transferred along with the adjacent strip of territory to the Gaekwar for a money compensation. But the Waghurs, now and again, disturbed the peaceful possession of the Gaekwar, and an expedition was sent against them, under the Political Agent Colonel Anderson. The little force gained a great success, though two valuable officers, lost their lives. In February 1868 a body of rebellious Bheels was defeated by a detachment under Captain Macleod. Some traces of Mahomedan disaffections were found but these were speedily suppressed. The Government of India had its attention directed to some disturbances between Muscat and Zanzibar. Lord Canning was called upon when in India to arbitrate between the Sultans of Muscat and Zanzibar with reference to their disputes. Lord Canning decided that the Sultan of Zanzibar must pay tribute to the Sultan of Muscat but would otherwise be independent of him. In 1865, the Sultan of Muscat was murdered, and it was suspected, his son Selim who succeeded him, had a leading hand in the murder. The Sultan of Zanzibar with the Shah of Persia took measures to dethrone Selim, the price paid to the Shah being the possession of the Bunder Abbas. The British Government was obliged to interfere as Muscat is a place of great importance to Indian trade, and was taking active steps to interfere, when another revolution took place in Muscat, Sultan Selim having been driven out by Azan-ibn-Shas. Captain Sladen headed an exploring party that was sent in the beginning of the year from Bhamo to Momein, and onward to the capital of Younan. Captain Sladen returned in September from Momein, having been unable to proceed further owing to the many disturbances in the Chinese Empire. The Chinese Empire was at the time fast disintegrating, the western provinces having set up the standard of of revolt and establishing as a separate power under a Moslem chief. This created a barrier in the highways of commerce between Burma and Western China and the disorganized state of Thibet and Southern Tartary and led almost to a total cessation of traffic between the British and the Celestial Empires.

GENERAL EVENTS.—Since the death of Dost Mahomed the Amir of Afghanistan in 1863, there had been a series of internal quarrels to get the throne among his sons. According to Dost Mahomed's desire, Shere Ali Khan, succeeded his father but his brothers Afzul Khan and Azam Khan rose against him. Both being defeated Azim Khan repaired to Rawul Pindee, Afzul Khan was taken as a captive. The latter's son succeeded in turning out Shere Ali, and seated his father on the throne. Afzul Khan died shortly after and was succeeded by Azam Khan, who in his turn was deposed by Shere Ali with the help of some external power. Though Shere Ali ascended the musnud by force there was a large party still in favor of his enemies, but the moral influence of the recognition of Shere Ali's authority by the British Government was great at Cabul. The hand of fellowship had first been stretched to Azim Khan but Shere Ali got the upper hand, and the Government at once entered into negotiations with him for a treaty of alliance. It was felt by the Government that all that was wanted was the neutralization of Afghanistan. In the treaty entered into between England and Russia Lord Palmerston had entirely neglected to insert any provisions as to the policy Russia would pursue in Central Assia. Russia cannot be bent on the conquest of Turkey in Europe, as that action on her part would be strongly opposed by the other great European powers. But in Asia, she can freely pursue a career of conquest and it cannot be overlooked that she has a direct eye on India.

15—2

The conquest of India was a vision of that great emperor to whom Russia owes her present greatness. The English cabinet, has often in times past forgot in their diplomatic relations with foreign countries, the fact that England was a great Asiatic power as well, and the mistake committed by Lord Palmerston in failing to insist upon the neutralization of Afghanistan, as a necessary condition of the peace between England and Russia is one, which must be set right by the Indian Government. Mr. Massey's budget exhibited a deficit which led Mr. Massey to reimpose the License Tax in its altered name, the Certificate Tax. If the Finance Minister had acted on the principle, laid down by the Secretary of State, of building the military barracks and defraying the expenses of other reproductive public works, from the funds available through the loans raised, or had he not calculated at a very low figure the expected opium revenue it would not have been necessary to reimpose the License Tax in any shape whatever. Mr. Skinner the non-official member in the Supreme Council fought hard to obtain the thorough recognition of the principle of charging reproductive public works to loans but the Viceroy and the members of the executive council were strongly opposed to him. Mr. William Gray wrote an able minute on the subject which did not see the light at the time. In March, this year, Hon'ble Mr. Massey retired. He had, as the permanent chairman of the ways and means committee of the House of Commons, brought to India a great reputation. He had great natural and acquired abilities and he showed considerable skill and knowledge in his encounter with Mr. Skinner. But Mr. Massey did not leave behind him, the reputation of a successful Indian financier. He was succeeded by Sir Richard Temple the first Civilian ever appointed to that high office, who was Sir John Lawrence's old friend and secretary. Sir William Muir was raised this year to the Lieutenant-Governorship of the N. W. Provinces and it was generally expected that under the administration of so able a scholar the cause of education, would receive a great impetus in the backward provinces under his charge. His place in the council was filled by Sir John Strachey, an officer who had risen by sheer force of ability, though his present lift was owing to the warm support of Sir John Lawrence. The question of affording increased facilities for paper currency remained under the consideration of the government. The money-order system worked with great success this year. The system is opposed in certain quarters on the ground that it interferes with the business of bankers, but there is little weight in this objection as the private bankers can if they choose enter into a competition with the Government and undersell it. The salutary practice was introduced of the Political Agents being bound to submit an annual report of the states under their charge, thus infusing a spirit of healthy emulation among the native princes, with reference to the good government of their states and the introduction of desirable improvements. The Viceroy exercised during the year the prerogative of the supreme power in the case of Tonk by unseating the tyrannical Nawab and placing his son on the throne. The British Government, is by its treaty obligations bound to uphold the native chiefs against external aggression and internal rebellion, and therefore a part of the duty of the same Government is to see that the subjects in the native states be not ground down by the oppression of a chief whom they are powerless to oppose. The year closed amidst the agonies of deaths from epidemic diseases in the greater portion of Upper India. The causes of these epidemic diseases are not far to seek. They arise from the neglect of the commonest rules of sanitation, that is to be found in the greater number of the Indian villages. Bengal lost this year her foremost orator in Babu Ramgopal Ghosh and her foremost lawyer in Prosonno Kumar Tagore. Babu Prosunno Kumar had served with great distinction as a councillor and his scholarship and acts of munificent liberality have earned for him and undying reputation among his countrymen.

The Oudh and the Punjab tenancy Bills became law during Sir John Lawrence's administration. The revenue policy of the British Government had always been, to find out the existing rights in the land and to recognize and protect such rights. Whether the land belongs to the zemindars or the tenants in the sense of each class having proprietory rights therein, is a question that had divided the revenue officers of India into two separate schools almost since the beginning of the British rule. Under the Permanent Settlement the zamindars are the proprietors of the soil, and settlement was concluded with them. The officers of the Bird and Thomason School in the N. W. Provinces on the other hand admitted village proprietors to direct engagements with the Government with reference to the land revenue. In Bombay and Madras, the normal state of the ryot was to hold of the crown, and wherever he so holds, says Sir W. Muir, without the intervention of any middleman, proprietary right is vested in the occupant of the individual fields. It might seem strange that during a long period of nearly three-quarters of a century the best revenue authorities should be at issue on a question of fact with reference to the revenue system. The fact was that one party of Indian politicians has always held that the Indian ryot was a mere tenant-at-will of the superior landlord and the other school has with equal tenacity urged that the landlord has no proprietory right in the soil at all, but that the peasantry, was, what is known in economic science, peasant proprietor under different designations in different localities. Lord Canning made a settlement with the Talukdars of Oudh, and granted to them sunnuds in which there is a condition that they should secure to those holding under them any subordinate rights that they formerly enjoyed. Lord Canning expressed an opinion that the Government was at liberty under the terms of the sunnuds granted, to define and record the rights of the inferior holders and to limit the demands of the Talookdars as against such holders during the currency of the settlement.

Lord Elgin directed the attention of the Chief Commissioner of Oudh to the complaint he had received, that tenants having rights higher than those of tenants-at-will were liable to be injured if the Government took no effective steps to protect them. Sir John Lawrence on his arrival in 1864 was informed by Mr. Wingfield the Chief Commissioner of Oudh, that no tenant-rights existed in Oudh. Sir John directed a fresh inquiry by Mr. Davies, the Financial Commissioner, and after a full and searching inquiry that officer reported that the tenant-rights did not exist and what privileges they possessed, they enjoyed by sufferance. These privileges the Talookdars would not recognize as rights. A compromise was then entered into between the Government and the Talookdars, by the provisions of which the Government withdrew from any assertion of the rights of occupancy on behalf of the ryots, but the ryots were thenceforth to hold by right certain privileges which they hitherto held by favor and might claim compensation for unexhausted improvements. The Talookdars however declared the Oudh Tenancy Bill to be a violation of the promise of the Earl of Canning, but Mr. Strachey asserted in the debate on the 22nd July, that the Talookdars, had approved of the draft Bill and acknowledged that it carried out faithfully all the engagements on the part of the Government. The provisions of the Punjab Tenancy Bill were disapproved of by a large section of the Punjab officials. Rights in land had always been incorrectly recorded in the Sikh rule previous to the annexation of the Punjab and in the troubled times that followed, it was far more profitable to be recorded as hereditary tenants rather than proprietors. But when during the peace and security of British rule rights in land became valuable, as the conviction deepened in the minds of the people as to the permanency of British rule, there was a flood of petitions to correct alleged errors. The first settlement having expired the officers engaged in it, were called upon to take cognizance of claims to rights, whether they were consistent or not with those recorded at the first settlement. In the Amritsar Division alone said Mr. Maine, in his speech in the Council, 60,000 heads of households had been recorded at the first settlement as entitled to beneficial rights of occupancy. At the recent settlement 46,000 of these tenents were held to be mere tenants-at-will, but the settlement officers allowed them a period of years during which they were to retain their rights of occupancy. The Chief Court disallowed this concession as one, which the officers had no authority to make and the decision of the Chief Court in the division of Amritsar alone affected no less than 22,000 cases. The Government added Mr. Maine, was threatened with an agrarian revolution to be be followed by an agrarian counter-revolution. The bill, as finally passed on the 21st of October, embodied provisions, that in the opinions of a section of the Punjab officials created new rights and tended to perpetuate a double property in the soil. The landed aristocracy accused Sir John of befriending the ryots at the expense of the private rights of the proprietors. We might close this chapter by recording the progress made in public works. Nearly fifty lacs were spent in commodious barracks and fortifications, and it was calculated that works of this nature will be completed in 1872, when the Public Works Department might devote its energies solely to the carrying out of those schemes on which the wealth and progress of the country depend. Before we pass on to the administration of Lord Mayo, we think it proper to take a general survey of the first decade under the crown, and estimate the progress the country had made in all directions. To this interesting topic we devote the next chapter.

CHAPER XI.

THE FIRST DECADE UNDER THE CROWN.

GENERAL PROGRESS UNDER THE EAST INDIA COMPANY.— It is well known that the Court of Directors, when retiring from the exalted functions with reference to the Government of India caused a memorandum to be drawn up giving a general review of the work done during the century of British rule in India dating from the Battle of Plassey. No one can doubt that that work had been of a character, unique in history of which England might very well be proud. It is not necessary to describe here at length the sad miseries and degradation of the Indian races at the close of the Mogul rule. These have received a fair measure of attention from many writers of ability and note and have been summed up in some of those brilliant paragraphs of Lord Macaulay, which served to diffuse a general knowledge of Indian subjects in London drawing-rooms. It shall be the duty of the historian, in the succeeding parts of this work, to refer more prominently to the problems that now await solution at the hands of the Government and to dwell according to his own lights, on the subject of the work that yet remains to be done by England in India. But it would be giving one side of the picture alone, were we ever deficient, in the pleasing duty of calling the attention of the Indians of all races and creeds, to the manifold blessings of English rule. The India of the modern age presents the interesting spectacle of the contact of the two types of civilization, that of the east and west, which according to the theories propounded by the master mind of Henry Thomas Buckle, were bound to exhibit diametrically opposite characteristics. The civilization worked out by the sober minds of the Rishis of ancient India and that, which owes its existence, to the

Islamic prophet, the Imams and the Caliphs are now in friendly communion with the more practical type, whose corner-stone was laid by the scientific minds of the west. Since the British rule was firmly established in India, the whole country is calm and tranquil and except the occasional outbreaks of the rude tribes on the frontiers, there is an unexampled peace. The readers of Indian History of the time of Lord Clive know very well, that the sea-board of India was infested by bands of pirates, and many pirate-rajahs held splendid courts out of the spoils gathered from the high seas. One of the first acts, of the British Government was to eradicate this evil which had made sea-voyage an extremely dangerous thing. Sir William Hunter, who has summed up the work of England in India with his usual ability and eloquence, has pointed out that British policy, energy and capital have been instrumental in reclaiming 13,000 square miles of frontier land. We learn from the writers who have dealt with the period covered by the administration of Warren Hastings, that at the time, the Regulating Act came into force there were standing camps of banditti, with whom the military and the police, had to fight vigorously and unceasingly before they were quite suppressed. Not only have these gangs almost disappeared but the criminal statistics of India show that "there is now less crime in India than in England." The professional stranglers, who took a pride, in their profession have now ceased to practise it, on the unwary travellers. Nor should we fail to remind our readers, of the freedom and immunity they now to a great extent enjoy from the ravages of wild beasts. The regularly paid military have no terrors for the law-abiding subject, and the police, though hardly in that condition of utility and integrity, which is worthy of British rule, have now to carry on their secret practices far away from the light of the day. The security of person and property is unbounded. Religious toleration, and liberty to every one to practise his religious observances, as long as he does not transgress the laws of the land, have been principles observed with fidelity unprecedented in the Asiatic continent. Not only has England performed the duties of keeping safe the person, the property and the religious beliefs of its subjects, but it had applied itself, at a time, when the native Indian subjects of England could hardly understand or appreciate her policy, to the task of ennobling the ruled and bringing fresh life and vitality to the dry bones of the valley. The cities of the Mahomedan Emperors, all grew round the encampments of the sovereigns, and were more like the cities of Feudal Europe. The cities of British India were all supported by manufactures and other industrial pursuits. The economic problem in India has assumed a complex aspect by the great increase of exports and imports, and the ordinary mind can hardly grasp the situation as regards the balance of trade. As with individuals, so with nations, the taste for everything higher and nobler can come only with the satisfaction of the ordinary wants of life, and the revival of the national faiths of India, the taste for developing a national literature, and a national press, which is evident since the last fifty years, satisfactorily testify to the fairly prosperous condition of at least one section of the community. In all the Presidency towns, high education had been introduced and though it was sometime before all classes of the community took kindly to the new system, the new power introduced into the land made itself felt, and the people who had been hitherto walking in darkness began to get some glimpses of the new light. In Bengal the efforts of several patriotic native gentlemen aided by Sir Edward Hyde East, a Chief Justice of the Supreme Court, had established the Hindu College and the influence of several of the best preceptors that the youth of India ever had, effectually gave a shock to the old superstitions of the recipients of the new training. Before the Government was transferred directly to the crown the English rule in India had accomplished great things. The Court of Directors claimed in 1858, that their Government of India "had been not only one of the purest in intention but one of the most beneficent in act ever known among mankind; that it had been one of the most rapidly improving Governments in the world." It is the duty of the historian to bring home to the minds of his readers the fact that during the thirty years of government under the Crown, the march of progress in India had been unprecedentedly rapid, and that the rule of the Crown has been as much for the benefit of the Indian people as in the good old days of the East Indian Company. This task we venture to accomplish in the reviews of the three decades which are to be found at the end of every ten years, and where we propose to enter into the details of the progress that is visible even to the casual and prejudiced observer.

EDUCATION.—The year 1854 forms an important epoch in the educational history of India. The establishment of the universities in 1857 and the regular organization of a system of state instruction, had given a great impetus to the cause of high education and the policy inaugurated by Lord Hardinge of giving a preference to English-educated natives of India, in the selection of all official appointments, made the natives of Bengal especially to resort to a system of education which became the high-way to worldly prosperity.

The higher classes in Bengal were at first holding aloof from high education and they did not, to a great extent avail themselves of the facilities placed within their reach even at the end of the present decade. In Bombay and Madras progress in this direction was slower than in Bengal but a very promising beginning had been made. In the N. W. Provinces, Oudh, the Rajputana and Punjab, the progress in high education was far inferior compared to Bengal. These provinces had come under British rule much later than the plains of the lower Ganges, and the English-educated youths did not receive in these provinces the same amount of encouragement that they did elsewhere. Rajputana, with her fighting clans, and peculiar constitutions, could be made to accept the altered condition of things, only at a very late day. The whole system of society in Rajputana, the heroic land of India, underwent a complete change when under the protection of British rule; the sword was sheathed there, and the ruling chiefs had no longer to depend on the co-operation of the leading men of the state and the chiefs of the fighting clans, for that security of their person and throne which was the choicest blessing they could have looked for. The Rajput clans, whose chief occupation was to be always in readiness to take the field against external invasions or internecine intrigues, and who from time immemorial had no venerated traditions but those connected with the battle-field, did take a long time to adapt themselves to the altered condition of things, and apply to the arts of peace the same energy and devotion that their ancestors had embalmed in the pages of history for generations together. At the end of the present decade the spread of education in volume can be well guaged from the information given in a readable shape to the Indian public by Mr. Arthur Howell, of the Civil Service in his note on the state of education in India in 1866-67. His figures show that at the close of the present decade, Bengal had a total number of 2,908 schools, and colleges with an aggregate number of 115,185 pupils under instruction. Bombay had 1687 schools and colleges, with 113,045 pupils. Madras, had 1391 educational institutions, with 48,865 pupils. The N. W. Provinces had 4,208 educational institutions with 152,533 pupils. The Punjab, 2,823 educational institutions with 97,698 pupils. Oudh 386 educational institutions with 15,154 pupils, the Central Provinces, 1,076 schools and colleges with 58,137 pupils. British Burmah had 248 schools and colleges with 7,599 pupils, Hyderabad 147 institutions with 6,644 pupils, Mysore 91 with 2074 pupils and Coorg 35 with 946 individuals receiving instruction. Mr. Howell had also given the annual expenditure per pupil incurred in these territorial areas, and this averages taking both, Government and other funds together from 19·8 in Bengal to

6·7 in the Central Provinces. It will be seen from the above figures that the total number of the Indian population receiving state instruction amounts to 622,342 students, a number which sinks into insignificance when compared with the total number of the Indian population. The main feature of the education despatch of 1854, was the laying down of the principle of state aid in support of voluntary efforts, for the first few years at least. The Court of Directors were always of opinion that the management of high education should be a concern not of a general state department but of local bodies and in 1857, confidently expected that the time will soon come when the Government might entirely withdraw from the system of high education and the cause of education be left in the hands of the more energetic portions of the local community. The expenditure of the state upon education did not however diminish in the decade under notice, but on the contrary rose to almost four times the amount spent for this object in 1857, and when this period closed several other educational projects involving a considerable outlay were under the consideration of the Supreme Government. Mr. Howell states that Sir Alexander Grant and Mr. Atkinson, the Directors of Public Instruction of Bombay and Bengal respectively, urged for the increase of the grants made for educational projects and their representations would have received favorable consideration, if there was any method of complying with their requisitions otherwise than by increased taxation. The hope of seeing first-class educational institutions started and managed entirely by native agency was not realized when this decade came to an end. Bengal can at the present day, afford us the spectacle, of first-grade educational institutions, manned entirely by educated natives of India, without any subsidy from the state, without any control of the department of Public Instruction and flourishing with hundreds of English-speaking scholars, and not only defraying all current expenditure but owning commodious habitations out of their own revenues.

Such institutions are the proudest monuments of British rule and the other provinces in India are now in a fair way to shew that they can imitate the example of Bengal in this respect. But the dreams of the Court of Directors were not fulfilled till a fair period of time had elapsed from the date of the inauguration of these serious efforts in this direction that date from the Education Despatch of 1854. The universities began from year to year to attract an increasing number of students and as the Local Governments and the provincial High Courts, always encouraged the educated young men of the universities, by opening up to them, and in some cases to them alone, the lucrative walks of life at their disposal, the influx to the portals of the universities, did from the very nature of things, increase continually. It was however seriously doubted in some quarters, whether university education as imparted in India was not mere cram, and not that sort of healthy mental sustenance, that alone produces sobriety of thought and intellect, and that finished Vice-Chancellor of the Calcutta University entered into a vehement defence of the system of education in vogue in one of his masterly addresses at the Convocation. Some instances of munificent liberality, in the cause of education were also exhibited during the present decade. The Talukdars of Oudh founded and maintained a College at Lucknow named after Lord Canning in grateful commemoration of his services to this country, and the Government also made an annual grant towards the funds of the College. Many of the merchant princes of Bombay, founded useful institutions at Bombay, Surat and Poona, and Mr. Prem Chand Roy Chand of Bombay made a liberal donation to the University of Calcutta, the annual interest of which was placed at the disposal of the Syndics of the University of Calcutta, to be spent as they thought fit. The lover of learning, who sees the best minds of the civilized countries of Europe and America, always allowed to continue their devotion to the Goddess of Learning, while freed from all the cares of the world by a system of liberal fellowships and professorships, will earnestly look for the day in India when our universities will be enabled to maintain a small and select band of scholars, who will imitate the example of the best trained minds of Europe and America by life-long devotion to the cause of literature and science. The Education Despatch of 1854 was followed by another Despatch in 1859, the substance of both has been very clearly given by Mr. Howell. The Despatches lay down that the best students in the schools and colleges should be encouraged by the grant of small sums in the shape of scholarships which are to be won in the lower school and tenable in the higher. Normal Schools were to be established in every province for the supply of schoolmasters, and the medium of all instruction for the greater number of the people should be the vernacular languages of the people, into which all the elementary treatises in English should be translated, and the English language is to be taught at every place where there is a demand for it. The institutions, where instruction is imparted in the classical languages of India are to be supported by funds as far as possible and every respect should be shown towards them. There are to be especial schools for the education in the special subjects such as law, medicine, engineering and agriculture. There were to be in each province a Director of Public Instruction and a large number of assistants and inspecting staff. The universities were established at the Presidency Towns and were to be on the model of the University of London, and they are not to impart any education but will test the education received elsewhere. The standard of the university education was to be such that every student of average ability and industry might be successful in getting through the prescribed examinations, while due provision should be made by which deserving students might acquire much more than the common degree of acquirements. The local officials were enjoined by the despatches to encourage high education, by giving them a preference in regard to public offices at their disposal, and even in the lower situations a man who could read and write to have the preference over one who cannot do so. During the period under notice the educational efforts of the state were always guided by these principles, though some of them had to be modified in practice and other were not applicable as being in advance of the times. We need not dwell here on the patent truth that the Government by encouraging the diffusion both of high and primary education, had been not only fulfilling the nobler duties of the state but as better discipline is always sure to prevail at every place where the schoolmaster is abroad, great facilities were also created in the discharge of the primary duty of all Governments—that of keeping peace and order within a community and effectively securing the protection of person and property. The historian reviewing the first ten years under the crown, cannot but be struck with the amount of progress visible at the end of the period in the matter both of high and primary education but he cannot fail at the same time to realize that great masses of the population were still in a condition of utter ignorance and the Government had a good deal to do with reference to them. The Government had placed a complete agency in the hands of those who wished to avail themselves of the privileges of high education, and Lord Stanley forcibly reminded the Government of the fact, that every effort should be made to impart a suitable education for every station of life, a principle which was further developed by the despatches of the Home Government of 1863 and 1865. The great Educational Despatches also laid special stress on female education which was to receive an unstinted support at the hands of the Government. The path of the progress of female education is beset with peculiar difficulties. The ideas with reference to the status and duties in life of the weaker sex differ materially in the east and the west. Though every one might not endorse in Europe the radical ideas on the subject of John Stuart Mill, that women are fitted for every occupation in life, the prevailing sentiment would give them the same liberties in society and the same cultured tastes that are in the east only the privileges of the sterner sex. The unsettled state of the country for many generations made it imperatively necessary that female honor should be guarded in strict seclusion within the walls of the zanana, and this sentiment had been sanctified by religious rules. To break through the barriers thus caused and impart to Eastern women a position and culture analogous to that enjoyed by her Western sisters, is an idea which the orthodox mind in India whether Hindu or Mahomedan, can scarcely assimilate. The arguments in favor of female education as represented by Western writers are many and weighty but the Eastern idea is that women are created to be the presiding deities of domestic affairs, and to shed their sweet influence on home life and that the restless inquisitiveness of mind caused by a sound education, would take them out of this sphere altogether, and impair their status in social economy. No theory can be more untrue and without foundation, than that we see stated in some of the periodicals from time to time that the women in the East are mere household slaves, whose treatment is brutal and who are the victims of every oppression that a rigid domestic despotism can give birth to. This may be the case in India, as in all civilized countries in isolated instances, among the lowest classes of the population, but among the higher classes, the women are the same domestic divinities that they are in countries, whose manners and social fabric are held up for our imitation. The tranquil life, and the innocent enjoyments of the Indian women, her devoted affection to her lord, and the cheerful performance of all the duties of domestic life, her inspiring influence, and her sacred musings, mark her out to be a being far different from that which she is represented to be, unfortunately too commonly, in the productions of those, who if better acquainted with the inner life of an Indian home, would have thought otherwise. That women may have some sort of training with advantage, is a truth of which the native mind in India was at first a very slow recipient. But the untiring efforts of the zenana missions whose energies were directed to impart everything worthy of the name to Indian women, have gradually succeeded in breaking through the sentiments of ages. The historian must give every credit to the enthusiasm and judgment of those who could hit upon the most effective method of influencing the apathetic mind of the east to anything like reconciling it to their advanced doctrines on the subject of female education. During the period under review not much progress was made in female education in any Indian province, though in Bengal and Bombay a beginning was made. Miss Mary Carpenter's visit to India in 1866, gave a great stimulus to the cause of female education, though the want of proper schoolmistresses and adequate inspection, stood in the way. The subject of female education is one to which we have again to recur in our review of the two succeeding decades and we reserve till then, a statement of facts and figures with regard to the progress in volume and the test in quality of female education in the present generation. With the spread of education, came social and religious progress among all classes of the population, which is a subject according to the true conception of history for the historian to treat of. The spread of English education and the great change in the face of the country by the railways and other works facilitating locomotion, introduced some improvements in the social condition of the people. Although the system of state education pursued in this country was based like the general policy of the Government on strict religious neutrality yet before the light of English literature and science many of the more unreasonable practices that were formerly sanctioned by religion are fast disappearing. In Bengal there had risen up a peculiar sect professing a Deistic creed, called the Brahmos, ever since the days of Ram Mohun Roy. The leadership of this sect was taken up by the venerable Maharshi Debendra Nath Tagore, the head of one of the principal aristocratic families of Calcutta and during the period under notice the great Indian orator and reformer Babu Keshub Chundra Sen was rising to prominence. But the complaint was common during the period under review as it is now, that English education while eradicating in many cases the old religious beliefs did not substitute for them any creed that would prevent the recipients from becoming the light-ballasted men that people always are, without religion. Though India owes a good deal to the energetic and unselfish labours of the Christian missions, it is an opinion publicly expressed by many of the best writers on Indian affairs that Christianity has not much chance in India. The bonds of caste have not yet given way though the prejudices with reference to it are gradually yielding. The first recipients of English education everywhere imbibed revolutionary tendencies, but since that time the educated Indians while essentially the same in home life as previously, have yet in all outward concerns and official life imbibed the true spirit of English culture. The belief in the old mythological fables, or the varied wiles of a subtle priestcraft, has been altogether swept away. When the decade closed, only the first batch of native gentlemen visiting England for purposes of education had come back, and the question of the social penalties under the alleged injunctions of religion had not yet seriously come into prominence. The large influx of European officers belonging to the new regiments, the introduction of barristers in the Muffassil, and the great development of the resources of the country which introduced Englishmen of ability and attainments in every part of the country, tended to change the tone of Anglo-Indian society. The political progress of the country during this decade was not so marked as during the two following ones. The establishment of the Talukdar's association in Oudh, chiefly through the efforts of Babu Dakhinaranjan Mukerji introduced the first political association of any consequence in Upper India. In Bengal the British Indian Association continued to do some useful work under the guidance of the able men who presided over its counsels, throughout the period under review. The history of this decade would be incomplete without a mention of the celebrated trial of the Reverend Mr. Long for libel, a case which arose from the indigo disputes and which stirred native society to its inmost depth. The historian should not perpetuate other cases, which attracted great public attention at the time they occurred and where there were some remarkable exhibitions of that frailty, which is the unfailing trait o' human nature. A good many improvements took place in the sanitary arrangements of the army in India. After the publication of the report of the Royal Commission under the leadership of Lord Herbert, the Sanitary Department of the state took every precaution to lessen the jail mortality of India and adopt in cases of cholera epidemics, removal, isolation and the destruction of the diseased discharges, which had been found the most efficacious means of preventing the spread of the disease and which had been strongly recommended by the commission under the presidency of Mr. Strachey. The malarious fever epidemics caused great havoc in Bengal. It was a peculiar sort of fever and raged with great vigor in the districts of Hoogly and Nuddea and the Northern and Eastern parts of the 24-Pergunnahs. It made its appearance in Rajputana in 1863, and also in some parts of the Bombay Presidency and Deccan in later years. The medical opinion was that this epidemic was brought about by the neglect of the ordinary principles of sanitation, and the allowing of decaying filths, and stagnant water to accumulate and infect the atmosphere around. The number of deaths caused by these epidemics was calculated at an enormous figure. There is no doubt that during the period under review, the sanitation of the Muffassil was grossly neglected and even now the state of things is hardly better. Without discussing as to who are responsible for this state of things, the historian might well dwell on this subject at some length. There is a remarkable saying of John Bright that a nation really lives in its cottages. The saying is true not only of England but of India. The cities represent but a modicum of the population of this vast country. In them are contained the wealth, the intelligence, the culture, and the enterprize of the surrounding territories; but the great bulk of the agriculturists upon whom the people depend for their daily food, whose bucolic pursuits are of that quiet nature, which attract no attention, live mostly in the villages. Many who were originally residents in the villages, have been gradually removing permanently or temporarily to the head-quarters of their districts and if they are in really affluent circumstances, to the metropolis itself. This habit has grown so much in some provinces that the remark is not wide of the mark that the villages are now being deserted for the city by all those who have the means of improving their condition. That many of the villages are still in a primitive state goes without saying. Their sanitation is much neglected, and their condition with reference to drainage, roads and drinking water so bad, that it behoves all who are interested in the welfare of the country to take this state of things into serious consideration. The towns are now all more or less improved. They have those facilities of communication and appliances of civil life that follow in the train of the higher ideals of living introduced by modern enlightenment and education. But the greater part of the nation is yet afflicted by the identical scourges, that existed in the country before modern science unfolded her marvellous pages, and thus an evil of huge magnitude still exists calling for remedy at our very doors,—an evil which is eating into the vitals of the people's existence, and threatening the economic conditions which govern the development of national industry and enterprise. Those villages that are situated by the side of either powerful hill torrents, or rivers which drain a large area, are often subjected to severe floods. These little communities have no system of drainage at all, and the course of natural drainage has been too often impeded by railway and irrigation works. Thus the superfluous rain-water of the season is often found accumulated into stagnant pools gradually being converted under the chemical action of the air, and the heat generated by the sun's rays, into pestilential vapours which bring in all the malarious fevers, and the out-breaks of Asiatic cholera, that have, in many cases, in Bengal, at least depopulated entire villages. The drinking water is often used in an unclean state and other important principles of hygiene and sanitation are either unknown or totally neglected. Thus a frightful loss of human lives is caused by preventible diseases. Lord Dufferin in his well-known speech at the St. Andrews Dinner which was characterized by a glowing eloquence made some very pertinent remarks on the subject but unfortunately while every care is taken to improve the cities, no effort seems yet to have been made, which has resulted in an appreciable improvement of the villages. The duties both of the authorities and of that educated Indian public, which ought on all occasions to be ready to succour their less fortunate brethern are manifold in this respect. Year by year the condition of the villages one way or another, when sorely afflicted by natural visitations of flood or famine or those pestilences, which ignorance of the laws of health so much tend to accelerate occupy a large measure of public attention. But the amount of good that any sincere well-wisher of the country can easily do by teaching the simple villager, some of those laws and principles of existence, that have ameliorated the conditions of urban life is really incalculable. The District officer or the philanthropic missionary in their tours, and those of the original inhabitants of a village that have made advancement in education or material life, can do much to improve matters—opportunities we heartily hope they will not neglect.

The Rajput clans, whose numbers are numerous, and who are to be principally found in those states ruled by the chiefs of these clans, present a most complicated social and political structure, which has to be carefully handled by any Indian administrator. Since the commencement of the British rule in India the conditions of the sovereignty and the relative positions of the ruling chief and his numerous sirdars are fast changing and a new social and political economy is being gradually introduced into Rajsthan. Sir Alfred Lyall called prominent attention to this fact in one of his masterly essays, in which he conclusively demonstrated how Rajputana with her wild ways of the past held out a promise of future development superior to that now afforded under the strong and centralized governments which are so deteriorating to her martial clans, improving during the period under review neither in intelligence nor education. For centuries after the Rajput States were established the chief occupation of the nobles, who were mostly kinsfolk of the reigning chieftains, was to be always in readiness to fight and to resist any undue encroachments on their privileges, by the royal authority. Indeed the conditions of Rajputana were such that the state of things could not be otherwise. But in these peaceful times their occupation is gone, and not being trained during the period under review in the arts of peace, they were gradually declining from the proud position they once held among Indian nobles, into a community unsuited to the times. As Lord Dufferin, very pertinently observed in his elaborate speech at the Mayo College, if Rajputana were still to retain in modern India the proud position, that was held by Rajsthan in ancient India, she will have to march at the head of the other Indian provinces, in all the arts of peace as she did in the arts of war through many rough centuries, in resisting the inroads of the Moslem and the Mahratta arms, and that the conditions of her life should undergo a thorough change. The Rajput States are the only states which can claim any antiquity in India. They originated in tribal sovereignty similar to that which obtained in Europe, according to Guizot, everywhere at the time of the downfall of the Roman Empire and though many capable Indian administrators have likened them to those feudal states, which sprang up at a later period, there is one very essential difference as Sir Alfred Lyall points out between the two. In Rajputana the privileges of kinship everywhere asserted themselves, and everywhere became predominant. The kinsfolk of the reigning family were the principal nobles and had the greater part of the land appertaining to the state, parcelled among themselves. When the the lands became insufficient a landless son of the chief was sent abroad, with other adventurers whose means were likewise scanty, to win territories abroad and to carry on an aggressive warfare in the unoccupied parts of the province. But the defensive wars were the principal features of the history of Rajputana. During the times of the Afghan Kings, raids and forays by the Imperial troops within the borders of a province that never fully submitted to the Imperial rule were the order of the day, and during the Mogul supremacy many regularly organized expeditions were sent into Rajputana. Following upon these were the Maharatta freebooters whose plundering expeditions kept the Rajput clans prepared to resist them at all times. But under the British rule which came just in time to protect the states from immediate dissolution, from internal faction, and external aggression, the country is secure and the power of the chief who has now no longer to depend for support almost throughout his reign on a turbulent aristocracy is gradually under British suzereinty becoming unbounded and centralized as it was never before. But all must sincerely deplore the gradual degeneration which the noblest of fighting clans of India is undergoing in these days. They must be trained up according to the new state of things, that is now prevailing, and the high political officers all over Rajputana should do their best to adapt them gradually to literary and commercial habits, so that they may take with their natural stock of energy the same leading part in modern history that their ancestors did in ancient history. The project of an Indian Sandhurst is not yet ripe, but should one be established the Rajputs will largely resort to it, and provide the best materials for officering the native army. The Rajput clans are a most interesting race. They have kept up their rugged independence, through a series of two thousand years, and every effort should be made to adapt them to the needs of the present times, for with their natural vitality and energy they will prove as successful in the arts of peace as they have been in the arts of war.

LEGISLATION—The legislation during the period under review, embraced a variety of subjects and a great many bills became law almost every year. In 1859, the number of bills that became law was twenty-eight, in 1860 fifty-three, in 1861 thirty-three, in 1862 twenty-four, in 1863 thirty-two, in 1864 twenty-eight, in 1865 thirty, in 1866 thirty, in 1867 thirty-seven, in 1868 twenty-eight, making a total in the ten years under review of three hundred and twenty-three. The constitutional historian of Europe or America dwells chiefly on the legislative enactments and has often remarked that these represent the true feelings and wants of the nation and the procedure connected with them throws the best light on the inner working of the constitution. Those who have gone through the sober pages of Hallam or the delightful ones of Erskine May are aware that they have dealt in full detail every parliamentary act from its first inception to its final passing. The historian of India should hardly attempt to follow at however great a distance their eminent example, because the history of legislation in India is not the constitutional history of the country. Some of the more prominent enactments which deal with large and wide-spread interests should receive a careful notice but as the legislation in India proceeds, from the very nature of things from the rulers themselves, there is little opposition finding vent through the regular channels of what Sir George Campbell calls the Executive Legislature of British India such as is necessary to elucidate the constitutional history of the country. The most important enactments of the year 1859, were the Civil Procedure Code, the Rent law and the Limitation Act. The Civil Procedure Code aims at introducing a system of uniform procedure throughout the Civil Courts in British India, and is so skilfully framed as to provide technical safeguards, while giving the greatest latitude to the presiding judges to act according to the principles of substantive law, or according to justice, equity and good conscience. Only a special procedure was reserved for the Small Cause Courts of the Presidency towns. The Rent law of 1859 was aimed at placing on a satisfactory basis the relation between landlords and tenants. When the Permanent Settlement came in force in 1793, the Government seems to have intended that as the landlords were to pay the same revenue to the state for ever the tenants were to pay the same rents to the landlords. But the great increase of population in Bengal consequent on peace, enabled the landlords to raise their rents immensely, and the land code of 1859 aims chiefly at restraining by means of law the enhancement of the rents of the tenants. We refrain from considering this subject at length here. We have to dwell on the Rent Act of 1885, at great length and the historian must in connection with that measure refer to the literature on the subject, to the opposition it evoked, and the arguments by which that opposition was sought to be met, and we reserve till then a full review of this vexed question. It has been asserted by many high authorities including the late Mr. Fawcett, that the permanent settlement was a great blunder, from the statesman's point of view. On the other hand another class of writers has sought to prove that this measure though involving some loss to the estate under the actual heading of land revenue, yet serves to foster the general prosperity of the people and bring in much money to the treasury through other sources. The whole discussion connected with this topic and the side-issues raised form one of the most interesting chapters of modern politics, and will be treated in its proper place. The Limitation Act of 1859 taught the natives of India that they must not slumber over their rights, that all claims with reference to real property must be prosecuted within twelve years and all claims with reference to small debts within three years, of the accrual of the cause of action. The most important enactment of the year 1860 was the Indian Penal Code, a work so exhaustive and dealing so comprehensively with every class of criminal acts, that it has been pronounced in all quarters to be a very satisfactory compendium of the substantive criminal law of the land. The Indian Penal Code had been elaborated through a long series of years beginning from 1833, by a body amongst whom there were some of the ablest jurists who ever came to India. It is applicable alike to all classes of the community. The only other measure of the year 1860 worth noticing is the Act of Indemnity whose provisions were rendered necessary by the mutiny and the disorder brought in its train. The Criminal Procedure enactment forms the most important feature in the year 1861, the procedure provided for the Criminal Courts is exceedingly simple and if its provisions are worked by competent men leaves but little room for comment. The Police Act supplemented its provisions, but this measure introduced but little appreciable improvement in the character of the police which remained as faulty and as much open to criticism as it had ever been. We shall see later on how the organization of the Police had been sought to be improved but still the nature of the work in which the Police is engaged is such, that unless in the case of men of solidity of character, the police is always apt to act unfairly, bringing discredit both on the individual men and the Government whose livery they wear. The police, as it has been constituted during the whole of the last generation had been much disliked by the better classes of the native population and

Lord Dufferin in one of his utterances bore testimony to the manifold imperfections of this department of the State. Act III of 1864 placed the foreigners resident in India under some sort of control of the Governor-General in Council, and Act VII of 1864 added whipping to the list of punishments provided for by the Indian Penal Code, being inflicted specially in the case of old offenders. Whipping is a punishment whose infliction involves a considerable amount of degradation in the eyes of the native community, and its operation should always be watched with great care by the superior authorities. Act III of 1864, dealt with the subject of the emigration of labour and the contracts entered into with and by the laborers. A short enactment passed this year also swept the appendage of the British Courts of Justice, in the persons of the Hindu and Mahomedan professors of law whose opinions were always sought for in questions of Hindu and Mahomedan law, as a part of the regular procedure of the Courts, by the presiding judges. The rulings of the Privy Council and the able text-books on the subjects of Hindu and Mahomedan law which had been written by many English lawyers, had, it was thought sufficiently elucidated the principles of Hindu Law and the necessity of maintaining Pandits and Kazees no longer existed. This step, though it might not have impaired the administration of justice, certainly took away the only patronage the state accorded to the learned men in the classics of India. The system of Government pursued in the non-regulation provinces came a good deal under discussion. There is no doubt that if the administration be officered by proper men, this system of administration is the best for unsettled provinces up to a certain stage of development. The Indian Succession Act of 1865 dealt with the succession to the states of intestates and testamentary succession in the case of all those who were not Hindus, Mahomedans or members of other established Indian religions. The Muffassil Small Cause Courts act provided on an extended scale the machinery for the recovery of the petty debts. The great increase in the number of Joint-Stock Companies made the legislature attend to them, and the Municipal Committee Act which was applicable only to the N. W. Provinces introduced the important principle that the head of the provincial executive could make the municipal organization compulsory in the case of any town he thought fit. The members of the municipality appointed under the Act chiefly by a system of nomination had the power of taxation. The rest of the work done by the legislative council, was besides some patchwork legislation, mainly confined to a Stamp Act and some provisions with reference to Christian marriages. The institution fees on suits levied by the new Stamp Act, were pronounced by the organs of public opinion at the time to be heavy and it was pointed out that this scale of fees would press heavily on two sorts of people, the very poor, and those who had contingent claims to great wealth. This Stamp Act also levied fees on ordinary petitions and complaints in criminal cases. The Oudh and the Punjab tenancy bills, excited a good deal of attention. With the establishment of the regular courts in the land, the legal machinery is often turned to purposes of private malice. The proverbial delay of the Indian Courts and the trouble attendant on every business to be transacted by the Courts, make it very easy for evil-disposed men to turn the prodigious power of the law to serve their unworthy ends. The jury system in India is a question of much interest but the consideration of this, we reserve till we come to speak of the Criminal Procedure Code of Sir Fitzjames Stephen.

Conclusion.—Since India came under the administration of the crown, the territorial acquisitions have been very insignificant. A narrow strip at the foot of the Bhotan hills, and some small tracts near Pishin and Quetta acquired for strategic purposes, and in 1886, the territory of Upper Burma complete the list of new acquisitions. The doctrine of lapse to the paramount power so much in the ascendant during the regime of Lord Dalhousie, was not acted upon in any single instance, and on the contrary the province of Mysore was restored after remaining fifty years under British rule. There has been little constitutional change during the present decade or the two following ones, in the constitution of the state except the appointment of a Finance Member, and a special Public Works member, while each Member is in charge of a department, the Viceroy in Council having to consider the more important matters. As the business of the country has been always increasing, the Local Governments have been sought to be relieved by the delegation of many useful functions to the local bodies. The English Government have sought to get the fullest information about the vast country under its rule and this object has been attained by the Trigonometrical, Topographical, Cadastral, Geological and Archæological surveys undertaken since the era of the administration of the crown. The first complete census of the British empire in India was held in 1871 and this was followed by another census in 1881 on which occasion most of the native states also numbered the people under their rule, thus the Government was furnished with complete statistical information about the inhabitants of this interesting country. Under the Indian Council's Act of 1861, there are now four or five members in each of the legislative councils which number from 10 to 18 members each. In each of the High Courts there is at present one native judge, and while thirty years ago, the Civil Service from which the superior administrative staff is drawn, did not contain a single native of India, in January 1888, that service contained 59 natives of India, out of a total of 964, the Subordinate Civil Service in Uncovenanted Departments consists mainly of natives of India. In native states natives of India have repeatedly filled the offices of the Regent or the Prime Minister, with advantage to the state and with credit to themselves. During the past thirty years, the administrative, judicial, revenue and executive business has more than doubled, and the judicious distribution of work, the giving of wider powers and responsibilities, to the local officials, and the gradual association of natives of India to some share in the administration of their country notably by placing a good deal of magisterial work to unpaid magistrates, subject to revision and superintendence, enabled the Government to go through the increased amount of work without any material addition to the strength of the Civil Service. The great majority of native Judges and Magistrates has made much progress in legal training and in uprightness of character. There now prevail generally a higher standard of probity and sense of duty among this class of officials and while a generation ago, this class was widely suspected and openly accused of corrupt practices, accusations of this sort are now more rare. All native judges and magistrates appointed in recent years have been mostly men of education and many are graduates in Arts and Law. The Police it is universally admitted continues to be a weak point in the administration but it is generally believed that since the organization of 1861, the status and the discipline of the police have much improved. The number of Criminal Courts having largely increased people have now to travel smaller distances to seek relief. The Jails everywhere have been constructed on the sanitary principles and though some abuses must exist as long as the character of the subordinate officials remains what it unfortunately now is, the death-rates are decreasing. During the past thirty years some revised settlements of land revenue were undertaken for long terms of years and the instructions of the Government have always been to make careful surveys and base the assessment on moderate and equitable principles. The railways have provided an outlet for agricultural produce and large sums of money now can circulate among the agricultural classes. The income of the Government excepting the item of land revenue falls under the following heads,—Salt-tax, Opium, Customs, Excise, Income Tax, Stamp duties, Forests, Post Office and Telegraphs. The system of registration of births and deaths came in use since the country came under the crown. The number of qualified native medical practitioners daily increased till now it amounts to a dozen times at least of the number available in 1857. The currency difficulty into which the Government of India had to fall ever since 1874 had not made its appearance during the decade under notice. The currency difficulty greatly increased the Home charges, and the expenditure that the Government of India has to incur in England, which is principally incurred under the following heads;—Interest of the Public Debt borrowed in England, interest on guaranteed railway capital, on account of arms and ammunitions and other materials bought in England, pensions to retired officers of the Civil and Military Departments, and the expenses incurred by the depots of troops in England. The difficulty arises from the fact that these items of expenditure in 1889 aggregated to 15 millions, and had to be defrayed in England in gold. We shall reserve for the future parts of this work a consideration of the public works, the trade and manufactures, the condition of the people, the political relations with Native States, and the progress made in Local Self-Government. The complex topics with reference to the Indian Army will also be detailed at another place. The vast increase of the population complicates every problem and is a source of unfailing anxiety to the economist and the administrator. We shall attempt to trace in the two following parts of this work the problems now confronting the Indian administrator and the work that according to the most approved opinions yet remains to be done in India.

End of the First Part.

INDIAN HISTORY

OF OUR OWN TIMES.

PARTS II AND III, (1869-88.)

BY

SATYA CHANDRA MUKERJI, M.A., B.L.,

Vakil, High Court, N. W. Provinces.

CALCUTTA :

PUBLISHED BY S. K. LAHIRI & CO.,

54, COLLEGE STREET.

1893.

[*All Rights Reserved.*]

CALCUTTA:
NEW TOWN PRESS,
10, PUDDOPUKER ROAD.

PART II.

This part of the "Indian History of Our Own Times" is, by kind permission, respectfully dedicated to His Excellency Lord Frederick Sleigh Roberts Commander-in-Chief of the Forces in India, that accomplished soldier and eminent statesman, who after having filled with conspicuous success every branch of the Indian military administration, had happily been selected to fill a position which enabled him during his tenure of that high office to bring upon the counsels of this great Empire, his judgment, equally clear and candid, which again had been fortified with a singularly wide knowledge of affairs.

SATYA CHANDRA MUKERJI.

PREFACE.

In presenting the second and the third parts of the "Indian History of our own times" to the public, I have to apologize for some unavoidable delay in the completion of the book. The profession, of which I have the honor of being a member, is a very exacting one and in nothing more so, than in the matter of constant attendance. Some personal misfortunes too, have delayed the finishing of this undertaking. Having however some time at my hands just now, I utilize it, in giving the finishing touches to this book which had a prominent place on my attention for the last three years.

I have, since the appearance of the first part, been favored with many suggestions with reference to the plan and the execution of this book. I have received an amount of help in the shape of materials from different quarters that it would be difficult for me to acknowledge all my obligations and where I am indebted to so many, it would be invidious to select a few for special notice. I have not thought it proper to burden the narrative with references to the authorities, although I am quite aware that a young writer's fame would chiefly depend on his getting access to the best materials. This method of work, however, would have expanded the limits of this humble undertaking to a considerable extent and I have, above all things, desired, while omitting nothing material, to confine it within such limits as might be acceptable to the busy public of our days. I have confined myself also strictly to the historical matter and have avoided any lengthened discussion on the problems of modern politics, which have not yet passed the regions of controversy. I have to do my literary work in the time that I can spare from my other duties and I have been unable to devote anything like an adequate amount of time and attention to this book, but it is much better that a native of India should attempt however imperfectly to give in a narrative form, this portion of Indian History, than that it should be left as a *terra incognita* about which one unacquainted with the subject would have found it difficult to know anything.

To the Press of this country, both European and Indian, I am sincerely grateful for the cordial reception they had been pleased to give to my humble venture. To many highly-placed European officials and Indian Princes and noblemen, I am equally thankful for the kind encouragement they have given me by subscribing to this book, aiding me with materials and favoring me with complimentary opinions. The Government of Bengal has been pleased to recognize that in writing this book I have consulted the files of the leading newspapers of the day and the published reports of Government. I am specially indebted to His Excellency the Marquis of Lansdowne, His Excellency Lord Frederic Roberts of Waterford and Kandahar and to Sir Auckland Colvin late Lieutenant-

Governor of the N. W. Provinces for having graciously permitted me to bring out respectively the third, the second and the first parts of this book under their kind patronage. To my many Indian friends who have looked over particular portions of this book my sincere thanks are also due.

I am aware that this book cannot pretend to be more than a manual of the principal events in the first three decades of Indian administration by Her Gracious Imperial Majesty. I happen however to be only in my 27th year at present and I can fairly expect that should time and opportunities permit, I shall attempt, later on in life, to enlarge it to the dimensions of a standard historical work. There are no doubt several faults and imperfections in the present book and my way of stating things might not always be approved, owing to the variety of human tastes, but I humbly trust that the present portion would meet with the same kind acceptance as the part that preceded it.

SATYA CHANDRA MUKERJI.
The 30th June 1893.

TABLE OF CONTENTS.

PART II.

Chapter	I (1869)	1—13
Chapter	II (1870)	14—27
Chapter	III (1871)	28—42
Chapter	IV (1872)	43—56
Chapter	V (1873)	57—70
Chapter	VI (1874)	71—84
Chapter	VII (1875)	85—98
Chapter	VIII (1876)	99—112
Chapter	IX (1877)	113—126
Chapter	X (1878)	127—140

PART III.

Chapter	I (1879)	146—156
Chapter	II (1880)	157—170
Chapter	III (1881)	171—182
Chapter	IV (1882)	183—194
Chapter	V (1883)	195—207
Chapter	VI (1884)	208—221
Chapter	VII (1885)	222—234
Chapter	VIII (1886)	235—447
Chapter	IX (1887)	248—260
Chapter	X (1888)	261—275

INDIAN HISTORY OF OUR OWN TIMES.

PART THE SECOND.

CHAPTER I.

1869.

THE EARL OF MAYO—Lord Lawrence was succeeded in the Indian Viceroyalty by Richard Southwell Bourke, the Sixth Earl of Mayo. He came of a family that had played a prominent part in Irish history from the Strongbow invasion downwards. His family had through several centuries of unrest, cast in their lot with the Irish people. He was brought up in the midst of the best sceneries of the Emerald Isle and in the accounts of the travels that he undertook to complete his education he had given evidence of a penetrative insight into character and a keen observation of affairs. During his Parliamentary career he had seldom spoken on any but Irish subjects and had filled the office of the Secretary for Ireland on three successive occasions when his party was in power. His success in this office was so conspicuous that the great leader of his party, offered him the charge of the extensive Eastern Empire of Her Majesty and spoke of the Viceroy-elect in terms of the highest praise. His party had gone out of power before he actually took charge of the Viceregal office, but the adverse political party confirmed the nomination. On the 20th December 1868 Lord Mayo landed in Bombay, and inspected everything of public interest in that city which under the auspices of British rule had expanded to magnificent proportions. He was accessible to the leaders of every section of the community and he took occasion to study as thoroughly as his short stay permitted, the harbour defences, the Municipal Taxes, and the Commercial enterprize of the capital of Western India. He then sailed down the coast to inspect the harbours of Karwar and Beypur. From the last mentioned place he crossed the Deccan plateau and proceeded to Madras where he conferred with the Local Government on many important questions. He was much struck with the peculiar system of irrigation by tanks and wells which is resorted to in the Madras Presidency. In personal discussions he elicited a mass of opinions on the scheme of the decentralization of the finances which he was then maturing. On the 12th of January 1869 he landed in Calcutta and took charge of his new office. The veteran Indian official who had got the credit for breaking the neck of the Sepoy revolt and who after forty years of Indian Service was now seeking the rest and honors of a respected old age made over the Empire in a state of profound peace to a successor who though unacquainted with Indian administrative details, was through his wide culture, his thorough grasp of principles and his capacity for unremitting labour, equal to the duties of the highest office outside the British Isles which any subject of Her Majesty might fill. The elevation of the Irish Secretary of the Conservative ministry to the Indian Viceroyalty coupled with the well-known success that had attended him in Ireland made some observations to be published as to the success that should attend Lord Mayo, in his new career from the similarity of circumstances in India and Ireland. The historian cannot too emphatically protest against the assertion of similarity in political status and condition that is so often made with reference to India and Ireland. India and Ireland are not at all alike. In India the native inhabitants are peaceful, docile and proverbially mild. In Ireland one section of the people at least has a strong tendency towards political crime. In India the conflict of religion is not half so keen and bitter as in Ireland. The Irishmen rise to all high offices either in the United Kingdom or in the colonies and dependencies and they have grievances only in matters of land tenure and the church. Years must pass before India can rise to the political status of Ireland. In the matter of the progressive advancement of the people it is already forenoon in Ireland about to usher in the bright midday while it is only the streaking light of dawn in India. It is a great mistake to place an Indian Civilian at the head of the administration of this country. The career of Sir John Lawrence in India plainly proved that notwithstanding an intimate intercourse with the first minds of Europe, the Civilian unconsciously imbibes a local bias and prejudice. His mind moves along certain defined channels. He is incapable of broad and statesmanlike grasp of the affairs of one-sixth of the human race. He is wedded to traditions and his previous friendships introduce an undesirable element in his dispensation of patronage. On the other hand the great English noblemen who have ruled India from the days of Lord Cornwallis to those of Lord Canning (we must except Lord Elgin who was too short a time in the country to leave any impress of his mind) notwithstanding their previous inexperience, have been successful and have given signal proofs of far-reaching and beneficent statesmanship. The Civil Service of India had certainly done great things in the past both in the way of conquering the country and consolidating British rule but like all close bureaucracies it has its defects in the way of limiting and narrowing the views and cramping the intellectual vision. Red-tape has its effects in all countries but those are remarkably well-defined in India. The Indian Government is a practical illustration of the well-known theory of the political philosophers, that a bureaucracy when presided over by a mind new to the subject but with a thorough grasp of principles, liberal views and acute mental vision, yields the best results, the strong points of each element being corrective of the deficiencies of the other. The system of the Viceroyalty being limited to five years has both its advantages and its disadvantages. The incumbents in that high office are too often seized with a desire to crowd too many measures to be able to occupy pre-eminent positions in History, thus sacrificing conscientious work and provident and timely statesmanship for the sake of eminence. This system is the main cause of too many important bills being considered and passed in hot haste, the work of years being compressed into weeks. The practical immunity and privileged position which a Viceroy attains after five years leads him to introduce too many administrative experiments more especially as he is sure that he and his descendants will not have to reap the evil arising from them. The necessity of years of local inquiries, of professional report and correspondence often dissuades the Viceroy from embarking on great and important measures. The systematic delay of references to England contribute a powerful cause otwards the same effect. The liability of the measures of one government being set aside by a Viceroy of a different cast of mind is a danger which though happily not often felt in practice, has yet in certain instances, produced an element of unrest and break of continuity in the Indian administration. The compensating advantages are bad Governor-Generals cannot distress the land for more than five years except if they be favorites of fortune like Lord Dalhousie and the bad measures of one administration cannot afflict the land for more than a certain number of years, as they are likely to be repealed if they be found iniquitous. One of the first acts of Lord Mayo was to invite Indian merchants to take a part in the grand Paris Exhibition of that year. The chief articles of Indian produce which attracted notice in the Queen of cities were silk fabrics, muslins, old armours, court-dresses, tables, saddle-cloths, marble-plates and bidree vases. The native chiefs sent special presents to His Imperial Majesty the Emperor of the French. The French nation appreciated the spirit of good-will thus exhibited and gave a suitable recognition to it. The exhibits from the native states captivated the intellect, the beauty and the fashion of Paris.

INDORE.—Maharaja Tukaji Rao Holkar was a model sovereign. Sir John Malcolm, the historian of the Holkars has given a graphic account of the peculiar characteristics of that race of princes but the present monarch seemed to unite a capacity for physical hardships with mental powers of no mean order. He discussed ably and with a good grasp of principles the merits and demerits of the land settlement in his territories with the British representative. He explained that the recent settlement had been effected after a thorough and careful measurement of the land and that the inclusion of the waste lands, whose rents were formerly exclusively enjoyed by the landed proprietors, into the class of assessed lands was the chief cause of its unpopularity. The Resident took another view of the question. He thought that the Maharaja having taken advantage of a temporary rise in prices had needlessly enhanced the assessed dues. The Maharaja effected great improvements in his mint with the aid of the Bombay Government. He established girls chools in many parts of his dominions and his schools for boys contained 1100 pupils. He completed a comprehensive and costly system of water-works and aqueducts for his capital city. He established a weaving and spinning mill on a large scale and under trained European management. He encouraged the cultivation of opium and cotton recognizing that in the opium-trade and the manufacture of cotton lay the great sources of wealth for his territories. His dominions increased forty per cent in population during the last half a century amounting in 1869 to 750,000 souls of whom a third were children. He expressed some very sound views on the political relations of the Government of India with native Indian states clearly recognizing the change of policy adopted towards them since the Mutiny and cautioning political officers as to the difficult and delicate duties entrusted to them in honestly interpreting the opinions of each government to the other and giving honest counsel to the Asiatic sovereigns. He justly remarked that the best thing the native chiefs could look to was such efficient administration as to draw the esteem of the Queen and the Houses of Parliament.

HYDERABAD.—This important state in the Deccan lost this year the chief that had ruled it for the last dozen years. Afzulooddowlah the Nizam ascended the *musnud* on the 11th March 1857. He, with the able assistance of Sir Salar Jung rendered important services during the Mutiny. He kept in check the furious Moslem subjects of his own territories who were thirsting for blood and vengeance. He kept within strict limits his own heterogenous and mercenary bands of soldiers who were eager for opportunities of plunder and distinction. He repelled an attack on the British Residency, rejected the tempting overtures of the mutineers, and above all quelled the rebellion in the Deccan by sending to the aid of the British troops the body of forces known as the Hyderabad contingent. For his signal services during the Mutiny, the Nizam was rewarded with the grant of those territories that his father had ceded to the British Government, got back the lapsed state of Shorapur, and one lac of rupees worth of goods, had fifty lacs of debt cancelled and was invested with the insignia of the first class of the Star of India. The state of Hyderabad remained under the management of the old pilot Sir Salar Jung. He had evolved order out of chaos. He had introduced the machinery of civilized administration. He had kept all the disturbing elements in the state in proper subordination. He had imported trained officials. He had been a terror to wrong-doers and to the habitual criminal classes. He had always vindicated the majesty of law and justice however high and powerful the offender. He managed all affairs satisfactorily during a long minority and the finances of the country were in a prosperous condition.

TRAVANCORE.—This State resembles a British Division more closely than any other native State. It is divided into districts and sub-divisions each with a regular machinery and a responsible chief. There are the different grades of the courts and the independence of the judiciary has been secured by elaborate precautions. There are commodious jails, cheap post, organized public work, registration and forest departments. There are museums and gardens where people may cultivate their finer feelings. Education is steadily advancing, the higher offices of the state are given exclusively to cultured and talented men. The finances of the country always exhibited a large surplus. This surplus the enlightened minister religiously declared would not be used in hoarding, but in the useful way of reducing land taxation, decreasing the export duty, and raising the pay of employes in petty public offices. The high offices of the state being filled with credit by the educated natives, it was evident that modern educated India is not dead to the art of statecraft. The Government is a mild and beneficent despotism and cases of oppression are heard of even more rarely than in British India.

THE OPIUM REVENUE.—The extensive cultivation of poppy in China and the appearance of the Persian drug on the Chinese market were powerful causes of the decreasing element in the Indian opium revenue. The growth of poppy in China was detrimental to the produce of the food-grains and the Celestial Emperor issued a strict order prohibiting poppy cultivation. But as Sir Rutherford Alcock writes from personal observations, the edict of the Government was obeyed more in the breach than in the observance. Persia became too a formidable competitor in the Chinese market. Her soil and climate were well adapted to the cultivation of poppy of good quality but she could not compete with India owing to the heavy cost of transport. Her Consul had always been soliciting privileges to send her opium to China through India but this request was not heeded. But the early close of the Abyssinian War enabled the Persian Government to charter some of the ships engaged therein and to transport opium. The Indian Government through fear conceded to Persia the long-sought privileges and she was able to transport her opium through India subject to a pass duty. This newly sprung-up trade between Persia and

China made India a serious loser under this item of revenue.

THE INCOME-TAX BILL.—Sir Richard Temple's budget which proposed both to borrow and to raise money by additional taxation for reproductive public works prepared the way for the bill introduced to impose an one per cent. income-tax for the present. The peculiar feature of this bill was that it had no provision for calling out returns of incomes, the assessment being based on rough guesses, and that in the case of under-assessment the collectors had the power to re-open the question in the middle of the year. The present bill held out a premium to Government extravagance and inflicted considerable hardship on the poor people. To be weak is to be miserable and the way of justice in India being paved with gold, the poor man is scarcely heard at all. The income-tax will be considered later on, from the standpoint of its suitability to India, but there is no doubt that it is a fruitful source of oppression in a country situated as India is. It was indeed a serious financial situation for the politician and the economist from year to year, with the revenues annually increasing by 20 per cent., with India's commerce at five millions with continued additions to the national debt. It is painful for the historian to contemplate that the unfathomable sink of the public works was causing all this deficit.

THE MILITARY AND THE FOREIGN POLICY OF THE GOVERNMENT OF INDIA—Lord Mayo's attention was early directed to the relations of the Indian Government with the neighbouring Central Asian States, Afghanistan, Beluchistan and Eastern Turkestan. All the three countries were the theatre of political intrigues and furnished cause for anxiety in view of the steadily aggressive policy of Russia in Central Asia. Beluchistan had been torn by internal dissensions between the actual occupants of the throne and the principal Sirdars, and Persian and Russian intrigues still further complicated matters. The State of Eastern Turkestan had been founded by a soldier of fortune who was eagerly looking for recognition to the Russians on one side, and the English on the other. During the wars of succession that followed the death of Amir Dost Mahomed the British Government espoused the cause of neither of the contending factions, but left them to fight out their own quarrels. At the same time it expressed its readiness to both the powerful rivals to recognize any of them that could succeed in establishing his position as the *de facto* ruler of Afghanistan. It went so far as to say that should it happen that both the rivals succeeded in ruling certain parts of Afghanistan and the kingdom was dismembered the British Government would silently acquiesce in the state of things and give its recognition to both. The Afghans thought this a mean and treacherous policy and it excited the exasperation of both the rival claimants to the throne. The summer of 1868 saw that the fortunes of Shere Ali were clearly in the ascendant and Sir Henry Rawlinson in an able despatch thought it politic for England to form an alliance with him. The details of the Afghan policy were being settled between Sir John Lawrence and the Secretary of State Sir Stafford Northcote, when Lord Mayo arrived in India. Lord Mayo entered heartily into the new policy and at once invited the Amir to a personal conference at Umballa on the then situation and for defining the mutual dealings of the two states with each other. The Amir came in state in March 1869 and he was received in India with splendid and royal honors. The Amir was deeply impressed with the material grandeur of British rule and he formed a high opinion of the efficiency of the British army. Himself a renowned soldier he discussed the whole subject of army improvement with keen interest and much sense with His Excellency the Commander-in-Chief. The Durbar at Umballa has been described to be an oriental edition of the Field of the Cloth of Gold. The Amir tried to persuade the Viceroy to enter into a definite treaty with him to recognize himself and his younger son Abdulla Jan as the rulers of Afghanistan and to support them against all odds. He wanted moreover an annual subsidy and assistance in arms and in men whenever he might solicit the same. The treaty demanded was of such a nature that it would have been extremely impolitic for Lord Mayo to have countenanced it, and he while courteously declining the same, managed to send away the Amir satisfied by friendly greetings, by presents and by absolute present recognition of his title. The Amir's formal visits with the Viceroy were of an agreeable nature and His Highness discoursed chiefly on horses and the army and made some reflections on railways, and on the best methods of administration in barbaric countries. Lord Mayo emphatically protested that England had no designs of territorial aggrandisement in Central Asia and that the peace and independence of Afghanistan should be scrupulously respected. At the same time, the Viceroy insisted upon Her Majesty's ministers to come to a formal understanding with the cabinet at St. Petersburg pledging it not to interfere in the affairs of Afghanistan. The boundaries of Afghanistan being uncertain, Russia was perpetually taking advantage of this fact. The question of Badakshan being included in the Afghan territories was settled by the Czar's acquiescence to its inclusion in the dominions of the Amir. In January 1873, Count Schouvaloff headed a diplomatic mission on the subject in London. Lord Mayo also meddled with the affairs of Beluchistan. He was unable however to bring his negotiations to any satisfactory conclusion though he had arranged for the arbitration of the long-standing disputes by a British officer. The mission to Yarkand whose only result was the collection of some statistical information about the country and people will be described later on. Lord Mayo's attention was also directed towards opening up trade-routes through Chang-Cheung valley, the defining of the eastern boundaries of India through a range of hills and forests and the placing the relations with Burma and Nepal on a satisfactory footing. The statesmen who had guided the affairs of India since the Mutiny had felt strongly the necessity of cutting down the numerical strength of the Indian army which had grown too large owing to the panic caused by the Mutiny. The ten years previous to the arrival of Lord Mayo saw a considerable reduction but the new and costly systems introduced by the English war office were the cause of a large increase in expenditure. The Duke of Argyll asked Lord Mayo to take up seriously the question of army retrenchment and to effect a saving under this head of a million and a half sterling, annually by economy in the military administration and the further numerical reduction of forces. With reference to the British portion of the army Lord Mayo was of opinion, that the European force was just sufficient for the requirements of the Empire and that it could not be decreased without imperilling the safety of the Empire. He tried however to effect a saving of half a million sterling under this head by diminishing the number of regimental head-quarters and keeping up the full strength of the fighting men in all regiments which would enable the government to disband several regiments. The Viceroy entered into the details of army administration with his military advisers, and tried to propose some retrenchments in the several Presidency armies without impairing their efficiency or offending their *amour propre*. Lord Mayo proposed to abolish the native gunners as well as the abolition of one regiment of Bengal cavalry and one regiment of Bengal infantry. The Madras sepoys who were mostly married men cost the state a good deal in transporting them to other parts of India. It was therefore necessary to keep the Madras regiments to their own presidency and by the adoption of this practice several regiments of cavalry and infantry were proposed to be dispensed with. By reorganizing the said horse and by deciding to disband four regiments of native infantry, considerable savings were sought to be effected in the Bombay army. The Secretary of State sanctioned only some of these proposals. The artillery reductions were sanctioned. With reference to the native army the Secretary of State suggested a different plan which led the Government of India to suggest a compromise which would have resulted in reducing the rank and file of the Native army by 9,000 men equally in the three Presidencies. Both Lord Sandhurst and Lord Napier of Magdala were dangerous army administrators, and their measures involved waste and extravagance. It is indeed difficult to act according to the principle enunciated by a high military authority as to the proper administration of the army viz. that waste follows excessive saving no less than excessive expenditure, that what is superfluous in the army is to be reduced but what is essential must not be starved. The military barracks that Lord Mayo inaugurated, were so carelessly managed that their construction was a heavy charge to the Indian Exchequer. The historian must painfully record that while Sir Henry Durand and Sir William Mansfield admitted that not more than three lacs had been actually spent in the barracks the budgets showed the expenditure at nearly twenty times that figure. The poor Indian tax-payer must however pay all taxation imposed without ever enquiring how things are going on.

GENERAL EVENTS—His Royal Highness the Duke of Edinburgh paid a visit to India in the closing weeks of the year. The provincial governors and many native chiefs came down to Calcutta to welcome the first prince of the Blood Royal that had visited India and His Royal Highness was everywhere received with gorgeous displays. The festivities in honor of the Sailor Prince in the metropolis of India defy description. The political effects of this visit was on a somewhat lesser scale the same that will be detailed in connection with the visit of the Prince of Wales. Nine scholarships were established this year by the Government of India to enable Indian youths to study in England. The Duke of Argyll was forced to admit that the great promises of 1833 and 1858 had remained unfulfilled that he established these scholarships as a partially compensating circumstance for the difficulties the natives of India laboured under in entering the Civil Service. The measure of justice was however too inadequate for a population of 200 millions in British India. The record of England's appointing natives of India to high offices under grave pledges and solemn declarations is a sorry one and so early as 1853, Lord Monteagle had raised his voice against the injustice of defeating the aspirations of the natives of India by artfully-framed rules, which escaped attention in England as mere matters of detail. Sir Henry Maine retired from his high office this year. His was the example of brilliant intellectual qualities absolutely wasted as far as Indian administration was concerned. He had a supreme contempt of the native intellect and he thought it beneath him to enquire as to whether the bills placed on the legislative anvil were in accordance with the recognized principles of civilized jurisprudence. He was always a partizan and he had done little good work except giving a general succession act. His immediate predecessors, Mr. Cameron Mr. Ritchie, Mr. Bethune and Sir Barnes Peacock had done good work in some direction or other but Sir Henry Maine threw away the splendid opportunities he had before him, and it is a sad task for the historian to record that the foremost exponent of ancient jurisprudence of the modern age, one who had done more than any other, to spread a knowledge of the village-systems of India in Europe should leave no substantial mark of his great mind behind in this country. The work connected with the Suez Canal was progressing fast under the direction of the French Engineer M. Lessops. By this canal brighter hope was expected to dawn on India and England than was expressed in the significant name of the Cape of Good Hope. The canal which was formally opened next year is one of the greatest triumphs of human engineering, and is an important event in the Indian history of the modern age.

CHAPTER II.

1870.

THE GOVERNMENT OF INDIA—One of the greatest changes introduced by the transfer of the administration of India to the Crown was the adoption of the cabinet system in the Imperial Government of India. Since the establishment of the British rule the supreme power had been vested in a Central Board with the Viceroy as President. Before the Regulating Act of 1773 and for some years after it the Governor-General was not the absolute President of the Council and the administrative system was often brought into great disrepute by such vagaries as those of Sir Philip Francis. Lord Cornwallis accepted office on the express and unequivocal condition that the Governor-General should be absolute within his Council and should have the power to overrule the other members on all topics of foreign policy and domestic administration. All questions of every department of the state had however to be referred for opinion to every member of the council and the progress of work was blocked up with much elaborate minute-writing and was very slow. After the Mutiny Lord Canning with the sanction of the Home Government introduced considerable modifications into this system. All business of a routine nature was disposed of by the Secretary and Under-Secretary of each department. The references from the Local Governments and all questions which involve general principles are disposed of by the responsible member in charge of the department while all important cases especially those which demand a departure from established rule must be laid before the Viceroy. These memberships of the council are mostly given to tried members of Indian Civil Service but the Law Department is always presided over by a distinguished member of the English bar, the Military Department by an eminent soldier who has given evidence of having paid sufficient attention to the administration of the army and the Finance Department sometimes by a financier trained in England. The secretaries to these departments are at the present day allowed to dispose of business which would have taken years during the times previous to the Mutiny. When His Excellency agreed in important matters with the initiating member responsible for the particular department the decision became final and was published as the order of the Governor-General in Council. Where however the Viceroy either differed or entertained some doubts on the point the case was circulated for opinion among all the members of the Executive Council who had to record their views on the subject. "After the papers of the case had thus completed their circuit in oblong mahogany boxes, the matter was brought for discussion in a meeting of the Executive Council. Some explanations and judicious compromises are tried to bring about an uniformity of opinion in case of any differences, and the collective views of the Government issue in an order of the Governor-General in Council. The Viceroy have however the constitutional right of deciding the action of the Government by his single vote, a right which fortunately had very seldom been exercised. Sometimes it is found impossible to come to an unanimity of opinion and in these cases the despatches to the Secretary of State mention the names of dissentient councillors and append in full such protests as they might choose to write." The personal duties of the Viceroy were not only to consider the important cases which pour into his room during the whole day from all the departments of State but also to meet his Chief Secretaries for all necessary information once a week, and his Executive Council too once a week for the transaction of business. The sittings of the Legislative Council which are ordinarily presided over by the Viceroy, are held when necessary, and when there happens to be any pressure of business once a week. The ornamental functions that append to the Indian Viceroyalty while affording some relaxation to the Viceregal mind after the hard labours of the day, are in themselves too many. The Viceroy has to receive and return the visits of all native chiefs, to confer with all foreign embassies to preside at all important meetings and open all public works of magnitude to lay the foundation-stones of all institutions which might do good to the people, to grant personal interviews to all distinguished either by wealth, valour or intellect, and to encourage by his august presence and eloquent words all suitable ceremonies fraught with far-reaching consequences to the millions of this great country. After night-fall the Viceroy has often to play again the part of the head of the State in receiving at state dinners, at balls and levees and other entertainments large and influential sections of the Indian Community. The Secretariat Offices to the Government of India minutely examine all questions of principle and all schemes submitted by the Local Governments and Administrations, and the Viceroy has to give a patient hearing to all these conflicting opinions and then to shape the course of his Government. The Suez Canal and the sub-marine telegraph which came in existence this year introduced a new element in the Indian administration by sensibly diminishing the distance between England and India. The Secretary of State is now consulted in all important matters by wire and his decisions which are often arrived at, by consultation with those statesmen who are his colleagues in the cabinet, have a great and preponderating influence on the Government of India. English statesmen accustomed to the free flow of Parliamentary eloquence have often expressed their surprize to the amount of business that is often got through with almost no speechifying by the Indian Executive Council and the rapidity with which decisions are arrived at even in the most momentous questions. The present system of the Government of India fully developed itself with the Suez Canal and the sub-marine telegraph in the time of Lord Mayo. It has been described to the minutest detail by Sir William Hunter and Sir John Strachey but the remarks we have made above represent fairly the leading features of it. Truly it has been remarked that the duties of the Indian Viceroy are so pressing, so momentous and of such far-reaching consequences and problem after problem so constantly occupies his attention that he has not, if he conscientiously works, breathing-time to give way to any unworthy considerations of temporary fame or personal popularity. From the time of Lord Mayo onwards increasing powers were conferred on Local Governments and Administrations to cope with the increasing business of the country, and public duty was sought to be delegated to local bodies. The weak point of the Government of India was (in the time of Lord Mayo) and still continues to be that no sufficient provision has been made in the constitution for the authoritative expression of such public opinion as exists in the country. There are no doubt many difficulties in the way but that some important change should be made in this direction, is a fact that has been admitted by a long series of right-thinking and enlightened statesmen, and the Government of India is moving at a snail's pace on the subject and with an evident want of sympathy with those just and honorable aspirations which the beneficent policy of England has called forth. We shall deal with this important question later on, in connection with the National Congresses of India which have made the reform of the councils the chief plank on its platform. No structural change has been introduced into the Government of India since the time of Lord Mayo.

INDIA IN ENGLAND.—The opening of the Suez Canal was destined to produce important social and political changes in India. It facilitated the way of commerce, it enabled the Englishmen in India to visit their homes frequently, it induced the Indians to make voyages to England to acquaint themselves with the details of modern civilization, it made it easy for English statesmen to be familiar with Indian affairs and it thus effected almost a revolution in the economy of Indian administration. During this year several visitors of importance and position from India were recieved with marked kindness by the English public. The Nawab Nazim of Bengal, who thought himself aggrieved by the treatment received by him and his family at the hands of the British Indian Government, visited England to rouse the authorities and the public to a sense of his wrongs. His agents contrived to make many members of the English press his advocates and they discussed with great breadth and impartiality the early history of England's power in the East and the services that had been rendered to the East Indian Company by the ancestors of the aggrieved visitor. Babu Keshub Chandra Sen the apostle of the Brahmo faith also visited England and all religious denominations united in giving a cordial welcome to the great religious reformer whose fluent English eloquence, controversial talents and grasp of subtleties drew forth crowds of admirers in every English city that he visited. The Maharaja of Kolapar a representative of the great Maharatta power that once dominated India, excited the attention that is usually given to an oriental prince who possesses intelligence and geniality of disposition. The Secretary to the Bombay Association Mr. Furdonji Nowroji did some service to his mother country by calling attention while in England to the gross mismanagment of the Indian finances and as far as his limited opportunities permitted keeping Indian subjects afloat before the British public. The East Indian Association whose fortunes were directed by its distinguished secretary Mr. Dadabhai Naroji, did much practical good in the way of collecting and disseminating information on Indian subjects in England. The question of the disestablishment of the Irish Church so thoroughly occupied the attention of the British Parliament that the Indian debates were few and far between and most uninteresting with the exception of the one on the Parliamentary Act of 1870 which laid down the principle that the Indian Gorvernment may under some restrictions and limitations appoint natives of India in India itself to the Civil Service. The scheme thus sketched out has subsequently developed into what is known as the Statuary Civil Service and whether owing to the inherent defects of the system or the imperfections of those who were selected under it to fill high and responsible offices, it has not been successful in solving the difficulty of allowing the educated men of India a proper share in the administration of their own country without denationalizing themselves for the sake of place and power. The Maharaja of Kapurtala one of the principal chieftains in the Panjab embarked for a visit to England, but he died on the way before reaching his destination. Her Majesty's Government and the English press noticed with great satisfaction the progress that was being made from year to year in many of the most important Native States in India. Nepal administered by Sir Jung Bahadur, Hyderabad by Sir Salar Jung, Travancore by an enlightened graduate of the Madras University, Cashmere under the guidance of its able minister Babu Nilambar Mookerji, Gwalior and Indore by industrious Maharatta chiefs who knew their business well, Jeypur by a Council many of whose members were cultured men, were all making rapid strides towards material improvement and Europeanized adminstration. The Native States of India who had exhibited steadfast loyalty in England's supreme hour of need came to be regarded with more and more confidence after the mutiny, and it is a pleasure to find many of the chiefs of these States, leaving aside the habits of oriental despots, minutely supervising all the departments of the State, carefully inquiring into and understanding public business, and keeping the finances of their dominions in proper order. The native chiefs were convinced that the days of Lord Dalhousie had passed away, and their just rights and privileges would be respected. Her Majesty's ministers repeatedly gave expression to the opinion that the native princes of India should be made to feel that they are trusted allies and integral members of a Great Empire. The dynastic difficulties at Chumba, Baroda and Kolahpur were considered at the India Office and its decision in at least the first two of these cases did not produce much satisfaction.

GENERAL EVENTS.—Sir Henry Durand succeeded Sir Donald Macleod in the Lieutenant-Governorship of the Punjab. He had the strong stuff of a veteran statesman in him and had supplied to the Indian Viceroys the ripe judgment of long years of personal experience in India. He was the foremost Haileybury civilian of his day and he exhibited on many occasions those amiable qualities and virtues which had made his school of civilians so dear to the Indian people. The retirement of Sir William Mansfield from the army and of Sir Barnes Peacock from the department of law and justice were notable events. Lord Napier of Magdala who succeeded as Commander-in-Chief of India was not a successful army administrator and it was also openly remarked in many military circles that his merits as a soldier had been considerably overrated. Sir Barnes was a valuable auxiliary to the Indian administrator by his great intellectual abilities, his keen sense of justice and his efforts to suit the administration of justice to the exigencies and requirements of the country. The Bengal High Court over which he presided for several years with such marked success, lost in him a judge and jurist whose like it has not yet been able to see. Lord Napier and Sir Henry Norman needlessly stirred up ill-feeling in the army by rejecting with a high hand many of its respectful requests with reference to its wants. The Governor of Madras Lord Napier had a very promising career in that presidency though he committed a mistake in introducing the Local Funds Bill which had to be withdrawn. Sir Willam Grey the Lieutenant-Governor of Bengal was the most fortunate man of his class since Bengal had, to use a very expressive phrase, ceased to be governed in the leisure-hours of the Governor-General. Sir Frederic Halliday had left almost amidst tears. Sir John Peter Grant retired with the loud execrations of one powerful section of the community who could make themselves heard, following him to his native shores, which Sir Cecil Beadon had to lay down his office while his reputation was under a sad blight by reason of the terrible

Orissa famine. Sir William Grey however retired amidst universal popularity. Though not a brilliant ruler, he was in every respect a cautious, safe and steady man and these qualities combind with his hard work and careful superintendence were the secrets of his success as a ruler. The Chief Commissioners in the minor provinces were following the well-known grooves, though loud complaints arose from some of those territories that their rulers had evinced partiality towards the Europeans wherever possible. The Supreme and Local administrations continued from year to year to bring in material progress and meet the administrative needs, by railways, canals, roads, improved public buildings, municipal institutions and a larger number of schools. The policy pursued with reference to primary education and the continued decrease of grants for high education excited considerable attention to the subject and great meetings were convened in Calcutta and other important towns which discussed the subject with great enthusiasm. At the Calcutta meeting delegates from 20 districts attended in defence of English education and this constitutional effort on the model of those found in the free countries of Europe, which promoted a healthy feeling of union and common work for the attainment of common good is a promising sign of the times which the historian must record with evident satisfaction. Sir Fitzjames Stephen during the current year, got four important legislative enactments passed, which were the Land Acquisition Act, the Income Tax Act, the Hindu Wills Act and the Penal Code Amendment Act. The Income-tax Act excited considerable opposition and it was passed with such haste and in such hole-and-corner fashion that it called forth indignant meetings and indignant protests to England. The Land Acquisition Act had many enemies who openly characterized it as a means of legalizing the spoliation by the Executive Government of private property in the name of real or fancied public purposes. The provisions of this Act were considerably modified in the light of the angry criticisms of the press but the way in which it is worked and the difficulties that are often felt in the way of an equitable adjustment of claims render it a source of considerable hardship and oppression. The Hindu Wills Act was considered as an unjustifiable interference with the testamentary privileges and usages of the Hindus guaranteed to them by their own religion. The Hindu community felt strongly on the subject and resolved to forward an appeal to England. The amendment to the Penal Code introduced the section with reference to the law of sedition in British India. That section is worded in such a vague and general way as to allow of considerable latitude of interpretation at the hands of the highest legal authorities and the law must still be said to be uncertain on the subject. The provisions of the Penal Code in this respect if worked by a repressive government, might, unless in the case of trials by exceptionally strong juries, succeed in taking away though by a circuitous process the liberty of the press conferred by Lord Metcalfe. In Bombay the Cotton Fraud Bill had to be abandoned as it was vetoed by the Governor-General. The legislation of the year was thus so much opposed to the existing public opinion of the country that Babu Kristodas Paul as its foremost representative was led to remark with regret that the country would not suffer much loss if the councils were shut up for some time. Gross blunders were discovered in the accounts of the Empire and the Finance Minister had to square matters by imposing the hateful $3\frac{1}{2}$th and by summarily stopping all public works. The finances of the Empire it was found were so grossly mismanaged that the state of things drew forth the indignation not only of the native public but of the powerful body of European merchants. The duty on rice and the unwholesome meddling with the commerce of the country which was then seriously crippled by the difficulties created by the Franco-Russian War, still further complicated the situation while the Indian administrators were beyond the reach of the protests of public opinion in the heights of Simla. The Finance Minister had bluntly to enter a confession of judgment and to carry out the decentralization, scheme as a remedy which will be detailed in the next chapter. Oudh lost this year the political leader of its landed aristocracy in Sir Raja Man Singh.

INDIAN AGRICULTURE.—The proposed establishment of a new department of the Government of India for the direction and supervision of Indian Agriculture turned a good deal of attention towards that subject. In India agriculture is the principal occupation of the people and the mainstay of the revenue system. The Famine Commissioners made a remark that is exceedingly near the truth when they said that 90 per cent. of the rural population of India are directly connected with the tillage of the soil while a considerable portion of the remaining 10 per cent. exist for their benefit. The Indian cultivator, though his methods may be pronounced crude and unscientific by modern thinkers, has through his experience of centuries, been able to hit upon the best means of making nature yield as good an outturn as is possible under the circumstances. He resorts to a practical method of watering the soil in every part of the country. He recognizes the advantages of fallows and of enriching the soil by manure. His methods have been adopted after due consideration of the peculiarities of the climate, the remarkable fertility of the soil on the broad river-basins, the perpetual sunshine and the regular periodicity of the seasons. Of course improvements are possible in his methods and probably some are necessay to support an increasing population, but these must be introduced judiciously and very gradually with a due regard to the scanty means and the chronic indebtedness of the Indian ryot. The rice crop is unknown in the greater part of India and it is not grown on any soil except those in the deltas of the great rivers and on the long and irregular strips of land on the borders of the sea. In those territories in which this crop is grown, the rainfall is ample or the water-supply from other sources is copious. It yields large pecuniary profits and it is staple food of 67 millions of the people. The food-grains of the other parts of India are wheat and millets. Wheat is one of the principle articles of the export trade of India and the wheat growing tracts of India together with those of America constitute the granary of the ill-favoured countries of Europe. In India wheat is grown almost in every district of the North West Provinces, the Panjab, and the Central Provinces. To a much smaller extent it is grown in Bombay, Sind and Behar. The total area under wheat cultivation in India is greater than even the total area of the United States devoted to the same object. The quality of the Indian wheat has been pronounced to be of the best description and only the wheats of some of the best tracts of Australia and California excel it. Wheat requires some irrigation in dry and parched regions which is supplied by the wells of the Indian peasantry. The Government canals have been of questionable advantage to that body. The wheat that is grown under the system of the Indian cultivators is more than sufficient both in point of quantity and quality for the food of the population, though it may not be so in view of those immense dimensions, which according to the imaginative enthusiasts on the subject, the Indo-European trade in wheat ought to attain. The staple food-grain of the lower classes throughout India excepting the rice-producing tracts are the inferior cereals known as *Joar* and *Bajra* or the great millet and the spiked millet, which are grown in equal abundance in Madras, Bombay, Rajputana and Upper India. There are known as 'dry' crops and require no other irrigation but that supplied by the local rainfall, and they constitute the autumn harvest. The minor cereals comprise the pulses, the oilseeds, and the Indian corn which form important articles of use. The Indian cultivator receives annually a very large outturn of these crops and as they require no great skill, his methods are best adapted to them. Besides these the Indian peasant has to bring land into cultivation for the vegetables, the fruits, the spices, the palms, and sugar, which enter so largely into the native diet in all parts of India. The department of agriculture has to look into these details of cultivation and try to better the state of things, it possible. Experience plainly proves that the Indian ryot knows his business far better, than those highly-salaried officers who are paid to make experiments in model farms. The best means of introducing into India a scientific system of agriculture has not yet been decided upon and the experiments and official papers in this direction which have cost the Indian taxpayer a very large sum of money, have left matters exactly as they stood twenty years ago. Lord Mayo's newly created department had also unlimited jurisdiction over the commerce of the country. That department has done little else than collecting statistics and information on all subjects connected with Indian commerce. The Indian cotton although its exports amounted to 37 milions annually during the American war, has considerably fallen off in the European market with peace in America, as the Indian crop has a very sort staple and does not serve the same purpose as the American cotton in spinning the finer qualities of yarn. The plains of Gujrat and Kattywar as well as the deep valleys of the Berars roduce the cotton which is known in the Liverpool market as *Surat* and *Dholera*. The experiments that have been made in India with the New Orleans seed have mostly failed with the exception of the district of Dharwar where the exotic plant is the chief staple. Jute which is the next in importance as a fibre crop is confined to the northern and eastern districts of Bengal. On the banks of the Brahmaputra and the other great rivers, jute is the principal crop, and the profits derived from its cultivation have largely increased the prosperity of the cultivating classes. The long fibres which are soft and silky and at the same time very strong are extracted out of the jute plant by rotting them to a degree so that the outer coats peel off easily, and the fibres are pressed and made up into bales for export. Jute is grown mostly on flooded lands which would otherwise have remained untilled and so this crop with its large profits does not interfere with the food-grains. The Indigo industry has declined in Bengal since the indigo ryots of 1860 but it is grown and manufactured to a considerable extent in Behar and upper India as well as in Madras. The opium of commerce is grown in a tract of land around Patna and Benaras, as well as well as in a fertile table-land in central India known as Malwa. In Malwa the poppy cultivation is free but the duty is levied when it is exported through British India. In Bengal it is a government monopoly. Opium is grown for local consumption in other parts of the country. The juice of the plant is collected after removing the petals by "scarifying the capsules with an iron instrument in the after-noon and scraping off the exudation next morning." Then the juice is dried and the opium is prepared into balls for the Chinese market at the central agencies. The soil and climate of India are favorable to tobacco but its quality is so inferior that it does not form an article of commerce. The cultivation of coffee is still largely conducted by natives. The tea-plant is indigenous to the southern valleys of the Himalayas and tea-cultivation owes its origin to the initiation of the Government. The tea industry in India is confined to Assam, the districts of Darjiling, Kumaon, Garhwal, the Kangra Valley and the slopes of the Nilgiries, and is now the chief field for European capital. The only other important article of commerce is cinchona which has been reared artificially from American seedlings, and which has proved a cheap febrifuge for the the fever-stricken millions not only in the Indian but also in the European plains. Its cultivation is the most successful experiment in arboriculture known in India. We must not pass over the silk industry of India which though a declining one in the country has yet an historic importance and celebrity. Sericulture and the cultivation of mulberry are now confined to the Rajshahe and the Burdwan divisions. It is carried on by the peasantry who are free to stick to it or to abandon it according as it pays or not. Indian silk however is unable to hold its ground in the European markets with the large productions of China, Japan and the

Mediterranean countries. A passing mention may also be made of the lac which is known in commerce both as a gum and as a dye and forms an important element in producing the regimental scarlet.

CHAPTER III.

1871.

The Decentralization Scheme.—We have shown above that the financial position of India was a perilous one during the first two years of Lord Mayo's rule. The Budget system then in vogue allowed of aggregate errors to the amount of 7 millions sterling on the wrong side, for in three years from 1867 to 1869, while the budget estimates calculated upon a surplus of $3\frac{1}{2}$ millions sterling the actual results showed a deficit to the same amount. The ordinary revenue had fallen short by $5\frac{3}{4}$ millions sterling to meet the ordinary expenditure, in the three years above named. The public debt had amounted in 1869-70 to about 193 millions sterling. This debt arose out of three different items, 50 millions represented the cost of first conquering and consolidating the country, 52 millions the cost of re-conquering and reorganizing India after the Mutiny and 91 millions the cost of guaranteed railways and canals. In 1869-70, Sir Richard Temple framed a very cautious budget (1869-70) estimating a small surplus £48,263, but item after item turned out much worse than had been expected until the deficit swelled to the vast sum of £2,542,861. As the Viceroy looked into the arithmetical tables composing the budget with a deeper scrutiny he found that the situation was much worse than had been anticipated and that the financial position was one of great weakness. Lord Mayo set himself to face the situation with great firmness. To struggle with the impending deficit he at once cut down the over-grown grant to the Public Works Department by £800,000 and curtailed by £350,000 the grants to the other spending departments. But even with these measures of economy the dismal abyss of a heavy deficit could not be bridged over, and Lord Mayo made up his mind to resort to the unusual course of resorting to additional taxation in the middle of the financial year. A permanent improvement in the finances to the extent of three millions a year was an absolute necessity and Lord Mayo's Government raised the income tax from 1 to 2½ per cent. in the second half of the financial year, and enhanced the salt duty in Madras and Bombay. These two additional burdens were estimated to add £500,000 to the Imperial coffers. In explaining his views on the subject to the Secretary of State, Lord Mayo said, that the policy of making good the ordinary annual expenditure by adding to the public debt was a very unsound one and that a permanent improvement in the finances must be resolved upon. This was to be done both by increased taxation and reduced expenditure. The sudden stoppage of public works involved much waste of materials and the addition to the burdens of the people might prove a cause of perilous discontent. Lord Mayo in adopting these measures felt that the Government of India had played its last card and there was absolutely nothing to fall back upon. In framing his budget for 1871-72 the surplus was estimated at £93,400, and in his speech on the subject he tried to defend his financial administration and vindicated the imposition of the income-tax. The number and variety of the returns submitted by the subordinate governments were not carefully compiled and digested by the higher officials and the central bureau, who were often ignorant of many important details. This system and the unpunctuality, in the submission of the returns by the Local Government made the whole system a most unsound one and demanded urgent attention. Lord Mayo remodelled the whole system and the Supreme Government was able to obtain every important information relating to the Indian finances month by month. Up to Lord Mayo's time the provincial governments had no independent financial powers and the practice was for each Local Government and administration to present towards the end of every year its estimates of expenditure during the ensuing twelve months. The Government of India after comparing these estimates with the expected revenue granted such sums as were reasonable. The defects of this system were glaring. The more a Local Government asked for, the more it got and as the money that was saved at the end of the year reverted to the Imperial treasury the Local Governments were but under little temptation to save. The government of Lord Mayo determined to introduce a radical change in this system and to invest the provincial governments with independent financial powers and responsibilities. On the 14th December 1870 a Resolution was issued by the Supreme Government which explained fully and authoritatively the principles of the decentralization scheme initiated from that year. A fixed yearly consolidated grant was to be made to each provincial government for the ordinary expenses of administration including the expenditure on public works. The army and several other departments were to be considered imperial and governed by the central government. These grants were religiously fixed for five years and nothing but severe financial pressure, would tend to reduce them. The sums thus placed at the disposal of the Local Governments were their absolute property. The Local Governments could save and spend as they liked without any interference from the Governor-General in Council. The services made over to the Local Governments and administrations were classified for official purposes as Jails, Registration, Police, Education, Medical Services, Printing, Roads, Civil Buildings, Public Works and the miscellaneous Public Improvements. The Resoluiton said that the Local Governments were effectually to have in their hands the responsibility of maintaining an equilibrium in their finances and that they could no longer draw upon a fund of unlimited and unknown depth. It was expected that under the new state of things the tendency to avoid waste would be the strongest, and that the Local Governments would have a very powerful motive for developing the local resources. The Supreme Government announced its intention resolutely to cut down the expenditure on every department to the lowest point compatible with efficiency. This system as tested by time would come under our notice again, but many high financial authorities of the time thought it best adapted to Indian administration. This system however was open to serious criticism in more points than one. It was virtually a permanent settlement of local finance and with the expanding claims on local governments, the means of defraying these should not have been fixed once for all. The most approved opinions on the subject among the ruled classes was that the system was unsound in principle, demoralizing in tendency, unrighteous in practice in as much as the Government of India should permanently fix certain allotments from the Imperial funds for local purposes and appropriate all future increase of revenue to its own purposes. The criticism was strongest in the Bengal papers, which with one voice declared that the revenues made over to the local administrations bore no proportion to the expenditure in those departments. The prospect was that the Local Governments would either starve the provincial departments, or would meet increased demands by increased local taxation. The defenders of the Government scheme loudly proclaimed that the chief end of this scheme was to get rid of objectionable taxation. But it was pointed out that local cesses were not less irritating than the imperial taxes and that while the income-tax did not press on small incomes, under the local rates it would hardly be so. It was feared that the Decentralization Scheme would lead to obnoxious taxes, which the poorer classes would have to pay and which would produce deep discontent. Such a course would discredit the Local Governments and necessarily the Supreme Government. It would prove, it was expected, a prolific cause of quarrel between the Provincial and Supreme Governments. The assignments had been made on the basis of the budget of 1870, which was an exceptional one, and should not hold good in years of plenty or pressure. It was clear from figures that the provincial allotment in the case of Bengal came short by half a million from the amount that was assigned two years ago and it was feared that further economy was not possible under the circumstances. The departments that had been decentralized were in the very nature of things such as to necessitate increased expenditure. The want of good prison-houses, the continual increase of jail population, the multiplication of sub-registry offices for giving due facility to all classes of the people, the reforms urgently needed in the Police department, the continued expansion of education, the want of good roads and other means of communication demanded that year after year large sums should be devoted to remedying the administrative defects in those directions. That influential organ of native opinion *the Hindu Patriot* described the scheme as developed by Lord Mayo as good in principle but a wretched patchwork in execution, as the assignments given bore no proportion to the area, the population the revenues and requirements of the different provinces, and it forcibly pionted out that its result would either be irritating local taxation or the starving of the provincial services. That Lord Mayo's decentralization scheme had not been arranged on a thorough and systematic plan is a fact, the truth of which must be admitted by the historian.

GENERAL EVENTS.—There was a bitter controversy on the legalization of the five-rupee note. The principal objection to the measure was that five-rupee notes being a legal tender the poorer classes would be forced to accept it, and in the absence of facilities for ready encashment would be obliged to pay a heavy batta for it. The finance minister answered this objection by saying that the employer of labour being absolutely at the mercy of the labourers these latter would be at liberty to refuse payment in five-rupee notes if they had to pay discount for it, and he further added that the Government would by providing a distinct cash reserve do everything in its power to afford adequate facilities for encashment. The poor labourers however were liable to be punished by law if they refused payment in five-rupee notes when such notes were legal tender, and Sir Richard by providing only one treasure chest in some districts would hardly be doing all that was needed. Lord Mayo also signalized the year by the creation of costly administrative departments which dealt with Agriculture, Archæology, Statistics, and Pisiciculture. The first of these designated the Department of Revenue, Agriculture and Commerce was to be devoted to twenty-five different subjects, although it was expressly avowed that the improvement of agriculture was its sole and main object. This gave rise to the not unnatural suspicion that a new department with handsome prizes for the Civil Service was all that was wanted. It was admitted that some little time would be necessary before the department could be raised to a position of usefulness though no definite period was given. The serious illness of His Royal Highness the Prince of of Wales which fortunately abated before the close of the year spread a gloom throughout the length and breadth of the land. Though England had been brought near to India by steam and electricity, the interest in England in Indian questions was not much. Professor Fawcett whose disinterested labours in the cause of Indian people had won for him the lasting gratitude of his voiceless constituents in the Indian Empire raised many important questions about Indian finance and discussed them with great ability. The grievances of the Nawab of Moorshedabad and of the Ex-Nawab of Tonk gave rise to many interpellations in the House of Commons. The Duke of Argyll, who was Secretary of State paid little attention to the affairs of India, and the members of the India Council were left to do as much as they liked. The raids of the Lushai tribe on the Eastern frontier made the government send an effective expedition against them. The British Government had to decide the succession to the States of Chamba, Nabha, Baroda and Kolapur. The British Government accepted as heir to the Nabha State the nominee of the Maharajas of Patiala and Jhind. The brother of the late Gaekwar who was in prison was raised to the vacant throne. The Maharaja of Kolapur had died in England where he had been on a visit and to the widow of the Maharaja was conceded the right of adoption. The British Indian Government was chosen as the arbitrator in the case of the boundary disputes between Afghanistan and Persia and a British officer was deputed to settle the matter. The debates in the Supreme Council were very animated and marked with very great ability. The subjects of debate were local taxation, permanent settlement, canalization and consolidation of laws. The Local Rates Bill threw upon the people fresh burdens for local requirements. These local taxes were certainly devoted to very good objects but they were levied from a nation the greater part of which is steeped in the most abject poverty. The Bill to consolidate the law of evidence was a very important measure and it presented a simple and admirable code in the hands of legal practitioners and judicial officers many of whom were unable to understand and appreciate the great text-books which contained the exposition of the English law of evidence. Some clauses in the Evidence Act do no doubt curtail the independence of the bar but the Act had been very useful in guiding the Indian judiciary along the right path and excluding many things that ought have no influence on the judicial mind. In the Northern India Canal Bill there was a clause that cooked widespread opposition inasmuch as it legalised the system of forced labour which had been unfortunately in vogue for some centuries. Mr. Cockerell the Bengal member entered an emphatic protest against the embodiment of such a disgraceful principle in legislation, but Sir Richard replied that the Indian people could not exist without it, and that as it was deep-rooted in the minds of the people long anterior to British rule, its sanction was not at all improper. Sir George Campbell recorded a strong minute in connection with the Criminal Procedure Code Bill advocating the placing of European British subjects in the Muffasil on the same footing in the eyes of the law as natives of India and placing the former under the jurisdiction of Native Magistrates. The minute of Sir George Campbell was conceived in the broadest spirit and it advocated a principle that ought to be affirmed in Indian legislation. The Brahmo Marriage Bill elicited a controversy that was unfortunately very acrimonious but the legislature settled the matter by passing the Civil Marriage Act whose the privileges could be availed of by all who did not belong to the recognized Indian religious sects and who would comply with the formalities required. The parties to such marriages were also participators in the legal rights conferred by the Indian Divorce Act, and the issues of such marriages were subject to the law of succession and consanguinity laid down in the Indian Succession Act. Sir George Campbell who succeeded Sir William Grey was an able man who had seen service in many different capacities. But he alarmed his subjects in Bengal by his imperious temper, his impulsive utterances and his sweeping reforms. He decided in a moment without even consulting his secretaries questions affecting the well-being of millions of his subjects. The proceedings of the Bengal Council under Sir George Campbell attracted great public attention as he often made an exhibition of himself in the Council Chamber. The Cess Bill was passed by the Bengal Council notwithstanding the strong opposition of the Bengal Zemindars who carried on their appeal in the first instance to the Viceroy and afterwards to the foot of the throne. Sir Henry Durand who had succeeded Sir Donald Macleod as Lieutenant-Governor of the Punjab met with an accidental death by a fall from an elephant. He was succeeded by Sir Henry Davies. Sir Ashley Eden who was appointed Chief Commissioner of British Burmah in succession to Colonel Fytche had a difficult work to perform in settling the primitive population of his province to peaceful and industrious habits. The return of the three native civilians from England— Mr. Romesh Chunder Dutt, Mr. Bihari Lal Gupta, and Mr. Surendranath Banerjee—marked an era in the history of the country. It was referred to by many high Anglo-Indian officials in their addresses on public occasions as an example worthy of all imitation. Mr. J. B. Norton, Sir Richard Temple, and Sir William Muir hailed this event as the dawn of a better day for India. The young men who had returned as Civilians were warmly welcomed and their success induced about a score of Indian students to proceed to England for purposes of education. The more orthodox of their countrymen however were hard upon their lapses in social demeanour. The death of the Hon'ble Justice Onoocool Chunder Mukerji, removed from the Native Society a judge devoted to his duties, a self-made man who had made his name and fortune by sheer dint of personal ability. On the 20th September a thrill of horror was sent through the whole of India by the assassination of Mr. Chief Justice Norman. As the Chief Justice alighted from his carriage and entered the threshold of the door of the Town Hall he was stabbed on the back by a Mahomedan ruffian. His Lordship sat down and said "I am killed." As he got up, another stab was given in the abdomen. The assassin was secured through the courage of those about the Chief. The Chief Justice was removed to the premises of Messrs. Thacker Spink and Co., where he expired at about 1-20 P. M. Many theories were afloat as to the cause of this murder and it was broadly hinted that it was the result of a dark political conspiracy. The question of the abolition of polygamy by legal enactments was hotly agitated in Bengal chiefly through the efforts of the first educationist and social reformer of Bengal the venerable Pandit Iswara Chandra Vidyasagar. The venerable Pandit had been working at the subject since 1856 and had almost completed his labours when Sir Doonarain Singh consented to present a bill on the subject in 1862. Lord Elgin was opposed to the measure and Sir Cecil Beadon advised that the Government should not interfere on the matter. Pandit Iswara Chandra got up a monstrous petition on the subject and a Committee was appointed to enquire into it. The literature on the subject was daily growing, and the Pandit issued a *brochure* on the subject which was worthy of his reputation and was a thorough exposition of his subject. The death of the worthy divine and eminent mathematician Archdeacon Pratt cast a deep gloom on all sections of the public, European and Native. He combined in himself the highest scholarship and originality with a genuine sympathy with weaker humanity, and a liberal culture of the heart that endeared him to all sections of the community.

MILITARY EXPENDITURE.—The short service system and the amalgamation of the English and the Indian army had greatly increased the burdens of India under this head. While the East India Company who had a local European force could sent efficient artillery and infantry recruits for £26 7s. 5d. per man the charges had increased to £136 13s. 11d. for cavalry and £63 8s. 5d. for infantry recruits. Eminent authorities are of opinion that this expenditure could be considerably reduced without impairing in the least the efficiency of the Indian Army. In criticising Sir R. Temples' budget for 1871-72 General Balfour showed that the military expenditure had been continually increasing, though this was not clearly shown in the accounts by transferring many items to the head of the expenditure incurred by India in England. General Balfour thought that the annual army expenditure was three millions more than what it ought to be. All criticism on the subject in the native press was sought to be silenced by the extreme Anglo Indian journals with the snub that army expenditure should be beyond the pale of native Indian criticism, as the loyalty of the natives of India was most dubious and they had an interest in diminishing the efficiency of the army and thereby impairing the political security of India. Mr. Fawcett reviewed the whole subject with a thorough mastery and incisive logic.

POLITICAL PROGRESS IN INDIA.—The continued progress and enlightenment of the educated classes brought the question of associating them more and more in the administration of the country to the front. There was an important debate on the subject some months later, in which a great many distinguished Anglo-Indians took part. Sir Bartle Frere advocated the direct representation of genuine native opinion in the local and imperial councils and this suggestion called forth a lively debate. Sir Mordaunt Wells while bearing testimony to the ability and integrity of the natives of India said that the recognition of this principle would gradually place more and more political power in the hands of the natives of India and that the principle if at all recognized, should be recognized under strict limitations. Dr. Mouat justly observed that the natives of India trained in the learning of the west had proved great successes in the work of practically administrating the law, that their untiring industry and thorough integrity were well-known and this fact qualified the selected few among them to the honorable distinction of occupying seats in the council through the suffrages of their fellow-countrymen. Dr. Mullens remarked that India was so vast a country with so many conflicting interests and nationalities, that the same principle was not applicable everywhere, and that while the advanced classes in Calcutta and Bombay could well be given a little political freedom it would be dangerous to apply the same principle every where. Up to the present year the native members of the Supreme Council had been either absolute princes or uneducated Zemindars, who were entirely ignorant of the language in which the proceedings of the Council were carried on and unfitted by nature and education to reflect native opinion. Sir Bartle Frere wound up the debate by the observation that the best course would be to extend political privileges to the more advanced classes and communities and train up the rest gradually in the duties of administration by entrusting to them work in the parishes, countries and provinces.

THE FEUDATORY STATES.—Previous to the mutiny the native princes were regarded with great distrust and suspicion by the British Indian Government. It was commonly thought that the native princes had at heart been hardly reconciled to the paramouncy of the British power and the Court of Directors in 1841 had laid down the principle that the Government of India was in no case to abandon any just and honorable accession of territory. But in 1857, in England's supreme hour of need when the Native princes stood fast by the British power and actively when aided in the suppression of that great military rebellion, the policy of dealing with them underwent an entire change. The Native princes were regarded as integral parts of the great Indian Empire and the interference with their vested rights and privileges was reduced to a minimum. This policy made the British administrators feel that they were responsible for the well-being of 600,000 square miles with a population of 50 millions. Lord Mayo impressed upon the Rajput chiefs and nobles that while Government would support them in their exercise of legitimate power it was expected in return that the princes would govern well, would develope the capacity to be rulers of men and would take to their charge with honest labour. Lord Mayo studied the whole question of the administration of native states and thought over the measures necessary for securing the blessings of a continued good government to the subjects of those principalities. He found that the Foreign office strictly regulated the courtesies of the Viceroy towards each chief but he impressed each ruling prince with the belief that his real friendship could be got only by an honest and conscientious discharge of duties, in the high positions which God had called them to fill. The principles which were to regulate the conduct of the Viceroy in Council towards the native chiefs were distinctly laid down. They were that the policy of non-annexation should be firmly resolved upon, that the British Government should leave to each native prince complete independence in internal matters with only a light form of control, that in cases of serious misrule, the ruling chief should be displaced and his place filled either by a worthy successor or by a council of Regency, and that the younger chiefs were to be educated according to the western ideas that they might fully enter into the spirit of the age and the principles of British administration. During Lord Mayo's tenure of the Indian Viceroyalty two important cases of Indian Feudatory States engaged his attention. In the great province of Kattiawar with its 117 chiefdoms Lord Mayo found that anarchy

and misrule had almost banished the ideas of security of life
and property, from the mind of the native population. Lord
Mayo found that that this state of things could be remedied
only gradually. He confined his interference to a leading
principality which he placed under the administration of an
experienced native minister and a chosen member of the Bombay
civil service and by this system of joint-rulers all necessary reforms were introduced with tact and judgment and without
much opposition on the part of the native population. A more
serious state of affairs presented itself in Ulwar. That state was
being governed by a Rajput chief who had just after attaining
his majority succeeded in the incredibly short period of seven
years to squander away a cash balance of £ 172,287 in addition
to the ordinary annual revenue of £ 200,000 and had made his
estate in debted to the amount £ 160,000. The crops of future
years had been previously hypothecated for the loan and the miseries of his subjects who were oppressed by worthless and rapacious
creatures of the prince, knew no bounds. The Rajput nobles
were insulted and the estates of those who incurred the dis-
pleasure of the chief were confiscated. The Rajput soldiery
which was for generations the pride of Ulwar was disbanded
and Mahomedan mercenaries were enrolled instead. The prince
proved incorrigible and when all entreaties and remonstrances
failed the nobles and the more powerful subjects of the state
took up arms against their ruler. Lord Mayo had to displace
this native ruler in the interests of his subjects and while retaining him the titular head of his kingdom with an allowance
of £ 18,000 a year for his personal expenses, placed all real
power in the hands of a Council of Regency with the British
Resident as President. The institutions of peace and civilization
were again opened and crime in all forms was suppressed by the
strong arm of the law. The chief however did not leave his
favorites and went on in the same reckless way as he did before.
Lord Mayo gave him plainly to understand that the only way
for him to regain his position was to show some signs of

repentance and try to improve himself. In the case of the Maharaja of Jodhpur, Lord Mayo thought that he had not proved a good administrator and he was visited with a severe rebuke and otherwise disgraced in the formal state ceremonials. On the other hand those princes who had been thought of well in the discharge of their exalted functions, were highly honored. The Begum of Bhopal who ascended the throne of her mother in 1868, had assiduously striven to reform abuses, and she was received by Lord Mayo with particular marks of distinction and presented with honor to His Royal Highness the Duke of Edinburgh. Lord Mayo also discouraged the practice of devastating villages and burning crops in the case of the frontier expeditions. He insisted upon a system of watchful defence and punishing all aggressions by means of a strong armed police. Lord Mayo set himself to elaborate a plan for the education of the young princes. He found that too often the scions of great and princely houses were reared up amidst the debasing influences of the zenana and did not receive that healthy education that would fit them for their position in life. The thought occurred to him of creating for them an Indian Eton where they would be able to associate with others of their age and rank and be trained up in healthy ideas and under healthy influences under the guidance and supervision of first-rate teachers and political officers. A scheme was gradually elaborated by those best skilled in the subject and the Rajputana chiefs and nobles showered money to make the project an accomplished fact. The college for the training of aristocratic scions was to have its seat at Ajmere with a council of management of which the principal chiefs of Rajputna were the members with the Viceroy as President and the Governor-General's Agent for Rajputana as Vice-President. The princes were to have their own quarters in the spacious compound of the college, to live under selected guardians and to be taught by experienced teachers. Those who have visited the Rajput chiefs' college at Ajmere named after Lord Mayo, whose fine marble statue stands to the west of it with its palatial residences for those who in the fulness of time would sway the sceptre of ancient monarchies, with its well furnished and commodious halls, the beautiful chains of the Aravelli Hills that surround it, the spacious compound dotted over with mansions each built in a separate style, the delightful avenues, and the distant prospect of the Taragarh Hill instinct with busy humanity, will agree with the writer that the Mayo College at Ajmere is one of the lovliest places in India. It had however to be broadly hinted by many a succeeding Viceroy that the principle that all play and no work makes Jack a stupid boy is too often forgotten there and though the Rajput princes develope fine English tastes they do not in all cases acquire solid qualities of head and heart.

CHAPTER IV.
1872.

LORD MAYO'S ASSASSINATION.—The Convict Settlement in the Andamans had been prominently engaging the attention of the Government of India for some time past. In these were aggregated 8000 of the worst criminals selected from all parts of India men cut off by their horrible crimes equally from the past and the future of their native country. The English officials who had to keep peace in those islands were in an isolated position and had to be aided by a strong soldiery. In such a convict colony the best arrangements, the strictest supervision and the most stringent discipline ought always to prevail. But unfortunately the state of things was quite otherwise. The convicts were always in possession of forbidden articles and in not a few instances they were found to be in possession of an unlimited supply of liquor. The convicts cost their mother country a good deal. Instead of being self-supporting they were very costly. Lord Mayo found that the charge of the colony to the Indian Exchequer had averaged £150,000 a year; each transported felon costing the country more than £1. 12s. per month. The convicts were mostly reckless men and they required to be managed with great tact and ability. Lord Mayo had been thinking, during the latter half of 1871, of developing the material resources of the Andamans by breeding domestic animals and extending cultivation on a large scale. An experienced officer of the British Army was placed in charge of this Convict Settlement and he was instructed to manage the whole business of the colony with such judgment as to be able to reconcile even the worst characters to their lot by opening up to them all the privileges and ambition of local citizens. On the 24th of January Lord Mayo left for a tour to British Burma intending to call at the Andamans on his way back and settle all weighty questions and experimental schemes in his presence. Sir Ashley Eden the first civilian Chief Commissioner of Burma did every thing to make the Viceroy's visit a pleasant one and the Viceroy was satisfied that a good deal had been done towards consolidating British rule in that province. On the 8th of February at 8 A. M., he anchored off Hopetown in the Andamans, with a brilliant party on board his own steamer and the attendant steamship. He inspected thoroughly every part of the convict colony paying especial attention to the Viper and the Ross islands where the worst characters were located. At about 5 P. M. the official inspection terminated but Lord Mayo intended to make Mount Harriet, a hill 111 6 feet high, a sanitarium where convicts suffering from ill-health might be temporarily quartered. Lord Mayo with a small party went up the hill and from its top saw the beautiful sight of the crimson sun of an Indian evening setting behind the horizon. When the party came down it was dark and torches had been lighted up. As the Viceroy had come to the bottom of the hill and was about to get up to the steam launch that lay in waiting for him a convict rushed with a sharpened knife in wild and reckless fury and "fastened, like a tiger" on the back of the Viceroy stabbed his Lordship twice on the shoulder inflicting two wounds either of them sufficient to cause death. The assassin who gave his name as Shere Ali was secured at once, but Lord Mayo breathed his last before he could be removed to his cabin in the frigate. Among the party there was a complete silence and steps had to taken at once for the devolution of the Viceregal office. The doctors embalmed the remains of His Lordship and Sir Barrow Ellis hurried with the intelligence to Calcutta while Sir Charles Aitchison directed his way towards Madras to bring up Lord Napier of Ettrick to act as Viceroy until the permanent successor arrived. The assassin was a hillman of great physical strength and commanding stature. He was about 30 and had won for himself good opinions by his brave conduct in the Sitana war and by faithful service rendered to many English officers. He had been convicted on the 2nd

April 1867 by Colonel Pollock Deputy Commissioner of Peshawar of murder for having slain his blood feud enemy on British soil. There was some doubt from the evidence as to whether he had struck the blow which had killed the deceased or his comrade had done it, and in his dying confession years afterwards he stated that he had only conspired to do the murder. He was sentenced to transportation for life but slaying a blood-feud enemy was a meritorious act in his own eyes and he rankled under a sense of injustice for having been punished so severely on account of an act that was not a crime in his own eyes. He therefore made up his mind to revenge himself for his grievance by killing some European officer of high rank. He soon established his character as a quiet man and was enlarged as a ticket-of-leave man in Hopetown. On hearing of the arrival of the Viceroy he sharpened a knife and patiently waited his opportunity. He silently crept through the jungle of Mount Harriet and when the Viceroy was about to get up on the steam-launch desperately rushed through the guards and succeeded in inflicting mortal blows. He said that he had done this act by order of God and stoutly denied that he had any partners or accomplices in his crime. He was tried for his offence and sentenced to death which sentence on being confirmed by the High Court at Calcutta was duly carried out on the 11th March. The remains of the Viceroy were brought to Calcutta in solemn state and imposing ceremonials celebrated this mournful event. Lord Mayo's assassination sent a thrill of horror through India and England. The inquiries that were set on foot proved beyond a doubt that these murders were not the result of a deliberate political organization but had been committed by desperate wretches in moments of fury. The native Indian subjects of Her Majesty were deeply shocked at the murder by such a cowardly and cruel act of Her Majesty's representative in India. They gave vent to their sorrow by many outward demonstrations, and as His Lordship's personal popularity stood very high the regret was genuine and universal. The public institutions tasked their ingenuity to the utmost in celebrating this sad event in a befitting manner and many speeches were delivered extolling the late Viceroy. Thus was cut off by the foul hand of an assassin, a frank, genial and kind-hearted statesman who had done long and faithful service to his party, who had performed with dignity and untiring industry the duties of his exalted Indian office, who had won the hearts of native princes and who had in the usual nature of things still a promising career to look forward to. Her Majesty the Queen was deeply touched by this melancholy event, the first statesmen of both the parties spoke with unfeigned regret of his services to his country and the English press as a body paid a deserved tribute to his long and distinguished public career.

LORD MAYO'S ADMINISTRATION.—The tragic end of Lord Mayo elicited such inflated speeches and articles about the merits of his Lordship's rule that the historian finds it difficult to estimate his administration by the colorless standard of history inasmuch as the contemporary literature affords him, but little aid, or guidance. There is no doubt that His Lordship's personal popularity always stood very high. Full of vigor and animal spirits His Lordship was peculiarly kind to all he came in contact with, and in social duties as well as in dispensing hospitality he performed his part with such an easy grace and so genuine a courtsey that he had completely won the affection and esteem of the higher circles of society both Native and European. His habits of industry enabled him to get through a large amount of work and he could personally direct and supervise every department of administration. Some of his views on administrative questions have been proved to be remarkably sound. He had written strongly about the efforts that were proposed to be made to teach the native agriculturist his work and improving his land by a system of costly manure. He rightly remarked that the rulers should be cautious in presuming to teach the native husbandman who had been doing his work for centuries and insisting on his adopting a more costly system of agriculture than his means allow. He found that the system in force with reference to the construction of public works by the special department in charge of them was faulty in many most important respects. The officers of the department had such large areas alloted to them for supervision and had such heavy office work and routine duties that the estimates were often a hundred per cent. wrong and the Government works were managed as badly as possible. He set about reforming this system and he emphatically placed on record his view that unproductive public works should always be constructed from the current revenue and not by a system of loans. That the Indian Public Works Department is too often guilty of the want of supervision, the want of personal management and too great haste in initiating the works is a truth which is patent to the student of contemporary history. The Public Works Department comes often to the forefront of the spending departments in India and the system in force there needs a thorough overhauling. Lord Mayo with the assistance of General Sir Richard Strachey initiated the project of the metre gauge railways constructed by the State. The broad gauge railways had been very costly. They cost nearly £20,000 per mile and the Government had to give a five per cent. guarantee on the capital invested to the companies who constructed them. Thus the Government was a full sharer in the losses and had nothing to do with the gains of these railway companies. The Government of India found that it could raise capital at 4 per cent. or thereabouts in the English market and the metre gauge railways could be constructed economically and worked with much less cost; necessitating an outlay of £6000 per each mile. Lord Mayo's Government therefore embarked on the project of state railways, which were all constructed on a narrow or metre gauge. The break of gauge thus sanctioned by Lord Mayo and his colleagues has been regarded in later times as a national misfortune. The losses and the heavy exponses of transhipment are justly considered to be a grievous inconvenience in the commercial circles and in the years to come many projects have been under consideration to repair the mischief thus done. Light provincial railways running to a short distance might well be constructed on the narrow gauge, but great arterial lines of communication which are the broad highways of commerce if constructed on a different gauge from the previously existing railways are a serious cause of detriment to the commercial prosperity of the country. Now that most of the feudatory states in Rajputana have linked their capitals with the railway that passes from Agra and Delhi through the historical cities of Rajputana to the capital of the province of Gujrat the cost of conversion of this important line to a broad gauge railway is heavy, but the commercial community is sought to be served by a standard gauge through a slightly different route. History must hold Lord Mayo responsible as the author of the metre gauge railways which in the then existing circumstances should according to the present opinions of the highest authorities on Indian railways and Indian commerce should never have been undertaken. Many of the most well-informed minds on the subject are now busily engaged in finding out the most economical way of undoing what has been done, and probably the Indian tax-payer will in the end be charged with heavier burdens for those railways that he would have been if they had been originally constructed on the standard gauge. Nor have the metre gauge railways brought any corresponding advantage to the state. They earn according to the latest accounts the same rate of profit as do the older lines, but any one who had witnessed, as the present writer had many occasions to do, the difficulties and heavy losses incident to transhipment at the important railway station of Ahmedabad which forms the junction between the route of Agra and the Panjab on the one hand, and the railway line which after traversing the rich cotton fields of Kathiawar, runs for many miles on lines constructed on bridgy foundations and after crossing the Narbudda and the Taptee on large and well-spanned bridges enters the city of Bombay and runs for a long distance on the side of and in full view of the Arabian Sea, will realize the truth of the remarks that we have made above. The Government of Lord Mayo also sanctioned a great many irrigation works as protective works against famine. He tried to organise education on a popular basis and he inaugurated some special measures for the education of the Mahomedans and the domiciled Europeans. The Mahomedans fancied they had all the grievances of an excluded class, and Lord Mayo justly thought this feeling was a source of political danger. Lord Mayo's administration was not regarded with favor by the ruled classes. He had to carry on his duties in the midst of unfortunate circumstances. The imperious Duke who was his master at the India Office, and the councillors who had their own way, who were thoroughly infused with the Punjabi spirit and with whose intellectuality he could not cope combined to make his position an unenviable one. Theoretically history must hold Lord Mayo responsible for all that was done in his name even in the face of the fact which is but too well-known that for many things His Lordship was but nominally responsible. The measures which were admittedly his own commanded the approval and sympathy of the public. His foreign policy and his policy in dealing with the Amir of Afghanistan were eminently successful. His desire to see everything with his own eyes before finally coming to a decision on an important question was commendable. If he had been spared he would have governed India in the true spirit of the proclamation. In his death the Queen lost a faithful and devoted servant and the Indian Society a genial and accomplished leader. His attitude was always dignified and he had impressed the Indian people with a real sense of the magnificence of the British power.

LORD NAPIER AND THE EARL OF NORTHBROOK.—After Lord Mayo's death the charge of the office of the Governor-General of India was held by Lord Napier, Governor of Madras, under

Sec. 50 of the Indian Councils' Act until the Earl of Northbrook arrived and relieved him. Lord Napier was very cautious in all that he did and he did not do more than finish the impending business left unfinished by his predecessor. Some of the most important bills which had been matured under Lord Mayo were passed by the Council under the presidency of Lord Napier, who did not think it proper to arrest their progress. The ordinary work of the Government of India was suspended for one month after the death of Lord Mayo and until the Countess of Mayo embarked for England with the remains of her noble lord, business was not resumed. Lord Napier created a very favorable impression in his position as Viceroy and rendered his short tenure of office remarkable by issuing the noble resolution on the Kuka executions. This resolution which had originated with Sir Fitzjames Stephen, was a document which laid down the important principle that the ordinary law is meant for quiet times as well as for periods of unusual commotion, that individual officers who presume to decide on the spur of the moment that they are at liberty to take any measures they deem proper, are guilty of usurping the highest prerogative of the Government. All offenders captured are to have a regular trial and it is the duty of the executive officers even in times of unusual excitement to hand them over to the regular tribunals for justice. Lord Napier had been unpopular with one section of the public at Madras but in Calcutta he won for himself very good opinions and when he retired from the Governorship of Madras he carried with him the good-will of the official and non-official public of Calcutta. The Earl of Northbrook who relieved him came of the well-known Baring family and had a good deal of training in Indian affairs. He was a warm admirer and disciple of Lord Halifax and in a speech on Indian affairs delivered in 1865 had uttered noble sentiments. In that speech His Lordship had quoted with approval the remark of J. S. Mill that the best way of governing India was to govern it in the interests of the Indians and make them feel that it is being so done. In the same address too he had emphatically pointed out the many important changes that Lord Halifax had introduced. These antecedents and his high reputation as a capable financier raised many hopes in the minds of the Indian people. Lord Northbrook naturally took some time to familiarize himself with the details of Indian administration and the rest that the land had under his rule was highly beneficial. His Lordship declared that nothing but a strong sense of duty could have made him undertake the immense responsibilities of his exalted office and that the Indian administrative machinery required to be handled with great caution.

GENERAL EVENTS.—Lord Napier was succeeded in the Governorship of Madras by Lord Hobart and Sir Seymour Fitzgerald the Tory Governor of Bombay by Sir Philip Woodehouse. Sir Philip's peculiar trait was that he did not vote in the debates of his Legislative Council on the constitutional principle that he should not do so as he had the power to give to or withhold assent from the bills passed by his Council. Sir Fitzjames Stephen passed the new Criminal Procedure Code just before vacating office in which he was succeeded by Sir Arthur Hobhouse. The Criminal Procedure Code won for him the execration of the native public which followed him to his native land. He did away with appeals in many classes of criminal cases and armed our Muffasil Solons with summary powers in many important cases. It is well-known that the Indian judiciary stand sadly in need of the correcting hand of the courts of appeal. Many of the provisions of the Code were opposed to the recognized principles of criminal jurisprudence and threatened the rights and liberties of the subjects in the Muffasil. His Grace the Secretary of State was implored in the petitions which poured on the noble Duke from India, to amend the Code as passed but the noble Duke refused to re-open the question. The Earl of Northbrook felt that there was much reason in the prayers of the petitioners and suspended the operation of the Act till the 1st January 1873 pending the consent of the Duke of Argyll. Sir Arthur Hobhouse in his speech in introducing the Obsolete Enactments Bill gave the people of India hopes that codification would proceed much more slowly than it had been doing and as changes bring unsettlement of society and the changes had been multiplied too frequently of late years, the land required some rest from over-legislation. The annual budget showed a serious diminution of the cash balances demonstrating plainly that more money had been borrowed and raised by taxation than was necessary. Lord Northbrook who was peculiarly strong in finance grappled with the question at once and issued circulars to the local officers to gauge the effects of taxation both imperial and local. He also took in hand the whole subject of army expenditure. The Government of India stopped the practice which had been obtaining hitherto of the Local Governments submitting their annual budgets to their legislative councils and thus gave the provincial rulers complete freedom in the matter of financial management which must be wisely used. The affairs of the Municipality of Bombay threw that city almost in a ferment. The powers that had been vested in the Corporation were small but the constitution proposed by the new Municipal bill left the elective element so small that there was a widespread consternation which found vent in the monster meetings that were held to appeal to the Viceroy to withhold his assent from the bill. The Bengal Municipal Bill which considerably increased the obligations of municipalities and thus necessitated much increased taxation was opposed clause by clause by the native members of the council and evoked general opposition.

Sir William Muir was succeeded in the Lieutenant Governorship of the North Western Provinces by Sir John Strachey. Sir William was an enlightened ruler and his strong views on the heavy settlement of the North-Western Provinces were remarkably true. He gave a great impulse to the progress of education and took an especial interest in the progress of the Mahomedan community whose leaders had collected a munificient sum for the establishment of a National College at Aligarh. Sir George Couper, the Homer of the Lucknow Siege, proved a most incapable administrator of Oudh and under his rule the country was torn by factions of the Talukdars. Lord Northbrook found out that there were many illegal taxes in the Central Provinces and he at once turned his attention to them. The Punjab was making rapid strides in enlightenment and civilization and Sir Henry Davis felt that it could no longer be ruled in the old executive spirit. Sir George Campbell came to be distrusted by all classes of the population that he ruled. He took most inadequate action to check the ravages of the fell epidemic fever that was then decimating Bengal. Sir George wrote a few high-sounding minutes on physical education, popular education and practical education but his action ended with the establishment of a few *patshalas* on the same lines as those founded by Sir John Peter Grant. His ill-advised move in the matter of the Sanskrit College and his notorious fight with the Calcutta University over the subject of the Urdu were hardly dignified. Mr. Fawcett delivered a very able speech on Indian Finance and Taxation, which though it had not any effect on the India Office extorted the admiration of the public by its clear analysis and wide knowledge of facts. Mr. Fawcett's outspoken utterances would it was feared endanger his position with his constituents and a movement was set on foot in India to present an address to his electors so that the "sightless champion of India" would be permitted to study and speak on Indian questions which address happily had the desired effect. Lord Northbrook followed up his predecessor's policy with reference to the native princes. His Lordship won the gratitude of the Indian people by opening up on a small scale a career for the cadets of good families. The native princes in many instances had to suffer from the meddlesomeness of their political agents, but they had on the whole no feelings but those of good will towards the paramount power, which feelings were given vent to with much warmth and in choice diction by Maharaja Holkar when he addressed the Viceroy at Burwar. There were some disturbances in Cashmere owing to the religious feuds of two Mahomedan sects but these were put an end to without much difficulty. In Joodpur there was a rebellion which cost much blood and treasure headed by the crown prince. The Viceroy's Agent however succeeded in bringing about a reconciliation between father and son and peace and order was restored.

LOCAL TAXATION.—There was an important debate on this subject in the House of commons on the 15th April this year Sir Massey Lopes who spoke on the subject with great ability pointed out that the gradual demand for local improvement continually increased the local rates and the people saw that there could be no relief from this sort of taxation but a continued addition to their burdens. This was exactly the feeling in India when local imposts for local requirements were first introduced under the scheme of Lord Mayo. This was apt to make the people suspicious and dissatisfied and the only sound policy in this direction was the keeping of a certain portion of the imperial revenues for local purposes and to have the proceeds of one particular tax say the income tax expressly set apart for local proposes in consolidation of all local rates and taxes. In these days of progress the British Government is bound to move in the general march for improvement and a general impost for local purposes while it would place the necessary funds at the hands of the Government would prevent arbitrary increase to it and reckless expenditure.

RELIGIOUS AND CHARITABLE ENDOWMENTS.—There is no country probably on the surface of the earth which has a greater number of religious and charitable endowments scattered over the whole length and breadth of the land than India. These endowments subserve the purpose of the elaborate system of Poor Law relief that obtain in other countries and enormous wealth is often placed in the many pagodas and mosques with which Indian piety has consecrated the land. But these endowments were often fearfully mismanaged and their funds diverted from the noble objects which the founders had in view. The Acts and Regulations that had been passed on this head have failed to produce that satisfactory management that is needed. This question was prominently discussed during this year and many suggestions were offered. The consensus of opinion however was that the administration of these trusts and endowments should be a branch of the Board of Revenue and experienced Deputy Collectors were to be appointed to administer the funds, apply them to the proper purposes and prevent the waste and misappropriation of the fund set apart for noble objects.

SOCIAL PROGRESS.—The natives of India are too often taken to task for not going on at any appreciably fast rate in the matter of social progress. But there are two difficulties in the way of the educated natives which have never been satisfactorily answered. It is well-known that the educated native of India whether Hindu or Mahomedan is confronted with a social system which is the evolution of centuries, which is deeply rooted in the feelings and prejudices of his countrymen and which if attempted to be changed wholesale would bring on social anarchy and disorder. The growth of English ideas has led to a revulsion of feeling against the caste system thus affecting the old industrial organization of the country in a way that is truly alarming and which has created a difficulty in relation to the bread problem, that it is exceedingly hard to grapple with. There is going on a great change in our social ideas and habits that is purely spontaneous. The change is of course not so rapid as enthusiastic reformers would wish but sensible change is going on. It has never been pointed out to us what social system we are to adopt as our own if we subvert the standing one. The only quarter of the globe where we could go for models and patterns is Europe but Europe herself is in a state of social anarchy and scepticism. Her best thinkers seem hardly satisfied with her existing social institutions, she is hotly discussing the gravest social questions and this makes her at the present moment an extremely unsafe precedent to follow. Time and inevitable circumstances must work many changes in the social system and will produce true and solid reformation.

Sir John Strachey's Minute on Lord Mayo's Rule.—Towards the close of the year Sir John Strachey published an elaborate minute eulogizing the administration of Lord Mayo and placing him in the front rank of Indian pro-consuls. The Indian public which was then recovering from the feverish excitement caused by the assasination was not found to fall in readily with those views. Lord Mayo it was thought allowed his councillors to have too free a hand. This is to be accounted for by the fact that he did not feel himself a thorough master of the situation, and that his haughty master at the India Office the Duke of Argyll belonged to a rival party and was notoriously under the influence of the great patron of the Punjabi councillors Lord Lawrence. Possibly if the statesmanship of Lord Mayo were allowed to blossom forth and not nipped in the bud by the foul hand of an assassin it would have regaled India with its fragrance. Lord Mayo's views with reference to high education had caused a just alarm. His measures spread discontent from one end of the country to the other. His proposal to make the land settlement a permanent settlement on the basis of a certain portion of the produce of the land would have proved iniquitious in practice. History cannot accord therefore to Lord Mayo a position in the same gallery with Cornwallis, Bentinck, Dalhousie (barring his annexation policy) and Canning, which had been accorded to him in Sir John Strachey's minute and later on in the elaborate works of Sir William Hunter which unfortunately give one side of the picture alone.

CHAPTER V.

1873.

RUSSIA AND INDIA..—Never did Lord Beaconsfield utter a truer remark than when he said that England by reason of holding India which is the brightest jewel in her diadem was more an Asiatic than an European power. The eternal complications that are arising every year from the presence and the continued progress of Russia in Central Asia occupy more than an ordinary share of the attention of the English cabinet and it is evident that the English Foreign Office has not been for many years past equal to the wily Muscovite diplomacy. Russia had been giving and repeating the most solemn assurances as to her pacific intentions in Central Asia but not a year passes when there is not some fresh accession of territory and what is more strange the previous assurances and negotiations are explained in such a way as to admit of the accessions in question without any breach of political faith. The domination of Central Asia and the invasion of India forms part of the chart of political greatness bequeathed by Peter the Great to the Russian autocrats and the great Northern Bear seems steadily bent towards that political programme. This year found that the neutral zone whose existence Russia had scrupulously bound herself to maintain, had ceased to exist and Khiba had been practically annexed. In the name of scientific expeditions she had been exploring new military and trading routes to Afghanistan and the North Western frontiers of India. She had been intriguing in Persia and had been successful in obtaining from His Imperial Majesty the successor of Darius many concessions advantageous to commerce and to the construction of railway lines. She had been playing not only the part of a conqueror but of a settled ruler and by giving some high military and civil appointments to the natives of the conquered territories, she had been doing her best to consolidate her rule. She had sent M. Lesseps the author of the Suez Canel to induce the Shah af Persia to run up lines of railway and telegraph through the dominions of His Majesty and to connect these lines with the Russian lines in Central Asia. All this portended mischief and the Indian Government had to pay especial attention to the frontier affairs, to the policy to be pursued in conciliating Afghanistan and to the keeping out of Russian intrigues from the immediate neighbourhood of the Indian frontiers. It is indeed a sad thing for the historian to see at every step English diplomacy outwitted by the Russian emissaries, and to find that no effectual means were taken to make Russia respect her own word. The jurisdiction of the principles of international law enforced by a comity of the Great Powers of Europe was the only effectual means in this direction. Russia greeted too with especial cordiality for political reasons the Shah of Persia on his visit to Europe. Armed collision between England and Russia, seemed to be inevitable but fortunately it was not imminent yet.

INDIA IN ENGLAND.—The address of gratitude forwarded by the British Indian Association to the electors of Brighton and to their representive in the House of Commons, Mr. Fawcett, was the first response made by the people of India to action taken on their behalf. It called forth a great demonstration at Brighton and one of the electors of Brighton who addressed the meeting justly said that never had there been a more interesting meeting than that one. The electors clearly recognized that the days of governing India Asiatically had long gone by and that although India might not be fit for a representative government, the principles which form the cornerstone of representative institutions should be the guiding stars of Indian rulers. England has risen to incomparable greatness not so much by the assertion of physical force as by moral grandeur and earnestness and the Indian people recognized the plain truth that India must fight her constitutional battles by the assertion of moral force. Mr. Fawcett truly remarked that a grave responsibility rested on

British electors with reference to their Indian fellow-subjects. They should see that India be not sacrificed to the party exigencies of politics that no charges be thrown unjustly upon India which ought to be borne by England, that those who waste the Indian revenues by administrative incompetency be called to account and that the finances of India be protected against the unjust demands of those who seemed to think that India had been especially created to supply cheap cotton for Lancashire and to afford an eligible investment for English capital. One of most gratifying signs of the times was the readiness with which the English people came to offer assistance to India when at the close of the year she was threatened with a famine. The *Times* newspaper as the exponent of the British nation called upon the English capitalists to untie their purse-strings to relieve the sufferings of their starving fellow-subjects on the plains of Bengal. Retired Anglo-Indians and English philanthropists discussed the subject in right earnest and made some valuable suggestions for the practical working of relief measures. The Lord Mayor of London called a meeting to raise subscription and the stream of English charity would have flowed towards this country but for a message from the India Office to suspend operations. The Indian Finance Committee continued its sittings and examined a number of witnesses the most notable of whom was Lord Lawrence. It requested the Government of India to send up native witnesses. The immense difficulties which attend the journey of a native of India to England made some representative men of all parts of India decline the honor of being deputed to England but still the moral revolution that had been going on had spread so far that many respectable men of position offered to go. The suspension of the labours of the committee however owing to political reasons did not necessitate the sending-up of those native witnesses who had been selected.

GENERAL EVENTS.—Steam and electricity having shortened the distance between England and India, the winter brought some distinguished travellers every season. The Hon'ble Mr.

Bourke M. P. (afterwards Lord Connemara and Governor of Madras), Mr. Smith M. P. and Lord William Hay M. P. came out to India and on their return they delivered addresses to their constituents full of sympathy with the people of this country. The first year of Lord Northbrook's administration was spent in mastering the routine of Indian administration. His Lordship however displayed a remarkable grasp of the financial situation, and at once invited the opinions of responsible officers on the pressure of taxation and the political effects of the recent measures of taxation on the people. The officers consulted condemned the income tax with one voice and the majority of them were of opinion that the newly-imposed local cesses produced a great hardship. His Lordship at once abolished the income tax and withheld his assent from the Bengal Municipalities Bill—the bill authorizing a non-agricultural cess in Bombay and took the whole question of local taxation into careful consideration. The Viceroy caused a forecast to be taken of the public works during the next five years and while sanctioning no unnecessary expenditure under this head he pushed on material progress by initiating and carrying on all measures of real utility. The finances being in a prosperous condition and there being no alarming rumours from abroad the credit of the government stood very high and the government promissory notes commanded a high premium all round the year. Sir Arthur Hobhouse rendered innocuous by radical amendments many of the bills of the preceding administration which were ripe for passing. The North Western Provinces rent and revenue bills and the Oudh Land Revenue Bill were passed in a harmless form and the sections introducing radical changes in the condition of the tenantry were taken out. The North India Irrigation Bill was first introduced during the time of Lord Mayo but it was so oppressive in many of its provisions that the Duke of Argyll was obliged to send it back for amendments. Lord Northbrook passed it in a form which would not cause much hardship if worked by honest officers. The new Governors of Bombay and Madras were exclusive in their sympathies and their administration though vigorous was unpopular with the ruled classes. The Punjab, the Oudh and the Central Provinces were under weak administrators and there were visible signs of decay. The case of the Mohunt of Tarkeshur, which excited a universal sensation througout India when orthodox Hindus pressed for the punishment of the head of an important shrine who had soiled his sacred cloth by polluting a young girl was a significant instance of the social and moral revolution that English ideas had silently created in the midst of an ancient society. The affairs of the Nawab Nazim of Bengal which had been aired in England during the past two sessions were quietly settled and an act was passed to give effect to the settlement. Bengal lost this year the foremost of her poets and the foremost of her dramatists Michael Madhusudan Datta, and Babu Dinabandhu Mitter. The former a barrister who had been converted into Christianity was the creator of the blank verse in Bengali poetry. Amidst trials and difficulties of no ordinary character his poetic genius has given to his countrymen some of most impassioned and sublime pieces of poetry that are to be found in their rising literature. Babu Dinabandhu Mitter took early in life to the worship of the Muses and in his works he has happily depicted the society of his day with an inexhaustible fund of vivacity and humour. Two veteran English writers of Bengal the first fruits of the Hindu College also passed away this year in the person of Kashiprasad Ghoso and Kissory Chand Mitter. The government of Bengal very unwisely offered to pay money to the Christian Missionaries to be spent in converting the aboriginal tribes to Christianity and there was a loud outcry against this precious idea, which was a clear departure from the principle of religious neutrality adopted by the state but this idea was not allowed to fructify.

THE MILITARY EXPENDITURE OF INDIA.—It was at the earnest desire of His Royal Highness the Prince Consort that the armies of England and India were amalgamated in 1862-63.

The amalgamation was effected to secure an uniform army for the whole British Empire, to do away with the need for a purely local army and to make India the training ground for the British soldier. Little did His Royal Highness think that this arrangement would be fraught with eternal evil to the people of India. While large reductions had been effected in the strength of the troops, the relief to the Indian Exchequer was not only nil but there was a considerable addition to the expenditure by reason of the measures that were adopted to effect an improved organization. Some apologists have tried to defend this enormous increase to the general rise of prices and the consequent additions to the salary of the officers. The Indian Government however, though the rise of prices has been general, has not thought it proper to increase the salaries in the civil departments except in rare and isolated instances. The most fruitful sources of this increase have been the Staff Corps system of promotion, which with increasing years increases the military rank and pay of officers in the army and the general staff, the general revision of staff salaries, the reorganization of the Army departments, the extension of hill sanitaria for European troops and the creation of appointments for garrison instruction and for instruction in Gymnastics and Army Telegraphy. There was considerable increase again in the military pay and allowances of the officers in the military accounts department and the personal staff of the Viceroy, the Governors of Bombay and Madras and the Lieutenant-Governors of provinces. The reorganization of the ministerial departments, the steps that were taken to lay in provisions and forage for the army, the attempts that were made to make supply and transport so efficient as to be able to cope with all sorts of military and political exigencies, the annual reliefs by railways instead of by road, the establishment of the Overland Troops service which necessitated the concentration of all European troops at Bombay and their conveyance by steamships at a considerable charge to the Indian Exchequer, were all attended with additional expense. The railways instead of tending to economy have indirectly increased the military charges, for while the railways are most frequently resorted to, the old transport establishments, have to be kept up in full to meet any emergencies in the interior of the country or beyond the Indian frontier where there may be no railways. There came to be considerable waste and extravagance in the supply of the army remounts whether through the government studs or by purchase in the local markets or by importation, in the cost of the clothing agencies whether under the head of materials obtained from England or the charges incurred in India in sewing, pressing, packing and transport, in the grant of money compensation in lieu of clothing under certain conditions, in the introduction of improved patterns, as well as in the barrack buildings, the barrack supplies and all charges connected with lighting cooling and conservancy. India a partner with England in this matter had to maintain her army on the same scale of expenditure as in England and the management of this department being ultimately in the hands of the English War Office it did not effect any considerable reform or retrenchment. The comparative statements of military expenditure in 1861-63, and 1871-72 show that although there had been a decrease in the strength of the European army by two brigades of artillery two regiments of cavalry and five regiments of infantry and a more than corresponding diminution in the native section of the army the aggregate military expenditure in the latter year exceeded the aggregate of the former year by nearly half a million. This growth of military expenditure engaged the earnest attention of Lord Northbrook and he examined all the above items of expenditure with close scrutiny.

THE EPIDEMIC FEVERS.—In noticing the condition of the Indian people, the historian must first of all give a regretful prominence to the epidemic fevers that had been decimating the fairest villages of Bengal. The Hon'ble Digambar Mitter in his minute on the subject which was published as an appendix to the report of the epidemic commission of 1861, took up the position that the epidemic fever was due to an obstruction of the surface drainage of the villages caused mainly by the construction of roads, railways and embankments, without a sufficient waterway for the ready discharge of rain and flood. The publication of these views by a man who though without any trained scientific knowledge, had an infinite fund of common sense and an accurate experience of the condition of the Bengal villages, led to great excitement and investigation. The circumstantial evidence that was brought to support this position in the shape of the actual condition of a series of villages through which a line of roads had been constructed recklessly, and the total immunity from fever of another series of villages similarly situated but lying beyond the influence of the road or embankment, was very strong. The medical profession was obliged by the very force of facts to admit that there was some truth in the theory and as the fell fever was gradually spreading to many parts of the country, and the lives of many thousands of Her Majesty's subjects were being sacrificed every year, the Government, while adopting other measures of relief instituted proper enquiries into this subject.

LORD LAWRENCE ON INDIAN MATTERS.—Freed from the shackles of office Lord Lawrence gave expression to some very sound views on Indian subjects in his evidence before the Indian finance committee. He spoke highly of the wisdom of Lord Cornwallis in introducing the permanent settlement in Bengal and spoke of it as the principal cause of that remarkable prosperity which Bengal in comparison with the other Indian provinces now enjoys. He advocated the extension of the Permanent settlement to all parts of the country under the condition proposed by Sir Charles Wood that eighty per cent of the lands of each village should have been first brought under cultivation. The imposition of local cesses was justifiable in his opinion in the permanently settled districts as Lord Cornwallis' arrangement did not include the idea of barring future improvements but His Lordship thought that such cesses should not have been imposed in the temporarily settled districts as in their case they were additions pure and simple to the land revenue. Lord Lawrence did not think that the decentralization scheme had any great merit. It would not tend to make the Local Governments more economical and the idiosyncracies and character of the individual ruler would be as great determining factors under this system as under the old one. The people of India would not be able to distinguish between local and imperial taxation. They identify the higher officers of the Local Governments with the Government of India and they were not likely to understand the principle that local needs should be carried out through local taxation. He thought that the practice of the Viceroy's communicating all his views on important subjects semi-officially to the Secretary of State and of their exchanging opinions with each other had a very salutary influence in as much as the Viceroy had the counsel of a statesman of the first rank with a thorough grasp of principles and the Secretary of State's theoretical knowledge was corrected and supplemented by information about practical difficulties and administrative details.

THE INDIAN PRINCES.—Lord Stanley of Alderley drew the attention of the House of Lords this year to the fact that there did not exist any competent and impartial tribunal which could be give a hearing to the grievances of the native princes. He said that the acts of the subordinate officials, accredited to the native states were often dictated by caprice and were accepted by the Government of India as acts of state. The supreme government felt itself bound afterwards by the position that it had taken up and had naturally to turn a deaf ear to the representations of the aggrieved princes. These princes cannot come before the properly constituted legal tribunals in British India, nor have they any *locus standi* to appeal to Her Majesty's Privy Council. His Lordship pointed out that a Supreme Court existed in the United States for the consideration of all matters in dispute between state and state and that in Portuguese India the government had to give a strict account of all its doings either in the matter of accounts or of general administration to the law officers of the Crown, and that these tribunals lead to no loss of prestige to the Executive Government. The Indian Princes have theoretically a right of appeal to the British Parliament, but Parliament with a standing majority for the Secretary of State is hardly a fit tribunal for such grievances, and the persistent calumnies and insinuations that are levelled against any member of the House of Commons, who takes up such cases have made the practical difficulties in the way of the aggrieved Indian princes, very great indeed. The Duke of Argyll combated these arguments by saying that it was necessary for the Government of India for reasons of policy and good government to reserve to itself the right of deciding in all cases of political treachery, political mismanagement and political crime. It would be, His Grace said, a serious source of disaffection and a blow to sound and enlightened administration in India, if the Government were ever to delegate these important constitutional functions to an independent tribunal, with a strong judicial element in it. His Grace conveniently forgot that the internal relations with the native princes should not be left consistently with reason or justice to the tender mercies of the Indian political department.

THE INDIAN FINANCE COMMITTEE.—The Indian Finance Committee, which went exhaustively into the condition of the Indian finances, expressed an opinion on the recommendation, that the Indian Financial year should end on the 31st of December and not on the 31st of March, so that the Secretary of State would be able to present the statement of Indian finances to the British Parliament before the Easter recess. The Committee stated that this practice of making a Financial statement to Parliament was revived in 1853, when the President of the Board of Control in giving the House a forecast of the measures necessary for the ensuing year, entered into an exhaustive review of the Indian finances before a committee of the whole House. The same practice was continued till 1858 when the new act for the Government of India was passed. The audited accounts on which the opinion of the House was based were accompanied by approximate accounts known as the regular estimate for the following financial year. In 1871, the complaint was first distinctly heard in the House that the Indian accounts were presented very late in the session when most of the members had left the town. The committee did not recommend the changing of the last day of the financial year. The Indian finances it was recommended should be presented to the House in an early part of the session but it would be the statement given in the Indian budget that would then be nearly a year old and discussions on that budget would have no practical value. The Finance Committee was of opinion that the evidence they had recorded had been chiefly derived from official sources and that competent native inhabitants likely to give useful information should be invited to place their views at the disposal of the committee. This invitation of the House of Commons to the educated natives called forth a virulent steam of abuse against them. Many Anglo-Indian writers of extreme views warned the English public against the educated native and went on to say that the native of India, who would come to England, sacrificing his caste and his religion would be no trustworthy representative of his countrymen. The authorities in England were opposed to the sending out of the commission to India, to record evidence on the spot. Such a step, they thought, would be regarded by the natives of the country as a virtual supercession of the authority of the local executive. It was contended by the influential representatives of native opinion, that the action of the English Government, in requiring the Indian subjects to go to England for the concession of rights and privileges to which they were entitled as citizens of a great empire, was unrighteous. The difficulties of the Indian in the way of his going to England were many and of different varieties and the English public which have no sympathy with the prejudices of the oriental mind could hardly be expected to appreciate all these difficulties.

The Wild Beasts of India—Lord Napier of Merchiston who subsequently assumed the title of Lord Ettrick did a public service to India by directing attention to the loss of life among the natives of India through the agency of wild beasts. His Lordship remarked, that the annual loss of life from this source was terrible and extraordinary and great loss and suffering were caused by the habitual terror exercised by these animals, by the limitation of cultivation and the interruption of traffic. Lord Napier suggested that a special service be organized of European sportsmen and native *Shikaries* who would be entrusted with a certain number of arms and that the State should reward them according to the actual number of savage and ferocious animals killed. His Grace the Duke of Argyll while admitting that the disarmament which had been going on since the mutiny had put a premium to the loss of life from this cause thought it extraordinary that the Indian people had not got the energy to destroy these wild beasts. The historian cannot indeed understand the force of His Grace's assertion. It was extremely unkind of the Secretary of State to taunt his Indian subjects with want of energy when he knew full well that the arms have been allowed only to a few of them under very strict limitations and that the Indian Government was responsible for the protection of the lives of its subjects.

Summary Trials—The investing of a large body of magisterial officers with summary powers was a grave source of dissatisfaction which was considerably deepened by the fact that these officers not unfrequently commit blunders and irregularities of an extraordinary character. These new provisions certainly served to effect their primary object that of strengthening the executive but this object was attained by the sacrifice of the liberty of the subject. When not a particle of evidence was required by law to be on the record, the chances of an appeal to the superior judiciary of the land were almost nil and every one having any experience of the Muffasil magistracy knows very well how frequently it stands in need of being corrected and rectified by the High Court. The remarkable independence of the Indian High Courts especially of the barrister judges, the technicalities whose benefit the Indian case law gave rather extensively and the stout championship of the barristers whose numbers were daily increasing made the judiciary an eyesore to those officers who had been trained in the Panjabi system of administration which was but another name for the strongest despotism. The sections with reference to summary trials continued to deface the Statute-book and although the imperfections of the magistracy were demonstrated in the clear light of day the Indian Government has not yet been taken this question into careful consideration.

MAHOMEDAN EDUCATION—Sir Syed Ahmed of Allyghur proposed to create a college in that city for giving special facilities to the Mahomedans to be instructed in English while combining with it a study of the Mahomedan theology. After considerable preliminary discussions the provincial committee appointed at the instance of Syed Ahmed came to the conclusion that as the Government could not guarantee religious instruction in any of its seminaries, and as the Mahomedans cared more for their religion than for anything else a separate educational establishment on an extended scale should be established where secular and religious training might be combined. The scheme progressed successfully and the Viceroy as well as the highest officers of the state accorded their patronage to the project. Native chiefs contributed liberally and before the expiry of the year about 20 lakhs of rupees had been collected for the purpose. A powerful opposition to the movement had however been organized, objecting to the proposed scheme on the ground that European science and literature entered into the curriculum of the proposed college and that its projector did not see any objection to eating and drinking with Europeans and an orthodox Mahomedan proceeded so far as Mecca to get a sentence of infidelity pronounced against the Syud, which he succeeded in getting done. The worthy Syed however persisted in his noble efforts and impressed upon his co-religionists the fact that they must move in these progressive times. The college soon after became an accomplished fact though it has not yet succeeded in imparting the standard of education necessary, except in rare cases.

CHAPTER VI.
1874.

THE FAMINE IN BENGAL AND BEHAR—Sir George Campbell was the first to draw the attention of the Government of India to the crisis of an impending famine throughout a great extent of his territories. The districts most threatened by the calamity were those of Behar and parts of the Rajshahye and Burdwan divisions. The reports from Patna showed that the rains had failed throughout a considerable part of the Behar districts, that the standing rice crop could not be saved, that caterpillars were doing a good deal of injury to the young plants and that the want of moisture prevented the sowing of the cold-weather crops. There was no hope of saving the paddy except in places bordering on streams, and to add to the difficulties of the situation a considerable part of the Benares Division was also suffering from draught with the same intensity as Behar. Lord Northbrook in concert with Sir George Campbell devised judicious measures for famine relief at once. Lord Northbrook was one of the members of the British Relief Commission which raised and administered half a million during the Irish Famine and Sir George Campbell had gleaned a good deal of information on the subject from his being the President of the commission that enquired into the famine in Orissa. Lord Northbrook issued a circular to the Local Governments directing them to curtail all expenditure that could be reduced, postponed or dispensed with, and aid the Government of India with the savings thus secured as a very large expenditure of money was necessary for the relief of distress and a serious loss of revenue was apprehended. The Government of India thought that the natural law of demand and supply would induce many traders to bring food to the famine-stricken districts. To facilitate this object the railway rates on grains were reduced by half, the local rates and tolls were abolished temporarily and the natural trade of the country was to be promoted by advances of money to the zamindars and planters on condition that they would import grain from a distance and sell it as near as possible at cost price all expenses included, as well as to traders of a safe and responsible character who would take the money at a moderate interest of 6 per cent. on condition that they would engage to import grain from a distance. To relieve those people who had neither money nor credit and who for want of work were unable to earn money or wages, the Local Government sanctioned a variety of local and emigration roads. Charitable relief was to be distributed to the old, to children, to persons in reduced health, and to others who might be unable to do a full day's work. The Government and its officers were to lay insufficient supplies of rice and other grain which would be forwarded as soon as possible to places of storage near relief works to prevent the support of a large body of laborers from being an additional burden on the distressed districts and the transporting agency was to be made as efficient as possible. During the dire famines that visited Bengal in 1769-70, 1837-38, and 1868-69 the Government had taken the most inadequate measures for famine relief although the mortality and beggary in many cases exceeded all descriptions. The British Government since its acquisition of India had within the last hundred years spent one million and three quarters of pounds sterling in round numbers by way of relief to its subjects suffering from famines. This sinks into utter insignificance when compared with the liberality of the imperial parliament during the great Irish famine of 1847. To Lord Northbrook belongs the credit of having distinctly recognized the responsibility of the state, of feeding the people in such times of distress and not surely to be content only with some remissions of revenue. He openly declared that it was his duty to anticipate distress without delay or hesitation and to prevent the loss of human lives as far as possible. His Lordship thought that the food supplies from other parts of India would be able to meet the scarcity in Bengal and Behar and his Government did not deem it necessary to stop the export of food-grains and to interfere with the free action of trade. But some extravagance characterized the relief operations and the money that was spent in the early part of the struggle was absolutely wasted. But through the energy, judgment, endurance and self-sacrifice of many high officers from the Viceroy downwards, the success of the relief operations was manifest. The stern reality of the crisis was fully apprehended and manfully met. It was remarked at the time with absolute truth that the success of the operations of the Government had been so complete that doubts were expressed as to whether they were at all necessary. In this dire struggle against this great natural visitation the English officers as well as the merchants and the traders of the country were shown to the best advantage and the address of thanksgiving that was presented towards the close of the year by the representatives of the people to the heads of the Supreme and Local Governments, gratefully recognized that the administration of famine relief in 1874 constituted a memorable and glorious chapter in the history of the British rule in India. The Viceroy deputed Sir Richard Temple to take the command of the campaign against famine, who carried out the humane policy of the government with a large-hearted sympathy. The famine though it put a serious strain on the finances of the country did not happily lead to any increased taxation. After the deputation of Sir Richard Temple, Lord Northbrook assumed the charge of the Financial Department and with reference to famine expenditure his Lordship remarked " that the condition of the finance had been so strong that an expenditure of 6 millions sterling on account of the Famine would be borne out of the surplus of income over ordinary expenditure in the three preceding years." " The Government of India" His Lordship added " are anxious to avoid the imposition of fresh taxes and any disturbance of the present financial arrangements of the country and it is with particular satisfaction that they arrived at the conclusion that notwithstanding the large and unexpected demand upon the resources of the state, no increase of taxation was necessary." The English people as soon as they learnt of the impending distress proffered substantial aid for the relief of the distressed millions. This generosity was gratefully appreciated by the Indian people in all parts of the continent. It is well-known that the heart of the British nation seldom fails to respond to the cries of distress however distant the scene of suffering, and although no actual aid was necessary the spirit in which the offer had been made added fresh lustre to the reputation of England.

BARODA.—Mulhar Rao has had been raised from a prison to the throne of Baroda but his administration of the state roused serious discontent among his subjects. Petitions went up to His Excellency the Viceroy bringing serious charges against the said administration and the Government of Bombay backed up these petitions. The Government of India determined upon the appointment of a commission to enquire into the state of affairs. The Government of India appointed the commission under its own immediate authority but it allowed the Government of Bombay to nominate two of its trusted officers as members of the commission, and with the European officers was associated the late Prime Minister of Jeypore who was thoroughly familiar with the difficulties that beset the administration of an Indian principality. Native Princes in India hardly welcome a commission of inquiry for the same reasons that would lead the Government of India to resent a Royal Commission. It lowers them in the estimation of the people and it brings to a deadlock the present administrative machinery. But the Government of India has a responsibility to the subjects of native states which are now supported in their just rights and privileges by British bayonets. The Gackwar was charged in his royal person with many scandalous acts, and his councillors with wholesale tyranny and oppression and there was every reason why the present enquiry should be promoted.

The commission after proper enquiry reported against the Gaekwar and Lord Northbrook gave a fair warning to the defaulting prince. The State of Baroda was divided into two parties—the Conservative Party and the Reform Party. The Conservative Party naturally desired the conservation of old abuses which meant a continuance of their own powers. The Reform Party while not desiring the supercession of the native dynasty wanted a thorough reform. The Viceroy gave the Gaekwar one year's time within which to reform all abuses with steady perseverance. The Gaekwar placed the state under the guidance of Mr. Dadabhai Naroji, who by natural intelligence, thorough practical experience and the conception of the duties of a state acquired by a long residence in England was wellfitted to cope with the corruption and intrigue that then infested the state. Mr. Naroji applied for the services of able native officers to second his efforts. Lord Northbrook committed a mistake in allowing the old Resident to continue, who unfortunately proved no friend to the new minister. Colonel Sir Arthur Phayre was highly unpopular in Baroda and he had created so many mortal enemies as to give a plausible color to the alleged plot to assassinate him which would come to our notice in the next chapter.

GENERAL EVENTS.—The events of the Fort St. George went on easily enough but the affairs of the Bombay Presidency excited a good deal of public attention. The Burial Bill passed by the Local Government was furiously opposed and it was vetoed by the Viceroy. A life of Mahomet published in Gujrati by a Parsi gentleman gave great offence to the followers of the Islamic faith and they applied to the Commissioner of Police to have the book withdrawn from circulation. This request was granted but even this concession did not satisfy the infuriated Moslem mob. They committed all sorts of outrages, singled out the Parsis for their special vengeance and for two days the capital of the Western Presidency was the scene of absolute lawlessness which was put an end to when the military was called out to restore order. Some other publications of the same author led to a renewal of the riots and the imbecility of the Local Government drew forth severe comments. Sir John Strachey who succeeded to the Lieutenant-Governorship of the North-Western Provinces gave the province some rest in the first year of his administration. This year the alleged capture of Nana Saheb by Maharaja Scindia caused a good deal of political excitement but the news did not prove to be true. The distinguished success of Babu Ananda Mohun Bose, the first Bengali wrangler of the Cambridge University was hailed as the dawn of a better intellectual era for India. Sir Arthur Hobhouse introduced an important bill entitled the Civil Appeals Bill which gave the right of second appeal both on grounds of fact and law though it took away the right of second appeal in cases of little value where there were concurrent judgments of the two lower courts. Those who have any experience of the Indian judicial system will admit that the allowing of second appeals both on grounds of fact and law is a desirable reform. The Moffusil Judges in not a few cases place implicit confidence in the weight that had been given to the evidence on the record by the lower court and in these cases, if no nice point of law arises there is absolutely no remedy. The law member justly held that the existing law was unsound because it separated law and facts by putting forcibly asunder things which nature had joined together. Lord Northbrook regulated the relations of the Government of India with the Native States in the true spirit of the Queen's proclamation. The complaint however with reference to the increasing interference of the British political officers became louder and louder every day. A small military expedition was undertaken against the Dufflas which was a mere punitive expedition and came to a conclusion without much bloodshed. Mr. Inglis held the financial portfolio for a short time during the deputation of Sir Richard Temple on special duty. The change of the ministry placed Lord Salisbury at the head of the India Office. His Lordship was a man of indefatigable energy and rare intellectual ability. As Lord Cranborne he had once before been Secretary of State and his Lordship's rule had proved most beneficient. He had strong convictions against the injustice done by England to India in financial matters and had manfully fought the battle of the Home charges. The General election brought the conservatives to power by an overwhelming majority and the loss of his seat in Parliament by Mr. Fawcett, though only for a time, was regarded by the Indian people in the light of a national calamity. The electors of Hackney however soon restored the sightless champion of India to his former sphere of usefulness. Bengal had to mourn this year the loss of one of her worthiest sons in the person of the Honorable Justice Dwarka Nath Mitter. He had been for many years the leading practitioner on the Appellate Side of the High Court and had adorned a seat on the bench of the highest Court of the land for nearly seven years. His untimely death at the early age of 39 was deeply regretted by all classes of the community and his colleagues on the bench paid a glowing tribute to his extensive acquirements, his varied learning and rapid perception, his keen discrimination and his instinctive love of justice. He had nobly vindicated the claims of his countrymen to high and responsible offices. He was succeeded on the bench by Sir Romesh Chunder Mitter a lawyer who has shed an undying lustre on his profession.

THE ADMINISTRATION OF BENGAL—Sir George Campbell's administration of the premier province of India was very severly criticized by the native press of Bengal headed by its able leader Kristodas Paul who reviewed the three years of his rule with great minuteness and a thorough grasp of the situation. That under this administration the ruled were estranged in a great measure from the ruler admits of little doubt and the provincial ruler left a name behind him that would be a warning to all coming after him. The eloquent words of Kristodas Paul under this head might well find a place in the pages of History which are as follow. There is scarely a class of this vast community

with which "he has not managed to be unpopular. He has been
" unpopular with his own service which at one time according to
" his own statement in the administration report, threatened to
" rise in rebellion against him. He has been unpopular with
" the uncovenanted service because he has given away its prizes
" to covenanted assistants, degraded its position and emo-
" luments and freezed its independence. He has been
" unpopular with the educational service the members of
" which he had repeatedly insulted by ill-merited snubs and
" reproofs. He has been unpopular with the judicial service
" the members of which from the highest to the lowest he has
" missed no pretext to attack or lower in the estimation of the
" public by an arrogant assertion of executive authority. He
" has been unpopular with the departmental heads whom he has
" sought to reduce to the position of correspondence clerks.
" He has been unpopular with the university authorities by
" waging a crusade against their legitimate authority and even
" questioning their intelligence. He has been unpopular with
" the medical profession by casting aspersions upon their in-
" come-tax returns and subverting the reforms in prisons which
" the representatives of that faculty had effected after years of
" thought, labour and struggle. He has been unpopular with
" the representatives of the legal profession whom he has
" literally abused in season and out of season. He has been
" unpopular with the independent Europeans for whose opinions
" and sentiments, he has shown the utmost contempt. He has
" been unpopular with the Zamindars whom he has denounced
" from his high place as " wolves". He has been unpopolar
" with the ryots whom he has saddled with an oppressive cess,
" and upon whom he sought to impose many more taxes and
" would have succeeded but for the humane interference of His
" Excellency the Viceroy, for whose health and life he showed
" the most cruel indifference by his utter inaction to remove the
" causes of the fell epidemic fever which has for years been
" decimating the fairest villages of Bengal though repeatedly

"urged to do so and against whose personal liberty he set a
"determined face by allowing the police and the magistrates
"to indulge in their freaks and caprices and by destroying
"those safeguards against abuse of power which the old law
"provided. And lastly he has been unpopular with the educated
"classes of the native community by putting them down with a
"high hand, by figting against their legitimate aspirations, by
"aspersing their character, and by prejudicing them in the
"opinion of the good and the true." The above passage gives
a summary of the indictments that can be brought against the
administration of Sir George Campbell. He had indeed been
adopting some measures whose tendency and ultimate effects
were the very reverse of beneficial, with reference to the ruled
classes. He centralized all powers in the hands of the Magistrate and Collector. The practical effect of this system was that
the District Chief who was usually an overworked officer, was
unable to exercise personal superintendence over many of the
departments and left everything to the judgment of the departmental head who in turn thus became the virtual possessor of
more authority than they had been under the old system
minus the responsibility that formerly attached to them. His
'parallel lines of promotion' had introduced the anomaly which
came to be felt so much in later times of making young
joint-magistrates almost without any experience of civil business,
to sit, on being promoted to district judgeships, in appeal over
the judgments of able officers, who have spent a life-time in
civil courts and whose judgments had been tested and found
correct in many weighty matters by the High Court and the
Privy Council. Sir George claimed the credit of having extended the Sub-divisional system whose foundation was laid by
Sir John Peter Grant, to effect which object he created the class
of Sub-deputies. The rule however that the Lieutenant-Governor tried to formulate that the Deputy Magistrates and
Collectors would be selected from the ranks of the Sub-deputies
and that men would not without good and special reason be taken

from outside for those places by any mere exercise of patronage was considered equivalent to the reduction of the initial pay of the Subordinate executive service to Rs. 100 a month. His land policy though conceived with a good motive was sought to be carried out with so little tact as to lead to the reopening of the land question and his proclamation to the ryots saying that it was perfectly lawful to unite to resist in a peaceable manner the excessive demands of the Zamindars had a bad effect on the impressible minds of the ignorant tenantry of Bengal who could hardly moderate their enthusiasm to the strict limits of constitutional opposition, and led to such outrages as the Pubna one. Sir George could not endure in peace the practice that was daily growing up of engaging able and talented barristers in the interior of the country, who checked the proceedings of an erratic magistracy and of the High Courts' interfering with its action. He denounced the lawyers especially the native section of it and the High Court judges with all the vehemance that he was capable of. He admitted the helplessness of the Government in the case of the police abuses and made the character of the police officials a peg on which to hang a general tirade against the nation from which they were generally drawn. Sir George was a hearty enemy of the educated natives of the country and he went so far as to say that he had a poor opinion of the inferior native courts of original civil jurisdiction in the matter of dealing thoroughly with facts. He forgot that this estimate was opposed to the recorded opinions of such eminent judges as Sir Barnes Peacock or Sir William Markby, and that the superior efficiency and character of the native members of the Bench had been freely admitted by those most competent to speak on the subject. His high-sounding rhetoric on the necessity of having a comprehensive system of primary education resulted in a three rupees monthly grant to the *gurus* of the existing *patshalas* and thus converting them into Government institutions. He tried to repress the educated natives whenever he found an opportunity and he openly and systematically reviled their organs of public opinion. In his last public speech he had almost pathetically declared that he deeply sympathized with the people of Bengal but this statement was traversed by an unanswerable array of facts and figures in the columns of the *Hindu Patriot*. The administration of Bengal is notoriously no bed of roses. With the spread of education, the influx of barristers trained in England and the vigorous criticisms of the native press, the work of the head of the Government is daily growing more complex and harassing and it has been suggested in later days by persons whose opinions influence the course of events, that the charge is too heavy for a single pair of shoulders and that the province should be cut up into two administrations. Sir Richard Temple who succeeded Sir George recognized at once that Bengal had passed the era of patriarchal government and that the progressive policy of the past had reared up a population which took an intelligent interest in the measures of the government. He had gained a deep insight into the best side of the character of the people of the province during the famine campaign and he used that to his best advantage. His first utterances on the education question, and the reform of Sir George's pet scheme of the native civil service were eminently concilliatory and tended to bring peace and harmony where there was discord before. Sir Richard Temple's operations during the famine were attended with great success and he completely restored confidence by energetically carrying out the humane policy of the Government of India.

Dr. BHAU DAJI.—The present system of Indian education has succeeded in producing so few men of originality in any department of thought or action that all real scholars deserve more than a passing notice from the historian. Dr. Bhau Daji of Bombay, the foremost scholar, leader and reformer of his generation passed away with the present year. Born of humble parents and educated under circumstances of considerable hardship, he not only succeeded in making his mark in the medical profession early in life, but managed to find out learned leisure for devoting himself to oriental researches. His activities in the field of researches into the antiquities of his native land soon acquired for him an enduring reputation which ultimately spread to Europe and America. He was a man of great public spirit and he took a leading part in founding the Bombay gardens, the Victoria and Albert Museum, the Bombay Presidency Association as well as the Bombay branch of the East India Association. He was honorably associated with many of the learned societies of the European continent and in the municipal councils, the university senate-house and the charitable society which he established he had rendered important services to the capital of western India. India lost in him a representative man who was regarded with equal respect by all the great communities in all parts of India.

LORD NORTHBROOK—Public opinion in India was entirely in favor of Lord Northbrook after about three years' experience of his Lordships' Government. His capacity for hard, patient and unremitting labour, the pains that he took in grasping principles as well as working out details, his just appreciation of the difficulties in the way of the Indian statesman and his sympathy with the children of the soil in whose interests alone he rightly thought the administration of India ought to be carried on, gained for him an universal popularity. His Lordship saw the evil effects of the estrangement that was apparent between the ruler and the ruled in Bengal, and he vigorously took up the whole matter and nipped the obnoxious projects of the provincial Lieutenant in the bud. There was the Municipalities Bill which was conceived with a double object of increasing taxation and repressing the educated classes, but Lord Northbrook came to the rescue and vetoed the measure. There was an unseemly squable between the Viceroy and Sir George Campbell as to the direction of famine affairs, Sir George desiring to lead the campaign himself and Lord Northbrook holding that he was physically unequal to the task. Lord Northbrook held that the government should act according to the advice of the competent medical men in organizing relief centres and distributing relief to the famished people but Sir George insisted that the doctors were wrong and that his own views should have free play. A reference followed on these matters to the Secretary of State but both the Duke of Argyll and the Marquis of Salisbury decided against Sir George Campbell, who immediately laid down the reins of administration. Lord Northbrook showed a commendable independance of his surroundings by overruling in many matters the impertinent and imbecile Government of Bombay. He enforced his measures of reform and retrenchment with a full sense of justice and in his distribution of patronage he was quite impartial and recognized merit in officers of every grade and standing in all departments of the Indian administration. We have dealt with his famine policy elsewhere. Never did the public and private virtues of the Viceroy shine more conspiciously than during those terrible struggles with a great natural calamity. He always sanctioned all important projects after a full personal inspection and he was thus not far wrong in the views he entertained. The Punjabi spirit of administration which had taken possession of the Government of India gradually gave way to just and righteous principles.

THE POLITICAL SITUATION IN INDIA—Russia notwithstanding its smooth professions and the pledge it had given by the marriage of the Czar's daughter with the Duke of Edinburgh had been steadily making advances in Central Asia. In the name of scientific expeditions it had been completing all military preparations and one by one absorbing all the kingdoms and khanates in Central Asia. It was forming secret alliances with Persia and Afghanistan. Afghanistan was a power divided against itself and the treacherous seizing of Yakub Khan by his father after having invited him by assurances of safety and protection tended still further to complicate matters. It was believed that Yakub Khan had proceeded to Cabul at the instance of the British Indian Government. He had staunch friends in Persia and Russia and he was much more popular with the Afghan tribe than his father and it was feared at one time that Persia, Russia and Yakub's party in Afghanistan would unite in demanding his release. There were some signs of internal trouble in Gwalior. The part that the Maharajah took in the capture of the supposed Nana was an impolitic one and gave great offence to his nobles and subjects. His Highness committed a serious mistake in surrendering the supposed fiend of Cawnpore without qualifying his belief in the identity of the man and his trying to make capital of that unfortunate man seemed to have filled his subjects and nobles with disgust.

CHAPTER VII.
1875.

THE TRIAL OF THE GAEKWAR OF BARODA—We have seen the lamentable state of affairs at Baroda in our review of the preceding year. Colonel Sir Arthur Phayre who was continued as Resident accredited to the Baroda Court, although an able and energetic man was hardly the right man in the right place and proved extremely obstructive in the way of the carrying out of many measures initiated by the new minister. It was not until the Governor General in Council issued direct orders for the recognition of Mr. Dadabhai Naroji as the chief minister that the Resident yielded. In Baroda there were two parties one of which sided with the Gaekwar and the other was perpetually busy in poisoning the ears of the Resident. The Resident suspected an attempt to poison him by means of arsenic and diamond dust, and at once came to the conclusion that the Gaekwar was at the bottom of this attempt. He also accused the Gaekwar of having tampered with his servants for securing private information and of having caused false entries to be made in his books and papers. The Government of India thought it necessary to enquire carefully into the whole matter and it decided that the enquiry should be held in the full blaze of public opinion as well as that the Gaekwar should have the benefit of a trial by his brother princes. It accordingly appointed a commission consisting of the Maharajas of Gwalior and Jeypur, Sir Raja Dinker Rao, Colonel Sir Richard Meade Mr. Philip Sandys Melville with the Hon'ble Sir Richard Couch as the President and Mr. John Jardine as the Secretary. Nothing could be fairer than the tone and spirit of the Proclamation appointing the Commission. It asked the Commissioners to confine their enquiries to the special charges before them and in no case to admit any evidence as to the general misrule of Mulhar Rao Gaekwar. It told Colonel Phayre distinctly that he would be called upon to contradict by trustworthy evidence the Gaekwar's statement that the present crisis had been brought about principally by his conduct. The Government of India temporarily took over the administration of the Baroda State and allowed the Gaekwar the fullest facilities in defending himself permitting him to draw the necessary expenses from the Baroda Treasury. Lord Northbrook also disarmed the annexationists by declaring that whatever might be the issue of the present trial the state would be restored to native administration. The trial commenced at Baroda on the 23rd February 1875. Sir Andrew Scoble (then Mr. Scoble) who was then Advocate-General of Bombay with Mr. J. Invararity conducted the prosecution while an old Bailey counsel Serjeant Ballantine with Messrs Purcell and Branson conducted the defence. Sir A. Scoble opened the case by stating that the Gaekwar had tampered with the Residency servants to obtain information and had instigated an attempt to poison Colonel Phayre with arsenic and diamond dust and said that he had witnesses to prove that the Gaekwar made payments of money to the servants at the time of the attempt to poison. The evidence was recorded during 15 sittings of the Commission and on the sixteenth day Serjeant Ballantine rose to address the Commissioners on behalf of the defence. He drew the attention of the court to the fact that the Baroda Police exercised a great authority over the witnesses, that they were mysteriously brought together in every 24 hours when just in the humour to disburden their minds and even contrary to law, the Police took depositions. He went on to say that the evidence produced was that of accomplices and was inadmissible in any English Court of law unless corroborated. He dwelt long on the nature of the corroborative evidence and contended that there was none whatever. He thought it improbable that the Gaekwar who had preferred certain charges against the Resident in a *Kharita* to the Viceroy asking His Excellency to remove Col. Phayre should attempt the life of the very man who would have to explain matters that formed the ground of complaint. He laid special stress on the technical pleas that the English law has provided for sifting evidence and characterized those technicalities as the bulwork of the liberty of the subject in a free country. He reviewed the evidence at great length and came to the conclusion that no witness has proved that the Gaekwar had any motive in acting as it was alleged he had done. Sir A. Scoble tried to show that the Gaekwar had a motive in attempting to poison Colonel Phayre. He believed that Colonel Phayre would prevent the recognition of Luxombai's son as he had refused to recognize the marriage and that the Resident would receive the support of the Government in this matter. The Gaekwar had admitted in his Kharita that he regarded Colonel Phayre as an uncompromising opponent and a persecutor. Serjeant Ballantine concluded with an eloquent tirade against those newspapers that had ventured to comment on the trial and to influence by their writings the opinions of the Commissioners to the prejudice of the Gaekwar. Sir A. Scoble ended with a forcible peroration saying that the witnesses had in the main told the truth, that the Gaekwar's guilt was established, that it would be the painful duty of the Commission to regard him not as a persecuted prince but as a criminal worthy of condign punishment. He finally prayed to God that the deliberations of the Commission might be brought to a just and righteous conclusion. The Baroda trial was the first instance of a straightforward and above-board policy in the matter of the political relations with the native chiefs and the finale of the Baroda drama was watched with great interest. The Commissioners were divided in opinion the native members concluding in favor of the Gaekwar, and the European members against His Highness. The Government of India issued the final orders on the subject on the 19th April 1875. The proclamation stated that the Commissioners being divided in opinion Her Majesty's Government did not base their opinion on the enquiry or report of the Commission but having regard to the gross mismanagement of the state by Mulhar Rao since his accession he should be deposed from the sovereignty of the Baroda state, that he and his issue would be precluded from all rights, honors and privileges thereto appertaining. " Her Most Gracious Majesty the Queen in re-establishing a native administration in the Baroda State being desirous to mark her sense of the loyal services of His Highness Khande Rao Gaekwar in 1857 has been pleased to accede to the request of his widow Her Highness Jumnabai that she may be allowed to adopt some member of the Gaekwar House whom the Government of India may select as the most suitable person upon whom to confer the sovereignty of the Baroda State". With the consent of His Highness the Maharaja of Indore Sir T. Madhava Rao then Prime Minister of that state was brought over to Baroda to assume the supreme direction of affairs and to form an administration. The orders of the Government had been telegraphed to the Marquis of Salisbury and His Lordship had approved of them on general grounds, in that Mulhar Rao was not fit to rule Baroda. The criticisms on the Gaekwar trial were directed to the sole point as to whether the government was justified in deposing the Gaekwar on the ground of misrule after having condoned his failures under that head and giving him time to reform his administration. The action of the government was somewhat inconsistent in the matter. Whatever his misconduct and misrule, they had been condoned by twenty months' grace and to make the old grounds a pretext for deposition in violation of the plighted word of the Government of India was a gross political perfidy, and a breach of faith which would be considered extremely reprehensible in the relations of private life. It broke a solemn assurance and it lowered the pledges of the Government of India in the estimation of the princes and the people. As the Secretary of State was evidently unwilling to concur with the verdict of the European element in the Commission, considerations of policy prudence and justice required the continuance of the probation of the Gaekwar. The evidence of Colonel Phayre was extremely damaging to the cause of the prosecution and even the leading journal of England the *Times* did not hesitate to refer to it in terms of unmeasured disapprobation. The *Times* distinctly said that the prosecution of the Gaekwar was the greatest blunder the government had committed since the Mutiny and that all the difficulties in India had arisen from the want of tact and discretion in men holding such responsible official positions as Colonel Phayre. There can be nothing more demoralizing than the practice which was fully laid bare in the Gaekwar trial of the native princes habitually coaxing the Residency servants in order to secure the favor of the Resident. The politicals have been vested with enormous power over the princes and they strike terror to the sovereign chiefs. The Indian press was very severe in its criticisms on the Baroda policy of the government and its tone frequently transcended the limits of moderation. The historian cannot justify the tone of all these criticisms but they were not entirely uncalled for. Lord Northbrook's action in the Baroda case in falling in at once with the views of the Resident and ordering an enquiry cannot be justified when we consider how slight was the evidence for the prosecution against the Gaekwar, the nature of which evidence was mercilessly laid bare in the emphatic protests of the Maharaja of Gwalior, the Maharaja of Jeypore and Sir Dinker Rao—themselves be it remembered three of the most loyal and conscientious men in India.

THE VISIT OF THE PRINCE OF WALES.—His Excellency the Viceroy announced at the Darbar held at Delhi that His Royal Highness the Prince of Wales, the future King of England with its colonies and dependencies would honor the Indian Empire with a visit in the month of November of the present year. About the same time His Royal Highness declared in a speech at the Mansion House that he looked forward with the greatest interest and pleasure to his intended visit to India, which had been the dream of his life. The princes and the people of India received this announcement with great pleasure and at once took in hand preparations to give a right royal reception to their august visitor. The name of the East India Company in whom the sovereignty of the country remained vested for nearly a hundred years was a mere abstraction which was not intelligible to the oriental mind. Since the direct assumption of the reins of the government by the sovereign of England, the name of the Queen was a mere sound, an echo. The masses of the people in India had never an opportunity to know by sight and imposing pagents the sovereign who is the arbiter of the destinies of one-sixth of the human race. The approaching visit therefore of the eldest son of Her Majesty, the heir-apparent to the British dominions and only second to his imperial mother in the respect and homage to which the sovereign is entitled, struck deeply the imagination of the oriental subjects of England and all classes and sections of the Indian people resolved to solemnize the occasion with fitting splendour. The reception of the Duke of Edinburgh was a great success, but the reception of the future king was naturally organized on a much grander scale. It was fondly expected that the impressions which he would carry away from his Indian tour and the knowledge that he will acquire about Indian affairs would one day be used to the best advantage of the millions of this country, that though the head of a constitutional monarchy His Royal Highness would be able to impress the government of the day with his views on Indian affairs. It was expected too that the Prince's visit would kindle greater interest in the affairs of India in England and that the knights of the pen who would represent the press would be able to impress the people of England with a sense of their responsibilities towards their great Eastern Empire. Bombay had the honor first to welcome the Prince of Wales on Indian soil and she played her representative part admirably. The scene at the Apollo Bunder where His Royal Highness landed on the 8th of November was as impressive as any that could be imagined. The officials of state, the corporation, the representatives of wealth, commerce and intelligence, the Native Princes of high lineage and splendid retinue, the army and the navy, the Parsi maidens and over ten thousand boys singing in a chorus formed the principle elements of a scene the like of which Bombay has never witnessed. After the usual round of festivities at Bombay His Royal Highness proceeded to Poona and thence to Baroda where the Prince witnessed the splendours of an oriental court and enjoyed those manly sports in the neighbouring places which had made India a coveted place to the true sportsman. Coming back to Bombay His Royal Highness proceeded to the Portuguese settlement of Goa and thence to Beypur where he was received by the acting Governor of Madras, the Resident of Travancore and other high officials. The Prince then proceeded to Ceylon where he inspected the various indigenous industries of that colony. His Royal Highness landed in Calcutta on the 23rd December. A grand procession escorted His Royal Highness from the Prinsep's Ghat to the Government House. On the 24th the Prince received the native chiefs then in Calcutta and witnessed the fireworks and afterwards drove through the illuminated streets of the city. After short visits to Barrackpur and the sporting fields near Calcutta His Royal Highness went through many formal ceremonies, conferred an honor on the Calcutta University by accepting the degree of Doctor of Laws from that body and was present at a grand entertainment prepared by the native nobility and gentry at the Belgatchia Villa as a spontaneous demonstration of loyalty. The personal demeanour of His Royal Highness made a most pleasant impression and brushed away those waves of ill-feeling which the bungling of officials clothed in a little brief authority always produces on such occasions. To the solemn dignity in keeping with his exalted position, he united a large heart, and a frankness in accord with his genial nature. At Calcutta His Royal Highness was met by a galaxy of native princes, each with a history of his own and the Prince's cordiality to these feudatory chiefs, bound them by silken cords of loyalty and affection to the paramount power. The native entertainment at a beautiful villa was eminently successful and its value lay chiefly in the fact that the people of the land had got it up without any initiative of the officialdom. His Royal Highness left Calcutta on the 3rd of January 1876 for Bankipur and Benares.

AFGHANISTAN.—We have seen in the last chapter how Yakub Khan was seized and detained by his father Ameer Shere Ali. The Government of India for the first time since the adoption of the policy of non-interference tried to interpose in the internal affairs of Cabul and addressed a *kharita* to the Ameer expressing regret for the imprisonment of Yakub Khan, the occupation of Herat by the Amir's troops and advising him to behave towards his son honorably and faithfully. This *kharita* was certainly a political mistake as it did go far beyond the policy that had been clearly laid down by experience as the safest to adopt towards Cabul. The Amir replied courteously but firmly. He said that it had been found necessary to detain Yakub Khan for disobedience of his orders. He denied that he had ever invited his son to his territories by giving him a safe-conduct. Shere Ali was a diplomat of the first order and by his tact and management of affairs he succeeded always in keeping the upper hand in Afghan affairs. The reply of the Amir could not but be regarded in the light of a snub to the Government of India and Lord Northbrook has to thank himself for it because he brought it about by his officiousness in meddling with matters which was clearly beyond the province of the Government of India. It has been and should always be its policy from which no departure should be permitted that the rivals for the throne should be left to fight out their own quarrels and that the British Government should form its alliance with the successful ruler when he becomes the rightful possessor of the throne.

GENERAL EVENTS.—Two small expeditions were undertaken by the Indian Government on the Eastern frontier of Burma one to avenge the murder of Mr. Margary and the other to quell the rather serious outbreak at Perak which resulted in the murder of the British Resident. The Chinese Government promised to render full reparation for the murder of Mr. Margary and there was no necessity for unsheathing the sword from the scabbard. A dispute with reference to the boundaries of the Karen country made a war imminent with Upper Burma but fortunately the difficulty was solved by a satisfactory settlement. In Bengal Sir Richard Temple's attention was engaged principally in allaying the discontent so rife under his predecessor's regime. The promise to restore two of the native colleges abolished by his predecessor, the Excise reforms that were inaugurated were measures in this direction. The Pubna outrages induced Sir Richard to issue peremptory injunctions to the District officers with reference to the peace of their districts and the battle between the zemindar and the ryot with reference to the rent question was fought out in the Law Courts. The first months of the administration of Sir Rivers Thompson in Upper Burma were marked by two unhappy events, viz., the gunpowder plot and the murder of the Inspector-General of Police when in the act of suppressing a dacoity. The ill-health of Sir John Strachey compelled His Honor to leave the greater part of the administrative work of the North-Western Provinces to his Secretaries, although whenever he did find it possible to apply his vigorous mind to any subject he dealt with it thoroughly. Lord Hobart whose administration of Madras was a very promising one was suddenly cut off in the midst of a useful career and was succeeded by His Grace the Duke of Buckingham and Chandos who arrived at the end of the year, Sir Rose Robinson acting as Governor in the interim. The public attention in the Western Presidency was chiefly occupied with the Baroda trial but the question of the land settlement also came prominently before the public there. The Indian economists are usually divided into two broad classes, one class advocating state landlordism, and the ryotawarry system and the other class egarding the zemindars as an useful institution which serve ran important purpose. In Bombay where cotton cultivation was the means of a perpetual influx of gold the Bombay ryot was in prosperous circumstances and that Presidency was held up as a model province. But when the value of land fell considerably and the assessments of land revenue were considered grinding and oppressive, it was found that the ryots of Bombay lived as much from hand to mouth as those in Madras and the North-West Provinces. The Bombay Government ordered some reduction in the land assessments, recognized the standing evil of the chronic indebtedness of the ryot to the money-lender and appointed a commission to enquire into the whole subject. Lord Northbrook's tour through Rajputana and Central India had a good moral effect on the native princes who always covet the personal friendship of the Viceroy. The most important financial measure of the year was the revision of the Tariff. It was passed at Simla which is impervious to the rays of such public opinion as exists in the country, and the revision of the tariff values of cotton goods, the repeal of the export duties except on three articles which had a hold on the foreign market the revision of import duties, the increase of duty on spirits and wines, led to a considerable loss of revenue amounting nearly to 50 lakhs a year. The Inland trade of the country was benefited by the reduction of some inland customs and by the abolition of others. The trade of the country was year by year becoming duller and duller. The active competition of many rival merchants in the great markets of the world had reduced considerably the profits of the large mercantile establishments and consequently led to heavy reductions in the managing staff. The Bill with reference to special appeals was suspended for the consideration of the suggestion of the Bengal Government with reference to the District Appellate Benches. The Indian Law Reports Act provided for the official reporting of the important decisions of the High Courts and appointed official reporters. The Indian Majority Act introduced into the council by the Maharaja of Vizianagram superseded the Hindu and the Mahomedan laws of majority. India occupied a very small share of the attention of the Imperial Parliament. The deputation of Sir Louis Mallet to elicit all facts and figures on the spot for the Secretary of State on the Tariff question, led to the apprehension that Lord Salisbury might interfere too much in the affairs of India and that the Home Secretary's views might overrule those of the Viceroy, and that the true interests of England might be sacrificed for the propitiation of Manchester.

THE DISCUSSION OF THE ANNUAL BUDGET—In making his financial statement Lord Northbrook explained the reasons as to why he did not summon his council for the last three years to discuss the budget. He said that according to constitutional rules the budget is to be laid before the council for discussion only in the event of a fresh tax becoming necessary, and His Lordship for one was exceedingly glad that such necessity had not arisen during the last three years. He added that in England the financial arrangements underwent considerable changes every year but India there did not exist any of those constitutional reasons for the annual discussion of the budget that existed in England. The wide publicity given to all items of income and expenditure, the ample explanations of the annual estimates and accounts were it was contended sufficient to take the Indian public into confidence. Lord Northbrook however overlooked that the presentation of the budget had one great advantage, it tended to elicit the views of the non-official members on the financial situation, views which in the case of those honorable members who were really representative men would be of great value to the government. The Indian government has advanced to constitutional semblances and a constitutional measure which would give an impetus to the political life of the country was of great importance. The practice of presenting the annual budgets for discussion has been recognized to be a very useful one in later times.

THE COST OF THE PRINCE'S VISIT TO INDIA—The debate on the cost of the Prince's visit to India in the House of

Commons was an important one. The oriental imagination which is apt to associate royalty with an absolute power over the revenues and which could but ill appreciate the grand theory that underlies the constitutional government of England, did naturally think the debate to be rather incongruous and disrespectful. Mr. Fawcett contended that the cost should not be charged on Indian revenues at all as the Prince was not coming out as a representative of the British power. Mr. Disraeli on the other hand moved that £ 30,000 should be charged on the Indian revenues for the fulfilment of the rites of hospitality by India to her future King. The Prince is the Prince of India as well as of England and the payment of his expenses, he added would not be agreeable to the feelings of the people of India. Mr. John Bright sided with Mr. Disraeli. He said that the Prince of Wales was the heir-apparent to the throne of the United Kingdom and he cannot in his travels be divested of that character and that position, that it was reasonable that the Prince of Wales should come to India at least in such state as would commend itself to the ideas the sympathies and the wishes the Indian subjects of Her Majesty. The English empire being greater than all the historic empires from the times of Alexander the Great to those of the Great Corsican hero, the heir to the sceptre of such an empire should travel in regal splendour. Mr. Bright anticipated another great advantage from the Prince's visit to India. He said that the Prince was by all accounts generous, kindly and courteous in a remarkable degree while the English officials in India were just the opposite in the main, in their dealings with the Indian population; that the Royal progress would impress the Indian people with the true character of their future king and the English officials were likely to be very much impressed with the frankness and cordiality of the Royal Tourist towards the Indian subjects of his mother and it would be a decided gain if the Indian officialdom learnt in however small a measure from the conduct of their future king, to be kind and courteous to the native population. This warning from the lips of the old and venerable John Bright would it was expected be listened to and acted up by those for whom it was intended. Mr. Bright had for many years studied Indian subjects with more than the interest of a politician, he had espoused the cause of the myriad millions of India on very important and trying occasions and the repetition of his remarks under the head of the treatment of natives by Europeans which had once found forcible expression in connection with Lord Derby's bill in 1858, amply showed that, in his opinion, the condition of things had not changed for the better. It was earnestly hoped that the Prince's visit would lead to a happy and enduring effect in this direction.

THE NATIVE CIVIL SERVICE.—The Parliamentary papers that were published in the month of July formulated the rules for the creation of a Native Civil Service. These rules aimed at giving the natives of India facility to enter the Civil Service without passing an open competitive test in London. They provided that no appointment should be made without the previous sanction of the Governor-General in Council, that every such appointment should be subject to disallowance by the Secretary of State within twelve months, that each selected candidate must pass a departmental examination within two years, that on the expiration of the probationary term of two years, the appointment would either be cancelled or confirmed, that in case of incompetency or misconduct the appointment might be cancelled before the expiration of the said two years. The power lodged in the Secretary of State was an anomaly as the Governor-General in Council might well be entrusted with the power of making the proper selections without any imputation of jobbery. The weak point in the whole system was the absence of a preliminary qualifying test and this made the series of restrictions necessary. With all these restrictions and with the new set of rules with reference to leave and pensions, the system was not expected to work satisfactorily. The members under this system in cases of alleged misconduct, were not to be tried by a commission but in a hole-and-corner fashion by the local and imperial governments.

THE YARKHAND MISSION.—Sir Douglas Forsyth has been charged with the mission to Yarkhand for the purpose of concluding a commercial treaty with His Highness the Amir of Yarkhand and Kashgar in 1873. The mission arrived at Karagalik the first place of importance in the territories of the Amir on the 5th November and reached Kashgar itself on the 4th of December. The account of the mission given by Sir Douglas is very interesting. He describes the signs of prosperity and civilization all along the way and especially notices the hospitality of the villagers. The first appearance of the English ambassador and his suite excited the lively curiosity of the inhabitants and during their whole stay they did not meet with the slightest rudeness or incivility, with no scowling looks or angry taunts. At the first interview with the Atalik as the chief was called, there was a long and trying pause and etiquette forbade the guests to speak much on that occasion. As the English officers scrupulously paid for every article they purchased they created a favourable impression and an advantageous commercial treaty was concluded. Mr. Disraeli was bent on strengthening the position of India with reference to foreign invasion and the mission to Yarkhand as well as the gaining of an immense influence in Egypt by purchasing the Khedive's shares in the Suez Canal were measures in this direction that were managed by the English foreign office in fulfilment of the imperial policy of the Prime Minister.

CHAPTER VIII.

1876.

THE PRINCE OF WALE'S VISIT TO INDIA—We have narrated in the last Chapter the progress of the tour of His Royal Highness in India. When the present year opened three fourths of the programme of his Indian tour had been completed. In the beginning of this year His Royal Highness visited Benares whence he come to Lucknow where the native soldiers who had remained steadfast in their loyalty to the British crown during the dark days of the Indian Mutiny were presented to His Royal Highness. From Lucknow the Prince of Wales proceeded to the latter capital of the Great Moghul, where had been assembled a large number of troops both for giving an opportunity to His Royal Highness who was a Field-Marshal in the British army, to judge of the appearance and efficiency of the vast body of soldiers before him and for the purposes of a great military demonstration, which it was thought necessary in a country under a foreign government and with perpetual complications on the western border. From Delhi His Highness' route was marked by a visit to the Panjab including a visit to the winter capital of the Maharaja of Cashmir. The Royal Tourist then came to Agra where he was splendidly received by Sir John Strachey the officials of the North-Western Provinces and the many ruling chiefs who had assembled there to meet His Highness. The series of entertainments given to the Prince at Agra were pronounced to be singularly brilliant and successful. His Royal Highness visited the capitals of the Maharajas of Gwalior and Jeypur, and then after a protracted stay in the Terai where Sir Jung Bahadur did his best to make the visit a pleasant one came down to Allahabad where many of the members of the Prince's suite received honors at the hands of the Indian Government and then proceeded to Bombay stopping at Indore on the way. He re-embarked for England about the middle of March. The Indian Historian, who must record this visit of one who is in the usual course of things, destined to be the future Emperor of India, must not stop with merely giving the details of the programme of the Royal Tour, or the unrivalled splendours that the imaginative and sentimental people of the East, displayed in honor of the Royal guest, but must attempt briefly to dwell on the actual and net results of the Royal tour. The average native mind in India could but comprehend with great difficulty that the Prince of Wales was not a representative of his august mother that he had no right while in India to attend to a petition, or to issue orders to remedy a grievance or to make any grants of money or land to any body who might please him. His only motive in undertaking this tour was to acquaint himself with the condition of the country and see with his own eyes the splendid Eastern Empire with its teeming millions over which he would one day be called upon to preside. But His Royal Highness' progress through the country gave the Indian princes and people a very fitting opportunity to display their sentiments of loyalty. Loyalty in the Eastern mind is always associated with the person of the reigning sovereign. As Mr. Walter Bagehot truly remarks, the masses of the people in every country can but little understand the principles of constitutional government and the feelings of devoted and abiding loyalty to the British crown, could fittingly, demonstrate themselves in the presence of the heir-apparent to the splendid possessions of the British crown. His Royal Highness and the members of his suite also distinguished themselves on all occasions by that courtsey and affability of manners, which is one of the most prominent characteristics of the genuine Englishman, and they brought soon after their arrival in England to the notice of the Secretary of the State, the fact that a wide gulf existed as regards all relations outside of the official sphere, among the European residents and the native subjects of Her Majesty. This is a condition of things, to whatever causes it may be due, that has been admitted and much regretted by all eminent thinkers who have grasped the situation. The Royal Tour produced a great addition to the amount of interest felt by England in India. The leading English newspapers had their representatives with the Royal camp to chronicle the doings of the Prince of Wales and although in some instances they had been misinformed as to certain matters, the amount of information which they had taken away with them would serve materially to increase the interest of Englishmen with reference to this country about which unfortunately such a large amount of ignorance prevails in England. Nor should we omit to record that although a large amount of money was spent in the displays which were undertaken to make the Royal visit an imposing one, yet a good many works of public usefulness were commenced in all parts of India as permanent memorials of the Royal visit. The only direct result ascribed to the Royal Tour in India is the assumption by the Queen of the title of Empress of India which was proclaimed with so much ceremony at Delhi on the first day of the next year. Some indirect consequences of the Royal visit were also of the undesirable sort. Some of the native chiefs who are always in a state of chronic deficit had to incur long journeys to meet His Royal Highness as well as to receive His Royal Highness in their Capitals and this additional strain on their already exhausted treasury had made them very much involved and in some instances their subjects had to pay heavier burdens. His Royal Highness and the members of his suite were also of opinion that the treatment received by natives of India at the hands of the English official classes was unsatisfactory. The Secretary of State and the Viceroy took up the matter, and instructed the average Englishman to treat the inferior and the weaker race with kindness and consideration. It is admitted on all hands that in the present state of things there cannot be complete social intercourse between the rulers and the ruled classes and nothing could be more lamentable than the wide gulf which separated the two classes in this country. The historian cannot shut his eyes to the fact that history affords no parallel of such complete isolation between the dominant people and the subject race. It goes beyond question that a thorough knowledge of the wants and feelings of the governed is an essential condition of the success of the governing body. In the old days of the East India Company, the European servants of that body adopted this country almost as their home. They could revisit their native land only at distant intervals and the natives looked upon them as their patrons being in turn looked upon as protege. But the improved furlough rules, the abundance of European settlers, the three week's passage to England, the telegraphic cable, and the assertion of the varied rights and privileges to which the natives of the country are entitled, have completely altered the state of things and the European now comes to the country with the intention of leaving it as soon as possible. It is also apparent that under the invigorating influence of that western education which our benign Government has provided, the educated natives of India are not prepared to carry on friendly intercourse with the European under the old conditions. It is universally felt, for many years past that something should be done to bring the two races together that they might meet as friends and acquire mutual confidence. It is well-known that a liberal education ought to be the best means for this end. It cannot be expected that a native of India who is not trained in the western methods, should appreciate European ideas or take delight in the rich conversation of well-informed Englishmen. There can be no doubt that Englishmen cannot feel friendship for those who see them merely for selfish ends, who are not ashamed to tell an untruth and whose demeanour is cringing. The foundation of the friendship between the two races must be on English education. Without this on the part of the native there can be no sincere and familiar intercourse between him and the Englishman, and the intellectual native knows very well that introduction to refined European Society will do him a great deal of good and is in fact the means to keep up culture and intellectuality in his case. The educated natives must learn and unlearn a good deal before they can be admitted to European Society. At the same time there cannot be a greater mistake than the one which is entertained by those Englishmen who are strongly prejudiced against us and which belief is unfortunately given currency to by the Press in times of unusual excitement that there cannot be a true gentleman among the natives. The natives had been trained under a different society altogether and many traits in their character which appear objectionable can be gradually removed. If the leaders of the community on either side should take their stand on a broad platform, and be prepared to overcome the strong prejudices of years, a most encouraging advance would be made. Of late years, some attempts had been made in the direction with a fair amount of success but that a good deal yet remains to be done is acknowledged universally. Let every well-wisher of the country hope that in years to come the matter would be placed on a much better and more improved footing than heretofore, and the question of any individual's being a gentleman would be judged not by the conventional forms peculiar to any nation but by these broad principles which are universally recognized.

Lord Northbrook's Resignation—Scarcely had the Royal progress come to an end when it was declared that Lord Northbrook had placed his resignation of his exalted office in the hands of the home authorities. The reason for this step was widely discussed at the time and appear to be some unfortunate differences of opinion with the Marquis of Salisbury. The noble Marquis has severely censured the Earl of Northbrook for having passed the Tariff Act at a brief sitting of the Legislative Council at Simla, in the absence of the non-official members and without any reference to the India office. It is well-known that the Marquis of Salisbury had in a moment of weakness pledged the Government of India to the abolition of the cotton duties and the sop that was offered by the Government of India to Manchester in the shape of the Tariff Act was contemptuously rejected by her. Lord Northbrook sought to vindicate his proceedings with reference to the Tariff Act and he stoutly maintained the retention of the cotton duties. Sir Louis Mallet was deputed by the Secretary of State to confer with the Viceroy on the subject which step Lord Northbrook took as an insult and he had no alternative but to retire from a position which he could not keep up any longer with any degree of self-respect. These proceedings of the Marquis of Salisbury raised the important constitutional question in England as to the amount of independence and discretion that the Viceroy is usually expected to enjoy. Lord Salisbury had moreover directed the Viceroy to refer all legislative and financial measures to the Home Government before they were laid on the Indian Council Board. Lord Halifax, the Duke of Argyll, and Lord Lawrence argued against governing India from England and thereby seriously diminishing the authority of the Viceroy. The debate on this subject was renewed by Lord Northbrook after he came from India when the Marquis of Salisbury conceded that while the initiative in all measures must rest with the Government of India no claim to independence on the part of that body could be entertained. It was also settled at the same time that the cotton duties might be retained till the Indian finances were sufficiently flourishing to justify this repeal. The British Indian Association of Calcutta organized a movement to do honor to Lord Northbrook and to commemorate his services in a grand manner. A public meeting of his Lordship's admirers was held under the presidency of Sir Richard Temple and a statue was voted to His Lordship.

LORD NORTHBROOK'S ADMINISTRATION —Lord Northbrook's administration was much criticised at the time of his retirement and almost diametrically opposite views were taken of it. It is the duty of the historian to view it as a whole without the passion or prejudice of contemporary critics and regarded in this light the impartial verdict of history must approve of several measures of his administration and condemn others. Coming after Lord Mayo when the ways and means of the Empire were administered with a rather light heart, His Lordship's merits as a financier stand conspicuous. He continued to enforce a strict economy and he maintained a healthy equilibrium between income and expenditure. Works of public utility were continued without having any recourse to additional taxation or raising inordinately heavy loans. There were remissions both of Imperial and Local taxation. The Income-tax was allowed to die a natural death, evoking the livliest gratitude throughout the country; non-agricultural cess was withdrawn in Bombay; the general house-tax was abandoned in Madras; the proposed increase of Municipal taxation was disallowed in Bengal; the pandari tax was reduced in the Central Provinces. The Southern Customs line was abolished. The Viceroy proceeded very cautiously in all matters relating to expenditure from the Imperial Exchequer and consequently a large reduction of taxation became possible. This was indeed a great merit in a Viceroy and history must give Lord Northbrook fullest credit for being an able financier. His Lordship's urbanity, his munificence, his steady and conscientious adherance to duty, his businesslike qualities, his single-minded devotion, his earnest anxiety to achieve in all directions the welfare of those committed to his charge, his entire subordination of all personal and selfish considerations to the public good, and his generous appreciation of similar qualities in others, are all universally admitted. In the reply that Lord Northbrook gave to the valedictory address, he said that he had introduced no new policy but had endeavored to adhere to those principles laid down by Her Majesty on assuming the direct Government of India. His famine policy, though involving much useless expenditure showed the purity and benevolence of his intentions and he certainly achieved a moral victory as great as any that shine conspicuously in the pages of history. In the matter of the cotton duties Lord Northbrook had no option and history cannot endorse the language of the valedictory address voted at the Calcutta meeting that it was a liberal or enlightened commercial policy or that it was dictated by the highest consideration for the best interests of India. Lord Northbrook's conduct of foreign affairs was hardly creditable to him. He was unwise in the remonstrance that he addressed to Amir Shere Ali, on his throwing his rebellious son into prison, to which representation the Amir paid but little heed. There was a widespread conviction that the deposition of Mulhar Rao was a foregone conclusion of the Government of India and though Lord Northbrook proved the purity of his intentions as regards further territorial aggrandisement by the restoration of native rule and placing a statesman of the stamp of Sir. T. Madhava Rao as the head of affairs, his Baroda policy was strongly condemned by even such temperate politicians as Kristo Das Paul. The Nizam of Hyderabad was strongly displeasd at Lord Northbrook's insisting on his presence at Bombay although he was unwell to receive the Prince of Wales. He mismanaged the affairs of Khelat which fell from bad to worse and it was not until the closing hours of his reign that he adopted the policy of reconciling the Khan to his rebellious sirdars by British arbitration a policy carried to a successful issue by his successor. We have the assurance of those who were associated with him in the task of administration, that he had the question of the more extended employment of natives of India closely at heart although he was unable to arrive at any satisfactory solution of the difficulty. His treatment however of the native civilian who got into a scrape during his reign as compared with his treatment of the two European civilians similarly situated showed a remarkable narrowness of mind. His rejection of the nomination by Sir George Campbell of the Editor of the *Friend of India* to a seat in the Bengal Council was hardly compatible with a genuine breadth of mind though he partially retrieved the error by the confirmation of the nomination by Sir Richard Temple of Kristo Das Paul, Editor of the *Hindu Patriot* to a similar honor. We have gone into these details to concentrate all the blemishes that have been ascribed to his administration. His administration on the whole however was satisfactory and when we reflect on the immense responsibilities of an Indian Viceroy we can scarcely with a reason complain against some occasional acts which we cannot bring ourselves to approve. History however must accord to him the highest credit for the purity of his intentions, even though he may have done some acts which all cannot approve of.

LORD LYTTON.—Lord Northbrook was succeeded in the Indian Viceroyalty by Lord Lytton. The son of a well-known peer who had written a number of delightful novels, he had imbibed his father's literary tastes. He had been brought up in the diplomatic service and had previously to his being sent to India occupied a number of high offices outside England. He had been offered the Governorship of Madras on the death of Lord Hobart but he had declined the offer on the ground of ill health. His Lordship was however prevailed upon to accept the Viceroyalty. As the appointment followed the unfortunate Tarff controversy and as Lord Lytton had been brought up in the Diplomatic service, the English press which is often too outspoken insinuated that the Viceroy would lack the brains to think and act for himself. The first acts of the new Viceroy gave unmistakeable proofs of his ability and independence. He broke through the usual routine practice by addressing the members of his Executive Council on his assuming office. He overruled the decision of the member of his Executive Council in the matter of the grant made from the provincial revenues by Sir John Strachey towards the erection fund of the Roman Catholic Cathedral at Allahabad, and approved the action of Sir John. His minute on the unfortunate Fuller Case excited a good deal of public attention both in England and India. It happened that the native press had been persistently keeping alive the fact that Mr. Fuller had been let off with a notoriously light punishment for killing his groom, that the medical report as to the man's having died of ruptured spleen did not extenuate his guilt. Mr. Fuller was charged at Agra by the trying magistrate with an offence under sec. 323 I. P. C. and very lightly punished. The matter had been disposed of six months before Lord Lytton had arrived in the country. But His Lordship found persistent complaints in the press that there had often been lamentable failures of justice in all cases in which Europeans were charged with having killed the poorer classes of natives in this country. He called for an official report of the affair from the Lieutenant-Governor N. W. P. who in turn took the opinion of the N. W. P. High Court. When all these papers had been laid before him the Viceroy severely censured the Magistrate who had tried Mr. Fuller, as well as the High Court and the Lieutenant-Governor because they did not think it their duty to take any notice of the Magistrate's conduct. The whole Anglo-Indian press came down upon the Viceroy and abused him in no measured terms. The Judges of the Allahabad High Court also remonstrated with the Viceroy for having exercised authority over them and strongly recommended a re-consideration of the case of the Magistrate who had tried Mr. Fuller. The Viceroy declined to remit the punishment which he had inflicted upon Mr. Leeds, and forwarded the remonstrance of the High Court to the Secretary State for disposal. The constitutional question raised by the High Court was one which was easily disposed of by the Secretary of State. He rightly held that the Judges had merely expressed an informal opinion, and that they had never considered the case in their judicial capacity. The Viceroy was therefore clearly within his powers in acting as he did. Lord Lytton however took a different line of action in the Thullier-Macdonald case. Colonel Macdonald had sought to serve the public by exposing the mal administration of the expensive department over which Colonel

Thullier presided. Instead of enquiring into the truth of the allegations made by Colonel Macdonald the Viceroy adopted the convenient and easy method of galling his mouth and punishing him severely as a warning to the officials who might feel disposed to follow his example. Lord Lytton also courted unpopularity by allowing his name to be associated with the Resolution of the Government of India which prohibits the public servants from memoralising as a body. Lord Lytton as might have been expected did display great ability in at once grasping the Foreign affairs of the Empire. Through his skilful management the Khan of Khilat was reconciled to his rebellious sirdars and solemnly ratified an agreement by which he and his chiefs bound themselves to refer all future quarrels to British arbitration instead of fighting with each other. If Lord Northbrook had adopted in 1872 the vigorous policy that he was forced by the Panjab authorities to pursue in 1875 some sort of responsible Government would have been established. The new Viceroy also displayed sound discretion in negativing the proposed expedition against the Afridis. If he had played himself into the hands of the soldiers who are only too anxious to obtain an easy occasion for making their name he would have sanctioned an operation which would have entailed much loss of blood and money without securing any advantage in return. The blockade that existed for sometime cost nothing and the blockaded Afridi tribe soon came to their senses.

General Events.—The Royal Titles Bill which empowered the Queen to assume the title of Empress of India caused a considerable amount of excitement in England. The English people were afraid that the new title would be used by the Queen in England, that this new title would imply some further stretch of prerogative and that the other members of the Royal family would assume other titles and claim greater allowances. The resentment of the English public was at last appeased by the assurance that the use of the new title would be restricted to India and that the members of the Royal family in England would retain their existing designations. The depreciation of silver excited also considerable attention in England and India. Lord George Hamilton announced that the Government would pursue the policy of masterly inactivity until a satisfactory solution of the complicated problem was discovered. Mr. Goschen who as chairman of the silver Depreciation Committee has had peculiarly favorable opportunities of forming an opinion on the subject declared that no living man could foretell the future of the white metal. The only satisfactory feature in the debate on the subject was the announcement that the Government has strongly set its face against what Mr. Fawcett happily termed "currency rostrums." The Secretary of State considerably modified Sir Barrow Ellis's bill named the Bombay Revenue Jurisdiction Bill which was a retrograde measure. The Oudh Land Revenue Bill was passed in October this year. The Talukdars secured some privileges under this act but the status conferred on the subordinate proprietors was far from satisfatory. The Belgian publicist M. de Lavalaya had made a statement that Lord Canning had purchased the support of the Oudh Talukdars in quelling the Mutiny in an easy cheap and convenient way by recognizing the position they had, during the misrule preceding the annexation, usurped. Lord Lytton attempted to answer this assertion, but the Indian public did not accept his statements in preference to the facts that history record. Sir Richard Temple left Bengal this year on special duty at the expiration of which he was appointed to the Governorship of Bombay. During the last year of his rule there were several miscarriages of justice, which excited considerable attention in Bengal. We need not keep alive in the pages of history the details of these cases, and the chief complaint of the Bengal press was that the officers concerned had not been adequately punished. The cyclone and storm wave on the sea-board districts of Bengal plunged upwards of two lakhs of human beings into a watery grave. Sir Richard Temple with his characteristic energy visited the scene of disaster and made arrangements for the relief of distress occasioned by the catastrophe. A change also occurred in the personal of the Government of the N. W. P. in the year under review. Sir John Strachey had never been in good health since he assumed the Lieutenant-Governorship and as a matter of course he could not do much work himself. Almost everything had been left to his Secretaries and Departmental heads. Towards the middle of the year he became worse and was obliged to apply for six months' leave to proceed to Europe to consult a first-class oculist. Sir John in spite of his acknowledged ability and vigor could not leave his mark on the N. W. P. A few days before he went on leave he completed the subordination of the District Superintendent of Police to the District Magistrate and reduced the former to the position of an assistant to the latter in the Police Department. Sir George Couper, Chief Commissioner of Oudh was appointed to that appointment. Sir George Couper had to apply himself at once to the task of retrenchment but with the exception of the abolition of three important appointments which affected the European bigwigs his operations were confined to unimportant reductions of the cheese-paring type. Sir Henry Davies the Lieutenant-Governor of the Panjab was granted a twelve months' extension of office, as there was no eligible man ready to take his place and he was himself too young to retire from public service. The question as to Simla being the summer residence of the Viceroy was discussed, it being decided to retain it and to improve its sanitation at considerable cost. Mr. Inglis who officiated as Chief Commissioner of Oudh during a considerable part of the year introduced two important changes. The Revenue instalments of the province were altered with very great advantage, and he abolished the costly special agency that managed the encumbered estates in Oudh. There can be no doubt that this latter was a step in the right direction. The creation of Assam into a separate administration was justified on the ground that the Chief Commissioner would devote his undivided energies towards developing the great natural resources of that territorial area but Colonel Keatinge the first Chief Commissioner did not fulfill the expectations that had been formed of him. The cost of administering Assam had increased considerably while no correspondig benefits could be shown. Sir William Muir proposed the amalgamation of Assam with Bengal, and though the subject was re-considered, the proposal was negatived. In the Central Provinces Mr. Morris did a great deal towards developing the coal and iron deposits of that territory. Mr. Morris also elaborated a very important colonization scheme. His plan was to draw the colonists from the famine-stricken districts of Madras and Bombay and to settle them in the Charwa jungle in the Hoshengabad district. The Sleepy Hollow as the Madras Presidency was generally called was aroused by the case of Mr. Weld who had offered a wanton insult to a dead *Sanyasi*, who was looked upon as a saint by his fellows. Under no circumstances could the exhumation of the corpse have been justified when the heirs of the deceased had offered to construct such works as might be considered necessary to prevent percolation. The Duke of Buckingham summoned a famine conference to consider the impending famine. In Bombay, in the Deccan and the Southern Maharatta country the famine attracted a good deal of attention towards the close of the year. In the early part of the distress the loss of cattle was fearful. The Government of Sir Philip Wodehouse made an almost useless appeal to the officers of the Forest Department to relax their strict regulations. A more practical step was taken when the Government helped the people to transport their cattle to the Ghats and provided pasture lands for them. The price of grain in the Bombay famine area was steadily improving at the close of the year. Relief works had been set-up for the able-bodied poor while the old and infirm were being charitably provided for. British Burmah made much quiet progress and there were considerable administrative improvements in Baroda, Indore, Kasmir and Jeypur. The young chief of Pattiala died and his state was placed under a Council of Regency.

CHAPTER IX.

1877.

THE IMPERIAL ASSEMBLAGE—The year opened with the Imperial assemblage at Delhi where it was publicly proclaimed that Her Gracious Majesty would henceforth be styled in all public documents as far as India was concerned by the title of *Empress*. The matter had been the subject of correspondence between the Viceroy and the Earl of Beaconsfield for a considerable time past and when the step was finally determined upon it was the theme of a lively debate in the Houses of Parliament. The Earl of Beaconsfield in his speech on the Royal Titles Bill, took up several grounds to justify the assumption of this title of dignity by Queen Victoria. It had been contended that there was no necessity for the step, that the mere change of title should not be proclaimed with unusual pomp and that this ceremonial would involve an useless amount of expenditure, which could be ill spared at a time when there was a famine scourging Southern India. Lord Beaconsfield however argued that a title went much with the people of India as with all Eastern people, that this step would cement the unity of the different parts of the empire and in view of the shifting phases of European politics such a demonstration was essentially necessary for the safety of England's position in the East. The Government motion carried the day and the 1st of January 1877 was fixed upon as the date for the assumption of this title by Her Majesty. In India the idea of holding the Imperial assemblage was opposed on several grounds. The native princes, it was pointed out had been much indebted by their lavish expenditure on the the occasion of the visit of His Royal Highness the Prince of Wales, the previous year and to require them at that juncture to proceed to Delhi was still further to embarass their resources. The famine had assumed a rather terrible appearance in the Southern Presidency and serious efforts were necessary to grapple with the distress in that quarter. It was urged moreover that the India of these days was not the India of old and that a mere pageant of this kind would not be thought much of by the thinking classes among the population who were the real leaders of native thought. But His Excellency the "Poet Viceroy" as he was called knocked all these objections on the head and with the dramatic instincts of a novelist and a poet, he resolved to have a show and a pageant in right Imperial fashion. The pangs of hunger of the starving peasantry of the Deccan were for a time shelved aside from the counsels of the empire and preparations began on a truly magnificent scale. The city of Delhi well lent itself for such an assemblage. It was the historical capital of India even in Hindu times, and it is popularly ascribed as the scene of many of those great incidents commemorated by the Mahabharata. Coming down to more recent times, it was the capital of Prithiraj the ruins of whose palace and fort are yet to be seen, not far away from the modern city. It was the central spot of Islamic history in India, the chosen abode of six successive dynasties who held imperial sway in a more or less scale. In the later days of the Mogul Empire, it was the most magnificent city in the East, the city of culture, intelligence and almost fabulous wealth. Its fame had drawn many a freebooter from the wilds of Tartary and Central Asia. It occupies a prominent place in all literature, in all poetry, in all history for six unbroken centuries. Its name appeals even to-day more powerfully to the imagination of the people in all parts of India than those of Calcutta or Bombay which have now far outgrown it in wealth and importance. Such was the city, the city of Kutub Minar and of Peacock throne where the Mutiny had its centre in recent times and which is still one of the most active marts, and beautiful cities in India that was selected for the purposes of this grand assemblage. The Presidency Governors, the Provincial Lieutenant-Governors and Chief Commissioners, many high Civil, Military and Political officers and about 70 ruling chiefs, and a vast concourse of spectators, including the Governor-General of the Portuguese settlements in India, the Khan of Khelat, the deputation representing the Sultan of Muscat, the envoy from Khasgar, the Ambassadors from the king of Siam and the Maharajah of Nepal, the Consular officers of Foreign Governments and nobles and gentlemen from every part of India were present on that memorable day to witness the proceedings. The modern city of Delhi could ill afford to accomodate such a vast number of illustrious guests, and the greater part of the dignitaries were encamped in the plains outside the city for many miles around. To give a solemnity to the occasion honorific titles and other marks of the sovereign's favor were scattered with sufficient generosity a number of prisoners both civil and criminal were set at liberty. An imperial banner was presented to each ruling chief, honors and titles were conferred on many of them and the salutes of a few were increased. On the 1st of January it was announced that henceforth the salutes for the royal flag and for the Viceroy and Governor-General would be 31 guns. The historian might well pass over the details of the ceremonial, the processions, the formal interviews, the formal durbars and the formal greetings and speeches. His Excellency's speech on the occasion though creditable to him as a scholar was hardly so as a political officer or a statesman of a high rank. It had been fondly hoped that the occasion would be availed of, for making a few graceful concessions to the claims of the educated public opinion in India the reasonableness of some of which had been admitted by the highest authorities and that some fresh declaration would be made in pursuance of the policy of the Parliamentary act of 1870, which as far as the employment of natives of India to high offices of the state went, had been as inadequately performed as the act of 1832. Lord Lytton admitted that the educated natives of India could reasonably aspire to a share in the Government of their own country and even went so far as to concede that this claim was founded on the highest justice, but he said that the natives of India had not yet deserved what they desired. He went on to add moreover that the middle classes had no claim to employment, that when those who by birth, rank and hereditary influence were the natural leaders of society had fitted themselves and their children for the honorable duty open to them by accepting the only education that could enable them to comprehend and practice the principles steadily maintained by the Government of Her Majesty it would only then be time to cordially welcome their co-operation in the work of administration. This view of the matter was not only in direct conflict with the principles reiterated by the most solemn resolutions of the sovereign and the Parliament but went to the root of the principle of competitive examination for the public offices in England and was one of those exploded theories which Sir Arthur Helps and Lord Macaulay almost disdained to notice when discussing the advantages of the competitive system. The historian is not concerned with exposing the hollowness of this view at this fag-end of the nineteenth century but the Viceregal utterances convinced the Indian public that the solemn assurances of the sovereign with reference to all employments under the state in 1833 and 1858 were almost on a par with those which the Sublime Porte held out for some time to its Christian subjects for the reformation of the provinces which they inhabited. Altogether the Imperial assemblage left behind it but little tangible results. The political philosophers say that it is occasionally prudent and politic to impress both the people of India and the foreign rulers with the grandeur and stability of British rule, and that this magnificent assemblage did something of the kind admits of no doubt. Only those who are in the secrets of the English Foreign Office can say whether in view of the existing state of things in Europe, this was a fit season for such an affair. In imitation of the grand doings at Delhi, smaller durbars and gatherings with attendant pomp took place at every headquarters of the Indian districts.

THE FAMINE IN THE SOUTHERN PRESIDENCY.—The Famine in Madras had been an accomplished fact long before the Delhi festivities were over, and Lord Lytton had to confer on the subject with the Governors of Bombay and Madras during their presence in Delhi. Sir John Strachey who had been appointed Finance minister had joined his post shortly before the assemblage and he disliked the method by which the Duke of Buckingham was grappling with the Famine. He converted Lord Lytton to his views and under his counsels Sir Richard Temple was appointed as the Famine Delegate with instructions from the Supreme Government as to how the famine was to be managed. The letter of instructions contained some allusion to the principles of famine relief, and it was laid down that the task of saving life irrespective of cost was one which the Supreme Government could not undertake. The truth is that the Government of India had up to that time no well-defined famine policy. Lord Lawrence went to one extreme in 1865-66, and Lord Northbrook went to the other in 1873-74. It was however evident that what the latter did could not be repeated. Famines were not rare occurrences in the country and if every famine was to be managed on the scale of the Behar operations of 1873-74, a sum of two millions sterling must be continually set aside for the purpose and there could be no doubt that the finances of India did not admit of this expenditure. It was certain that from the very necessity of the case there would be a reaction in a short time against that policy, which was first assailed by Mr. Eustace Smith's motion in the House of Commons for enquiring into the management of the Behar Famine. The principal thing to which Sir John devoted his attention was to secure economy. He protested against making promises of remissions of land revenue to people suffering from the famine, he summarily sent away from the relief works women who wore any ornaments and men who were thought possessed of some resources of their own and he restricted admission to those works, and above all he invented the famous "bare subsistence" scale of wages. The Government of India took offence with the Madras Government not for neglecting the famine but for doing too much. One pound a day was declared sufficient to sustain human life and operations being carried on on this basis, the mortality was returned within a few months at half a million deaths. The Madras Government on the advice of their Sanitary Commissioner protested against this scale of subsistence and the Marquis of Salisbury after consultation with the medical officers of the India office sent instructions to modify the "Temple subsistence" scale of wages. These instructions however arrived late and before they arrived a good deal of mischief had been done. The North-East Monsoon rains again failed and the Duke of Buckingham being dissatisfied with the way in which the famine was being dealt with appealed to private charity in aid of the sufferers. The matter then assumed an aspect sufficiently serious for the Viceroy to go there in person. With Lord Lytton's visit to the south which had unfortunately been too long deferred came a better state of things. Good understanding was restored between the Imperial and the Provincial Governments, and the Duke of Buckingham cordially accepted the famine policy of the Government of India. He assumed the management of the famine with General Kennedy as his personal assistant. Under this system much good was done and real relief was given to the suffering people. Lord Lytton definitely shaped his famine policy in a minute dated the 12th August 1877, in which he said that the Government was determined to avert death by starvation by the employment of all means practically open to the resources of the state and the exertions of its officers. Extensive works in which a large number of laborers could be concentrated under professional supervision were directed to be opened. Gratuitous relief was to be subsidiary to the main object of getting people on the relief works, and the Viceroy explained that he did not think it fit to call upon the people for contribution because they would have to bear the burthen of taxation for famine purposes. Lord Lytton also visited Mysore, where the famine administration had been placed in the hands of Mr. C. A. (afterwards Sir

Charles) Elliott, and where the number of victims was considerably less. All these measures were too long postponed and the want of timely measures had kept the local authorities altogether unprepared to meet the catastrophe. As it was, the entire affair was a sad one. The human victims of the famine numbered by millions, the immense cost incurred on relief works produced no permanent results, and the famine administration of Southern India would remain in the eyes of posterity a deep blot on the reputation of Lord Lytton, whose intentions however were always good.

THE FRONTIER QUESTION.—The Frontier Question assumed an unusual complexity during this and the next year. Lord Lytton had been expressly entrusted with carrying out what afterwards came to be known as the "forward frontier policy" of the Beaconsfield cabinet which consisted in the apt words of Kristo Das Paul, in shaking England's fist in the face of Russia across the Indian border. The Russian was displaying at this time unusual activities in Europe. The Sultan at Constantinople did not pay any heed to the clamour of his Christian subjects for the reformation of the provinces inhabited by them and these Christians who were members of the Greek Church openly asked for the assistance of the Russian sovereign. Russia was only too willing to avail herself of any plausible excuse for interfearance and if possible for open hostilities with Turkey. The Great European powers could not look on with unconcern at any disturbance of the balance of power in Europe which was certain to take place in case Turkey was allowed to fight Russia single-handed as the old man of Europe was sure to be foiled in such a struggle. A conference of the great powers took place at Constantinople, in which England was represented by the Marquis of Salisbury. Nothing came out of this conference. It was expected that the great powers would not be able to agree as to the terms to be imposed upon Turkey, but though this agreement was arrived at, Turkey displayed an unusual vigor in refusing to accept the terms proposed. It is said that Turkey was supported in this refusal by the Earl of Beaconsfield. The people of Russia had become pledged to the deliverance of their oppressed brethern and had determined that if that object was not to be attained by means of diplomacy it must be attained by war. It has been said that Russia had from the first made up her mind to appeal to the sword and that her professions to preserve the peace of Europe were utterly hollow. But it has been established by the most recent investigations that the Russian Government had not finally decided on war until a very short time before the actual declaration of hostilities. It was not till the beginning of April that any serious measures were taken. The peace-loving Alexander II was placed under the painful necessity of declaring war on the 25th April last. The war it was anticipated would be a mere "walk over" to Constantinople. The veteran military heads all over Europe laughed at the idea of the Turks having anything of the ancient stamina left in them to encounter effectually the legions of the Cossacks. But the Turks did in reality offer a stubborn resistance. They had many advantages as compared with the Russians. They did not fear death, in battle they were more anxious to lose their lives than to save them. They were savage barbarians and were not much hampered by considerations of humanity. They were little troubled with impediments, their food was simple and they were but nominally paid. It is not necessary for the Indian Historian to enter into the details of the war which are in themselves sufficient to fill a volume. When the present year closed the war had been going on for several months with varying fortune in Erzeroum, Armenia and the adjoining provinces. Plevna after sustaining heroically a siege of five months had just surrendered unconditionally to the Russians. We, who live in times when the movements of the Russians absorb almost the whole care of the Supreme Government can readily understand that in the days of the Russo-Turkish war, the Government of India and the English Foreign Office were unusally vigilant and every slight trace of Russian influence in Afghanistan was resented. Early this year it appeared that the Government of India and the Amir of Cabul were not on the best of terms. Shere Ali had refused to attend the Delhi Imperial assemblage. Before the arrival of Lord Lytton in India Major Sandeman had been deputed by Lord Northbrook to place the relations between the Khan and the Sirdars on a satisfactory footing. Lord Lytton on arrival suspected Russian intrigues in Beloochistan and made that a pretext for occupying Quetta. This step naturally unsettled the Amir of Cabul who looked upon it as a direct menace to his country. He demanded explanation from the British Government and the Peshawar conference was the result. Syed Noor Mahomed the Vizier of Cabul came to Peshawar to confer with Sir Lewis Pelley about certain new arrangements proposed to be entered with Amir Shere Ali. The British Government through its plenipotentiary produced a treaty empowering it to establish a permanent resident at Cabul and to occupy Herat and Kandahar in the event of a Russian advance on Merv. Shere Ali himself shared in the profound distrust of his subjects with reference to the English people and he seems to have been of the opinion that if he once allowed the English a footing in his country they would end by annexing it. Under such circumstances it is a matter of little surprise that the treaty was declined. The British Government on Shere Ali's declining the offered treaty informed him that the verbal promises made to him at Umballa by Lord Mayo in the spring of 1869 were no longer binding on the Government of India. This reply was taken by the Amir as a direct threat to declare hostilities and he began to make military preparations. The public mind in India was considerably disquieted and every sort of rumour was circulated in the bazaars. On the occasion of the budget debate Lord Lytton made a speech to explain the real state of the border affairs. The Viceroy said that the Government of India wished to have a belt of independent states on the frontier where the British name would be honored and trusted, forgetting that the rude tribes on the frontier and in Afghanistan would not trust the British. The Viceroy however assured the public that the military preparations on the border were not intended for a great military campaign against our neighbours and that "to rush into purposeless border warfare or to provoke hostilities with any of our immediate neighbours would be an act of insanity." In order to bring border politics under his direct management Lord Lytton proposed to combine the Panjab and Scinde frontiers into one administration under the immediate control of the Foreign Department. The publication of the Khelat blue-book showed that the object of the occupation of Quetta was solely to checkmate alleged Russian intrigues in Beloochistan. As a similar attempt with reference to Cabul failed, the Government went to the length of asking the sublime Porte to intercede on its behalf with Amir Shere Ali. An envoy extraordinary accordingly came to Cabul from Turkey but could not convince the Amir of the desirability of forming an alliance with the English against the Muscovite. The press which was in the secrets of the Government began to talk about the end of the year, of having discovered Russian intrigues at Cabul with the evident object of preparing the public mind for a second invasion of Afghanistan. It will be seen from the above resume of events that Lord Lytton was the first to introduce into India that forward Imperial policy which has since become almost a factor of Indian administration. What the merits or demerits of that policy are, it does not become the historian to discuss at this stage. The Afghan people have, it is idle to conceal, a profound distrust of the British. They are not in the same state of civilized and stable Government, as the people of India are and the Amir has not often more than nominal authority over his turbulent and unruly subjects. The steady advance of Russia in Central Asia, the dreams of Russian statesmen as to one day exchanging swords with the British on the tops of the Hindu

Kush make the situation one of extreme complexity which has been occupying the serious and supreme attention of the ablest of Indian administrators and military authorities for the last dozen years. With little variations the policy of the Government of India in this matter seems to have been to keep English influence paramount in Afghanistan, to interpose a friendly state between India and the Russian foe and at the same time to be ready with her preparations, her military defences and transport on the Indian frontier. With the later developments of that policy we shall deal further on.

GENERAL EVENTS.—Sir John Strachey this year further extended the decentralization scheme which had been initiated at his instance during the rule of Lord Mayo. Besides the services transferred in 1871 a few departments—Excise, Stamp, Law and Justice, and some other miscellaneous items were made over to the Governments of Bengal, the North-Western Provinces, Oudh, the Central Provinces and Bombay. The arrangement would be revised after the lapse of five years. Another principle which the budget embodied was the enforcement of local responsibilty for the management of many of the great works which had been constructed or were under construction, and for meeting the charges which those works entailed. Under this arrangement the Government of Bengal was required to pay 20 lakhs annually and the Government of North Western Provinces 5 lakhs annually for the purpose of paying interest on the capital spent on the construction of canals and railways. Sir John rightly held that expenditure for the relief of famine should be looked upon as ordinary charges and therefore met out of ordinary income. The revenue was estimated at £52,192,700 and the expenditure at £56,442,400, the deficit being proposed to be met by loans. Lord Lytton distinctly told the Indian public in his speech on the budget that India had no option in the matter of the remission of the cotton duties, which were to be repealed as soon as the situation permitted. Sir John also sketched out some other financial reforms such as the abolition of the Inland customs levies and sugar duties, the equalization and reduction of salt duties throughout India. To meet the extra amount that was necessary for contribution to the Imperial Exchequer, the Bengal Government brought forward two bills—a Public Works Cess Bill and a compulsory Water-rate Bill, the N. W. P. Government with Sir George Couper at its head imposed a license tax on trades and professions. The Public Works Cess Bill passed into law in spite of the strong opposition of the British Indian association. Lord Lytton made a speech as Chancellor of the Calcutta University which had a great political significance. He admitted that the Government had never conscientiously endeavoured to fulfil the obligation it had incurred in the matter of giving a fair share of appointments to the children of the soil and assigned as a reason for this that the Government had signed an incompatible agreement with the Civil Service. His Excellency forgot in uttering these words that the obligation contracted with the members of the Civil Service was with particular individuals, whose removal by death or retirement terminated that obligation; while the obligation with natives had been contracted with a whole people and was therefore permanent in its character. The Government of India resolved on financial and other grounds to combine the administration of Oudh with that of the North-Western Provinces. The powerful Talukdars of Oudh vehemantly protested against this measure but they were silenced with the assurance that the simple mode of carrying out this measure would be to transfer the chief executive authority from Lucknow to Allahabad leaving matters otherwise as they stood and that the Lieutenant-Governor would be required to reside at Lucknow during a portion of the year. Scarcely was the ink with which these pledges were given dry when the business of uniting the departments in the smaller province with the corresponding ones in the bigger one was zealously proceeded with. The Oudh departments of police public works, education, jails, dispensaries, registration and excise ceased to have separate existence. A very important movement was set on foot in the course of this year in connection with the Civil Service Question. This was a national movement organized by the Indian Association of Calcutta to protest against the changes in the rules for the admission of candidates to the open competitive examination for the Indian Civil Service ordered by the Marquis of Salisbury in his Despatch of the 24th February 1876. One of the changes was the reduction of the maximum limit of age from 21 to 19, thereby practically barring the natives of India. As the change was most prejudicial to the prospects of our countrymen the Indian Association called a monster meeting at the Town Hall in Calcutta to petition Parliament against the said change. The meeting was very largely and influentially attended and expressions of sympathy with the object were received from all parts of India, from associations and from public men. By this movement the hopes of an Indian Union upon the common platform of loyal and constitutional action for the redress of our grievances and the assertion of our rights and privileges were immeasurably strengthened. As there was a large deficit in the resources of the Government the various Divisional Commissioners were instructed to invite native Bankers to accomodate Government with some fifty lakhs of rupees at 6 or 7 per cent. Considerable hardship was felt by this class in withdrawing their money from more profitable investments and in a great many instances borrowing money at a considerably higher rate to be able to respond to the invitation of the Government which was tantamount to a command. The Civil Procedure Code Bill which in its original shape had aimed at lowering the status of the subordinate judicial officers and putting a stoppage to the execution of decrees of Civil Courts underwent considerable modifications. There were two small penal expeditions during the year against the Jowakis and the Afridis and these tribes were reduced to submission. A prolonged scarcity visited the N. W. Provinces and a famine appeared imminent but the fall of general and heavy rain in October happily averted this danger, but until the gathering of the rabi harvests the distress continued. The abolition of the Delhi College, the closing of the Bareilly College, the abolition of the Anglo-Sanskrit Department of the Benares College, the withdrawal of grants from Anglo-Vernacular subscription schools filled the public mind with alarm and anxiety. These measures were deemed as blows to high education and excited a considerable amount of criticism. In Delhi the feeling ran unusually high and subscriptions were started to save the College. The expedition against the Angami Nagas ended successfully. The feudatory chiefs were called upon to subscribe to an Imperial loan of eighty lacs. The native Coinage Act came in force in Alwar and negotiations were in progress for the transfer of salt-producing tracts in Rajputana and Central India to the paramount power.

CHAPTER X.

1878.

THE SECOND AFGHAN WAR—We have seen in our review of the preceding years a good deal of Afghanistan, Amir Shere Ali and the Russian conquests in Central Asia. Russia had contrary to her engagements with England sent an embassy to Cabul and this embassy had been received with open arms. The English cabinet on being informed of this fact instructed the Government of India to send a similar embassy. The Amir had been completely won over by Russian intrigues and he refused to acknowledge or answer the Viceroy's communications. The English embassy was ordered to proceed on its way without any definite replies from the Amir asking it to come but the Governor of Ali Musjid gave the English envoy plainly to understand that he was to proceed beyond that station at his own risk and peril as the Amir was unable to guarantee the safety of the mission. The escort that had accompanied the envoy was but of ordinary strength and the British embassy had to turn back. The English cabinet and the Government of India felt naturally deeply mortified at this repulse and an ultimatum was sent to the Amir fixing a date whose expiry would relieve the British Government from all obligations of keeping the peace. The date expired without any reply and hostilities were commenced at once. A spirited proclamation told the British Indian subjects of Her Majesty that the Amir had proved himself to be an enemy of England by his diverse hostile deeds and the Afghan subjects were told that they would have every support from the British Indian Government if they did not attempt to support the reigning Amir. Meanwhile the English cabinet by a stretch of diplomacy secured the neutrality of Russia and not even a shot was fired before the Russian embassy had been withdrawn from Cabul. The conduct of both of the great nations of Europe, England and Russia towards the

Afghan chief had hardly been worthy of themselves. The Afghan chief had repeatedly turned to the British Government for a treaty of protection and of offensive and defensive alliance but he received no response. When Khiva fell under the dominion of the Russians he renewed his solicitations and sought earnestly for the coveted protection but the British Government offered him arms and ammunition instead. The cordiality of Lord Mayo had a great effect upon him and he did not turn to the Czar until he had been completely disappointed in the hopes he entertained of English protection. The Wily Muscovite fed him with false hopes and then completely deserted him in his hour of need. The Russians found it extremely inconvenient to imbroil themselves in a war with England while the flame of the Russo-Turkish war was yet ablaze and when her forces had been to a great extent disabled by sickness and recent losses. So they left the Amir completely to his fate and quietly withdrew from the scene of action, when deluded by their false promises he had courted the open onmity of England and the English artillery was actually thundering at his gates. The Afghan complications called forth an outburst of loyalty from the native princes and people which was graciously recognized by the Queen and the Viceroy. The British troops were divided into three separate columns known respectively as the Kurram valley, the Peshawar and the Quetta columns, which in all numbered about 35 thousand men. The season selected was not at all suited to such warfare for the snows of the mountains were as bad enemies to the advancing British force as the stout-bodied and fanatical Afghans. But the Amir probably relying upon Russian promises of aid was totally unprepared to meet the invasion and after two successes of the British force at Ali Musjid and Peywar Kotal, the progress of the British troops was very rapid. The military part of the campaign had been condemned on scientific grounds by high military authorities, the commissariat arrangements were exceedingly defective and the information and observation of the

British commanding officers had often been far from accurate. The progress of British troops found Afghanistan itself torn by internal dissensions and a revolution took place resulting in the flight of Shere Ali and the succession to the throne of his son Yakub Khan. The Afghan war excited a good deal of attention in England and it called forth a strong condemnation of it from Lord Lawrence. Lord Lawrence who had an exceptionally good knowledge of the Panjab frontier, thought that the war had been too hastily undertaken that very possibly Shere Ali had very good reasons for refusing to receive the British embassy and his officer had not insulted the British envoy at Ali Musjid but received it with as much courtsey as was consistent with refusing it from proceeding to Cabul, and that England should have waited from commencing hostilities till these reasons had been clearly explained. His Lordship further contended that nothing substantial was to be gained by the Afghan war and that the war was not necessary for the sake of British prestige according to the most approved canons of international law. The effect of the open pronouncement of such views coming as they did from a statesman of such ability was to range public opinion in England against the Afghan policy of the British cabinet. Lord Beaconsfield was obliged much against his will to summon Parliament to consider the Afghan question. Lord Beaconsfield in defending the war did not refer to national honor or to Shere Ali's unfriendliness. He took his stand upon a different ground altogether. He said that the present Indian frontier though a safe frontier by nature and difficult to attack by even a powerful invading army was a haphazard and not a scientific frontier and that it was necessary to rectify this frontier. Sir James Stephen considered that the war was necessary for the fact that in the interests of the British Indian Empire the British Government should have a paramount influence in Afghanistan. He admitted however that the Amir had not been treated with justice and fairness and that England is now obliged to effect through much loss of blood and treasure what she could have easily done if she had taken time by the forelock. Sir James Stephen also justified the war on the ground that the principles of international law were not applicable in our dealings with Asiatic powers and that England must be the sole judge of what was necessary in the interests of her British Indian Empire. Lord Northbrook in his speech at Winchester fully reviewed the situation in Afghanistan. He denied that during the administrations of Lord Mayo and himself the question of the rectification of the frontier had never been brought to the notice of the Government by such experienced military advisers as Sir Henry Norman, Sir William Mansfield and Lord Napier of Magdala. The question had been fully considered during the Viceroyalty of Lord Lawrence and it was then decided that the British Government should strictly keep within its frontier that it should not cause irritation, hatred and defiance in the minds of the Afghans by the forcible or amicable occupation of any advanced post in their territories. Lord Northbrook after fully reviewing the course of recent events was of opinion that the war was not necessary and nobly vindicated the honor of England by enunciating the principle that even while dealing with weak Asiatic states England should not swerve one inch from the path of justice. Mr. Fawcett boldly asserted that though the crown and the cabinet has the unquestioned prerogative of declaring war without the consent of Parliament, in this particular instance such a course was not necessary as there was no emergency and there was plenty of time to consult the country in the person of the representatives of the people in Parliament. Mr. Fawcett also raised his voice against making poor India pay the expenses of the war. It was he contended an Imperial war and England should bear its burdens. The great leader of the Liberals Mr. Gladstone also raised his voice against the war. Rectification of the frontier he said was a convenient diplomatic phrase meant to conceal an annexation of territory which it was not convenient to avow. Before the end of the year it had been decided to saddle India with the expenses of the war on the ground that there was no reason why England should render any assistance to India. The Indian press was in a body opposed to the policy of the Government which culminated in the declaration of the war.

THE VERNACULAR PRESS ACT AND THE ARMS ACT—The greatest blessing that the Indian people enjoy under British rule next to the security of life and property is the freedom of speech and writing. This blessing was conferred in 1835 and was taken away only for a time by the terrible events of 1857. But on the 14th March at a single sitting of the Council, without any previous notice to the public a law was passed which took away this liberty from one section of the people. The English press and those journals that used the English language as the vehicle of expression were left untouched. This law was unfortunately passed by a Viceroy whose eminent father as well as himself were distinguished votaries of literature. There is no doubt that some members of the Vernacular press were guilty of unworthy conduct and of inexcusable follies and indiscretions. They sadly departed from the enlightened criticism based on precise information and careful thought, which all civilized Governments welcome as a valuable auxiliary and were misled into expressions which were not only disrespectful and intemperate but if they created any great effect on the minds of the ignorant masses would endanger the very foundations of the Government. But considerable difference of opinion existed on the point as to whether, even admitting that some Vernacular prints which were mostly obscure had transcended the proper limits, the Government was justified in enacting a law in which it should be the judge in its own cause and be empowered to annihilate the paper which it thought to be guilty. His Excellency the Viceroy while protesting that such a measure was absolutely necessary for the proper maintainance of the British Raj went on to declare that the present law of sedition was uncertain and the temper of the jury could not always be relied upon so as to make a conviction certain in every case where the Government desired it and the chief end of the law was that in such cases it was better to prevent seditious appeals than to punish the offenders after the crime had been committed. The provisions of the act, the speeches of the members of the Government in support of the measure and the manner in which it was passed produced a wide discontent in India and influential meetings were held in many important towns to protest against the measure. There was an animated debate on the subject in the House of commons. Mr. O'Donell an Irish Patriot made the first move in the matter and characterized the Vernacular Press Act as an engine of oppression which could not be equalled in the worst-governed countries of Europe. Mr. Gladstone followed him declaring that he had received the tidings with great pain and that the action of the Indian Government had been unwise and unfortunate. The ex-premier lent a powerful tongue to the dumb millions of India and his voice at once arrested the attention of the British public. He was backed up by a speech from Sir George Campbell. Lord George Hamilton defended the Act on the ground that the existing law of sedition in India was very severe and that an amendment was necessary. He forgot that nobody had complained of the severity and that the defence clearly exposed the utter hollowness of the pretext for enacting the law. Sir John Strachey had declared from his place in the Council that the better classes of native journals were free from the faults against which the present Act was levelled but the educated native community of Calcutta was considerably excited when the provisions of the act were made to have a retrospective effect and some of the important vernacular papers were served with notices to enter into bail-bonds. The Calcutta meeting against the Vernacular Press Act was a crowded and enthusiastic one. It recorded its deliberate opinion that having regard to the devoted loyalty of the Vernacular Press the Act was altogether unnecessary and uncalled for that its provisions were calculated to interfere with the freedom of discussion, to shut up the natural outlets of popular feeling and thus to aggravate the evils of popular discontent, and that the act will by arresting the growth of oriental literature deal a serious blow to the cause of native progress and good Government in India. Some influential English journals condemned the press law in ringing sentences and many high authorities on Indian affairs took a calm dispassionate view of the situation and regretted the extreme haste with which the measure had been passed. The agitation against the measure spread far and wide both in India and England and the Liberal party strongly denounced this piece of repressive legislation. It continued to deface the statute book till repealed by the Government of Lord Ripon.

The Arms Act of the present year was in consonance with the spirit of the Vernacular Press Act. The existing law on the subject necessitated a judicious discrimination between the loyal and the evil-disposed, the peaceful and the unruly and the loyal and proclaimed districts. But the New Arms Act swept all these distinctions between natives of the country and while making an invidious distinction in favor of the Europeans and Eurasians prohibited all classes of the native community from bearing arms except under a license obtained from the authorities. This measure was justly considered as casting an unfounded slur on the loyalty of the natives of India. The carrying of arms being clogged with conditions the loss of lives from the depredations of wild beasts would, it was feared, considerably increase for in actual practice it would not be always easy to secure a license. It was justly remarked on all sides that while the Government always generously acknowledges the conspicuous loyalty of the people of India on all fitting occasions it has, in practice, recourse to repressive and retrogressive legislation indicating the utmost distrust of their loyalty. Sir William Robinson truly remarked that the policy of this Act was a libel on the people of India and it was regarded in that light throughout the length and breadth of this country. It formed the subject of many protests and memorials all of which had no effect.

GENERAL EVENTS—The Government of India had to engage its attention in the middle of the year to the despatch of the Indian Sepoys to Malta for the purpose of a military demonstration in Europe, to overawe Russia to agree to the terms proposed at the Berlin Congress. The Indian Sepoys felt proud of the fact that the English Cabinet had thought them worthy in point of valour and capacity for endurance to measure arms with the Cossac hordes. They nobly responded to the call of duty and although sea-voyage was forbidden in the case of many of those called upon to go, they cheerfully obeyed the behests of their sovereign. The relations with the native princes were generally of a cordial character though there was a passage-at-arms with the Nizam of Hyderabad on the question of appointing a Private Secretary to Sir Salar Jung. Holkar received the cession of certain tracts of territory as a reward for his services during the Mutiny. The native princes gave notable proofs of their loyalty on the occasions of the Russo-Turkish and the Afghan wars. His grace the Duke of Buckingham and Chandos ruled the Southern Presidency wisely and well in a spirit of independence liberality and even-handed justice which made him highly popular. Sir Richard Temple adopted a very cautious and conciliatory policy after the Surat scandals. Sir George Couper was the very type of a beauracratic administrator and his narrow-mindedness and illiberal views put the clock of progress back in the N. W. Provinces. Sir Robert Egerton was a routine administrator and his administration of the Panjab was marked by little vigor or progress. Sir Rivers Thomson succeeded Sir Edward Clive Bayley in the Supreme Council being in turn succeeded in Burma by Sir Charles Aitchison whose sterling ability and thorough knowledge of and sympathy with the people made him a valuable ruler in the province in his charge, where organizing ability was so much needed. The question of the restoration of Assam to

Bengal was again under consideration. Assam had so much in common with Bengal that her separation from the sister province was only justified on the ground that large financial grants and separate and close supervision were necessary for developing that province. Sir Ashley Eden courted some unpopularity by his support of the Vernacular Press Act and by denouncing the elective system but his rule was otherwise marked by great vigor and resulted in substantial progress. There were important changes in the administration of Mysore which was made ready for being transferred to native rule. In Bengal there was a wide schism brought about by the progressive Brahmos owing to the marriage of the daughter of Keshub Chandra Sen with the Maharaja of Kooch Bihar according to Hindu ritual and while the girl had not yet arrived at the recognized marriageable age in that sect. Some of the best-educated and most earnest of the Brahmos seceded and set up a separate church according to republican principles. Early in the Parliamentary session a select committee was appointed to enquire into and report on Indian Public works under the Presidency of Lord George Hamilton. The Committee collected a mass of valuable information and came to the conclusion that the Indian public works were not always managed on good principles and that many of the Indian railways and irrigation works were not paying concerns and were heavy burdens on the Indian tax-payer. The Home charges increased to a considerable extent by the heavy burdens which the war office by a clever manipulation of figures managed to throw on the India office. This growing military expenditure evoked a loud protest from Indian tax-payers who could no longer acquiesce in this gross and growing injustice and in an influential public meeting at the Town Hall adopted a petition on the subject which was presented to the House of Commons by Mr. Fawcett and to the House of Lords by the Earl of Northbrook. Lord Salisbury after his five year's tenure of office as Secretary of State retired from the Indian Ministership which fell to the lot of Lord Cranbrook.

Lord Salisbury had raised high expectations but his imperious temper coupled with great change of views since he first came to the India office produced wide discontent and all classes of his Indian subjects were impatient of his domination. Mr. Whitley Stokes announced during the course of this year his ambitious projects at codification and the Viceroy felt that the legal element should be strongly represented in the Council. He appointed the Advocate-General of Bengal and Mr. G. H. P. Evans a leading member of the Calcutta Bar as additional members of the Council.

The Famines.—Several famines of great magnitude had developed in important portions of British India and the country had been struggling against these adverse circumstances for a considerable time past. The famines in Madras, Bombay, North-western Provinces and Mysore had been very severe, had caused considerable sufferings and had been of very long duration. Mr. William Digby who was thoroughly familiar with the famine campaign in Southern India clearly proved that the Government of India was at first unwilling to believe the magnitude of the calamity that was depopulating Southern India by the most horrible of all deaths, and persisted in its scepticism that the disaster had been magnified. The stern reality forced itself to the attention of the Government of India and the presence of the famine delegate did not improve matters. His Excellency the Viceroy's presence improved matters but a good deal of mischief had already been done. The figures which the census of the famine-stricken districts showed, exhibited a lamentable decrease of population, the greatest number of deaths having occurred in Mysore. The North-western Provinces famine was fearfully mismanaged but no notice was taken of the conduct of Sir George Couper at this crisis. There is food enough in this vast country to meet the most fearful dearths in particular localities and if there be good means of communication between the different parts of the country, and the management be carried on under proper supervision there need be no death from scarcity and starvation. A commission under the presidency of General Sir Richard Strachey was appointed to consider the whole subject of famine administration. The money that was raised by additional taxation was to have been devoted religiously to a separate fund for the prevention and relief of famine in British India. Sir John Strachey however announced that its object was to increase the general revenues of India for public works and other purposes. He had declared that the interest on famine loans was first of all to be paid off from the proceeds of additional taxation. Subsequently he fixed upon the capital charge as what was meant to be paid off from this source. But again he scouted the idea of creating the proceeds of additional taxation into a separate fund. He justified this action of the government by saying that Government has to meet famines by judicious measures, in the same way as it is under obligations to provide proper courts of justice, police, education and so forth, that as no separate fund existed for the above objects, there was no necessity for a separate fund to provide against famines. He added that if the proceeds of additional taxation were constituted into a separate fund, and then by a sudden change in the circumstances of the country, there be a considerable falling-off of revenue the government would have to choose between increased taxation or the abrogation of the law constituting a separate insurance fund. But when these taxes were imposed Sir John Strachey spoke in a different note altogether. He said "so far as we can now speak for the future the Government of India intends to keep this million and a half as an insurance against *famine alone*. We consider that the estimates of every year ought to make provision for *religiously applying the sum I have mentioned to this sole purpose*. The subsequent utterances of Sir John Strachey are sadly at variance with these declarations. When in defiance of all principles of reason, justice and equity England resolved to throw upon India the costs of the Afghan war, the government of India found itself unable to keep this solemn pledge and had to look for ways and means in every direction. The additional taxation consisted in the imposition of a Licence tax which did not spare incomes even so low as Rs. 100 per annum. In practical working it was a great hardship and it often produced serious discontent. The character of the subordinate officials in India who are charged with the administration of these taxes, is hardly of that sort which would make its working an easy one. In Surat its introduction led to serious riots. Everywhere it produced a considerable amount of suffering, and even the extreme Anglo-Indian organs condemned this tax in no uncertain voice. The License tax was characterized as iniquitous on several grounds. The first was that it fell exclusively on trades and industries and exempted all classes of the salaried officials of the government. The second was that the government was wrong in their theory that trades and industries generally benefit from famines and that therefore they should be called upon to pay so large a proportion of the annual tribute demanded by the state as protection against such famines. The third was that the inquisitorial inquiries of the municipal authorities, and the schedules required to be filed which went into the every detail of the shopkeeper's business no less the high-handedness and extortion of the tax-gatherers justly produced exasperation. The fourth was that in actual practice the work of assessment was entrusted to enumerators, kanungoes and sub-deputies whose discretion could hardly be trusted, over whom there would be little check and against whom the poor traders would not venture to complain for obvious reasons. In addition to the License tax the salt duty was enhanced almost 50 per cent. in Madras and Bombay and to secure symmetry the salt duty in the Bengal Presidency had been lowered resulting in a loss of nearly sixty lacs of rupees. Lord Lytton's estimate of the proceeds of the addition to the salt duty in Bombay and Madras did not exceed 30 lacs. In 1868, Lord Lawrence proposed the equalization of the salt tax in India but His Grace the Duke of Argyll reasonably set his face against it. His Grace remarked that salt in India was the only thing which could occupy the places of those articles of consumption which formed so large a part of the taxable commodities in the English financial system and the Duke thought that the existing rates should not be altered. Lord Northbrook attempted a slight increase to the salt duty in Madras and Bombay in 1873 and 1874 but his proposal was disallowed by the Secretary of State. Lord Lytton by the terms of salt convention with native states secured their consent to tax their subjects under this head for the convenience of the British Government, and he made the salt duty in all parts of India uniform on the ground that differential rates lead to smuggling and therefore necessitate the maintainance of the salt cordon, which produces great hardship and oppression. His Lordship forgot that customs barriers would still be maintained in the great cities of Northern India for the collection of the octroi duties, and in Bengal the barrier could not be wholly done away with, as even under the present system the Bengal duty would be higher by six annas than it would be in the other provinces thus leading partially to the contingency of the cheap salt of the other provinces superseding the imported salt of Bengal. The revision of the salt duty balanced the gains and losses of the Government and kept the necessity for the License tax still unaltered. By taking over the salt business of the native states the British Government extended its monopoly through the length and breadth of the land and the subjects of the Native States had to be taxed at the same rates as those leviable in British territories which was neither equitable nor righteous.

INDIAN LOANS—The great difficulty caused in all transactions between England and India since the rates of exchange were altered so much to the disadvantage of India attracted attention to the question as to whether the Indian loans could not be raised in India. It was however found after a considerable amount of discussion that the preponderance of advantage for the State would be found to lie with the plan of taking up the loans in England. As was observed by a very high authority it was obvious that loanable capital must be much more plentiful and cheaper in England where the usual rates of commercial interest range from three to six per cent. than it can be in India where it is from seven to twelve per cent. The advantage of taking up a loan in India are first that a large loss is avoided in remitting the annual interest in sterling to England and that the gain to the government from this source must be estimated at the cumulative and compound interest during the whole period, and secondly that a large gain would accrue from the same cause when the time came for the repayment of the whole loan. The Indian market would be unable to take up the loans except for a considerably higher interest than what the English money market offers. Should England give her imperial guarantee to the Indian loans there would at once be a sensible reduction in the rate of interest. The gain to the Indian exchequer by taking up the loans in England is often considerable.

The End of Part the Second.

INDIAN HISTORY OF OUR OWN TIMES.
PART III, 1879-88.

PART III.

By gracious permission this part of "Indian History of Our Own Times" is dedicated to His Excellency the Marquis of Lansdowne, Viceroy and Governor-General of India in grateful recognition of the kind interest taken by His Lordship in this humble undertaking by his dutiful subject.

SATYA CHANDRA MUKERJI.

INDIAN HISTORY OF OUR OWN TIMES.

PART THE THIRD.

CHAPTER I.

1879.

THE THIRD DECADE UNDER THE CROWN.—We have in the foregoing parts taken a rapid survey of the more important events during the first two decades of Indian Administration by Her Gracious Imperial Majesty. We propose to bring down the contemporary history of our country to the close of the administration of Lord Dufferin which ended on the 13th December 1888, when the Indian subjects of Her Majesty passed under the rule of the Marquis of Lansdowne, the reigning Viceroy. Our readers must have observed that we have scrupulously resisted the temptation of going beyond the limits assigned to this work and while omitting nothing material have refrained from branching out into the less important details. That plan we would observe in the following pages too, and should all circumstances be favourable, it is our earnest wish to continue this narrative to the end of the Fourth decade of Her Majesty's Indian Administration as soon as that decade ends and all the necessary papers are forthcoming.

THE AFGHAN WAR.—We have considered in our review of the last year the progress of the war so far as it was comprised within the last decade. Lord Lytton's Afghan War was, so far as the military operations went, eminently successful. His generals went, saw and conquered. With the exception of very slight resistances, the British army had practically a walk-over.

The astute ruler of Afghanistan Amir Shere Ali was in a very critical position. He had all along been relying on promises of support from the Russian Cabinet which to his misfortune was withheld from him even at the moment when the English army was actually knocking at his doors. The victim of the jealousy and diplomacy of two first-class European cabinets, Shere Ali's position cannot but excite a deep sympathy in the minds of all right-thinking observers of the situation. Difficulties confused him and he left his capital and throne and courted a sad fate in exile. With him vanished all hopes of the Afghans ever meeting the British in the field with success. His son Yakub Khan was noted for his abilites and tact but with an empty treasury, with troops almost mutinous for heavy arrears of pay, he thought the best thing would be to patch up a peace on the most favourable terms obtainable. He therefore invited the British Government to propose negotiations which ended in the Treaty of Gundamuck. Lord Lytton summarized the military aspects of the campaign that was ended by the Treaty of Gundamuck in a triumphant despatch to the Secretary of State in the month of August. The Viceroy laid special stress on the fact that while the standing army of the Amir had been defeated and dispersed, his Sirdars and his warlike subjects had made no serious and strenuous efforts at resistance, his towns had received the British force with open arms, the boisterous mountainous races on the frontier which were always considered to be a source of immense strength to his dominions had with the exception of a few harmless reprisals remained almost neutral and the Amir's subjects whom no European could approach without imminent personal danger, had permitted the telegraphic communications to be established and remain unbroken all the way from Peshawar to Jellalabad along the entire length of the Khybar pass. Lord Lytton also considered that the political effect of the campaign had been all that it was desired to be. By the treaty that was concluded between the two powers, the Amir accepted the proffered friendship of the British Government in terms that could no longer be mistaken. The entire foreign relations of Afghanistan were placed at the absolute control of the British Indian Government, the command of the principal passes and three important districts was surrendered to the Government of India. The location of a permanent British Resident at Cabul with the right to depute special officers to any part of the Afghan territories, as occasion might arise, was conceded in unequivocal terms, Lord Lytton added that this new state of things was a decided improvement on what used to be our relations with the foreign powers on the North-West frontier ever since the celebrated Umballa conference from the time of Lord Mayo downwards. The Viceroy anticipated that this treaty would lead to an abiding and permanent peace from the fact that the Bolan pass had been guarded by British troops for a considerable period of time past and yet there had been no disturbances, and that the Amir cheerfully accepted the provisions of the treaty recognizing it as making his position substantially much more strong than it had ever been. Lord Lytton little knew when he penned this triumphant despatch that within a few weeks his political forecasts and anticipations would be scattered to the winds. The Viceroy forgot most unaccountably to take note of the fact that since the first Afghan War the Afghans had lost all faith in the English. The Afghans can never trust an Englishman. The history of British India showed to them by what slow and sure steps a company of merchants had founded a splendid empire and they alike distrusted all the diplomacy and all the professions of the Government of India. This view of the state of things, history must record to the credit of the Native Press, (which was then led by the veteran politician Kristodas Pal), was put forth in many organs of native public opinion, but Lord Lytton seriously erred as a statesman in completely overlooking this aspect of the question. He selected Major Sir Louis Cavagnari for the delicate and difficult duties of the British Envoy at Cabul and ordered him to lose no time in proceeding to his destination. The selection met with the approval of all sections of the Indian public. Major Cavagnari was well-fitted for the duties he was entrusted with, both by nature and previous training. Soldier by instinct he had made himself fully acquainted with the language the literature and the resources of Afghanistan, within a few weeks of his arrival at Cabul. There was a mob rising uncontrolled by the authorities and the British officials with the gallant Major at their head were hacked to pieces in the selfsame quadrangle where Sir William Macnaughten and his suite had perished in 1841. The tragedy stood revealed to the civilized world before the vote of parliament thanking the Indian army had arrived in India or the honors for the successful campaign had been blazoned forth in the London Gazette. Lord Beaconsfield had on receiving intelligence of the details of the Afghan war publicly boasted that the "scientific frontier of Afganishtan had been accomplished and achieved with a precision of plan and a rapidity in execution, not easily equalled in the annals of statesmanship or war." Scarcely had this boast been uttered than the Indian Government and the British Foreign Office were called upon to face a new state of things. To retrieve British prestige, General Roberts proceeded immediately to Cabul with a large body of troops. He entered Cabul almost without any opposition and the city, the fort, the treasury passed under his dictatorial control. Yakub Khan was made a prisoner of state. General Roberts after having made the British flag wave over Cabul was attacked by the Afghans in great numbers, and he was obliged to abandon Cabul and to entrench himself within the Cantonment of Sherpur. This disaster was again rapidly retrieved. The Afghan war takes a new aspect from this point and we shall take up the thread of narrative in our next chapter.

FOREIGN AFFAIRS—Besides the Afghan war the attention of the Government of India had to be directed during this year to several important questions of foreign policy. The tract of country which lies between Chittagong and Burmah was a *terra incognita* to the Indian Foreign Office before the time of Lord Mayo and it was sanctioned after the Lushai expedition by the said Viceroy that anything like a precise Eastern frontier should be marked out. On that frontier the Nagas had been committing some raids and had also succeeded in making a considerable advance into the British territories. The Nagas were driven back after a sharp struggle by the British troops with a Manipur contingent under Sir James Johnstone. The old king of Burmah having died, the kingdom passed into the hands of his son Theebaw who signalized the beginning of his reign by several acts of cruelty which might better be omitted. The representative of the British Government at the Court of Mandulay was openly insulted by the Burmese king, and he gave himself such airs in his intercourse with the British Government that it was determined to withdraw the British Resident from the Court of Mandalay. The Government of India made up its mind to enter into open hostilities with him but the Home Government had its hand already full of foreign complications and did not think it prudent to embark on new adventures. The conduct of the Burmese king had filled the authorities in India with just indignation and it was only accidentally that a war was averted. The Burmese king did not however learn moderation from this forbearance on the part of the Indian Government but six years later repeated his agressive acts and provocations on a scale which cost him his throne. The state of Kashmir came prominently before the Indian and English public during the present year. That Valley of Roses, is probably considered, by the extreme section of the party who are still in favor of England adding to her territories in the East as too important and too beautiful to be left to a native ruler and some leading papers in England began to advocate its practical annexation for alleged neglect in the matter of a famine that was raging within its borders. The Maharaja had done his best in the crisis but the distress was too deep and widespread to be grappled with complete success. It was alleged too that some Kashmir officials had been guilty of heartless murders, and that some suspicious correspondence with the Russians had been discovered. A small rising at Gilgit was also made an indictment against the Maharaja who it was said must be responsible for all unruly and inimical tribes on his border. The primary object of all this agitation was annexation and it is to be feared that if the Conservative Government had been in power sometime longer than it was, the conference that had been arranged between Lord Lytton and the Maharaja would have ended in practically arranging for the Government complete control in the internal affairs of that state.

THE FINANCES.—Sir John Strachey's budgets since the day when he took charge of the office of the Finance Minister in the last week of December 1876, had been received by the Indian public with unfavorable criticisms. The budget of 1877-78 was a development of the decentralization scheme in which the old conditions were revived and extended and local responsibility for reproductive public works was enforced. The budget of 1879-80 showed that the deficit during the past four years amounted to £24,863,000. Another feature of this budget which alarmed the Indian public was the entire disappearance of the Famine Insurance Fund, though Lord Lytton had given an emphatic and solemn pledge to the effect that not a rupee of the proceeds of the new taxes would be applied to any purpose other than insuring the country against famine. In the teeth of this pledge the famine fund was deliberately swamped up in the general revenues of the country. It was applied to defraying the expenses of the Afghan War and to remitting the cotton duties partially. This was considered at the time to be a gross breach of faith on the part of the Government of India nor can history acquit the Government of this charge even after the explanations that have been given of this course of conduct in subsequent years. It was contended that there was no necessity for keeping up a separate famine fund as the general revenues of the country were charged with all operations necessary for the prevention of famine. But the public both European and native had refused to be convinced by this logic. The Government however discerned the necessity of enforcing a strict system of economy in all departments. Parliamentary pressure was brought on the Government in this matter and a commission with Sir Ashley Eden at its head was appointed to consider in what way the military expenditure could be curtailed without impairing the efficiency of that branch of the state. The commission submitted its recommendations in the course of the current year proposing several organic changes which adopted would lead to a curtailment of the expenses by a million and a quarter per annum. Sir John Strachey also found that the License tax had been most unpopular in its working. It fell heavily on the poor and it affected in his own words, a large class that ought to be exempted. The reason he continues, for exempting them is that the numbers brought under taxation have been far larger than was anticipated and experience shows that it was not politically wise or financially worthwhile to collect from a great multitude of people fees small as those which were imposed on the smaller incomes by the License tax. The difficulty of preventing extortion and oppression on the part of the petty officials entrusted with the duty of collecting the tax has proved in some parts of India serious and it is impossible to doubt that there has often been reason for the numerous complaints that have been made. Sir John therefore thought it politically wise to amend the law. The year closed with some better prospects for the Treasury to the extent it about two crores, *viz.* saving of loss by Exchange 76 lacs, additional revenue from opium 77½ lacs, additional revenue from Railways 40 lacs total 193½ lacs, besides which the salt and other branches of public revenue exhibited an increase. Sir John Strachey had also been trying to abolish the Inland customs line, a measure which stood accomplished during the next year. He equalized the salt duties throughout India and suppressed the manufacture of salt in the native states. In 1887 Mr. Allan Hume was charged with the duty of persuading the Chiefs of Rajputana and Central India to surrender the salt-producing sources in their respective territories and to acquiesce in the imposition of a salt tax of Rs. 2-8 a maund on their subjects. By this arrangement the British Government was a great gainer financially. It has saved the the cost and trouble of maintaining the customs line and has at the same time profited by the imposition upon the people of Rajputana and Central India of a salt tax at the same rate as that which prevailed in the British territories. Sir John compensated this burden by the remission of the sugar duty—a duty which was paid only by well-to-do classes and which was a poor compensation for a tax on an article that was a necessary of life. In securing theoretical symmetry and excellence Sir John Strachey threw away 20 lakhs of rupees by reducing the salt duty in Northern India of which no body ever complained and which relief, the 130 milions of Northern India scarcely felt, while the poor people of the Madras and Bombay Presidencies felt heavily the increase in the salt duty. It had been the dream of Sir John Strachey's life to make India a free port by gradual abolition of all customs. The first step towards the carrying out of this measure was the exempting in March 1878 from import duty, the coarser yarns, and the goods made of such yarns at a sacrifice of revenue amounting to £12,227. At the same time many articles were removed from the import tariff. The order of March 1878 was found unworkable in practice and in 1879 a Committee was appointed to consider and report on the matter. The Commission reported that the yarn employed in manufacture in the India mills rarely exceeded 27s, but Sir John Strachey exempted all cotton goods not containing yarn of a higher number than 30s, at a sacrifice of revenue to the extent of £2,00,000 at a time when deficit was plainly staring the Indian Government in the face. Even the Secretary of State had laid down that the abolition of the cotton duties should take place only at a time of financial surplus and Lord Lytton had declared on taking office that he never contemplated to abolish these duties at the risk of adding one six pence to the revenues of the country. But the sacrifice of this important branch of the public revenue was only filled up by the unpopular License tax imposed a year before with an ultimate eye to fill up the contemplated gap. Sir John, however, defended this measure as undertaken in the true interests of the people of India. Sir John Strachey's measure had been so cleverly framed that the Lancashire Cotton Lords could bring in the bulk of their goods within the exemption clauses and thus the historian is obliged to record with regret and shame that under a great and civilized Government the interests of India were deliberately sacrificed to gain the Lancashire votes for the Conservatives in the General elections then pending. If those elections had given the Conservatives a fresh lease of power, another measure which aimed at the abolition of the octroi duties that form the bulk of the Municipal revenues in the greater part of India would have been passed into law and the Indian Municipalities would have been under the necessity of resorting to fresh taxation to recoup the loss thus caused. But an opportune swing of the political pendulum in the United kingdom saved them this necessity. The budget of 1879 had discovered a heavy deficit and the opposition leaders brought this serious state of the Indian Finances so prominently to the notice of the Houses of Parliament that the friends of India in England were considerably alarmed. This was a most undesirable state of things and six weeks before the next official year expired Sir John produced his famous "Prosperity Budget." In this document the expenses of the Afghan war were so under-estimated that to all appearances the finances of India looked to be in a quite normal state. The public however suspected that there must be a serious error somewhere and Sir John was obliged to confess that the **expenses** of the war had been under-estimated by 4 millions sterling. This was again found not to be the whole truth for Sir John was obliged to make a second confession that the expenses of the Afghan war had been under-estimated by 10 millions. The fact speaks for itself and needs no comment from the contemporary historian.

GENERAL EVENTS.—This year is memorable for the interest evinced in England with reference to Indian affairs. The Conservatives had ruled India through Lord Lytton in a manner which could not but excite deep discontent in India and which led even statesmen of the rank of Mr. Gladstone to study the subject and inveigh against it with merciless severity. The Conservatives in older days had given to India the Queen's proclamation but Lord Lytton with the sanction of his official chiefs Lords Salisbury and Beaconsfield had sacrificed principle honesty, humanity and liberality in administering this country under the new ideas of Imperialism. The liberals advocated justice for India and her people. We know it too well that several high authorities both among Englishmen and Indians had regretted the fact that India should be the sport of party politics. The question is indeed one of serious importance and the contemporary historian is expected to deal with it and give his opinion with reasons. We for one are quite prepared to admit the many and serious deficiencies of party government but the fact is unmistakeable that notwithstanding these serious shortcomings England flourishes as the first country in the civilized world. We believe in the words that Kristodas Paul used in 1880, that it is far better that India should retain her vitality through the animation of English party politics than that she should die of mere inanition from the want of party sympathy. Whatever may be the cause that might lead any English political party to take India under its special shelter, we should eagerly welcome the advent of powerful intellects and still more powerful eloquence to the exposition of Indian wrongs and grievances at the bar of the English nation. Mr. Gladstone turned his attention from the classic land of Homer to the classic land of the Aryans and John Bright and Henry Fawcett brought all important matters regarding the Indian administration to the notice of the British public. During this year Mr. Lalmohun Ghose exposed the wrongs of the Indian people with reference to their admission to the Civil Service of their own country. His powerful eloquence and earnestness of purpose produced a great enthusiasm amongst his hearers and he was so powerfully backed up by the voice of John Bright that an immediate scheme was propounded on the part of the responsible authorities in India for creating what is known as the Statutory Civil Service. The local governments made quiet progress during the year. With the exception of the Rumpa rebellion in Madras there was little that was exciting. The Bombay Presidency continued under the rule of Sir Richard Temple who at the end of his administration was liked by all classes of his subjects. With indefatigable energy he visited every nook and corner of his dominions, helped the Government of India in the transport arrangements during the Afghan war, was a friend of education in every shape and form and when he retired at the end of the next year his subjects voted him a statue. Sir Ashley Eden brought his unique knowledge of the province that he ruled to do much work in the matter of opening up improved communications, and carrying on the work of reform in a quiet and steady manner. The province of Lower Burmah developed considerably under the wise and energetic rule of Sir Charles Aitchison. The administration of Sir George Couper was forcely assailed and by all accounts he proved himself to be a narrowminded unsympathetic and incapable governor. Sir Robert Egerton's government of the Punjab was a fair success though he never tried to introduce any liberal improvements in his province. The true conception of all history comprises an adequate notice not only of the doings of governments but also of all sorts of activities visible among the people. This year the historian can record that there was an amount of literary intellectual and moral activity among the people in all parts of the country that it was cheering to the philosopher and the philanthropist. Societies, associations, anjumans, and sabhas were springing up on all sides for the purpose of focussing the scattered energies and activities of the people and trying to improve by united effort their intellectual moral, social and political well-being. The political associations did their work wisely and well; the revival of political life and aspirations was full of promise in the fulness of time. The various nationalities of India were shaking off their lethargy of ages, and a visible impulse of nationality and ardent patriotism was discernible on all sides. Bengal was deeply agitated this year over the question of the Durga Poojah holidays which extended to 12 days but which the Commercial Associations in Calcutta wanted to cut down to four. Lord Lytton unhappily gave his sanction to this measure. Calcutta mourned this year the loss of two of her prominent citizens, who had raised themselves to positions of great influence with the Government and were links between the rulers and the ruled, Raja Digambar Mitter and Nawab Amir Ali. The Law Commission of which the Law Member, Sir Charles Turner and Sir Raymond West were the members recommended that the process of codifying wellmarked divisions of substantive law should continue, that English law should be made the basis of all future codes, sufficient recognition being given to local and special customs, that the law of wrongs, the law of property and the rules for the interpretation of statutes should be systematically undertaken. The Deccan Agriculturalists, Relief Act was passed this year. It was an unsatisfactory measure and delivered the debtor entirely to the hands of the creditor.

CHAPTER II.

1880.

THE AFGHAN WAR.—The last year closed with the occupation of the city of Cabul by Sir Frederick Roberts. But the Afghan troops could hardly be checked by the British force and they were living on open plunder and rapine of the citizens. The flying column organized by General Roberts committed many excesses by burning every village within a distance of ten or twelve miles from the city whose inhabitants were suspected of having fought against the British authority during the late outbreak. In his New-year's day speech Lord Lytton declared that his orders had been to extend clemency to the refractory and the proclamation of a general amnesty. But some executions had taken place in Cabul before this proclamation had been issued and were daily taking place even after it, of those who had fought against the British troops, after the establishment of a dictatorial authority by General Roberts on the 1st of October last. The offenders were declared guilty of treason but it was forcibly pointed out by English Judges that there can be no treason for waging war against the authority of a belligerent power. The Government of India had no intention of annexing Afghanistan and so the political officer specially deputed, Sir Lepel Griffin opened negotiations with the members of the Royal family of Afghanistan for a ruler strong enough to hold his own. Sir Lepel declared at a meeting of the Afghan Sirdars that the British Government intended to divide Afghanistan into provinces that Kandahar and Herat should be separate from Kabul and Turkestan and that Yakub Khan who had proved false to his treaty engagements with the British should be permanently deposed. The plan of the partition of Afghanistan could hardly have been expected to be acceptable to the Afghan Sirdars and though at a subsequent meeting this programme was considerably modified, the Afghans commenced hostilities again and gave a severe fight to General Stewart whose position was insecure and caused grave anxiety till another brigade joined him. The Afghans were ultimately defeated south of Ghuzni. The Ministry in England had changed before these operations were over and the Liberal Cabinet then in power determined to modify the programme of the Conservative Viceroy and to make over Afghanistan to a ruler capable of administering its affairs without imposing any condition whatever. Negotiations were opened by the same political officer with Abdur Rahman grandson of Amir Dost Mahomed, a distinguished member of the Barakzai family and who was reputed to be an experienced soldier and able statesman. The Liberal cabinet determined to withdraw the British troops from Cabul and Kandahar as soon as possible and to establish something like a settled government without reserving any power of interference on the part of the British Government. Only a general understanding was come to with Amir Abdur Rahman with reference to his foreign relations. No formal engagements were entered into. A subsidy was promised and very conciliatory terms were offered with reference to the actual state of things caused by the war. The fortifications at Sherpur were allowed to stand, and the guns taken by British troops were restored. But there unhappily happened another disturbance at Kandahar immediately. A son of Shere Ally, Ayub Khan raised the standard of revolt at Kandahar and with the aid of the local Sirdars established his authority and besieged the British troops stationed there. General Roberts immediately proceeded to Kandahar with a strong column and reached that place without a single hitch. He struck a signal blow at the rebellion headed by Ayub Khan and British prestige was again fully restored in Cabul and Kandahar. The Afghan operations concluded here and the British troops evacuated Cabul and Kandahar as soon after, as was found possible. The Afghan war that was thus concluded was hardly a wise act of statesmanship. The war cost the Indian taxpayer many millions of money and some of the bravest soldiers. There was even less excuse for undertaking it that there was for that unfortunate one undertaken by Lord Auckland. The idea of a scientific frontier seized Lord Lytton's mind and he subdued every other consideration for the accomplishment of that idea. The actual results attained by war could have been achieved much better by diplomacy without turning the Afghan people into implacable foes of the British Government. The idea of a scientific frontier was thought commonly at the time to have emanated from Lords Beaconsfield and Salisbury and Lord Lytton was merely thought to be a tool in the hands of those eminent men. But the historical researches of later years have conclusively proved that the idea was imbibed by Lord Lytton from his Military Secretary Sir George Pomeroy Colley and forced by him on his distinguished chiefs. Sir Erskine Perry who had assisted towards the elucidation of the subject by an able minute has proved from official documents that the idea of a scientific frontier emanated from the Indian authorities and was only approved of by the Home Government. This theory had led to all the political and financial embarrassments of the Afghan war and unless distinctly repudiated by the Home Government it would be the source of countless evils in the future. The Afghan war proved that the Russian interference in Afghanistan so much mentioned abroad was an entire delusion, that the Afghans though not able to offer an effective resistance to British troops, yet have no liking for the English and will avail themselves of every opportunity to strike a treacherous blow. Throughout the Afghan war the bravery and gallantry of the native troops and officers and the loyalty of the native princes showed themselves conspicuously and this was the only satisfactory feature of a series of campaigns barren of any political results over which the historian would gladly draw a veil, if possible.

THE FINANCES.—The Afghan war created a serious drain on the Indian Exchequer. Sir John Strachey in presenting his budget this year observed that if India were ever to have a separate national existence she must have self-respect and self-reliance and that this magnificent country ought to bear its own burdens. India should only expect justice from England. She should never ask for charity. Sir John showed that there was no cause for alarm but only a few weeks after, the great demand on all the frontier treasuries and the want of all precise knowledge on the part of the Government of India as to the actual expenses of the war placed it in a very serious position. Mr. Gladstone exposed this state of things in the House of Commons with irresistible logic and eloquence and Lord Cranbrook the Secretary of State addressed a scathing despatch to the Government of India on the serious position that the country had been placed in by the financial genius of Sir John Strachey. Borrowing had to be resorted to by the new Finance minister Sir Evelyn Baring to deal with the legacy of deficit bequeathed by his predecessor. The new four and a half per cent. loan was taken up eagerly by a Syndicate of French capitalists and the credit of the Indian Government stood high in the European markets. This enabled the Indian Government to tide over the crisis. The last act of Sir John Strachey was the remodelling of the Accounts Department by which the higher grades were reserved for the Covenanted officers and ministerial grades for the uncovenanted officers. The native of India is an accountant almost by instinct and this measure was on a piece with the measures of repression during the administration of Lord Lytton. The license tax was also placed on a new footing inasmuch as as the taxable minimum was raised to Rs. 500. With these measures the Indian career of Sir John Strachey came to an end. The famine policy which he had inaugurated was pronounced to be a failure even by the Famine Commission and all his measures which he could carry into practical execution under the Governments of Lord Mayo and Lord Lytton were directed by a simple love of crotchets and untried notions and theories regardless of their actual results.

He lacked the essential quality of an administrator, viz sympathy with the ruled. He never loved the people of India, he never made their welfare his first care and object. His unquestioned abilities and great energies produced a series of measures which the historian must even at a distance of time unqualifiedly condemn and it needed very great efforts totally to undo the mischief caused by them. He will however be gratefully remembered by posterity for one single act viz the restoration of many objects of great beauty and interests both of Mahomedan and Hindu architecture in the districts of Agra and Muttra. He left India unregretted by the people.

LORD LYTTON'S ADMINISTRATION—On the 8th of June 1880 Lord Lytton laid down the reins of Indian Government, on the change of ministry occurring in England. He had been an Indian Viceroy for exactly forty-nine months and his administration was much criticised at the time both in England and India. Lord Lytton assumed charge of his high office with a speech from the throne. He said that though the obligations of the Viceregal office were heavy he did not shrink from the task as he might well rely on the counsel of his experienced advisers and the loyal support and co-operation of all classes of Her Majesty's subjects. These were noble sentiments and all India gave the Viceroy a fair trial. When he left India however, he had completely sundered himself from these and similar high traditions of English statesmen and he was held responsible for disastrous war, financial calamities, popular dissatisfaction and discontent. Of course his councillors were a good deal to blame for the advices given but as the responsible head of the Government the whole discredit of the measures that issued in the name of that body must be attached to him. His administration was characterised by a retrograde policy in every department of state, by crooked measures, high-handed proceedings and repressive acts totally at variance with those lessons of statesmanship indelibly impressed on India by some of England's noblest sons. Lord Lytton was a first-rate scholar, had great powers of oratory and still greater capacity for work, and he has left on record some of most elaborate and best finished minutes on the different departments of state. He began well by showing sterling independence in the matter of the Fuller Case but he was early subjected to a process of deterioration, and the jarring elements of his council still further increased his confidence in those who had the tact and the capacity to lead their august master by the nose. The foreign policy of the Viceroy was his own work and his acts have been proved to be grand mistakes by the light of subsequent events. The occupation of Quetta, the Embassy to Cabul and the War with Afghanistan in which there were serious military and diplomatic blunders, must have shipwrecked his reputation as a statesman before the bar of history. He can not be exonerated from all blame by the excuse put forward for him that he was only carrying out the behests of the great English Statesmen then in power. To be such an ignoble and pliant tool in the hands of others is hardly creditable to the immediate successor of that high-minded statesman Lord Northbrook but the question has been set at rest by the researches of Sir Erskine Perry among the documents of the India office which have led to his fixing on Lord Lytton the entire responsibility of the political and financial calamities incidental to the war. The ill-fated idea of a scientific frontier had cost the Indian Exchequer many millions irrespective of the frontier railways whose entire cost has not yet been estimated. The military demonstration in Afghanistan had called forth the spontaneous loyalty of the native chiefs and princes when the state of things became critical but otherwise it had hardly served the purpose so much bruited abroad of strengthening the hold of the English on India. Lord Lytton had however ill rewarded the loyalty to the native princes by proposing to cut down their armies and reduce their dignity and position. The people of India many of whom had been educated up to a standard that enabled them to understand the motives and the actions of their rulers, were, without almost an exception highly discontented with Lord Lytton's administration. His famine policy in the Deccan swelled the death-roll to an enormous figure. He held the Delhi rejoicings at a time when he had sufficient warnings of the day of sorrow at hand and he heeded not the sufferings of the starving wretches in the jungles of the Deccan till it was almost too late. When His Lordship visited the famine-stricken districts in person the affairs had turned for the better but incalculable mischief had been done before that. He will be ever remembered as the author of those obnoxious repressive measures the Arms Act and the Vernacular Press Act. These measures though not vigorously enforced during the present administration were so much opposed to all accepted traditions of the Indian Government, and to all principles of civilized jurisprudence that they were sufficient to damn the administration in the eyes of the educated natives of India. These measures produced a widespread discontent and an organized agitation spreading to many parts of the country tangibly evinced the pervading dissatisfaction. In the Public Works deparment there continued to be a wasteful expenditure till it was checked by the committee of the House of Commons that sat to enquire into the state of Indian public works. The financial administration of the country has been fully reviewed in the foregoing pages and it can not be denied that it was an entire *fiasco*. The people of India clearly perceived that Lord Lytton wanted to carry everything with a high hand. The Government of India is a despotism but it had always been the accepted policy that this despotism should be tempered by public opinion. Lord Lytton made a distinct departure from these traditions and the snub that he gave to some important political bodies in the land when they approached him in reference to public questions, with patriotic supplications did not heighten his reputation among the ruled classes. The Viceroy did take some interest in Mahomedan education, and in the education of the domiciled Europeans and Eurasians. He also earned the gratitude of the Hindu community by restoring the Durga puja holidays. The late Hon'ble Kristodas Pal in reviewing his administration said, "If he had more faith in his own judgment and less in Sir John Strachey's if he had been less imaginative and more practical, less ambitious and and more moderate, less aggressive and more prudent, less theatrical and more real, less diplomatic and more direct, less continental and more truly English, he would have undoubtedly made a successful ruler of the millions whose destinies were committed to his charge. That he has failed is patent enough but he has failed not only because of his own shortcomings but also because his Council was literally a bear garden. With some of his colleagues he was hardly on speaking terms and a house thus divided could not stand." The historian must endorse the view of Lord Lytton's rule contained in the above lines. Here was an eminent example of how the finest qualities could be of no avail to an administrator without sympathy with the people that he ruled. He took some part in the debates of the House of Lords to vindicate his own reputation as an administrator but he said nothing new to enable the historian to do otherwise than assent to the view given above.

The Marquis of Ripon—The elections in the United Kingdom ended in a decided Liberal victory and a Liberal Ministry was formed. During the elections hardly any Indian question except the Afghan war attracted any attention but Mr. Gladstone did not lose sight of her myriad millions. In one of his Midlothian speeches, on the 2nd April, he delivered a spirited speech in which he showed how the vernacular press of India had been delivered bound hand and foot as much under the control of the Viceroy as the Russian press is under the control of the Czar. This state of things he argued was serious in a country where the native of India would scarcely meet the European as his equal or speak out his mind freely to him but where the press is the only means to get at the truth with reference to the real feelings of the ruled classes. Mr. Gladstone formed a new ministry with the Marquis of Hartington as the Secretary of State for India. The choice for the Indian Viceroyalty fell on the Marquis of Ripon a nobleman of high descent and great experience in the public life of England. He had served as Under-Secretary of State and Secretary of State for India and had occupied seats in the Cabinet as Secretary for war and Lord President of the Council long before he retired from active political life in 1873. In 1874 His Lordship became a convert to the Roman Catholic Church. This step brought on him showers of abuse from the English press but it revealed his Lordship as a man of sterling conscientiousness. During the first six months of his rule the Marquis of Ripon distinguished himself by winning the respect and confidence of all classes of Her Majesty's subjects by a broad-hearted statesmanship which contrasted admirably with Lord Lytton's procedure which had forfeited the sympathy of the natives of India. We have narrated above the steps taken by the Marquis of Ripon to bring to an end the Afghan War and to repair the financial calamities which had been sought to be concealed under pomp and circumstance. The old council under Lord Lytton had nearly gone out before the year expired. Sir Andrew Clarke who admitted in his valedictory speech that he had done nothing in India during his tenure of office as Public Works Minister was the first to leave. Sir Alexander Arbuthnot next followed suit. A distinguished Madras civilian and educationist he lent himself to the repressive measures of Lord Lytton's rule. Sir John Strachey and Sir Edwin Johnson who were mainly responsible for the financial blunders of the late administration left about the end of the year. Sir Evelyn Baring, who came from one of the first houses of business in Europe, and who had Indian experience as the

Private Secretary to Lord Northbrook was appointed the new finance minister. With an almost new council the Marquis of Ripon earnestly commenced his responsible task.

GENERAL EVENTS.—Sir Richard Temple resigned somewhat before his time with a view to enter the House of Commons. His administration of the Bombay Presidency was very popular with certain classes who voted a statue to him. He was succeeded by Sir James Fergusson, who was being initiated into the mysteries of the Indian Government during the first year of his rule. In Madras His Grace the Duke of Buckingham laid down the reins of office at the close of the year. His Grace stood high in the estimation of the public of the Southern Presidency. His large-hearted sympathies with the ruled, his unfailing business habits and judicial temperament had endeared him to the people whom he ruled and the movement in his honor to express the respect and gratitude of the people was a genuine and spontaneous one. He was succeeded by Mr. Adam who had been very useful to the Liberal party in the matter of organization. All these nominations proceeded from Mr. Gladstone who had been advocating the cause of the Indian people with an earnestness that had endeared his name to them. Mr. Gladstone drew frequent attention to the Indian grievances in the course of the electoral campaigns in Scotland. He condemned the Arms Act as casting an unmerited scur on the loyalty of the people and as coming in force curiously within a very short interval of that period when the confidence of Her Majesty in the loyalty of Her Indian subjects was loudly proclaimed at Delhi. He denounced the Vernacular Press Act as a "contradiction to the spirit of the age in which we live and a disgrace to the British authorities." Referring to the pledge given with reference to the License Tax he pointed out that the pledge had been utterly broken and that the money had been used upon the " ruinous unjust and destructive war with Afghanistan" with reference to which war he said " A meaner act, a shabbier act, a more dastardly act is not to be found than that by which this government forbearing even to remonstrate with Russia, that is to say accepting from Russia the most feeble and transparent excuses, with ostensible satisfaction reserved all its force and all its vengeance for the unfortunate Amir of Afghanistan." The great Liberal statesman on coming into power, closed the Afghan War, and promised to divide on an equitable basis the expenses of the war between India and England. The new Viceroy who was a quiet, and steady man without any love of show in him, was requested to examine all the cardinal questions of Indian policy for the proper instruction of the Liberal ministry. There was also considerable attention bestowed on Indian questions by the English public. The first-rate magazines opened their pages to the discussion of Indian questions and lectures on Indian subjects were delivered not only by Dr. Hunter the Earl of Northbrook, Sir Arthur Hobhouse and Sir Richard Temple but also by Mr. Lal Mohun Ghose whose speeches made a capital impression on the British public. The reception given in England to Mr. Lal Mohun Ghose was a just cause of patriotic pride on the part of the educated natives of India. Religious excitement coupled with some dread of the census operations then in progress roused the Santhals of Bengal to a state of open distatisfaction. Sir Ashly Eden who brought himself first into public notice by suppressing the first Santhal rebellion managed the situation with so much tact and energy that the excitement was suppressed without much cost of powder, shot and blood. The census rules were relaxed and other welcome concessions were made which quieted Santhalistan. The Rent question was brought to the front in Bengal during the year. The landlords of Bengal complained to the Government of the increasing difficulties in the way of realizing rents as well as of the cesses which they had been commissioned to collect for the Government. Several measures were framed with this object but none met with success. At length a Commission was appointed to simplify matters and the whole subject of the Rent law in Bengal was taken into consideration. The Rent question in Bengal is beset with unusual complexity and the respective relations of property and labour, capital and intelligence were to be readjusted. The Commission submitted its recommendations which would be considered in detail later on. The cotton industry of the city of Bombay had reached such extensive developments as to cause serious anxiety to the English mercantile classes. Those who have been to that magnificent city of Western India and have looked down upon the whole area of that commercial mart from the chosen points of vantage so well-known to all, could hardly meet with a more agreeable spectacle than the edifices of numerous mills streching for many miles together in all directions as far as the eye can reach. The outturn of these mills was considerably appreciated in the Indian market and some legislative projects with reference to them were put before the Council but ultimately abandoned. One of the results of the extended scheme of decentralization introduced by the late administration was that many charges were thrown upon the local resources which ought in justice to have been met from the provincial revenues. In Bombay the community which is chiefly commercial was so much distinguished for intelligence public spirit and independence that the local affairs were managed with conspicuous success. One administrative change which was much emphasized about this time was that the officers should have as minute a knowledge of local affairs as possible and should always undertake tours of inspection. There can be no doubt that much is to be gained by the central Government of the country from the local knowledge of all the officers under it and there is also much advantage in the minute acquaintance of the heads of administrations with all portions of the territory under their charge. The local officers are kept constantly vigilant and the people can always approach their rulers with their grievances under this system. But it is extremely doubtful whether the official tours are performed as they ought to be and whether they are not at present more fruitful of evil than good. The cities of Calcutta and Bombay showed their gratitude to Mr. Fawcett, the sightless champion of India by raising a sufficient fund to meet his election expenses. The grievances of the third class passengers by the Indian railways excited considerable attention. It was universally admitted that the third class passengers who pay the most towards the railway earnings are treated in a way which is a disgrace to any civilized administration and a conference was arranged to remedy this state of things from which no practical benefits were derived. Jeypore mourned this year the death of Maharaja Ram Singh, the enlightened ruler of that state and Travancore lost its model prince. In British Burma which is essentially an agricultural country the area under the plough was steadily increasing especially in the Pegu division. The main cause of the prosperity of British Burma was the moderation of the Government demand on commerce and the high speculative rates which were offered for rice on account of keen competition. Labour earned very good wages in Burmah and it was thought desirable that some labourers from the more crowded parts of India whose lot is as hard as could be borne, should be imported into that province. The expansion of the sea-borne trade of British Burma also established her internal prosperity. The Vernacular Press Act although on the statute-book was practically a dead letter since its enactment with the exception of one isolated instance of vigour. The historian will have to record during the course of the next few years the visible organization through which the Natives of India of all races and creeds meant to carry on the work of constitutional agitation, and it would not be out of place to remark that the political associations all over the country displayed a healthy activity and interested themselves in all public questions. There can be no prouder monument of British rule than that an ancient and fallen race should work out its political regeneration. This was the dream of those noble statesmen who realized that the English in India are for a high and noble purpose and who with the motives of philanthrophy introduced the beneficent policy of English education.

CHAPTER III.

1881.

THE POLITICAL ASPECTS OF THE COUNTRY.—The year 1881 will ever remain memorable in the history of Indian administration for the restoration to native dynasties of the two important Feudatory kingdoms viz. Baroda and Mysore. These acts on the part of the paramount power evinced the sincerity of its professions and cemented the loyalty of all the feudatory chieftains. They were both acts of pure justice and proved beyond a doubt the sense of duty of the English people. Lord Dalhousie had, for pretexts much flimsier than those which were available in the above cases, made large and important annexations. The Maharaja of Mysore was installed by His Excellency the Governor of Madras on the 25th March. He owed this happy consummation to the righteousness of his cause aided by the sense of justice of that eminent statesman Lord Halifax. The father of the Maharaja who was installed had tried his best to get back the kingdom and to induce the British Government to redeem the promise given half a century ago that the Raj would be restored as soon as equilibrium of the finances had been secured. But it was not until Lord Halifax was in charge of the portfolio of the India office that the truthfulness of His Highness's claim was admitted, and it was decided that the young Maharaja should be installed as soon as he completed the eighteenth year of his age. The kingdom of Mysore had got into debt owing to the late famine and the conditions of the treaty of transfer had been arranged with great moderation. The Mysore state was to pay an annual subsidy of 24 lakhs for the first five years and then an increased subsidy by 10 lakhs, if the state of the finances permitted its being paid and was to observe the usual conditions as to the building and repairing of forts of importing and manufacturing arms, of increasing military force, of introducing separate coinage, of employing Europeans as well with respect to the manufacture of salt and opium, the construction and working of railway and telegraph lines and continuing the existing laws of revenue settlement and existing system of administration. His Highness the Maharaja on ascending the throne issued a proclamation in which he expressed his willingness to observe the above stipulations and indicated the mode of administration that he would follow. This was by a council of which Dewan Ranga Charlu was to be the President. The Maharaja reserved for his own consideration all questions with reference to legislation and taxation and all important measures with reference to the administration of his territories and the well-being of his subjects. As the Mysore state was in debt the Maharaja wisely determined to employ cheap native agency instead of the British agency which was expensive. He fully realized that Mysore having been under British rule for more than fifty years would greatly lament any deterioration from that absolute security of life and property which is the greatest blessing of British rule. Sir John Gordon who had arranged the transfer business was appointed British Resident and the Maharaja accepted cheerfully that officer as his guide and philosopher in all questions of difficulty. The Maharaja also gave his subjects a sort of informal Parliament and on the 7th of October two hundred representatives from all local taluqs met to criticise the administration of the past year and to offer suggestions with reference to the coming year. About the end of the year the Governor of Bombay installed the Gaekwar of Baroda. It was a conclusive proof of the will of Her Gracious Majesty that all native states should be continued in integrity and independence. Since the unfortunate proceedings with reference to the Baroda state in Lord Northbrook's time, that state was being administered with conspicuous success by the native statesman, Sir T. Madhava Rao. It is a matter of regret that under the British rule the natives of India have very little opportunity to exhibit their fitness in the highest duties of administration. The Moslem rulers offered commands of armies and pro-consulships of provinces to their conquered Hindu subjects and great statesmen and financiers could spring up under that rule. It is unfortunately quite otherwise under the British regime and it is in the feudatory states alone that native statesmanship can flourish to any great extent. The work which Lord Northbrook entrusted to Sir T. Madhava Rao was one of equal difficulty and importance. The Baroda state was suffering under accumulated grievances arising from past maladministration of the sirdars bankers, ryots and others, the treasury was empty and the country was torn by internal factions. The local sirdars and people were jealous of the new prime minister who had to proceed with the utmost tact, firmness and caution. During the five years that the state was under his charge he maintained public order and tranquillity with firmness and moderation, he established a proper and sufficient machinery for the administration of justice in both its branches, he provided a police commensurate with the extent and density of the population, he executed necessary and useful Public works, he provided for popular education, he gave suitable medical aid, he reduced, re-adjusted and where necssary abolished taxes, he enforced economy, he restrained waste, he kept the expenditure below the receipts and he generally strengthened the executive establishments. The young Gaekwar at the same time developed a thoroughly healthy moral nature and steady mental virtues. The highest political authorities agreed that the very highest appreciation was due to the unwearied labours of Sir T. Madhava Rao for the good of the State and people and cordial acknowledgements were also due to the heads of departments who were all native gentlemen of high attainments. The Gaekwar acknowledged his obligations to Mr. Melville and Sir Richard Meade and let it be mentioned to the credit of the Maharaja that he has maintained his splendid kingdom in the same state of efficiency in which he received it. The relations of the Government with Amir Abdur Rahman remained very friendly all through. The British government did not give him any help in the matter of suppressing the insurrection of Ayub Khan though it looked very anxiously on the situation. Ayub Khan was ultimately defeated and his troops dispersed and Abdur Rahman ruled Afghanistan with a strong hand which was necessary to keep down the contending elements in that disturbed country. Lord Ripon made a tour in Rajputana during the current year. His Excellency observed that the Government of India as the paramount power was under a sacred obligation to see that the subjects of the native states do not suffer from misgovernment or oppression and he aimed to effect this object not through force and coercion but through the elevating, humanizing and civilizing influence of education. In Rajputana the Native States were enjoying fairly prosperous years and the work of administration had been going on smoothly. In Oodypur a new land settlement was completed under the supervision of Mr. Wingate of the Bombay Civil Service. In Jeypur there was a growing absence of that mutuality and harmony in the Council, so necessary for a good administration since the death of the late Maharaja. In Bharatpur the Government was under the direction of His Highness personally and the administration, it was universally admitted was carried on with less consideration for his subjects than was shown by other native rulers. The young Chiefs who had been trained under English tutors or at the Mayo College did not fulfil the expectations of their subjects as they gave too great attention to sport and the out-door amusements and too little to the duties of the State. The finances of several Native States such as Tonk, Bikanir and Karowlee were in a state of sad confusion. The Government at Marwar was reported to lack strength. The general closing of the "Khari" works in Jeypur which supplied salt of a sort which though not generally edible was a part of the food of the camels and the horned cattle produced general dissatisfaction. The Maharaja of Bundi issued an edict prohibiting the marriage of old and infirm persons with young girls. This edict was welcomed by his subjects though in British India such an edict would be deemed as undue interference.

THE FINANCES.—The exchange difficulty had been gradually making the financial position of India insecure, owing to a variety of causes the principal of which was the superabundance of the silver mines recently discovered as compared with gold mines and a great decrease in the demand for silver. The relative values of gold and silver were much disturbed in the markets of the world. India which had to make fixed annual payments to the English Government which are unalterably fixed in gold was a great loser by the depreciation of silver and this circumstance hung as a deadweight upon her revenues. The only hope in the matter of escape from this difficulty is from the increasing popularity of silver and she always looks with an wistful eye to the results of those international conferences which are arranged for the purpose of introducing bi-metallism in certain European and American countries. This year an international conference met at Paris to discuss with a view to practical action this question in which India was vitally interested. India was represented by Sir Louis Mallet who supported bimetallism but Mr. Gladstone was still in favour of the orthodox doctrine of monometallism. The question was however discussed by the highest economic authorities during the course of the year and many of them declared themselves to be in favour of bimetallism. Sir Evelyn Baring in his budget speech said that this loss by exchange coupled with the precariousness of the opium revenue and the periodical outbreak of famine made the financial position of India quite insecure and he made a departure of policy by carrying out several measures of real economy. He reduced the salaries of the High Court Judges, he effected the double object of enforcing economy and at the same time encouraging local industry by coming forward to purchase Government stores in India. He also did a great deal of good in inducing the great English capitalists to apply their capital in Indian railways and canals, and it is to him that India owes the accession of the famous Rothschilds to the guild of Indian enterprize. He reformed the whole system of accounts and did his best to ensure accuracy in the despatch of business. England contributed £5,000,000 representing one-fourth of the total cost of the Afghan War and the bulk was to be paid by the Indian Treasury. This was a great disturbing element in Indian finance and with this deadweight hanging over it the Indian Government could not attempt any final changes during this year. The Afghan war was a war for purely imperial purposes, and the English Foreign Office had alone been responsible for the policy of the war and there can be no question that the contribution made by England represented most inadequately her share in the transaction. The Parliamentary committee had justly cut down the amount to be spent for Indian public works and the new policy of the Finance Minister to encourage the application of private capital was very generally approved. Major Baring gave bodily form to the Famine Insurance fund and his famous circular about purchasing the Government stores in India if carried out in the same noble spirit which actuated him and Lord Ripon would do much towards resuscitating the decaying Indian industries. There are men and capital enough in the country and the only thing wanted is adequate encouragement. It is indeed a thing of deep regret that the Indian industries which in times past have produced many things that are the just admiration of the civilized world should now die out of the country and how to revive those industries is one of those problems that are pressing themselves on the attention of the enlightened Indian official and non-official alike. It is indeed idle to conceal that those industries are flourishing to a much greater extent in the feudatory states being under the patronage of the native chiefs and nobles, but in British India their practical extinction is but a question of time. If the Indian Government should use the produce of indigenous industry in all their requirements in the various departments and administrations as far as practicable and should also employ indigenous labour for the erection of Government buildings to a much greater extent than is now the case the skill of Indian workmen which at one time produced the Tajmahal of Agra and the famous embroidery so much appreciated in Europe would remain in the country. It is much to be regretted that this duty on the part of the Indian Government remains as yet unfulfilled.

LORD RIPON'S INTERNAL ADMINISTRATION.—Lord Ripon won the universal respect and confidence of all classes of the natives of India by the liberal way in which he ruled over them. He was a capital man of business and after having familiarized himself with the preliminary duties of Indian administration, he took a broad and statesmanlike view of things and in all matters of importance before the Executive council His Lordship explained the facts of the case himself. He took a warm interest in his work and he discharged the duties of his high office thoroughly, conscientiously and in perfect accordance with the spirit of the Queen's proclamation. His Excellency studied the complicated question of Indian famines in disposing of the report of the Indian Famine Commission. He revived the Agricultural Department, and undertook land assessments on an improved plan in several parts of the country. But His Lordship will have an eternal claim to the gratitude of the people of India by the step that he took in the course of the year for extending the principle of local self-government which is almost one of the inevitable results of the extension of the decentralization scheme under Lord Mayo and Lord Lytton. Lord Ripon declared in plain terms that his government would introduce the policy of local self-government in the matter of the administration of the local funds. The measure was conceived in the spirit of the best and greatest rulers our country ever had and the whole country welcomed it with unfeigned satisfaction. It is the first step towards the political education of the people on a large scale, and the only effective means that has been yet adopted for associating the people of the country in the administration of their affairs. Under the inspiring influence of Lord Ripon the local governments agreed to give the measure a fair trial. The only weak point in the measure that was conceived was the power that it proposed to vest in the District Magistrates, who would be the chairmen of the District Boards. In the less advanced parts of the country it was feared that the District Magistrate would be the practical head of affairs and that the whole system would end in a failure as far as its real object was concerned. It was suggested in many influential quarters that it would be far better to make the District Judge the chairman if the Government was not prepared to allow the Board to elect their own chairman. But Lord Ripon devised a constitutional measure which if worked in a sympathetic spirit by the District officials and with energy and integrity by the representatives of the people would familiarize them with the primary duties of administration and pave the way for the larger association of the educated natives of the country in the provincial Councils and ensure their future political advancement all along the line. Lord Ripon took an enumeration of the people of India and the work though managed by a central head was carried out in such a way as to dissipate the foolish notions as to the motives of the Government which the ignorant always see in such a step. The most pleasing feature with reference to the census operations was the hearty co-operation of the people, and the educated natives freely rendered their services as unpaid enumeratosr for this work. Lord Ripon also took interest in the question of the education of European and Eurasian children. The lot of the domiciled European and Eurasian who had not the means to send his children to England was in many respects an unenviable one, and Lord Canning had declared that unless something was done in this respect it would be a standing reproach to Government. The same educational institutions which imparted such a high-class education to the natives of India would equally suit the Europeans, but as these communities had availed themselves but little of those advantages, Lord Ripon placed some special facilities within their reach to enable them to better their condition. Lord Ripon also did conspicuous services in the matter of the reorganisation of the Punjab University, and in withstanding the effects of that mischievous agitation which was opposed by the educated natives of the Punjab. Lord Lytton in 1879 had declared at Lahore that the education which could be imparted without causing any harm to the physically weak Bengali is not suited to the hardy races of Upper India. The internal peace lead to social and material progress. Many important lines of railways were completed and several other projects were matured under Lord Ripon's beneficent rule, the political aspirations were steadily expanding, the Native Press had been increasingly active, the public associations were in the full tide of their activity and the social and political problems of India were being earnestly discussed with a view to practical action. The whole country rejoiced at having a statesman so just and so righteous at the head of the Indian administration

GENERAL EVENTS—Mr. Whitely Stokes introduced into the Supreme Council several ambitious projects of legislation, the principal of which was the Transfer of Property Bill. The codification measures of Mr. Whitely Stokes would, it was feared, throw the Indian public more completely at the mercy of the lawyer. However perfect the English systems of administration of justice might theoretically be considered to be, its practical results are often lamentable. The delay and expense attendant on the British courts contrast very unfavourably with the summary methods of justice to which the great masses of the people of every country are by instinct attached. Some of Mr. Stokes' measures were based on English statutes and the wide difference in the state of things in England and India caused the apprehension that such measures, as the Indian Companies' Bill did not fit in well enough in this country. The Negotiable Instruments' Act which was passed this year caused little excitement as by its provisions all native hundis were still to be regulated by local usages and customs. The Inland Emigration Bill and the Hindu Wills Bill caused considerable commotion in Bengal. The former was, in deference to the timely protest of the Hon'ble Maharaja Sir Jotindra Mohun Tagore and of the public bodies of Bengal referred back to the Select Committee. The Liberal leaders redeemed their pledge with reference to the Vernacular press of this country by a bill which provided for the unconditional repeal of the Vernacular Press Act of the previous administration. The country was not yet ripe for a scientific treatment in respect of all legal problems and Mr. Stokes' measures would it was feared increase the stream of litigation. The restraints of office prevented many of the best Parliamentary friends of India from taking any part in the debates on Indian affairs and consequently they were not of that animated nature they were expected to be from the importance of the subjects dealt with. The sentimental philanthropists of England protested against the Indian opium trade forgetting that India would lose an extensive revenue by the suppression of that trade and humanity would not benefit thereby as China would have her opium supply from other sources and that unless Parliament was prepared to make good the pecuniary loss expected, the English public should not raise this question. Lord Hartington promised not to interfere with the opium trade but to consider whether the Government monopoly in this respect could not be dispensed with. This step, His Lordship was convinced later on in the year would prove very mischievous as without any appreciable benefit it would result in the loss of two millons of revenue. The question of the abolition of the India Council in London was discussed. There is no doubt ample room for improvement with reference to that Council particularly by placing on its body experienced Indian gentlemen of enlightenment and education but there is little doubt that in these days when India is practically governed by telegraphic wire from England, the abolition of the India Council would place India at the mercy of the waves of party conflict in England and that the Secretary of State would lack that counsel, the result of years of Indian experience in all departments to which he ought to pay deferential heed before making up his mind with regard to Indian questions. Madras lost her energetic Governor Mr. Adam who during the short tenure of his office had proved to be an energetic and sympathetic administrator. He was succeeded by Sir Monstuart Grant Duff a liberal statesman of high rank. The Governor of Bombay Sir James Fergusson greatly disappointed his subjects. Some of his legal measures had been so high-handed and capricious that they were disallowed by the Secretary of State. In domestic matters he showed much narrow-minded bigotry and most of his actions were characterized by indifference to the interests of the people. Sir Stuart Bayley was removed from Assam to the Residency at Hyderabad and he was succeeded by Mr. Charles Elliott who developed the resources of the province with characterstic energy. The Bengal Government proposed that important measure of legislation known as the Rent Law. The Rent question was treated as a whole and some provisions from the Irish Land Act were bodily introduced into Bengal. The Zamindars of Bengal and Behar through their powerful association, the British Indian, then led by some of the foremost politicians of Bengal, Rajah Rajendra Lala Mitra, Hon'ble Kristodas Paul Maharaja Sir Jotindra Mohun Tagore, Maharaja Sir Norendra

Krishna, and the Maharajas of Durbhanaga, Domraon, Hutwa, and Bettiah, set on foot an influential agitation both in England and India and the literature on the subject grew to such proportions that it is difficult to compress the whole subject within reasonable limits. There was an insurrection during the year among the Bheels but it was effectively managed by timely force and diplomacy. The intrigues that were discovered at Kolhapur were magnified into a grand conspiracy the hollowness of which theory was revealed at the trial of the conspirators. The debate on the Afghan war in the House of Lords was opened by Lord Lytton and he was supported by Lords Salisbury and Beaconsfield the last of whom succumbed this year to the cold hand of death. But no one was convinced by Lord Lytton's speech although it was a finished one that the Afghan war was a righteous war. The arguments of the Conservative party were satisfactorily answered by the Duke of Argyll, Lord Granville and Lord Selborne. The London *Statesman* under the management of Mr. Knight and Col. Osborne enlisted the sympathy of some of the foremost public men of England towards Indian grievances and aspirations.

CHAPTER IV.

1882.

THE EGYPTIAN WAR.—The Egyptian War was a purely Imperial war and the Indian historian is compelled to make a brief reference to it because of the help that India in response to England's call gave her, in the shape of an Indian contingent that nobly did its duty, the alacrity shown by the loyal offers of the native chiefs with reference to placing their own troops at the disposal of the Indian Government and the burden that the Indian exchequer had to bear in spite of the manly protests of Lord Ripon and Major Baring as to the amount of the expenses incurred by the contingent sent from this country.

The war in Egypt was of the nature of a Civil war, in which the aggressive party were the Nationalists whose object it was to keep all foreign influence out of Egypt. The English and French fundholders who had made large advances to the Egyptian Government exercised a predominant influence in every department of state and this fact led the Nationalists to combine to keep everything in their own hands. The English Government lent its support to the Khedive and bombarded Alexandria on the ostensible plea of keeping safe the world's commerce that passed through the Suez Canal. The leader of the Nationalists Arabi Pasha, showed no mean capacity or skill but his organization broke down and the British force whose action was sharp and swift carried the day. The war having ended the whole political fabric of Egypt was re-cast. The Indian contingent did the allotted work well and gloriously. The metal it showed was duly appreciated in England, and Indian military training, and the attachment of Indian troops to the British standard was vindicated before the eyes of Europe and Asia. The case of the Indian tax-payers with reference to saddling India with the cost of the Indian contingent to Egypt was put in a noble and manly way by Lord Ripon and Major Baring but the protest was of no avail and the Liberal Government of England disappointed the hopes of the people of India by throwing the above burden on the Indian Treasury.

LORD RIPON'S DOMESTIC POLICY AND THE LOCAL SELF-GOVERNMENT SCHEME. We adverted briefly in the last chapter to the general features of the Local Self-Government scheme but during this year it was practically introduced into Local Governments and administrations. Sir Ashley Eden the Lieutenant-Governor of Bengal perceived that legislation of an extensive and complicated character would be necessary to sanction the excercise of the powers to be conceded in the different departments to the District Boards as well as for the proper powers of control and inspection to be reserved to the State. His Honor however as a beginning increased the grant for primary education by one lakh of rupees and made liberal allowances to the District Road Committees for the execution of well-considered projects. He relieved the Muffasil Municipalities of all police charges directed them to apply the funds thus set free to judicious expenditure in the matter of conservancy, lighting, drainage, water-supply and similar public works and expressed his willingness to extend experimentally the elective system to all first-class Municipalities. Lord Ripon had vindicated in the warmest terms the capacity of the people of this country for Local Self-Government. His Lordship said that the people of India have no doubt been to a great extent tolerant of existing facts but with the spread of education a class of public spirited men have come into existence whom it should be sheer folly not to utilize and who would be able to a considerable extent to reduce the overwork that is the general complaint of District officers. The scheme, His Lordship, added was chiefly desirable as an instrument of political and popular education, and if allowed a full and fair trial without any direct though well-meant official interference the results, would be very gratifying. Lord Ripon emphatically stated that the gradual introduction of the elective system was the main object of his Government, though he left it to the Local Governments and district officers to devise the best means for this object. His Lordship also laid down the general views of his Government as to control in that there must be effective supervision but the members of the Board must be free to such an extent that they might feel that real power had been placed in their hands, and the organization of this delicate machinery was left to the discretion of the Local Governments. Sir George Couper who was the very type of a narrowminded provincial Governor did his best to thwart the benevolent intentions of Lord Ripon and to reduce Local Self-Government within the narrowest possible limits. He bluntly declared that the people in his satrapy had no liking for the elective system and he would therefore only cut down the number of official members, increase the number of non-official numbers to one-half of the entire body and the non-official members were to be nominated by the district officer, approved by the Commissioner of the Division and confirmed by Government. The District Officers of course would continue to be the chairmen of the said bodies. This was merely an attempt to shuffle the cards a little leaving the regular officials of the district in full possession of their ample powers. In his further orders on the subject Sir George Couper limited and defined the duties and responsibilities of District and Municipal Committees in a such way as to reduce the whole scheme to a mere sham. Sir Charles Aitchison on the other hand dealt with the whole question with a breadth and liberality of view that cannot be sufficiently admired. That high-minded statesman laid down the important principle that local bodies must be trusted, their powers and responsibilities must be alike real, there must be no illusion about the one or the other, that it must not be assumed that the people were unfit for the duties of election and that they must be trained to acquire the intelligence, the honesty, and the capacity to choose their representatives. Sir Charles Aitchison introduced elections at once in the more considerable towns upon the English model. The Chief Commissioner of Assam Mr. Charles Elliott fell in cordially with the views of Lord Ripon and he treated different parts of his province in different ways. As Local institutions were of recent growth in Assam and complications arose from the presence of a large and powerful section representing the tea industry, he had framed his recommendations with great tact and judgment. The Government of Bombay did not take any steps forward in giving extended power to the District Boards regarding the administration of District and Provincial funds, but it took a really broad view on the subject of Municipal administration. Thus Lord Ripon planted in the Indian soil the roots of a system that would in the fulness of time be productive of the highest good. There was a spontaneous feeling of gratitude for a ruler from whom the measure emanated with such good grace and with the utmost generosity. Lord Ripon's aim was not only to make the Municipalities and Local Boards efficient administrative units but to make them instruments for the political education of the people. Lord Ripon also earned the gratitude of the Indian people by the repeal of the Vernacular Press Act. His Lordship ascertained from careful enquiry that the State would not be put in danger by reason of this repeal and he carried out the measure quietly but firmly. The native public all over the country gave His Lordship their warmest thanks for this act and a very influential meeting in Calcutta concluded that agitation with reference to the obnoxious Act which might fairly claim to have been eminently successful. At that meeting Mr. Lalmohan Ghose and Babu Surendra Nath Banerji gave powerful expression to the feelings of the Indian public with reference to this measure. It was the cardinal aim of Lord Ripon's policy to exert his great talents to secure the victories of peace, and to encourage indigenous talent, indigenous industries and indigenous institutions. His Lordship with the active assistance of Major Baring and Mr. Ilbert appointed Mr. Justice Romesh Chandra Mitter the senior puisne Judge of the Bengal High Court as officiating Chief Justice in spite of the opposition to that step from influential quarters on political and administrative grounds. Mr. Justice R. C. Mitter had after a most successful career in the High Court Bar been elevated to the Bench and had established the highest character for himself by his ability, industry, honesty and that judicial patience and calmness of temper which is the first characteristic of a judge and his appointment to the officiating Chief Justiceship of Bengal was hailed with profound satisfaction all over the country. Lord Ripon also gave an Indian judge to the N. W. P. High Court in the person of a Mahomedan barrister of great culture. His Lordship also advanced Rai Saligram Bahadur, a tried officer of the Postal Department, to the appointment of Postmaster General of the N. W. Provinces, an office never before filled by a native of India. The Madras Government at Lord Ripon's instance appointed a native gentleman Mr. Justice Muthuswamy Aiyer to the Bench of the Local High Court. In the humbler situations, in Government offices and state railways the employment of indigenous agency was to a great extent, given effect to. Lord Ripon had laid the foundation of a revived national industry and by his judicious regulations on the suspension and remission of Government revenue in bad seasons advanced the interests of the agricultural population.

The extension of education had received the earnest attention of Lord Ripon's Government. He appointed an Education Commission with Dr. Hunter as its president whose object was to extend primary education without in any way interfering with the progress of high education. The Commission owed its birth to the agitation of a powerful clique in England which was opposed to the spread of high education in India and it was therefore at first looked on by the natives of India with great suspicion but the honest utterances of His Excellency soon dispelled all doubts. His Lordship showed the utmost deference to public opinion, particularly to Indian public opinion. He invited the leaders and representative men of every community to submit their opinion on all important matters and measures. Lord Ripon also took in hand the question of giving the utmost publicity to Legislative measures. Of course the utility of this project was to have been tested by the measure of the attention which the Government would bestow upon the opinions which might be elicited. The credit of the scheme of Local Self-Government is entirely Lord Ripon's own. It was with difficulty that His Lordship converted the Secretary of State to his views and he appealed with a rare sincerity of heart to all men of influence and education to take their proper place in the administration of the country. It was recognized on all hands that Lord Ripon had been not merely a ruler but a friend of the people. Lord Ripon devised a liberal system of agricultural loans and set his face resolutely against taxation of the articles of food in any form. The restless chief of Upper Burma almost necessitated the declaration of hostilities by the headlong course that he pursued. An embassy waited on His Excellency to open negotiations to settle the differences but no real work was done. As his own Foreign minister Lord Ripon improved the relations with the Feudatory princes by the same high-minded statesmanship. He placed the young Maharaja of Jeypur on the throne with proper safeguards and highly approved of the administrations of the Gaekwar and the Maharaja of Travancore. His noble policy was appreciated by all the Native Chiefs and they became more devoted in their attachment to the paramount power.

THE FINANCES.—The second budget of Sir Evelyn Baring showed that he had a firm grasp both of the financial situation of India and of sound economic principles. The accounts for the last official year closed with such a surplus that the Finance minister with the sanction of Lord Ripon was able to make large reductions in the taxation of the country. The Patwari cess of the N. W. Provinces was abolished involving a remission of revenue to the extent of £316,000, the cotton duties and the import duties were abolished, the taxation being reduced to the extent of £1,219,000, the salt duty was reduced to Rs. 2 all round involving a remission of taxation of £1,400,000. Major Baring improved the prospects of the Subordinate Executive Service by an annual cost of £50,000. The Finance Minister justly remarked that the Native Deputy Collectors formed the backbone of the British administration in India and that the Government looked to them for ability and efficiency in quiet times and for energy, resource and fortitude in times of difficulty, that this service should consist of the cream of those who are willing to embrace an official career in this country and that they should be in receipt of adequate salaries throughout their career. Major Baring remarked that the government of the country could not be carried on without a cash balance of £8,5000,000. He also improved the prospects of the Subordinate Judicial Service and arranged the provincial contracts on a liberal basis. The new policy enunciated was to provincialize three-fifths of the revenue and one-fourth of the expenditure of British India. Major Baring truly observed that if the opium revenue were taken away from India the country would soon become bankrupt. The policy of remission of taxation at this stage does not seem by the light of subsequent events to have been a prudent step. All the three sources of revenue that came to be abolished did not press very hard on the poor and were comparatively unobjectionable and if the Government had not sacrificed these three millions it might have more effectively aided the advancement of the project for local self-government which must have ways and means as an essential condition of its success, or it might have carried into effect the recommendations of the Education Commission with reference to primary education or taken in hand the numerous administrative reforms that are so needful. Of course the cotton duties were doomed from some years past. Lord Lytton explained at Manchester how the entire abolition of the cotton and import duties must follow in the train of that tortuous policy that his government had followed in this respect, and there can be no question that although Lord Ripon prided himself on the fact of his having given complete free trade to India he too must be considered to have been a party to the sacrifice of Indian interests for the sake of a few merchants and manufacturers of England. The Famine Insurance Fund was restored from the general revenues and it was to be applied for famine relief and the execution of public works. The Government of India under the influence of the Public Works Minister Sir T. C. Hope introduced the experiment of stock notes which however was not attended with the desired success. It failed to attract the capital of the rural and industrial classes for whose benefit it had been principally designed. The Finance Minister was obliged to float a loan of two and a half crores principally to meet the burdens thrown upon India by the war expenditure in Egypt. The loan was not so successful as might have been expected, and it was taken up at a discount. The reduction of the military charges of India and the English taxation on Indian silver work also drew masterly minutes from Lord Ripon's government.

LEGISLATION.—The Assam Emigration Bill was passed into law this year. It was characterized by the Hon'ble Kristodas Paul as the Slave Bill and its two objectionable features were the fixing of the maximum wages of the coolies at Rs. 6 per mensem and the contract to subsist for a period of five years. After passing the act the Government went into the subject of coolie emigration as a whole and issued instructions and framed bye-laws which if they were strictly carried out would prevent the abuses arising from the Act to a great extent. Mr. Whitley Stokes was to vacate his office in the middle of the year and he passed in hot haste the codification measures introduced last year as well as the Easements Bill. The provincial governments for the most part repudiated the Easements Bill so it was at first confined only to the Central Provinces. The Criminal Procedure Code amendment Bill was an improvement upon the similar efforts of Sir Fitzjames Stephen. Mr. Whitley Stokes was unquestionably a great lawyer and a sound jurist but he lacked the practical talents of statesmanship and gave the country many measures which did no practical good. He was succeeded by Mr. Ilbert, the youngest lawyer who has ever held that high office, an academician of great repute and a trusted pupil of Sir Henry Thring and under him there was no legislation at high pressure.

GENERAL EVENTS—The Lieutenant Governorships of Bengal, N. W. Provinces and the Punjab changed hands during the current year. Sir Ashley Eden had long been a 'prominent figure in Indian administration and he had left his mark on the administration of the province where he served. His admirers voted him the high honor of a statue and taken all in all his administration was a fair success. The duties of the Bengal pro-consulship were daily becoming more and more arduous, and the advancing intelligence of the people made a thorough moral rectitude, a high standard of ability and an insatiable appetite for work the essential qualities of the administrator. Sir Ashley Eden was to a great extent opposed to the rising hopes and aspirations of the educated classes but in the ordinary duties of administration he effected many and enduring improvements. He established separate Rent Courts and divided the public service into two branches, the judicial and the executive to ensure a better training for the officers and to improve the administration of justice. He had carefully managed the resources of his province and under him the treasury was flourishing. He had been most active in devising roads railways and canals and if his resources had not been crippled he would have certainly done much more. He gave encouragement to high and primary education and was specially interested in female education. He took some forward steps in the matter of the employment of natives to the higher offices of the state, and he took some special measures to ameliorate the condition of the Behar ryots. Sir Ashley Eden substituted Hindi the vernacular of the people for Urdu as the language of the courts. But his administration sadly lacked in sympathy with those feelings and aspirations of the educated middle classes which it had been the chief object of Lord Ripon to foster and encourage. The Rent Bill which was introduced at his instance in the Supreme Council was a measure about which the best-informed opinion of the country was almost equally divided but there was no doubt that he had been actuated in framing it by a sincere sympathy with the Bengal Ryot. Sir George Couper whom the people of the united provinces used to call the "clergy governor" was succeeded by Sir Alfred Lyall. An accomplished man of letters with intimate knowledge of many important departments of the State he came as a distinct improvement on his predecessor. Sir Rivers Thomson who succeeded to the Bengal administration had previously had a varied experience and was considered to be a conscientious officer. But the Indian Civil Service could well be proud of the literary abilities, the varied capacity and the broad-hearted statesmanship of Sir Charles Aitchison who became this year the ruler of the Punjab. There being many projects for railways and canals under the consideration of the Supreme Government the office of the minister for public works was revived in the person of Sir Theodore Hope who had the reputation of being singularly industrious and independent in his views. Lord Hartington did not find the duties of the India office congenial to his mind, as he was not at all acquainted with the details of Indian administration. He exchanged the War Office for the India office and the Indian Secretaryship fell on the Earl of Kimberley, a nobleman who was quite familiar with the details of Colonial administration. Before the end of the year Sir Charles Aitchison was able to signalize his administration by services to the cause of high education, by remodelling the University on improved lines and by throwing open the sub-executive service to the educated natives. Sir Alfred Lyall was called upon to face the question of the abolition of the Agra College whose existence was not justified by the results. The true facts with reference to the Agra College and the splendid endowment from which it originated were brought to the notice of Lord Ripon through a series of well-reasoned articles in the columns of the *Hindu Patriot* and a laudable move on the part of the Agra public to maintain the College on their own responsibility induced the Government of India to make it over for a limited period provisionally to a local committee under the superintendence of the Executive officers of the district. The sufferings of the Deccan ryots engaged but little attention of the Government of Sir James Fergusson, who was entirely under the influence of the dominant Civilian clique. Sir Grant Duff proved a failure in the administration of the Madras Presidency. He retained his usual flippancy and though he wrote and talked much he did very little solid work. He made fearful mistakes in the case of the Chingleput affair and the Salem riots and his attitude towards the educated natives had been systematically inimical. The Khond rising in the Central Provinces was speedily suppressed. Sir Charles Barnard conducted the administration of Burma in an enlightened spirit though he could not keep the dacoits fully under control. During the year several cases of high-handed and arbitrary proceedings on the part of the Civilian officers came to light especially in Bengal. With an ever vigilant press, with a rapidly rising class of educated natives, with advancing ideas as to the rights and privileges of the subject, the Bengal officers had to feel their way most cautiously and any erratic proceedings on the part of those officers were fiercely exposed to the light of day and brought their authors to certain grief. The Mahomedans submitted a petition complaining that they had not got a fair share of the loaves and fishes of office, which memorial was referred for report to the Local Governments. The long minority of the Nizam had caused the affairs of the State to be administered by a statesman whose capacity for business, steadfast loyalty to the British Government and powers of organization were undoubted and who at the time when the British power was shaken to its foundations had sharply come with his resources to uphold the prestige of the British name. This was the last of the many years of administration of Hyderabad by Sir Salar Jung. The historian of the modern age must record with pride the grand example of Indian statesmanship exhibited in Sir Salar Jung who joined the great majority early next year. Lord Ripon when installing His Highness the Nizam paid a warm tribute to the capacities and the loyalty of Sir Salar Jung and asked the young chief to continue in the footsteps of that illustrious statesman. To keep under proper control the conflicting elements in the Hyderabad State, to carry on the work of administration smoothly by his commanding qualities, to be careful about the finances of the State, to keep the judiciary above all suspicion, the army under the necessary discipline, the police in a high state of efficiency, were some of the acts of Sir Salar Jung and those only can appreciate the full extent of his success who are familiar with the tangled web of intrigues and the thousand conflicting influences which unfortunately are too often the invariable incidents of an Oriental Court.

CHAPTER V.

1883.

THE CRIMINAL JURISDICTION BILL.—This year must remain memorable in Indian History for the remarkable agitation that was set on foot by a majority of the Anglo-Indian community in India with reference to a bill introduced in the Legislative Council for the purpose of removing the race disability imposed on Native magistrates and judges by Chapter 33 of the Code of Criminal Procedure. The measure was a small one and even if it were carried out in its integrity it would not have affected more than a half-a-dozen or so of Indian Covenanted Civilians. But this Bill was selected as the battle-ground to fight the wider question as to whether the liberal measures introduced by the Liberal Viceroy with the support of the Liberal majority in England should be allowed to pass quietly through the Council in the teeth of a bureaucracy tenacious of their privileges and an Anglo-Indian community who are not over-burdened with sympathy in regard to the hopes and aspirations of educated India. Since the question of the extension of the jurisdiction of Muffasil criminal courts over European British subjects was first raised in Parliament, many changes and improvements had taken place in the country and the objections which were valid then could not be valid now. On that occasion many illustrious English Statesmen of whom the father of Lord Ripon was one, had declared that the Natives and Europeans should be placed on a footing of perfect equality before the law. Under the direct rule of the Queen-Empress all courts were Queen's courts. The High Courts established by Royal Charter observed no distinctions in the trial of Europeans and Natives. In all the Presidency Police Courts, magistrates who are both Europeans and Natives try Europeans and Natives alike. The present efficient condition of the Muffasil courts which are

more or less filled with trained lawyers removes objections
which could formerly be urged on the ground of competency
and fitness. The privilege now enjoyed by the European
British subjects amounts in many cases to a denial of justice
to the aggrieved native of India. Such had been the considerations that brought this problem within the field of practical politics. Sir Ashley Eden proposed to do away with the
disability in the matter of trying European British subjects
in the case of Indian Covenanted officers who had entered the
service through the open door of competition in England and
who had attained a certain standing in the service. This proposal had been circulated confidentially for an expression of
opinion to the Local Governments and Administrations and it
had been generally approved of by them with the exception of
the Chief Commissioner of Coorg. Fortified by this consensus
of opinion in favor of removing the disability in the case of
Covenanted Officers Mr. Ilbert introduced into the Supreme
Council the Criminal Jurisdiction Bill. The question had been
raised in 1872 and though the progressive step in this direction was supported by the Pro Tem Viceroy with several other
members of the Executive Council the motion was lost by a
majority of two. After the present Bill was introduced into
the Council an agitation was set on foot both in England and
India, the like of which in organization, in demonstrativeness
and continuity the Indian historian has not had yet to record.
The real issue which the Bill proposed to remedy was lost
sight of and the Independent Britons were so furious and
maddened over the affair that they went far beside the real point,
raised all sorts of side-issues, and poured forth the bitterest
invectives against the children of the soil through their recognized organs in the press and from the platforms in every
part of the country. No one denied the right of the European
British subjects to agitate in a loyal and constitutional manner
to prevent the passing of any law which they considered mischievous but the tactics which they employed were such as

no reasonable man approved of at the time and which history must unequivocally condemn. We shall do no service to our contemporaries or to posterity by keeping alive in these pages the rancorous abuse that was showered against all classes of the natives of India or the insulting language that was heaped even on the devoted head of the august Representative of our Gracious Sovereign. But we must record with pride that though the children of the soil received the amplest provocations they did not retort or organize a counter-demonstration and with the solitary exception of Mr. Lalmohun Ghose's vigorous speech on the subject at Dacca, which happily did not find an echo in any other town or village, the Indian community displayed the most admirable patience and calmness. The main objections urged against the Bill were that it was not wanted by the natives, that it would be detrimental to the interests of justice and that the time was not ripe for it. The English champions of the Bill satisfactorily answered all these objections. They showed that Sir Ashley Eden on the motion of Mr. Behari Lal Gupta c. s. pressed the question for solution to the attention of the Government of India and that all the Local Governments and Administrations had agreed to its necessity, that the Bill had received the support of the leading native members of the Council, the leading organs of the native press, and the leading representative Associations. They pointed out that the native judges and magistrates who would be invested with the jurisdiction under the new law were not likely to be found wanting. The native Subordinate Judges and Munsifs who already exercised jurisdiction over European British subjects were universally pronounced to have done their duty well nor had any abuses of power been brought to light in the case of the native magistrates who try European British subjects in the Presidency towns. The British Government in this country had been steadily progressing towards equality in the eye of the law and the reform sought for was not the work of a day but the result of continued progress through a century and a quarter. At the meeting of the Supreme Council on March 9th 1883, the question was thoroughly discussed and even the responsible officials who dissented from the action of the Government could not but express their indignation in the most emphatic terms, at the foul allegations against the natives of India, and the malicious and scandalous personal attacks at the Viceroy. The Hon'ble members of the Council condemned in no uncertain terms, the wicked and criminal attempts that had been made to excite disaffection against the Government in the army. The agitation was carried to England and an influential deputation waited on the Earl of Kimberley who plainly said that there was no hope of the Bill being withdrawn though it might be modified in some respects in conformity with responsible official opinion. There were many meetings in the large towns of England to support or condemn Lord Ripon's policy and the English journals and periodicals teemed with articles on the subject. The leaders of thought in England openly expressed their sympathy with the progressive policy of Lord Ripon. The debate in the House of Lords on the subject was begun by Lord Lytton who described his successor's policy as the policy of gradually transferring political power to the natives of India and he was supported by Lords Cranbrook and Salisbury. The specific points raised were answered by the Lord Chancellor, Lord Northbrook and Lord Kimberley. The Lord Chancellor spoke highly of the ability, the legal training and acumen of native judges, from the experience derived from his extensive practice in Indian cases before the Privy Council. Her Majesty's Government declared that the principle of equality before the eyes of the law must be strictly observed in British India and Lord Ripon was but giving effect to the settled policy of the British nation, as declared in the Queen's Proclamation. The opposition in the English press was led by Sir James Stephen who forgot himself so far as to assert that the Queen's proclamation of 1858 was a merely sentimental document and was not binding on the

Indian Government. His Excellency had declared that his Government would not be influenced by any taunts, threats and menaces but would consider any reasonable objections against the measure. On referring the measure to the Local Governments and Administrations a volume of opinions was elicited on the subject which showed that the majority of the Anglo-Indian officials were as uncompromising and unyielding up to this date as they had been when that high-minded statesman Lord William Bentinck subjected the Europeans to the jurisdiction of the ordinary Civil Courts. On the return of the Government to the capital, negotiations were opened with the leaders of the opposition for a satisfactory solution of the question, and an agreement was at last effected at the instance of Sir Auckland Colvin. Lord Ripon explained that having reference to the strength of feeling on the subject his Government has been able to adhere to the principle of the Bill as far as circumstances permitted. The *concordat*, as the technical phrase for the above agreement went, confined the privilege to Native District Magistrates and Sessions Judges and settled that the European British subjects would have the privilege when charged before District magistrates or Sessions Judges to require that they should be tried by a jury of which not less than half the number should be Europeans or Americans or both. The discretion given to the Local Governments to authorize junior Native Covenanted officers to try European British subjects, in the original Bill was done away with and the suggestion of the Bombay Government about extending jury trial was accepted. On the motion of the Hon'ble Amir Ali the option was given to an accused person European and Native alike to demand a trial before another Magistrate or the Court of Session when charged with an offence under clause (C) of Sec. 191 Cr. P. C. The Hon'ble Kristo Das Paul from his place in the Council showed that this was an unsatisfactory solution of the difficulty in as much as the race distinction while abolished in one direction had been deepened in another, that the difficulty of empanelling a jury in remote districts would lead to great administrative inconvenience, and that the European Magistrates had been placed on an equality with their native colleagues by the curtailment of some powers which they had enjoyed since a long time. Lord Ripon replied that his Government was pledged to this settlement and he could not reopen the discussion. The original Bill thus amended was passed by the Council and received the formal assent of His Excellency. The *concordat* deeply disappointed the native community and although they appreciated the noble intentions of the Viceroy and were thankful that he was able partially to give effect to the original principle of the Bill, they could not but regret that His Lordship had not proved equal to the arduous task, that the appalling difficulties in his way had led him to send a message of peace to a furious community. They regretted that no adequate political results had been achieved from the bitter discussions of the immediate past and that the question had been kept in such a state as to accentuate race-distinctions based on the status of the accused more deeply. Yet they felt that the Viceroy deserved their cordial support and heartfelt gratitude for his noble vindication of the Proclamation of the Queen and for his earnest and sincere desire to govern India for the benefit of her people. The historian must accept this view as the verdict of history. The political results of the bitter controversy were certainly small but that the Viceroy was placed in a critical situation and received but little support from those who were engaged in the actual duties of administration in all parts of the country, admits of no doubt. The anomalies created by the *concordat* would remain on the Statute Book for a long time yet to come and the historian cannot but wish that Lord Ripon had acted like Lord William Bentinck who carried his Black Act in the teeth of a fierce opposition, to which Act however the Independent Britons soon grew reconciled.

THE "BENGALEE" CONTEMPT OF COURT CASE—There was

another remarkable agitation during the year which was confined to the ruled classes but which had spread to every Presidency and province of India. The Editor of the "Bengalee" was hauled up before a Full Bench of the Calcutta High Court for having committed Contempt of Court by publishing in his paper certain articles reflecting on the conduct in a certain case, of a Barrister Judge of the Court. He raised the important question about the summary jurisdiction of the High Court in cases of this sort and expressed his regret for what had appeared in his paper, which was founded on the information supplied by another paper. He was sentenced to two months' simple imprisonment on the Civil side notwithstanding the calm and judicial course recommended by Mr. Justice Romesh Chandra Mitter for which he cited some precedents. The trial of this case raised several grave issues and it took place at a time when the whole country was in a state of excitement owing to the Ilbert Bill and its result spread a panic among the ruled classes who were agitated to the inmost depths. Babu Surendra Nath Banerji, the Editor, had done great services to his country's cause. Possessed of almost marvellous energy and wonderful powers of persuasion he had laboured unremittingly and devotedly to spread the ideas of civil and religious liberty among the Indian people. He had been chiefly instrumental in founding the Indian Association, a public body which had done much for the political education of the people. An orator, whose mastery of the English tongue and whose magnificent eloquence can not fail to produce the deepest impression, an educationist who is one of the first to realize the prophecy of Lord Halifax as to the educated natives taking charge of the high education of their fellow-countrymen, a man of sturdy independence and a steadfast friend of the oppressed and the down-trodden he, had already established his name as one of those who would take a conspicuous part in those fights for the subject's rights and the privileges of the people that were just commencing. The sympathy for him was deep and widespread and the agitation that was set on foot to consider the grave issues raised by the Contempt of Court case was of such a character that the leaders of the community remembered no parallel. All sections of the Indian community and all portions of Indian continent held demonstrations to express their sympathy with the Babu in the hour of his distress. A moral force was acting at the root of this agitation in the shape of the students in all parts of Bengal who devoted their best energies to stir up their countrymen. The sight of an agitation spread over all classes of Indians whose ancestors had fought for centuries, to express sympathy for one who had labored in their cause is the most pleasing spectacle that the historian of the Indian people can behold. Under the beneficent rule of Her Majesty, Indian unity which had been a dream in past ages was becoming an accomplished fact and the same influences, the same waves of thought were acting in different parts of the country. This made possible only two years later the spectacle of a National Congress which notwithstanding its shortcomings is the proudest achievement of British rule, where many of the best intellects of every Presidency meet together to devise measures for the good of their common country. On being appealed to the Privy Council, their Lordships of the Judicial Committee held that the jurisdiction of the Courts of Record to commit summarily for cases of contempt appertained to the Indian High Courts established by Royal Charter and declared after an examination of the provisions of the adjective criminal law of India that this jurisdiction had not been interfered with by the Indian Legislature. The whole question of political agitation was becoming a pressing one from day to day. The labours of our public men for the quarter a century following the Mutiny had established the position that the rulers are not alone to perform the duty of thinking for the ruled but that the ruled might suggest what is to their best advantage, and could respectfully ask for many concessions from the grace and good-will of the Government.

The rapid spread of education increased the number of public questions and it was felt by those best competent to form an opinion on the subject that every province should have its association where all questions affecting it might be discussed and only important questions of principle affecting the whole of India should be considered by a central body and that the bounds of constitutional agitation should never be overstepped.

LORD RIPON'S DOMESTIC POLICY.—The Local Governments and Administrations were engaged during the year in extending to the territories under their charge the boon of Local Self-Government which had been conferred by the Supreme Government. Sir Alfred Lyall appointed a Committee under the presidency of Mr. C. P. Carmichael to consider the scheme suited for the United Provinces and the scheme he finally adopted was a great improvement upon that which had been sketched out by his predecessor. He adopted the principle that the right of election was not to be exercised by the general public but by a consultative electoral body nominated by the Government and the Board were given the power to elect their own chairman if they chose to do so. The Government also provided some safeguards for the abuse of powers by the Local Boards which unless worked in a very liberal and sympathetic manner would reduce the Boards to the position of nonentities and place them at the mercy of the Executive. The Punjab Act was more of an enabling than than of an enacting nature and left a good deal to the discretion of the Local Governments. This Act also empowered the Local Government to impose additional burdens on the people for purposes of Local Self-Government and though the Viceroy and Sir Charles Aitchison explained that that provision would be worked with the greatest consideration it was an unfortunate feature as it led the shrewd oriental nature to suspect that the burdens of the people would be increased under this new scheme. The Local Self-Government Bill for British Burmah gave the people greater freedom in their own affairs, though the rural tracts were exempted from the operation of the Act. The Imperial Council passed this year the Central Provinces Local Self-Government Act. This was a small measure but on the occasion of the discussion of the Bill in the Council Mr. Gibbs, hailed the measure as a harbinger of reform and as the legitimate outcome of England's enlightened policy in the East. He said that the District officers should do their best to work the scheme in a perfectly fair and sympathetic spirit, that there should be no dictation and unnecessary interference on their part and that the people of the country should deem it a privilege to make the scheme a success by their honest and intelligent efforts in this direction. In Bombay the Local Self-Government Bill was introduced in the Council but two able native members of the Council Mr. V. N. Mandalik and Mr. Baduruddin Tyabji showed that those provisions were not calculated to advance the cause of Local Self-Government. The Central Provinces Land Act first recognized in Indian legislation the principle of compensation for improvements which was borrowed from the Irish Land Act and about whose satisfactory working in Ireland there was such a conflict of opinion.

The Bengal Rent Bill was finally introduced into the Council this year and the zamindars kept up a steady agitation against the measure which they described as one of spoliation and confiscation, and as utterly inconsistent with the pledges of the Government embodied in the Permanent Settlement Regulations. Lord Ripon took special measures for the publication of all legislative measures and for inviting well-informed opinions on the same. The policy of supplying the place of imported articles by country-made articles received a vigorous extension during the past year. Lord Ripon made a mistake in interfering with the Jail manufactures of Upper India. The comparative cheapness of jail-made articles interfered with the profits of some European mill-owners and on their representation jail manufactures were suppressed summarily. The step was an unfortunate one, as native manufacturers never complained of the cheapness of convict labour, and manufactures are regularly carried on in the English prisons. The Government of India granted a fixed annual subsidy of twelve lakhs a year to the Amir of Cabul to make him independent of Russian influence and to enable him to rule strongly. The Government however thought it wise not to enter into any hard-and-fast treaty engagements with the Amir. The serious differences between the Maharaja of Bikanir and his Thakurs ended in open rupture. These differences arose from prolonged misrule and all intercessions of the Political Agent proved to be of no effect. The march however of a small number of British troops and the destruction of the stronghold of the Thakur of Bidasur who headed the rebellion quieted matters. A strong Government was established and the Political agent was invested with fuller authority. The young Maharana of Dholpur was installed during the year. The Government of Lord Ripon sustained a great loss by the transfer to Egypt of one of its main pillars, Sir Evelyn Baring. He had rendered great services to India as the Private Secretary to Lord Northbrook and his warm sympathies with the people and rare financial abilities was a great strength to the Government of Lord Ripon. He had consistently supported the Viceroy in his liberal measures and his solid intellect for business always led him to suggest the most practical plans. He was succeeded by Sir Auckland Colvin of the N. W. P. Civil Service, an officer whose abilities and antecedents led the Indian Public to expect the best results from the appointment. He had very strong views on the periodical revision of the settlement of the land revenue in the N. W. Provinces and as a Member of the Deccan Ryots' Commission he had recorded a powerful minute on the subject. As a member of the Supreme Government it was one of his first acts to give effect to those views and to establish something like a fixity of of settlement in the N. W. Provinces. He announced his policy in this direction in his first financial statement and to him the country owes the recognition of several important principles in this direction. These were that all improvements made either by the landlord or the tenant should be exempt from assessment that lands which had once been properly classed and valued should not be revalued or reclassified, and that revision of settlement should be based only on three specified grounds viz. increase of the cultivated area, improvements executed by the state and the rise of prices. There can be no doubt that if these principles could be carried out without any undue sacrifice of the general revenues there would result considerable agricultural prosperity. The incalculable mischief caused by the periodical revision of settlement was pointed out to the Secretary of State by Sir Auckland Colvin and after a good deal of correspondence the important principles stated above obtained the recognition of the India Office. No fiscal charges were introduced during the current year and though the Indian treasury had to make an iniquitous contribution of £797,000 towards the expenses of the Egyptian War, the finances of the country exhibited a surplus without any fresh loans or additional taxation. The wheat trade of the country was sought to be stimulated by reducing the railway freight between the two great wheat marts of Upper India, *viz.*, Delhi and Agra and Bombay.

GENERAL EVENTS.—Sir John Morris retired this year from the Chief Commissionership, of the Central Provinces after 15 years' rule during which he did much solid and useful work, being succeeded by Mr. W. B. Jones. The rising of the Akas on the North-Eastern frontier led to the despatch of a small punitive expedition which suppressed the rebellion in a short time. The Report of the Education Commission which was a masterly document was referred to the Local Governments and Administrations with a view to taking practical action. A grand International Exhibition was opened in Calcutta during this year which enabled the natives of all parts of the country who came to witness the imposing spectacle, to appreciate the natural products and the varied industries of this wonderful continent. The collection of interesting objects ranged from every department of nature and art, indigenous and foreign. The Government of India also recorded an important resolution for the proper preservation of the ancient monuments of art in all parts of the country. The administration of Mysore which had been going on very smoothly with a cheap native agency sustained a great loss in the death of the first minister Mr. Ranga Charloo. Sir James Fergusson showed great strength of mind in dealing with the Ratnagiri shooting case though he did nothing to mitigate the sufferings of the Deccan ryots. The chronic indebtedness of the Indian ryot being a crying evil. Lord Ripon proposed to encourage private capitalists to lend sums at moderate rates of interest. His Royal Highness the Prince of Wales evinced great interest in Indian affairs while presiding at the ceremonies at the Imperial Institute and the Northbrook Indian society. His Royal Highness expressed his warm desire to draw closer the bond of union between England and India. His Royal Highness the Duke of Connaught came to India to command a division of the Indian army, and the Duke who was accompanied by the Duchess received a loyal and enthusiastic welcome in every part of India. Some spasmodic efforts were made to establish a regular organization in England for the ventilation of Indian grievances and though some of the leaders of English public opinion warmly seconded these efforts, no substantial scheme was given effect to. Mr. J. K. Cross succeeded Viscount Enfield as the Under-Secretary for India. He had taken an interest in Indian affairs and had mastered the question of Indian Finance.

CHAPTER VI.

1884.

LORD RIPON'S ADMINISTRATION.—Lord Ripon's administration closed practically with the Ilbert Bill though he remained a few months more at the head of affairs to suit the convenience of his party at home. The estimate of his administration is perhaps the most difficult and delicate task that falls to the lot of the contemporary historian in India. His Lordship's aims had been so noble, his motives so high and pure, his intentions were so consistently to govern in the spirit of the Queen's proclamation that it really pains the historian to think that his administration when tested by the only test that history can apply, that of accomplished results should be so disappointing to the critical eye of history. The high-souled statesmanship and the single-minded desire to consider in every instance the true interests of the children of the soil which had characterized Lord Ripon throughout his Indian career must be duly appreciated and the grand popular demonstrations in his honor in every town and city of India through which he passed during his last tour plainly showed that the nation's grateful feelings had been stirred to their utmost depths. The administrative machinery of India is so complex, so few of those who are carrying out the actual duties of Government in every Province are throughly saturated with the spirit of the age, so deep-rooted are many of those traditions of the Government that formed its cardinal principles in those days when the people were unable to think for themselves, so great is the deference that the Viceroy must always pay to the opinions of his constituted advisers, that it is impossible for the noblest English statesman to introduce any radical changes in Indian administration smoothly and within a short time. In the matter of the Afghan War Lord Ripon must have the credit of using his influence with the Liberal Cabinet in the way of putting a speedy end to the War, though Mr. Gladstone's desire to confer "institutions" on Afghanistan led the British forces to be kept there for some time longer than was desirable, Lord Ripon used a wise discretion and exhibited a keen insight into the affairs of that troublesome kingdom, in leaving the Afghan people free to construct their own administration and in leaving the Amir unfettered by any hard-and-fast treaty engagements. Lord Ripon evinced a sincere desire to improve the welfare of the people by making large remissions of taxation when circumstances permitted. In the matter of the cotton duties His Lordship was unable to resist the India Office influence though he tried hard to convince the people of India that their abolition had been for their benefit, the hard fact remained that England, the great apostle of free trade raises £83,000 by duties on Indian imported silver-ware, notwithstanding the strong advocacy of Mr. Gladstone in his budget of 1881-82, for the purpose of protecting the English manufacturers who might be undersold by the Indian artificers. Experience proved however that Lord Ripon's Government had not acted rightly in the selection of the two taxes to be abolished and that the License Tax, which as it stood then, was an anomalous and an obnoxious tax and the export duty on rice which prevented the normal expansion of the export trade of India should have been knocked on the head. The Viceroy was actuated by the purest motives in the matter of issuing orders, for the substitution of imported articles by those produced by indigenous manufacturers, but the India Office influence backed by the interests of the English manufacturers proved too strong an obstacle in the way and His Lordship could not materially reduce the amount of the stores obtained from Europe. At the outset of his administration, Lord Ripon propounded a policy of encouraging private capitalists to undertake Indian canals and railways, but His Lordship found to his regret that although a considerable amount of English capital was being yearly wasted in worthless and fraudulent foreign investments, the English capitalists would not embark on Indian Public Works without a Government guarantee. His Lordship was therefore compelled to submit proposals for constructing 3896 miles of railway within the next five years at a cost of $33\frac{1}{2}$ millions and he added that the Famine Insurance Fund might be applied to this purpose. A Committee of the House of Commons investigated this matter and examined a number of witnesses. Dr. Hunter, Major Conway Gordon, and Mr. Westland who represented the Indian Government took a cheerful view of the financial aspect of Indian Railways and the House of Commons sanctioned all the proposals of the Indian Government with the exception of that which related to the appropriation of the Famine Insurance Fund with the condition added that there should be no addition to the burdens of the people. The doubtful condition of the Indian finances, which is seldom prosperous in bad years and the new lines being along the less important channels of communication made this policy to be watched with great care by the native publicists. In dealing with the report of the Famine Commission, Lord Ripon revived the Agricultural Department and recommended the establishment in each Province of a Board on the model of the Central bureau. Lord Ripon could not carry out to the fullest extent the principle of a remission of state demand in bad years and though he was actuated in this matter by the Sincerest sympathy with the Indian ryot he could only prescribe a sliding system of suspension, the successful working of which would depend in a great measure on the honesty and efficiency of the subordinate staff. In the matter of conferring the boon of Local Self-Government, Lord Ripon was acting in the spirit of those eminent statesmen, who had laid down in the earlier years of British rule the principle that England was not in India merely for the purpose of collecting taxes and giving security to life and property but for a higher and nobler purpose, the regeneration of a fallen people.

Though various Local Governments did their best to minimize the boon conferred by the Supreme Government, history must give Lord Ripon the credit of having widely extended the principle which had been to some extent recognized by Sir Charles Trevelyan's minute in the matter of the appointment of Honorary Magistrates in 1862—a principle which in the fulness of time would admit the natives of India to a fair share in the administration of their own affairs. Lord Ripon had introduced this system and it was left to his successors to develope it with care. The mass of evidence elicited by the Education Commission placed before the public an interesting amount of facts and information with reference to that important problem and the Government came to the decision that with reference to secondary education the efforts of the state should be confined to the development of the grant-in-aid system. Lord Ripon also perceived the injustice of saddling the Indian taxpayer with the maintenance of the Christian Church but his enlightened action in this matter was nullified by the strong opposition of his colleagues in the Council. We have already referred in detail to the legislative measures of his administration and we need not repeat our remarks here. Sufficient it is to say that His Lordship's views had always been to secure the real welfare of the ruled. In this noble work His Lordship had to work almost single-handed. He was deserted by those whose duty it was to have given loyal support to him and when His Lordship took up this noble work he little thought of the appalling obstacles in his way. His administration convinced the people of India that a Viceroy however strong he may be in his own convictions and in the justice of his policy, can not ride roughshod over the views, the opinions and the protests of those who claim administrative experience, who are after all the real rulers of the people placed under their charge and who are not disposed to acquiesce in any material alterations in the system of administration pursued up to date. The noble policy of Lord Ripon and his noble utterances, enthroned him in the eternal gratitude of the Indian people and though the actual and net results, His Lordship could accomplish, were but little, his Indian subjects clearly recognized the efforts that he had made on their behalf, the great difficulties in his way and they did not hesitate to accord to him the highest honors. History will recognize in him a ruler of the highest conscientiousness and of the noblest aims, though he lacked the practical turn of mind to reconcile conflicting interests. A friend to all that was high and noble, he made the people of India feel that they ought really to be ruled in their highest interest and in the spirit of those pledges which their gracious Sovereign had given to them on a memorable occasion.

THE EARL OF DUFFERIN—The Marquis of Ripon laid down the reins of office on the 13th of December and on the same day the Indian millions passed under a new ruler the Earl of Dufferin. His Lordship who had succeeded to the family title and estates while yet a minor had been for some years a lord-in-waiting on the Queen and an attache to Lord John Russel's mission to Vienna. As Under-Secretary for Indian affairs from 1864 to 1866, he had been initiated into the mysteries of Indian administration under Lord Halifax and had ample opportunities of studying Indian questions from a standpoint favourable to the Indian people. He held the Governorship of Canada from 1872 to 1878 where he was universally pronounced to have been a successful administrator. He had been British Commissioner in Syria to enquire into the massacre of the Christian people, he had been the accredited agent of England at the Court of St. Petersburg in the trying times following the Russo-Turkish War, he had managed the delicate task of negotiating the Egyptian matters in the Court of Constantinople and he had represented British authority in Egypt when the task of reconstruction was left to the English, after the collapse of Arabi's rebellion. The experience that he thus had of so many alien people and alien forms of Government, his rare diplomatic abilities, his eloquence which was not unworthy of a grandson of Sheridan, the tact that he displayed in ruling so many races and reconciling so many conflicting interests in Canada, induced the English press generally, to approve warmly of His Lordship's appointment. He had been trusted by both the great political parties in England and his experience had taught him to face men of various shades of opinion and interests and to reconcile interests of the most conflicting character. He assured the Indian people just after landing in Bombay that he would keep unimpaired the loftiness of aims and intentions and that even-handed justice which ought to be the cardinal principles of the Indian Government.

THE RELIGIOUS AND POLITICAL MOVEMENT IN INDIA—Two of its greatest men were lost to the country of their birth by death, during the current year. Keshub Chundra Sen and Kristo Das Paul died respectively on the 8th January and the 24th July. Each represented in his own sphere the highest development of the two important movements, which had been going on in India as the result of the beneficent system of education that England had introduced. Ram Mohun Roy was the first exponent of the new forces that had been created. He perceived the absurdity of many of the dogmas of later Hinduism and he sought to bring back his countrymen to the pure monotheistic creed of the earlier religious writings. His work was taken up by Maharshi Debendra Nath Tagore, who by his indefatigable efforts and the unexampled purity of his character secured a large following. Babu Keshub Chandra Sen was one of his enthusiastic followers in his earlier days, but later on, set up a church and creed of his own. Possessed of high oratorial powers, of a commanding personality, and of all those qualities that enable one to make religious tenets popular he laboured in the cause of religious and social reform all through his life and in his efforts he received the warm and active sympathies of many officers of high position. He repeatedly explained to his countrymen the beauties of the character of Jesus Christ and held in sublime admiration many of the teachings of that great Book, the Bible. Kristodas Pal, whom the best men among the ruling and the ruled classes equally delighted to honor was the life and soul of all public movements for the last quarter of a century in Bengal. The legislation of the period both Imperial and Provincial bears the stamp of his master-mind in many important particulars and he was a tower of strength to the Government and to his fellow-subjects in faithfully interpreting the motives and wishes of each party to the other. The *Hindu Patriot*, which he conducted with such marked ability and the British Indian Association of which he was the life and soul and which was for many years the only political organization of its kind in Upper India had done a good deal in the matter of securing concessions for the people during the quarter of a century immediately following the Mutiny. The historian of India, if he were conscientiously to perform the arduous duties inherent to that position, must turn eternally to his writings, for correct and precise information and guidance on many matters of importance. The trusted representative of the landed aristocracy of Bengal, a sober, hard-headed and practical man of business thoroughly conversant with all the facts and figures relating to every department of administration and the honest and fearless spokesman of the people, he was the highest exponent of that system of political agitation which had done great good in the past, which depended entirely on the grace and good-will of the Government, which appealed respectfully and in moderate terms to the good sense and sympathies of the higher officers of the state, which did its work in a quiet and unobtrusive way, and did not seek by appealing to the people to bring pressure in a constitutional way on the decisions of the Executive Government. The sincerity of his character, moral and intellectual, his unfailing temper and remarkable self-control, his infinite fund of information, enabled him to pursue with the highest success a career which has been and will be pursued with more or less success by hundreds of his countrymen. In a country, situated like the India of to-day with diverse and conflicting interests, his perfect balance of judgment enabled him to discharge the difficult and delicate duties of the leader of what has been called "H. M's opposition" with a degree of tact, prudence and discretion which could be fully appreciated only by those who had comprehended the situation in all its aspects.

THE AFGHAN QUESTION—The gradual advance of Russia in Central Asia had caused great anxieties to the English Cabinet. This year the absorption of Merv into the dominions of the White Czar, made the public feel that no faith could be placed in the solemn promises of the Russian Cabinet. The annexation of Merv was a direct encroachment on the Afghan territories and an infringement of the boundaries of Afghanistan as settled with Russia in 1873. Amir Abdur Rahman desired the intervention of England in this matter and expressed a wish to be furnished with a map showing the precise extent of his dominions. As no such map existed the Cabinet of St. James arranged with the Cabinet at St. Petersburg that some chosen Commissioners should represent each Government on the spot and have a precise settlement of the boundaries of Afghanistan, the overstepping of which by either Government would be a distinct *Casus Belli*. The public felt that British influence must predominate in Afghanistan and that an independent and friendly Afghanistan would be the best barrier between England and Russia. This result would be achieved, it was clearly laid down, not by reducing the Amir to the position of a protected Indian Prince but by leaving to the Amir entire freedom in the matter of internal administration and having certain matters of foreign policy under the direction and control of the British Indian Government. This was the origin of the Afghan Delimitation Commission. The British Commissioner, Sir Peter Lumsden took his route through the

Beluchi Desert, as the Amir could not guarantee his party a safe passage through Afghanistan. He arrived at Sarrakhs in November but had to wait a considerable time before his Russian colleagues arrived. The Liberal Government adopted the policy of Lord Lawrence, Lord Mayo and Lord Northbrook— a policy of non-intervention in the internal affairs of Afghanistan, and without having recourse to force or coercion make the Amir accept the position of a friendly ally acting in the interest of England. No British outposts were to be established in Afghanistan and nothing was to be done that could in any way wound the national feelings of the proud and unruly subjects of the Amir. The idea that originated with Lord Beaconsfield's cabinet of having a British Resident at Cabul, of holding the passes between Afghanistan and India by British forces, and perpetually intermeddling in the internal affairs of Afghanistan was finally dropped. This idea which had been the chief cause of the two disastrous wars with Afghanistan was based on a fundamentally wrong conception of the Afghan character, and nothing was more calculated to turn the Afghans into our bitterest enemies. Both the Liberal and the Conservative Governments however agreed as to the necessity of having the North-West frontier of India strongly secured by a chain of fortifications and by a net work of strategic railways which would serve as an easy means of transport in times of difficulty. The Afghans cannot trust an Englishman and this fact should be the keynote of the Afghan policy.

GENERAL EVENTS—On the 10th November Lord Napier and Ettrick presented a petition to Parliament from the people of Madras against the practice of the Local Governments spending a great part of the year in the Hills. This gave rise to an interesting debate. The withdrawal of the headquarters of the Local and Imperial Governments from the plains for the greater part of the year is attended with grave administrative inconvenience. The system not only throws a heavy burden on the Indian Exchequer but it removes the Indian Governments from all touch of the chief centres of population of the country. The practice had grown to such proportions from the days of Lord Lawrence, that the heads of departments and the offices joined in the general migration to the hills. There is no doubt that the English Statesmen who came out as Viceroys and who are generally past the middle age of life, might seek the comfort of a salubrious climate such as the hill-stations afford but there could be no question that when in good old days the Anglo-Indian officers could work for 30 or 40 years in the plains without any long leave worthy of the name, the extension of the privilege to a considerable number of officers and their assistants was a gross abuse of the system. The high rate of salary paid to the Anglo-Indian officers is distinctly admitted to be due to the fact that they have to work in an uncongenial climate, and should the salaries be reduced in the case of those who always enjoy an English climate the system would not find so many defenders as it does now. The Exodus question began to attract a great deal of public attention in India and the injustice to the Indian tax-payer of the system is so apparent that Lord Kimberley hinted that he would take up the question and prescribe a limit to residence in the Hills. The Indian budget continued to be presented year after year at the fag-end of the Parliamentary Session, and was read mostly to an empty House. This system showed a sad unconcern towards Indian affairs by the English House of Commons which was in the final resort, the arbiter of the destinies of the millions of India. Alderman Fowler had brought forward a motion in 1883 to improve this state of things and though it was accepted by the Liberal Government, it failed to bring about any perceptible results. The questions that were asked by independent members of the House of Commons regarding Indian affairs were continually on the increase and this fact imbued the local rulers with a wholesome dread of Parliamentary agitation. Mr. Stanhope in the course of his speech on the Indian budget pointed out that the expenditure of India was on the increase and that it could be curtailed in several respects without impairing the efficiency of the administration. Sir Auckland Colvin as the responsible Finance Minister rendered some explanations. Lord Ripon had assured the Indian public in his reply to the address of the native community at Madras that the rules both with reference to the Covenanted and the Statutory Civil Service were capable of considerable improvements. The agitation with reference to the Civil Service Age question had been carried on consistently and vigorously ever since the announcement of Lord Salisbury's new rules. These rules operated with peculiar hardship on the natives of India, for very few Indian youths could be expected to leave home and succeed in a most difficult competitive examination conducted through a foreign tongue at the early age of nineteen. Lord Ripon succeeded in persuading his colleagues that the raising of the age of the Civil Service candidates was desirable not only in justice to the natives of India but on broad and general grounds in the case of all candidates. Lord Ripon's Government addressed therefore a despatch on the subject to the Secretary of State. The appointments under the Statutory Civil Service had given but little satisfaction. This was due to the fact that the Local Governments in making these appointments did rest the selections exclusively on family connections, and ignored the amount of culture the recipients had. The Supreme Government urged on the provincial administrations the necessity of making proper selections for those offices, and the Governments of Bengal and Madras introduced a system of limited competition while the other provinces yet stuck to a system of nomination pure and simple. Lord Ripon also threw open every fourth vacancy in the higher grades of the Opium service to the natives of India and decided that the candidates for this service should be selected by a system of nomination. Every fourth vacancy in the Survey Department was also thrown open to the natives of India, and the Surveyor General was directed to frame bye-laws for the proper selection of candidates for employment in his department. The filling of the Indian Services by Cooper's Hill engineers had caused the Government of India to make some concessions to the Indians by the famous Rurki resolution, but under the pressure of Anglo-Indian agitation and outcry the boon was considerably minimized. By the Public Works Re-organization scheme, the prospects and pay of the Executive and Assistant Engineers were considerably improved. The Punjab reorganization scheme created a number of well-paid new posts and the block in the promotion of the Covenanted and the junior Civilians was removed. The scheme originally included the making over of a good number of high judicial appointments to the uncovenanted service but this step which would have conferred a substantial benefit to the natives of India was disallowed. The police functions of magistrates had led to the union of judicial and executive powers in the same officer. The interests of good government imperatively demanded that this system of things should no longer continue as it had been the prolific source of all those evils in the administration of justice which arise from the functions of the judge and the prosecutor being united in the same officer. Lord Ripon placed Mr. J. W. Quinton on special duty to report on the Police functions of magistrates and recorded an important minute on the subject. The question however remained unsettled at the time when His Lordship laid down the reins of office. In the practical carrying out of the Local Self-Government scheme, the principle of election was established on a firm footing but the choice of the local bodies in the matter of their chairman fell generally on the District or the Sub-Divisional Officer. The Government of India had aimed at preventing this result but no one who is actually acquainted with the practical working of Indian Districts could have failed to foresee that no one who had a stake in in the District could possibly oppose the election of the District or Sub-Divisional Magistrate to the chairmanship of local bodies. The question of providing ways and means for the spread of secondary education was dealt with unsatisfactorily. The Local Governments were told that the newly-established Local Boards would be able to do much in the way of spreading the elementary education of the masses. The Supreme Government gave indeed a broad hint that the Local Boards were to impose additional burdens for this object forgetting that such a step would bring into discredit the whole system in the eyes of an oriental people. The Salem rioters who had been sentenced to severe punishments for their alleged offences were proved to be innocent beyond all doubt, and the evidence on which they had been convicted to be false and perjured and the prisoners were all released as an act of grace. In Bengal there were many cases of magisterial high-handedness, of which the Krishnagar students' case in which a number of students had been prosecuted on what proved to be no offence whatever, attracted the greatest degree of public attention. The case was an example of the evil arising from the system of uniting police functions in magistrates. The Bengal Government had to degrade and transfer these officers for their proved high-handedness, The receptions given to Lord Ripon all over India during his winter tour were most enthusiastic. They showed a political activity and upheaval that was very significant and full of hope for the future of India. The cause of Municipal Government in Calcutta received a terrible blow by the Lieutenant Governor's superseding the Calcutta Corporation for not properly performing its duties with regard to sanitation. There was a power reserved to the Local Government under Sec. 28 of the Municipal Act to institute enquiries in cases of gross negligence and although the Corporation contended that they had done everything that was possible for sanitary improvement with the limited means at its disposal, Sir Rivers Thompson played himself into the hands of the coterie inimical to the Corporation in spite of the emphatic protests and entreaties, of the ruled classes. The spread of the methods of constitutional agitation all over

India brought into the field a new power of influencing the decisions of the Indian Government. It was felt that the English elector should be instructed more about Indian affairs through his representatives in the House of Parliament. The costliness of British as compared with Native administrations, the method of taxation regarded necessary by British costliness, the poverty of the Indian people, the misleading statements and garbled telegrams from the English official sources, were some of the questions to which the attention of the British elector was invited by powerful appeals. As the greatest dependency of England, India has high claims to her consideration and if humanity, justice and far-seeing policy could have their way, there need not be the smallest doubt that such consideration would be adequately shown. At the next General Election Bengal, Bombay and Madras sent delegates to lay before the electors of Great Britain the disabilities, disadvantages and grievances, the natives of India laboured under. This system of political agitation had not yet had its full trial and it is reserved to the historian of the future to deal with this topic in all its interesting aspects and to declare what solid and permanent results it has been able to achieve for the Indian people.

CHAPTER VII.

1885.

The War with Upper Burma.—One of the most important political events of the year was the third Burmese war. The king of Upper Burma had brought the Indian Government to the brink of a war with him several times since his accession to the throne. The actual war broke out from the sudden adoption of a vigorous policy towards the North-East frontier which contrasted very much with the policy adopted in dealing with Russian advance and Russian diplomacy on the North-West frontier. The Chambers of Commerce all over England, particularly the London one kept up a persistent agitation on the subject of extending British trade in Upper Burma and openly hinted at the annexation of that part of Asia in the interests of commerce. Two enthusiasts on the subject Mr. Colquhoun and Mr. Holt Hallet sketched a programme for railway extension through Upper Burma to the frontiers of China, a project that was eagerly taken up by the Chambers of Commerce and forced upon the attention of the Secretary of State. Lord Kimberley set his face resolutely against annexation, and in the replies that he gave to the deputations that waited upon him, His Lordship gave a blunt answer saying that he would not favor the policy advocated by the Chambers of Commerce. The Indian Government however took up some of the grievances of the Bombay Burmah Trading Corporation. They remonstrated with the Mandalay Durbar on the injustice and impropriety of its conduct, and hot disputes arose between the two Governments. The Indian Government sent an ultimatum to King Theebaw which was required to be complied with, within ten days. The document unequivocally demanded that the kingdom of Upper Burma should accept the protectorate of the Indian Government, and allow an officer of that Government to act as the arbitrator in the matter of the disputes with the Bombay-Burma Trading Corporation. The compliance with these demands was inconsistent with the position and privileges of a Sovereign State as defined by International Law, and the Burmese Government showed no disposition to comply with them. On this, hostilities were commenced at once. No formal declaration of war was issued explaining in detail the circumstances that had led to the war but General Sir Henry Prendergast was ordered to cross the frontier and advance on Mandalay. No resistance was offered to the advance of British troops and the campaign was an almost bloodless one. The King of Upper Burmah tendered an almost unconditional surrender and he was at once made a prisoner of war and deported to British India. General Prendergast took over the Government of the country pending the decision of its fate by the English and Indian Governments. The provisional Government was subsequently taken over by Sir Charles Barnard, and the future of Upper Burmah remained for some months under consideration. Lord Dufferin visited Burmah with a view of studying all sides of the question on the spot and in his minute on the subject dated the 17th February 89, he after discussing the matter comes to the conclusion that the territories should be annexed to the dominions of Her Majesty. Lord Dufferin at first considered the question of making Upper Burmah a "buffer" state but this course he deemed unpracticable as it would prove an impediment in the way of free commercial intercourse with China, and that it would lead England into other complications with China. Lord Dufferin then discussed the question of making Upper Burmah a fully protected State like the feudatory States of India. His Lordship came to the conclusion that no eligible prince of the Alompra dynasty was available. The princes who were men of ability and commanded any following had made themselves objectionable by intrigues with the French or by brutal murders. His Lordship also inferred from the fact that General Prendergasts' march had been unopposed that the Burmese had not any objection to the blessings of British rule being extended to them, and that the pacification of the country would not be the same difficult task it had proved in Lower Burmah which took full ten years to conquer. Lord Dufferin therefore recommended that Upper Burmah should be annexed and this recommendation being sanctioned by the Home authorities the announcement as to the annexation of Upper Burmah was made public. The historian can not but regard the whole affair with reference to Upper Burmah as singularly unfortunate. Theebaw was certainly a bad neighbour and there might have arisen from time to time complications with reference to Upper Barmah from his cruelty and unwise measures. But these could not be made the plea of depriving a people of their liberty. As long as the annexation of their country was not determined upon, the people of Upper Burmah remained quiet. But a furious resistance to British authority was organized as soon as it was known that that Alompra dynasty would rule no longer. The difficulties in the way of holding and pacifying the country were found to be much greater than had been anticipated when annexation was determined upon. The army in British Burmah was nearly doubled and the military police was considerably increased in numbers, but within a few weeks, after the Burmese began to offer resistance to the British power, in the greater part of Upper Burmah, the authority of the British did not extend beyond rifle range from their fortified posts. The disturbances in Upper Burmah although described in official language to be dacoities were nothing less than a national rebellion organized as best it might be under the circumstances. The administration of the country was conducted also in a manner which could not fail to make the British name unpopular among peaceable and law-abiding citizens. The administrative staff for Upper Burmah was hastily recruited from among officers of but little training and experience and the correspondent of the *Times* had to point out their misdeeds in many cases in the strongest language. In places which were administered by tried officers of the British Commission in India, the work went on with smoothness but in the case of the greater part of the country, high-handed and illegal proceedings were to a great extent rife. The situation in Burmah had rendered military operations on a large scale necessary and Sir Herbert Macpherson was sent there with a large body of reinforcements. The original estimate of the cost of annexation had been thirty lakhs. This estimate was largely exceeded and although some members of the House of Commons urged England to bear a share of the burdens as Burmah had been annexed solely in the interests of British trade and the Indian interests had benefited but little by that step, Sir John Gorst declared that the decision of Mr. Gladstone's Government as to throwing the entire cost of the operations on India must be considered final. The historian must record with regret the undeniable fact that England had never done financial justice to India. She has thrown upon the unrepresented and dumb millions of this country all the charges which she possibly could. The poor Indian tax-payer has even now to pay the charges relating to the Brittanic Majesty's establishments in Persia and China although these establishments are under the control of the Home Foreign office and the Government of India has nothing whatever to do with them. If the adjustment of charges between England and India had always been made on principles of equity and justice, the financial condition of the country would have been far different from what it unfortunately now is. Mute and Helpless India does not even now meet with justice at the hands of that great nation which under the orderings of providence, is the final arbiter of its destinies. The work of the pacification of Upper Burmah proved a long and tedious one and continued through the succeeding year.

AFGHAN AFFAIRS.—The Russian Commissioner for the purposes of the delimitation of the Afghan frontier did not arrive for a considerable period and while Sir Peter Lumsden was waiting for that functionary the Russian troops under General Komaroff advanced first to Pul-i-Khatum on the Hari Rud and then successively to Sari Yazi on the Murghub, the the Zulfikar Pass, Akrobat and Pul-i-khisti close to the junction of the Murghub and the Hari Rud. The British Government remonstrated and demanded that while the delimitation had not yet been carried out the Russian troops should be ordered back. The Russian cabinet refused to agree to this demand and only conceded that pending the delimitation there should be no further advance on either side. Within a few days however of this agreement which was concluded in the middle of March, there was a fight between the Afghans and the Russians and General Komaroff had seized and occupied Panjdeh. This act was universally considered to be one of unprovoked aggression and extensive military preparations were made both in England and India for the war between England and Russia which appeared imminent. The Army Corps in India were placed on a war footing and a vote of credit of eleven millions sterling was granted by the House of Commons without a division. The Government of Mr. Gladstone however soon came to an arrangement with the cabinet at St. Petersburg which provided that Russia should give up Zulfikar to the Amir, continue in possession of the territories she had seized and the territory which Russia at first claimed as a neutral zone she should obtain in her own right with an acknowledged title to possession. Its foreign policy was the weakest point of Mr. Gladstone's administration but this arrangement was simply a surrender, or as some characterized it, even worse, a capitulation. Russia having thus gained an important point appointed Colonel Kuhlberg to meet Sir West Ridgeway who had been placed at the head of the Boundary Commission in succession to Sir Peter Lumsden and the delimitation work proceeded slowly. While the excitement continued of an impending war between England and Russia there was a spontaneous outburst of loyalty from one corner of India to the other, and the Feudatory princes vied with each other in placing the resources of their states at the disposal of the Paramount power while loyal offers of being allowed to serve their country as volunteers went up from all sections of the Indian people. The war party in Russia has always a favorite theory to rely upon *viz.*, that the Indian people are discontented with British rule and the appearance of the Russians on the Afghan frontier would be the signal for a general internal rising in India. That this theory was entirely false and groundless was proved to demonstration by the genuine feelings of loyalty so conspicuously displayed by the princes and people of India. There can be no doubt that though the British Government must have like all human institutions, many defects, the subject race s in India feel that it is the best foreign government they are likely to have and they have every thing to lose and nothing to gain by a change of masters. The offers of the Feudatory princes were accepted not in the shape of pecuniary help but of a stated number of well-trained troops capable of taking their pl ace by the side of the Imperial troops while unfortunately the loyal offers of the people in the matter of volunteering were considered inadmissible.

THE FINANCES—Sir Auckland Colvin in laying his budget for 1885-86 before the public pointed out, that the revenues of the Empire were but barely sufficient to meet the current expenditure and that any extraordinary burdens would have to be met from other sources. Lord Randolph Churchill in laying this budget before the House of Commons a few months later announced that the abnormal expenditure consequent on war preparations had completely upset the calculations of the Finance Minister. The frontier railways and the war expenditure had amounted to $4\frac{1}{4}$ millions of which $3\frac{1}{2}$ millions were borrowed in England and the remainder provided by cutting down the allotments for public works and by other retrenchments. Lord Churchill stated that the outlook of the Indian finances was far from what it ought to be, and that if the Conservatives remained in office next year they would ask the Parliament for the appointment of a Commission into the working of the Government of India since 1858. The increasing difficulties of the situation in Central Asia had made the permanent addition of ten thousand effective troops to the European Garrison and of twenty thousand men to the Native Army, thus adding, together with the cost of the strategic railways on the frontier, two millions permanently to the military expenditure of the Indian Empire. This permanent increase in the military charges led the authorities to think of increasing the burdens of the people and Lord R. Churchill in his budget speech indicated that the new tax would take the shape of an extension of the license tax to the official and professional classes. This idea was an old one and Lord Lytton and Sir John Strachey had actually introduced a bill with this object in view. But the outcry that had been raised by the influential classes to be affected by the proposed measure led the Government to abandon it. On the 4th January 1886, Sir Auckland Colvin introduced a bill which proposed to levy an Income Tax of four pies per rupee on all incomes of Rs. 500 and upwards and of five pies per rupee on incomes above Rs. 2,000 a year. This tax was to extend to incomes of all and every kind excepting income from agriculture but not excepting funded stocks. Sir Auckland Colvin explained in a masterly speech the circumstances which had led to this taxation, but did not meet the objections which had been advanced against this particular form of taxation. Lord Dufferin explained in an able and sympathetic speech that a deficit had been caused and that provision must be made for it. The history of direct taxation in India had proved the utter unsuitability of this form of taxation in India. Lord Canning had been so much convinced of the discontent that the rogueries of the subordinate officials engaged in collecting the income tax spread through the land, that he remarked that he would gladly govern India with 40,000 European troops without these taxes than with 100,000, with them. Mr. Samuel Laing, had emphatically placed on record that that while the good policy of the British rulers had gone a great way to conciliate the Indian people the practical difficulties in the way of the assessment and collection of the income-tax had been making British rule unpopular with the people. During that animated debate which took place on the Income tax in the Council of Lord Mayo, Mr. John Inglis had boldly and fearlessly exposed the evils arising from the Income-tax, evils the existence of which was practically admitted with reference to the territories under his rule by Sir William Muir. Lord Mayo, we have it on the authority of Sir William Hunter, had placed it on record, just before starting on the fatal trip to the Andamans, that the income-tax had well-nigh become a source of political danger. Lord Northbrook had in the first year of his administration collected a mass of evidence on the practical working of the income-tax which clearly showed that great hardships were inflicted on the people in the matter of the working of the income-tax. It is an unfortunate fact too well-known that the proper machinery for the honest and conscientious working of such a tax, cannot be secured in this country, and that the subordinate officials are but too prone to harass for their own purposes those who are not liable to the tax and for whose welfare the Government shows such praiseworthy solicitude. The protests against the measure, of important public bodies were unheeded and the suggestions that had been made for the re-imposition of the import duties were hardly considered practicable. The bill was passed with the assurance from the Viceroy that a Finance Committee would be appointed to examine all branches of expenditure and to effect savings where possible so as to obviate the necessity of making this impost exist longer than absolutely necessary. The Committee was shortly after appointed with Sir Charles Elliott as President and Sir Henry Cunningham, Sir William Hunter, Mr. Mahadeo Gobind Ranade, Mr. Westland, Mr. Hardie Mr. Bliss and Col. Filgate as members. The field before the Committee was vast. Its jurisdiction extended over expenditure in all departments, Imperial and Provincial not excluding the Army. The Committee was to assemble at Simla hold conferences with heads of departments when necessary and submit its report early in the cold weather of 1886.

GENERAL EVENTS.—In the early part of the year there was held a conference at Rawul Pindi between Lord Dufferin and the Amir Abdur Rahman, in which the Afghan Chief distinctly gave the British Government to understand that the Afghan people would not tolerate the presence of the English on Afghan soil even as allies and that the only help that could be accepted was money arms and ammunition. This conference led to a better understanding between the two Powers, and convinced Lord Dufferin that constant interference in the affairs of Afghanistan would make an honest alliance between the Afghans and the English almost impossible. The despatch of Colonel Lockhart's mission tended to place the defences of the Empire on a sound footing in the case of a Russian invasion from Gilgit or Chittral. On the death of Maharaja Runbir Singh the British Officer on special duty at Kashmir was converted into a Resident with full powers to interfere in the administration of the State although Sir Henry Hardinge had given a solemn pledge to Golab Singh that no Resident would be imposed on the State. Lord Canning had promised that the fortress of His Highness, ancestors should be restored to Maharajah Scindiah when no longer required for the safety of the Empire. This promise had been confirmed by successive Viceroys but it was reserved for Lord Dufferin to do this act of justice to the Maharajah. The effect of this graceful act was to a considerable extent marred by His Highness being compelled to pay a heavy compensation for it. His Highness Maharajah Scindiah had been administering some of the most fertile lands in India under his charge with conspicuous success during a long reign. His habit of doing every important business of the State in person, his proper appreciation of the cares and the duties of a responsible ruler, the economic way in which the administration was carried on, which always left at his disposal a large annual surplus, his choice of wise ministers, his personal interest in the army of the state had made Gwalior a model kingdom with a prosperous treasury and a contented people. This year will also remain memorable for having witnessed the project for the supply of medical aid to the women of India. The project which was taken up by the Countess of Dufferin sought to remove the grievances of the women of India by the supply, through an association, of trained female medical aid and by imparting medical tuition to the female population of India. It was a well-known fact that the Indian women owing to their habitual modesty would not freely seek for medical aid at the hands of the male practitioners, and the association which starting under the patronage of the Countess of Dufferin was largely supported by the Indian princes, nobility and gentry has done an immense amount of good work from year to year. The question of the employment of the Mahomedans in the public service engaged the early attention of Lord Dufferin who from his experience of Islam in Syria, Egypt and Turkey was peculiarly well-fitted to deal with it. From the statistics collected through careful inquiry it was found that the complaint of the Mahomedans of not getting a fair proportion of the appointments of the public service had no foundation in Madras, Central Provinces and Northern India and that in Bengal and Bombay the Mahomedans suffered because appointments were determined by strict educational tests. The Mahomedans were given to understand that Persian could not be revived as the official language of the country and that they should qualify themselves by high education for the appointments which they sought. Sir Charles Aitchison signalized his administration by appointing Pandit Ram Narain, a native of the Punjab to an officiating seat on the bench of the Chief Court. Bengal suffered from several natural visitations. There was a famine in the Burdwan division, the floods caused great destruction to life and property in several districts and a terrible stormwave and cyclone swept over Central Orissa causing extensive damage. The close monopoly that still existed in the N. W. Provinces and Oudh in the case of the Subordinate Executive service for men of the Amla class was a fruitful source of administrative evils. It has been very tritely observed that one who breathed the corrupt atmosphere of amladom all his life would not suddenly turn an honest man because his pay and status had been raised. This class of officers, having little or nothing in the way of English education as their equipment in life might prosess native energy and natural talents but cannot in these progressive days prove equal to the duties and responsibilities created by a complex state of society. Lord Reay the new Governor of Bombay created a very favourable impression by his sensible action in the case of Broach riots, the railway incidents and the working of the Forest Laws in the Tanna District. Lord Dufferin introduced an important departure in the matter of the education of the " poor white " by making it obligatory to recognize passing by the standard in their case as equivalent to passing the Entrance Examination of the Calcutta and the Punjab Universities. The reason assigned for this step was that the Entrance examination was not sufficient practical. Lord Dufferin passed the Bengal Tenancy Act in spite of the strong opposition of the Bengal Zamindars. His Lordship had not had sufficient time to study the question but he accepted the conclusions of his constituted advisers and gave his assent to a measure, which to say the least ought to have been grounded upon more complete statistical information about the rural economy of Bengal. It is indeed too early to discuss the practical results of the law. It will takes many years to show whether it stands approved or condemned by the light which practical working throws on its provisions. The Indian tax-payers had to bear the costs of the Indian contingents that were despatched to Suakim. The Under Secretary of State in proposing that Indian troops be despatched to Suakim added that they should still be on the Indian establishment with a view to throw their ordinary expenses on the Indian exchequer. For the first time in the history of this country, a native of India Mr. Lal Mohun Ghose sought the suffrages of the British constituency of Deptford at the General Election and although he was defeated he secured a very large measure of sympathy and support at the hands of his electorate. Several Indian delegates visited England with a view to influence the British electors to induce their members to take a lively interest in Indian affairs. A new guaranteed company was formed in England under the name of the Indian Midland Railway Company which found some difficulties in the way of getting the necessary capital in the English market. It was evident that with the British capitalists the investment in Indian railways, was not at all popular and even with the Government guarantee the Indian railways could not attract capital with the same rapidity as many other foreign investments. A large amount of English capital is annually wasted in a variety of worthless and fraudulent investments but the English capitalist would not invest a rupee in Indian railways without a Government guarantee. Sir Donald Stewart retired from his office as Commander-in-Chief of India before the expiry of his term, having accepted a seat in the India Council and being succeeded by Sir Frederic Roberts. Upon General Roberts devolved from the very commencement of his career in this office, the task of placing the frontier defences of India on a proper footing. A systematic chain of forts and military outposts were established on the N. W. frontier and strategic railways and other ready means of of transport were also undertaken on an extensive scale. There can be no question but that the Government of India would be neglecting its legitimate duty if it did not do all it could to be always in readiness for that collision beyond the Indus which seems inevitable in the course of time and although these defences cost India an enormous sum, her people would feel their utility in times of danger should ever any such come.

THE NATIONAL CONGRESS—The closing week of 1885 saw the birth of that useful organization known as the National Congress, which is the first beginning of an informal Indian Parliament and where many of the representative men of every part of the country meet and deliberate on political questions of common interest. The different sections of the Indian people had long been divided by everything that can separate man from man, but under the blessed influences of English education, common feelings and sentiments had been growing up. Several years before the actual assembling of the National Congress the idea of such a gathering where the enlightened men of all parts of the country would meet for purposes of common good and submit proposals to Government, in a respectful manner for such reforms and improvements, as they considered necessary had been entertained by the wisest minds. During the last week of December 1885, the first of such gatherings took place in Bombay under the auspices of the enlightened leaders of public opinion of that city, and presided over by a distinguished barrister of Calcutta Mr. W. C. Bonnerji. The unique spectacle was witnessed of representatives from many parts of the Bombay and the Madras Presidencies and from some of the great towns of the Bengal Presidency laying aside their petty differences, and putting their shoulders to the wheel as one man for the benefit of their common motherland. The Congress was the beginning of a new era in the history of Modern India. It represented the first efforts of an ancient nation regenerated under the noble influences of western civilization, to work out its own improvement and to strive loyally and constitutionally for the full and free enjoyment of those privileges, a capacity for which had been developed during a century of British rule. If it be the true function of history to delineate every change in the feelings and condition of the people, the historian cannot but attach sufficient importance to the Congress, its work and its methods.

CHAPTER VIII.

1886.

POLITICAL ASPECTS OF THE COUNTRY.—The Burmese who had been keeping up a sort of guerrilla warfare made the work of pacification of Upper Burmah as distant as ever. The peculiar geographical features of the country, its dense forests and its hilly regions made the work of the dacoits an easy one and the British Military and police had a very difficult task in the way of tracking out the culprits. The work of introducing British administrative machinery in the comparatively simple state of society existing in Upper Burmah, and of settling down the disorderly population to habits of peace and industry was a difficult one and required the utmost tact and energy of many British Officials. The annexation had revealed the fact that nearly twice the amount of the original estimate for the Burmese war would be necessary for the pacification of the country and the throwing of the whole burden on the Indian treasury introduced a disturbing element into the Indian finances. Two important chiefs of Feudatory India who descended from Maharatta warriors had displayed great administrative abilities, died during this year. Jayaji Rao Scindiah died leaving a minor son who was placed on the throne under a council it Regency, of which Sir Ganput Rao Khudkey the trusted Prime Minister of the late Chief, was the President. Under the treaty concluded with Maharajah Scindiah last year, the fort and town of Morar were evacuated. The Gwalior territories were to be administered by the Council of Regency during the minority of the young Chief and the Council was to act in consultation with the Resident in all important matters of State. The death of Maharajah Tukaji Holkar placed his eldest son Bala Saheb on the throne who began his administration by initiating many useful reforms. The late Maharajah Holkar was always unhappy for the suspicions which the Foreign Office entertained with reference to his loyalty during the Mutiny. He had tried repeatedly to vindicate his reputation by re-opening the question and proving that the charges brought against him by the then Resident Colonel Durand were groundless. But His Highness had never succeeded in his endeavours even though Lord Ripon had expressed himself at one time willing to rehear the case. The career of these Maharatta chieftains plainly showed that they could in the present altered times display that wisdom in consolidating their rule and administering their territories according to civilized principles that their ancestors could exhibit in the exciting scenes of the field of battle. His Highness the Maharajah of Kashmir paid a visit to the Viceroy in Calcutta in the early part of the year and he returned to his territories deeply impressed with the necessity of introducing reforms in many departments of administration. With the advice and assistance of his able Finance Minister Babu Nilambar Mookerji, he abolished many odious taxes and obnoxious imposts and effected many important changes in the revenue and judicial systems. These reforms naturally excited the opposition of those who profited by those abuses and of officials of the old school who did not appreciate the noble motives which dictated the new policy and these persons soon succeeded in gaining a complete ascendancy over the Maharajah and thwarting the much-needed reforms. Finding that it would be difficult to discharge conscientiously the duties of his high post Babu Nilamber Mookerji tendered his resignation which was reluctantly accepted by his master. During a career of nearly twenty years Babu Nilamber Mookerji had evinced the capacity of an educated native of Bengal for the practical conduct of affairs in the highest and most difficult situations of public life, and though he at last found his way beset with difficulties through the intrigues which formed a chief factor in oriental Courts, his long and useful services to the Kashmir State had made it much better in many respects than it was when he first joined its service. Some excitement was created by the sudden deportation of Dhulip Singh to Europe when on his way to India. Dhulip Singh had obtained the permission of the authorities to return to India but he had done many foolish things when setting out on his journey and for political reasons it was thought expedient to stop him at Aden. He might have been allowed to lead a quiet life somewhere in Southern India but the Government resorted to very vigorous measures with reference to him. The despatch of the Lockhart mission created grave misgivings in Russia. The Muscovite suspected the English of aiming at the occupation of Badakshan, a suspicion wholly unfounded. The results of the Lockhart mission were to recognize the political importance of Chittral which was just on the south of some of the most important Himalayan passes and the occupation of Dir a small Pathan state by the son of the Chittral Chief. The work of the Delimitation Commission proceeded smoothly as far as Dukchi and the remaining thirty-one miles of frontier, will, it was announced, be settled between the two Cabinets, the joint Commission being in the meanwhile withdrawn. Russia claimed Wakhan to be Non-Afghan territory but the English Cabinet expressed its determination to support Afghanistan in case Russia laid claim to Wakhan. The negotiations with reference to the Afghan frontier were reopened at the close of the year between Sir West Ridgeway and M. Lessar in London. The complications with China at one time assumed a threatening aspect, and the British Government had to make two important concessions. The shadowy claims of China to suzerainty over Upper Burmah were recognized by agreeing to send tribute missions from Mandalay to Pekin at prescribed intervals and the Tibbet mission which had already cost the Indian treasury a large sum of money was countermanded. China at the same time consented to give substantial facilities between India and Thibet and Burmah and China. The question of the exact boundaries between China, and Burmah was not definitely settled at this time. Risings in Afghanistan plainly showed that the hold that Abdur Rahman had on Afghanistan was yet far from complete. The sons of the late Mush-Ki-Alam who had besieged General Roberts at Sherpur in 1879 led the rising but it was speedily suppressed. The Ghilzai tribe who aided this revolt was severely punished.

GENERAL EVENTS.—The Houses of Parliament being too busy over the Irish question the attention paid to India was small. This Select Committee for enquiring into the administration of India came to an unexpected end. The Upper House selected 15 members and sent a message to the Lower House to appoint their Committee. Mr. Gladstone had taken but little interest in this matter and the motion being strongly opposed was thrown out. The debate on the Opium traffic had become an almost annual institution. Opium traffic was attacked with the arguments, as to its immorality and as to the wickedness of corrupting the Chinese. The debate came to nothing but it was pointed out by Sir Richard Temple that as long as the Chinese were bent upon using opium it was far better that they should use the first-rate Indian article than the second-rate indigenous one, and Mr. Lewis McIver justly remarked that if the British people wanted to be virtuous by suppressing an immoral traffic it must be done at the cost of the British tax-payer and the loss to the Indian revenues must be made good. The Indo-Colonial Exhibition which was held in London this year revealed to the common public of England the vast material resources of India. Her Majesty took the deepes interest in the Indian Court and in the Hindustani craftsmen who had been taken to the Exhibition. The frequent changes in the Ministry at home led to the seal of the India office constantly changing hands. When Lord Salisbury formed his administration Sir Richard Cross was appointed to the India Office with a peerage, with Sir John Gorst as Parliamentary under-secretary. Sir Alfred Lyall signalized his

tenure of office by establishing a Legislative Council for the
N. W. P. and Oudh and his term was extended by six months
for the purpose of enabling him to complete the arrangements
of a separate Univesity for the United Provinces. The question of a separate University had been discussed for a considerable number of years since the time of Sir William Muir.
The grounds set forth for a separate University were that the
high officers of the Government of those provinces had no
voice in the deliberations of the Senate, that special and local
requirements were never brought to the notice of the governing
body, that the Calcutta University framed its rules in utter
disregard of such peculiarities, that the North-West students
felt the hardship of being compelled to come to Calcutta and
had not the privilege of that encouragement which an assembly
like the Convocation imparts to the student mind. The
Calcutta University had tried to meet these objections as far
as possible and had empowered the Lieutenant-Governor of the
N. W. P. to hold a convocation at Allahabad for his own
territories ; but still a separate University was thought to be
a necessity by the official world and Mr. Quinton introduced
a bill for the establishment of an University at Allahabad.
The bill showed one improvement in allowing a certain number
of Fellows of the University to be elected by the Senate and
and approved of by the Chancellor. Sir Alfred Lyall in opening the University said that it was a step towards the recognition of the principle of self-government although it was
apparent that the University was to all intents and purposes a
department of the Government. He also explained that in the
existing state of things a teaching university was not possible
in India. Many of the independent organs of public opinion
looked on the whole project with great misgivings and regarded
it merely as a means for lowering the standard of high education which the N. W. P. officials could not do as long as a
separate University did not exist. It is evident however that
the real reason why education is yet backward in the United

provinces lies in the fact that educated natives do not get there the same encouragement that they did in the older provinces. In Bengal from the time of Sir Henry Hardinge preference is given to English-educated natives in the choice of all official preferments, but in the United provinces, until very lately the most important offices under the Government, open to natives of India, were filled by uneducated men of the old school while the graduates were pining for want of employment. The average graduate in every country looks to education not for its higher blessings but for its material advantages. Until very lately the men of the old school without any tincture of English education were thought fit for the most responsible duties in the United Provinces but happily there is now a change for the better. The theory of social weight was often used to give preference to aristocratic mediocrities and to shut out the educated natives, and it was often forgotten that a good social position did not compensate for the absence of educational qualifications. The closing year of the administration of Sir M. E. Grant Duff was characterized by many scandals. He was succeeded by the Hon'ble Mr. Bourke brother of Lord Mayo, who was shortly after elevated to the peerage under the title of Lord Connemara. The most important administrative measure of the year was the appointment of the Public Service Commission to examine the conditions under which natives of India could be admitted to the higher posts in the public service and after considering the whole question in the light of the materials at hand to submit their recommendations with some degree of finality. The Commission was presided over by Sir Charles Aitchison and with him was associated an English lawyer in the person of Sir Charles Turner. The Government of India declared in their resolution that any scheme for the admission of Indians to higher employment in the public service to be entirely satisfactory would require Parliamentary legislation. The Commission was coldly received by the native press and Lord Dufferin warmly referred to this subject in his reply to the address of the Puna Sarvajanic Sabha. The Public Service Commission commenced its sittings at Lahore on the 15th December and proceeded on to other great towns to collect evidence. Lord Dufferin also took into consideration the question of jail manufactures. The Government of India concurred in the views expressed by the Prison conference of 1877 that jail labour should in the first place be applied to the production of those articles which were necessary for the various State departments and that jail labour should be interfered with only where it was manifest that by the competition of jail labour private trade was being interfered with. The Excise question engaged the attention of the Bengal Government. The question of combining a maximum of revenue with a minimum of consumption had always been a difficult one to solve and the Bengal Government had appointed a commission to enquire into the results and practical working of its excise policy. Effect was given to some of the recomendations of the Excise Commission and central distilleries were re-established at some of the larger towns. The Commisson had recommended that stills should be grouped outside the inhabited parts of the town and that care should be taken in selecting the place for the shops within the town, but the Bengal Government did not think any such stringent orders to be necessary. The efficiency of the excise staff was considerably increased and all shops were prohibited under heavy penalties from selling liquor to children under 12 years of age and ordered to be closed at nightfall. The Education Commission had recommended the policy of the gradual withdrawal of Government from higher education leaving the work to enlightened public spirit where practicable. In pursuance of this recommendation the Bengal Government announced its intention of closing the Berhampur and the Midnapur Colleges unless arrangements had been made before the first of May 1887, for the transfer of their management to local bodies. These two important provincial towns were able to take charge of their colleges thus fulfilling in one important respect the expectations of those who had introduced the present system of high education in India. The munificence of that noble lady Maharani Surnomoyee C. I. of Cossimbazar, which had already shown itself in substantial donations to works of public utility, was chiefly instrumental not only in keeping up the Berhampur College to the standard of its former efficiency but of still further increasing its usefulness. The question of techincal education engaged the attention of the Government but nothing was practically done to spread this useful branch of knowledge. The Finance Committee occupied itself mainly with the revision of the provincial contracts and recommended large reductions in the provincial assignments. The Finances of the Empire were hardly in a hopeful condition. The Revised Estimates for 1885-86 exhibited a deficit of nearly 3 millions while the Budget Estimates for 1886-87 showed a small surplus of £182,200. Sir Auckland Colvin announced that the only hope for a better state of things lay in the fact that the Government of India had been able to press the silver question, which had permanently crippled the resources of the Indian Empire, upon the attention of the English Cabinet which had promised to appoint a Royal Commission to enquire into the matter. The real solution of the silver difficulty lay in the hands of the powers of Europe and the United States. Unless by the combined action of those powers, the demand for silver vastly increased, there was no hope of the relative values of gold and silver being adjusted to the advantage of India. The large annual payments in gold which India has to make introduces large fluctuations in her accounts even if the rupee were to fall by a trifling fraction of a penny. An important measure was passed this year by the Supreme Council with the object of amending the Oudh Rent Act of 1868. The present act provided that all tenants in Oudh would have a statutory right of occupation for seven years at the rate which they were paying at the last settlement and that the landlords could enhance at the end of that period at the rate of one anna per rupee or 6¼ per cent. Thus occupancy rights were intoduced in full force in Oudh although Sir Henry Davies had reported during the administration of Lord Lawrence that they did not exist there in any shape. It was openly asserted that this bill was a violation of the engagements of Lord Canning with the Talukdar class. The compromise of 1868 provided that the Government would not claim occupancy rights on behalf of the Oudh tenants. The peace of the country was slightly disturbed by serious riots between the Hindus and the Mahomedans, at Etawah Delhi, Umballa and other places. The question of imprisonment for debt was discussed in connection with Mr. Ilbert's bill abolishing imprisonment for debt. The bill was strongly opposed, it being pointed out that imprisonment was often the only means to make a dishonest debtor pay and persons who by secret deeds had transferred the legal ownership of their estates to others while in ostensible possession of property on the credit of which they might take large advances, deserved the condign punishment of imprisonment. The press unanimously thought that the gradual abolition of imprisonment for debt would make the execution of money decrees almost impossible. The sad condition of the imported coolies in Assam excited great attention. Poor and ignorant, they were often made the victims of wily recruiters, and made to enter into contracts the terms of which they did not understand. In many cases their treatment in the tea-gardens furnished the cause for just commiseration. The necessity for amending Act I of 1882, which regulated the importation of labour into Assam was forcibly pointed out by the advocates of the voiceless coolies.

THE NATIONAL CONGRESS.—The National Congress met in the closing week of the year in Calcutta, and delegates duly chosen from many of the most important cities of all parts of India came down at considerable expense and personal self-sacrifice to respond to the call of duty to their native country.

Such an assemblage was the proudest monument of British rule and would have been impossible under a Yudhistir, an Asoka or an Akber. The men that were engaged in this good work, were, to use Lord Beaconsfields expression, all men of light and leading, the flower of India's intellectual aristocracy, men who have proved the stuff of which they were made by pushing themselves to the front in the active struggle of life and who were not the mere accidents of birth. They were welcomed by that ripe scholar and antiquarian of European reputation, Rajah Rajendralala Mitra who saw in this assembly the realization of his life-long dream that the scattered units of his race might some day coalesce and live as a nation. The deliberations of the Congress were presided over by the eminent economist and veteran publicist of Bombay Mr. Dadabhai Naoroji under whose guidance the work of the Congress was conducted in a thoroughly practical and business-like manner. In the resolutions adopted by the Congress the foremost place was given to the reform and reconstitution of the Legislative Councils. The changes advocated by the Congress with reference to the Councils were of two sorts, functional and structural. The functional changes demanded were that the yearly budgets be laid before the Legislative Councils for discussion and that the right of interpellation be conceded to the members. In the first of these demands the Congress was supported by almost the entire body of enlightened public opinion in the country. The right of interpellation is enjoyed by members of the Ceylon Legislative Council and had been conceded by Lord Dalhousie to the Legislative Council of 1854 when it was withdrawn owing to its abuse by certain European members. The Congress expressly exempted from interpellation all subjects connected with the army, the foreign policy of the State and the dealings with Local Governments and also reserved the right of the Executive to with-hold an answer for State reasons. The structural changes advocated were that the proportion of non-official members be raised from a third to a half and that the elective principle be introduced. It was at once recognized that under the existing circumstances a complete representation of the people in the Councils was impracticable but it was universally felt that the nomination system although in some cases it had given us extremely good men to represent our interests, did not afford that guarantee for the independence of the non-official members which an elective system did. The solution of this problem is an extremely difficult one *i. e.* that of getting at an organization which would return to the Councils, members who could fully represent all sections of the community. The proposal for the separation of the judicial from the Executive branch of the administration, was in Lord Dufferin's words, a counsel of perfection in the carrying out of which some extra cost, and some decrease in the present powers and privileges of Magistrates and Collectors were necessary. The other resolutions of the Congress dealt with the removal of the restrictions that pressed hard in the case of the natives of India with reference to the Covenanted appointments, the extension of trial by jury into non-jury districts, of giving finality to verdicts of juries, the desirability of permitting natives of India to enlist as volunteers and other questions of public interest. In the discussion of these matters "the stalwart Sikh, the sturdy Pathan, the proud Rajput, the hardy Maharatta, the amiable Madrasi and the versatile Parsi mixed freely with the sons of Bengal in brotherly emulation to serve their mother land and the good feeling that prevailed was all that could be desired." The Congress was looked upon with different feelings by its numerous critics. It was recognized that the English Government by its beneficent policy had "reared up a great educated class, nurturing them in the doctrines of English liberty, grounding them in the work of administration, disciplining them by the practical teaching of local self-government, admitting them to some of the highest offices of the State and publicly consulting them on every large legislative measure, and this powerful class thus exercised and inured to the duties of British citizenship, now asked to be more fully associated in the work of British rule. The duty of the Government was to accept this new order of things, to recognize frankly the changed aspect of the country and to provide means for the requirements of the times. But other critics spoke of the Congress and its work in a different spirit altogether. The claim of the educated classes to represent the masses was entirely denied. This argument however would not bear examination. The educated classes have always been recognized by the Government to be the interpreters of the feelings and wishes of their less fortunate countrymen and it is absurd to say that our educated men could not represent accurately the feelings of those who speak the same language, have exactly the same social institutions, and the same wants. The people of India were again described to be unfit for those institutions which they sought as they could not within less than the life-time of a generation have reached to anything but political babyhood. This argument ignored the fact that the Indians had enjoyed a glowing civilization in the past, that our religious and political brotherhoods and village communities were as old as the hills and that both under Mogul and English rule we had evinced capacities in all departments of civil administration of a high order. But the fiercest attacks were made upon the advocacy by the Congress of the elective principle. The critics failed to recognize that in this matter the Congress proceeded with extreme caution. It did not want to begin at the point that England had reached after many generations of constitutional Government, but asked only for a gradual advance in the line of loosening the bonds by which England held India. All movements of this sort have to pass through various stages, of opposition, of abuse, ridicule and misapprehension of its aims and objects, but the Indian public respectfully prayed for certain concessions confident in the sense of justice and righteousness of the English people, and should they only succeed in establishing the truth of their cause, the concessions were certain to come in the fulness of time from the hands of that nation which had always been the foremost in championing the cause of civil and religious liberty.

CHAPTER IX.

1887.

AFGHAN AFFAIRS.—The protracted negotiations with Russia with reference to the settlement of the boundaries of Afghanistan were brought at last to a peaceful termination. In the final arrangement that was arrived at, Russia agreed to abandon her claim to the Khojah Saleh District in consideration of a strip of pasture land in the Khusk valley, and this state of things was finally embodied in a protocol. The settlement that was arrived at brought the Russian outposts 11 miles nearer to Afghanistan, but this was immaterial considering the fact that the territories of Herat and Afghan Turkestan have been for some time at the mercy of the Autocrat of all the Russians. Thus Sir West Ridgeway brought to a conclusion the delimitation business. The activity of Russia in Central Asia was magnified by bazaar rumours in India and there was a good deal of uneasiness. The attitude of the Russian press tended to intensify the popular excitement. The Ghilzai rising in Afghanistan assumed formidable proportions and was succeeded by the Herat mutiny which made Abdur Rahman's position rather insecure for a time. These risings which were probably due to Russian intrigues were suppressed before Ayub Khan raised the standard of revolt on the confines of Afghanistan. The rule of Abdur Rahman did not seem to be at all popular with his subjects and the revolt of Ayub Khan seemed to be a grave source of political danger. The surrender of Ayub Khan to General Macleane towards the close of the year removed the most powerful rival of the Amir. Ayub Khan was brought over to Rawul Pindi and being safely interned there was placed beyond the possibility of committing any mischief. A few months later Ishak Khan who was the Governor of Afghan Turkestan raised the standard of revolt in the north of the Hindu Kush and being defeated by the promptness and gallantry of Amir's troops fled to Kerki. This rebellion was followed by the rising of the Shinwarics who were put down also without considerable difficulty. It was expected that some difficulties would arise in interpreting and giving effect to the boundaries settled by the Delimitation Commission. The wily Muscovite was always too prone to avail himself of any ambiguities and loopholes that might be found as was the case with Lord Granville's arrangement of 1873. But happily the task of rectifying the boundary line laid down in the Khusk valley was smoothly and satisfactorily performed by Major Yates. Russian influence also showed itself in Persia where the Shah greatly curtailed the privileges gained through the diplomacy of Sir Drummond Wolff in the matter of throwing the Karun river open to trade. The only satisfactory course in dealing with Russia in Asia is to draw a hard-fast boundary line and to let her plainly understand that any encroachment on her side will be regarded and resented as a *Casus belli* and this policy was at last adopted by the Government of India.

HER MAJESTY'S JUBILEE.—The most important political event of the year was the celebration of the Jubilee of Her Majesty the Queen Empress which called forth an unprecedented outburst of loyalty and enthusiasm from one part of the country to the other. The idea of a Jubilee is as old as the time of Moses and it had been given practical effect to by the great dignitaries of the Roman Catholic Church at stated intervals. In Asia where the monarchs were mostly arbitrary despots and had but little hold on the hearts of the people the idea never took a deep root. In India only the illustrious Akber reigned considerably over fifty years and that was the only opportunity for the celebration of the Jubilee. In England too, such opportunities had been exceedingly rare, occurring on an average only once in three hundred years. But the completion of the fiftieth year of the rule of Her Gracious Majesty, Queen Victoria, made her subjects in every part of her vast empire, willing and anxious to celebrate the auspicious event in a befitting manner. They were all earnest and sincere in the cause of loyalty and devotion to their Sovereign and each was willing in his humble way, to contribute his mite to so noble a cause. History does not record a nobler or more glorious reign than that of Queen Victoria. Her subjects are identically one in their devotion to their Sovereign and the period embraced by her reign has truly been the Augustan age and has witnessed the continual extension of the domains of knowledge and the alleviation of human sufferings. The charity and purity of the life of our Sovereign are unexampled. She is never weary of visiting the huts of the poor. She feels the deepest concern in the welfare of all her subjects smitten by distress and always subscribes freely for relief. She is the asylum and home of all goodness and domestic virtues that can adorn an individual and she has realized in her life the noblest idea of Hindu widowhood. The initiative was taken by the people in all cases and the Jubilee was celebrated far and wide in the land in all possible varities of fashion which fertility of imagination could create, exuberance of loyalty could suggest, or the largeness of purse and heart could provide. Durbars were held in every important Indian town for the celebration of this auspicious event and rejoicings that were due to the unprompted impulses of the people took place in every form. At the Calcutta Durbar which was a very grand affair, Lord Dufferin delivered a speech worthy of the occasion and worthy of his reputation as an orator. His summary of the blessings of the reign of the Queen-Empress was neat and appropriate. In graphic language he depicted how the reign of the Queen-Empress had brought justice to every cottage-door, how it had bridged the floods and pierced the jungle, how it had converted millions of barren acres into well-watered plains, how it had diminished the risks both of famine and pestilence how it had lit a hundred lamps of learning in every chief centre of population and how it had placed within the reach of the humblest Indian student the accumulated wealth of western learning, science and experience. His Excellency then touched on the burning question as to the aspirations of the educated natives to be associated more extensively with their English rulers in the administration of their own domestic affairs. His Lordship declared in emphatic terms that he would be glad and happy if he should during his tenure of the Viceroyalty be permitted to place on a wider and more logical footing the political status which was so wisely given a generation ago by that great statesman Lord Halifax to such Indian gentlemen as by their influnce, their acquirements and the confidence they inspired in their fellow-countrymen were marked out as useful adjuncts to the Legislative Councils. This authoritative expression of generous sympathy with the most important reform demanded by the educated voice of the country evoked sentiments of lively gratitude throughout the country and encouraged the hope that Lord Dufferin would take up this question in a broad and liberal spirit and solve it on the lines indicated in his Lordship's speech on this solemn occasion. The prison gates were widely opened on this occasion and 23 thousand of those who were not past reclaiming were set free once more to gladden their hearths and homes. Some Native princes sent deputations to England to convey their congratulations to the Queen-Empress, others attended in person and many Indian noblemen visited England on this occasion. With one exception the Indian chiefs and nobles came back well-satisfied with the reception that had been accorded to them. Funds were collected in almost all the principal Indian towns for the purpose of raising permanent memorials of the Jubilee and a decent sum was sent to England to serve as India's contribution to the Imperial Institute. In many parts of India the Jubilee has been commemorated by works of charity and benevolence. The Jubilee in India was celebrated on the 16th of February by order of the Viceroy, and the demonstrations that were

… in India were quite worthy of the noblest Sovereign that ever reigned.

FEUDATORY INDIA.—His Highness the Nizam of Hyderabad made a magnificent offer of sixty lakhs of rupees as a free gift to the Government of India for strengthening the defences of the Empire. The offer was significant in more ways than one. It plainly showed that the Native Chiefs had now begun to recognize their position as integral factors of a great and united Empire and desired to be actively associated in the external defences of the Empire. It showed moreover that the theory upon which General Skobeloff had founded his whole scheme for the invasion of India, namely that the Russians would be aided by the princes and people of India was utterly without foundation. The princes and the people of India may have many grievances to redress but they know fully well that India must yet continue for many centuries under foreign rule and the British are indisputably the best masters they are likely to have. Self-interest therefore, if no higher consideration should always make the princes and the people of India declare for the continuance of the British rule. The question as to whether the Nizam's offer should be accepted or not was for a long time under the consideration of the Government but Lord Dufferin came to the decision that the resort to a system of benevolences would be unworthy of the Government of India and that should other native states follow the example of the Nizam it was quite possible that the people of those states whose condition was financially none of the best would have to bear extra burdens for the defence of the Empire. This might lead to discontent in the natives states which were being already taxed to some extent under Sir John Strachey's salt arrangements. The Chief of Kapurthala made also an offer of five lakhs to be devoted to the object of strengthening the defences of the Empire. These free gifts were handsomely acknowledged but they were not formally accepted. Lord Dufferin decided upon making the native states keep a small body of well-disciplined troops commensurate with the resources of the state and thus instead of having half-armed and useless rabbles there was likely to be a body of troops which would prove a strength to the empire. Thus a great addition was made to the fighting strength of the Empire without any extra cost to the British Exchequer. In acknowledging these offers a broad hint was given which was readily taken up by other native states. There were some important administrative changes at Hyderabad. Nawab Salar Jung II was obliged to relinquish his post and Nawab Sir Asman Jah was appointed in his place. Colonel Marshall who had been appointed Private Secretary to the Nizam acquired great influence over His Highness who resolved to introduce the Cabinet system in Hyderabad. The Gwaliar state which had been practically under British management was made to advance a sum of three and half crores as a loan to the British Government at four per cent. The Gwaliar treasury was full and this amount was taken from the accumulated savings of years. The Travancore state which is always a model state carried out the important reform as to the separation of judicial from executive functions. The Mysore Representative Assembly met in October and took a most important step, in protesting against His Highness spending a large portion of the hot weather away from the head quarters at Otacamund. The affairs of Cashmere were gradually coming to a difficult pass. The Resident was a strong supporter of Dewan Lachman Das in whose hands all real power was centred and the complaints against his arbitrary and high-handed proceedings were bitter and loud. The young chief of Jhallawar was deprived of his powers for political reasons. The affairs of Bhopal were the subject of a good deal of public attention and the conduct of Sir Lepel Griffin was sharply criticised in some quarters, but the Government of India on Sir Lepel's applying to prosecute his critics gave an unqualified approval to all his proceedings with reference to the Bhopal state.

THE FINANCES.—There was a revision of the Provincial contracts during the year which was based mainly on the recommendations of the Finance Committee. The Government of India found it necessary to diminish the provincial allotments. Under the Decentralization scheme the Government of India while handing over certain departments to the immediate financial control of the Local Governments, has uniformly reserved in its own charge the great spending departments, involving large expenditure. Instead of the Local Governments managing their own finances and making certain assignments for Imperial expenditure such as the Military and Home charges, the burden of exchange, the payments to Railway Companies, it was the Imperial Government which maintains its prior claims upon the receipts of the main revenue Departments and sets apart so much of its revenues as it can reasonably spare to meet the civil expenditure placed under provincial control. Under this system the Local Governments had sometimes to incur the odium of supplementing their resources by imposing additional burdens. But partly by the increased economy and partly by the natural expansion of many of the items of revenue the Local Governments had in most cases been managing their affairs satisfactorily. The Government of India found that the annexation of Upper Burmah had added considerably to the burdens of the Empire and the Finance minister had to resort to the expedient of diverting the Famine Insurance Fund from its original object to meet the ordinary charges of the Empire, and of starving the Provinces. The first expedient was defended on the ground that the diversion did not involve any breach of faith on the part of the Government. The Government of India defended the lowering of Provincial assignments on the ground that the empire must always be looked at as a whole and not as a collection of separate and semi-independent states. The Local Governments had not thus the benefit of all normal growth of their revenues and of any economies which they effected in their expenditure, and this principle naturally took away all motives for exercising economy and for increasing revenues by good administration. The income realized from Upper Burmah fell far short of the expected sum and the expenses under all the heads, considerably increased. Thus the Financial position became most disheartening. The steadily falling exchange still further increased the embarassments of the Government and it was generally, thought that the income tax would be raised to meet the deficit. The Finance Committee's recomendations were submitted and the Committee was dissolved. Sir John Gorst declared that these recommendations were under the consideration of the Government with a view to speedy action.

GENERAL EVENTS.—The year opened with a disastrous fire in the People's Park Fair at Madras which burnt to death about 400 persons. This was followed by other disasters by sea and land and by terrible epidemics which counted their victims by thousands. The railway accident at Umballa caused the loss of many lives. The *Tasmania*, the *Sir John Lawrence* and the *Retriever* were lost within a few days of each other and later on the *Maharatta*, the *Earl of Jersy*, and the *Arcot* were wrecked. The loss of the *Sir John Lawrence* brought gloom and disaster in many a home in Bengal. That ill-fated vessel left Calcutta on the 25th May with 700 Hindu passengers to the holy shrine of Juggernath and nothing was heard of it ever afterwards. It had evidently been wrecked in the Bay of Bengal where a terrific storm raged about the time that the steamer left Calcutta. The Viceroy and the Lieutenant Governor of Bengal despatched telegrams of sympathy to the sufferers and steps were taken for the relief of those who had been left destitute and helpless by the occurrence of this calamity. Inquiries were also instituted to find out whether the vessel was in a sound and sea-going condition when it left. The first branch of the enquiry entrusted to the Public Service Commission, having been completed, a sub-committee of the commission dealt with the special departments and in the closing week of the year its report was finally completed and submitted. The Government of India proposed the raising of United Burmah into a Lieutenant Governorship but the Secretary of State did not sanction the proposal. The Local Governments and Administrations were asked seriously to consider the question of abolishing imprisonment as a method of enforcing a decree for the restitution of conjugal rights and to consult public opinion on the subject, as well as to offer suggestions for laying down a standard measure of length in India. The question of Jail Administration was brought to the attention of the Government by the loud complaints as to the misconduct of the jail officials and the Government of India recorded an important resolution on the subject. The Government of India found it as a fact that the punishment of whipping was too often unnecessarily inflicted in Indian jails and it was laid down that whipping should be sparingly inflicted and reserved as a last resource of discipline against contumacy. The necessity of taking measures for the better accomodation and preservation of the health of the prisoners was strictly enforced upon the attention of the Local Governments. All the Lieutenant Governorships, in the Bengal Presidency changed hands during the year. Sir Rivers Thomson was a most unpopular ruler and he departed without any public or popular demonstration. Sir Stuart Bayley whose antecedents were in his favor succeeded to be the ruler of the province whose administration was daily becoming the most difficult in India. Sir Stuart in his durbar speech at Bankipur, laid down the the important principle that local officers were to co-operate with the newly-created local bodies in a sympathetic spirit, that that the people were to be gradually trained up in the duties of administration. Sir Alfred Lyall was succeeded by Sir Auckland Colvin whose durbar speeches told the people of India that they were yet in the lowest forms of the political school, that they should occupy themselves with the petty affairs of their own localities and that the higher administrative questions were altogether beyond their range. Sir Charles Aitchison was succeeded by Sir James Lyall, who though partial to the members of his own service ruled on the whole wisely and well. Lord Reay was called upon to deal with the case of Mr. Wilson, a member of the Civil Service, who was charged with having sent improper proposals to the Dewan of Cambay in regard to his daughter. The decision of the Special Commissioners who found Mr. Wilson guilty was not accepted by the Secretary of State but Mr. Wilson was made to retire from the service. Lord Connemara made an extensive tour through his dominions in the course of which the Governor made himself acquainted with the real state of the country and the people. Lord Connemara succeeded in repairing the mischief that had been done by many indiscreet acts of his predecessor and his strong sense of justice restored to office many of the native officials of Tanjore who had been unjustly dismissed. In Burmah Sir Charles Barnard was succeeded by Sir Charles Crosthwaite who applied himself vigorously to the task of suppressing organized dacoities in Upper Burmah. The action of Mr. Ward in Assam in the matter of curtailing the privileges of the poorer classes who had always enjoyed the rights of collecting certain articles of forest produce, caused great hardship. The Panjab Tenancy Act was aimed at converting the superior tenants into inferior proprietors and prescribed the methods for acquiring statutory rights in the land. The Panjab had all along enjoyed the village system and the aim of the new act was to introduce a ryotwari tenure as had been recommended by the Famine Commission. Should the act bring its train annual and fluctuating assessments varying directly with the crop in the place of those fixed for a considerable period, as well as the granting of suspensions when necessary, it would bring in a great reform in Revenue administration, Lord Stanley of Alderley drew the attention of the House of Lords to the wrong that had been committed to the Arnigadh Zamindars who had been turned out of property worth twenty thousand rupees for a sum of rupees five thousand for the purpose of providing a better Botanical Gardens for Mussurie as well as to the conduct of Sir Alfred Lyall in attacking in a circular letter to his subordinates a judgment of the Chief Justice of the North Western Provinces. But Lord Cross declined to interfere in these matters. The Indian National Congress held its sittings at Madras this year under the presidency of Mr. Buduruddin Tyabji a leading Mahomedan barrister of Bombay and was attended by six hundred delegates from all parts of India. Sir T. Madhava Rao as the foremost representative of the intellect of Madras welcomed the delegates. The business of the Congress was confined mostly to the consideration of the sub jects which had engaged the attention of its previous sittings. A most indiscreet act was committed with reference to the published report of the Third Congress which embodied two pamphlets that contained many passages which to say the least did not commend themselves to the judgment of the educated section of the Indian people and which pamphlets were from their being published along with the report could be taken to be the work of the whole Congress. Sir Auckland Colvin in criticising the work of the Congress next year pointed out how objectionable many of the passages in those two pamphlets were and what evil effect they might likely have on the minds of persons who were likely not to think of the other side of the picture at all. Lord Dufferin too took exception to those pamphlets and while sharply criticising the Congress, though on incorrect information, on the eve of his departure from India, gave a prominent place to those pamphlets, which according to the statement made in the report had been distributed by thousands.

INQUIRY INTO THE ADMINISTRATION OF INDIA.—While India was being ruled by the East India Company, there used to be an exhaustive inquiry into Indian administration at the time of each renewal of the Company's Charter. Since however India had passed to the Crown no such inquiry had been held. The people of India had prayed the Houses of Parliament to grant such an enquiry but the prayer was unheeded. The prayer was first for a Royal Commission with an adequate number of native members on it, who would come out to this country and enquire into the details of Indian administration and the conduct of the local officers. There were however several grave objections to a Royal Commission being appointed although such a Commission was the best method for eliciting all the facts. The protest that would be made by every officer from the Viceroy downwards that such a Commission would destroy the prestige of Indian administration, the inevitable delay with which alone a large body inquiring into multifarious details can move, were grave objections in the way. On the other hand a Parliamentary Committee composed of experts, submitting its report within the session which had seen its appointment and dealing with a limited number of witnesses would be able to do the requisite work without stopping the clock of progress in India for a decade or two such as a Royal Commission must inevitably do. A Royal Commission could scarcely complete its work in less than a decade and a considerable period of time must elapse in the references to local officers and the Parliamentary discussions. The prayer therefore of the people of India for a Royal Commission was substituted by one for a Parliamentary Committee.

TAXATION IN INDIA.—There was an animated discussion in the leading periodicals of England with reference to the incidence of the taxation in India. Mr. Dadabhai Naroji who had made the economics of India his life-long study pointed out that the average incidence of taxation amounted to 5s. 8d. per head whilst the average income of the population is about 40 shillings per head. The official theory is fully set forth in the report of the Famine Commission. This view is that a native of India who does not trade or own land or consume spirituous liquour has to pay only 7d. as taxation on account of the salt that he consumes. The view of Mr. James Wilson the first Finance Minister that rent, and the opium revenue do not represent taxation proper was adopted by the Famine Commission. It is contended that the Government has from time immemorial a prescriptive and unquestioned right to receive from the occupier of the land whatever portion it requires of the surplus profit left after defraying the expenses of cultivation, and thus rent does not represent taxation proper. The opium revenue which it is alleged was derived from foreign customers did not also represent taxation proper. But it appears to us that both these views are untenable. Should the opium monopoly not exist, the growers of Indian opium would command their own terms with the merchants and unless it is shown that the price paid by the Government to the growers was as much as they would receive if there were no State monoply, the opium revenue must be considered as a tax imposed by the State on this branch of agricultural and commercial industry. That the Government has never asserted a general right of ownership in the soil is proved by the fact that when the Government conceded land to the railway companies it could not do so by a mere notice to its tenants to quit but it did so by an elaborate course of legislation in 1850, 1857, 1860 and 1870. The claim of the State is distinctly limited by Manu the oldest authority on the subject to only a fixed share of the produce and on this theory the whole system of British land revenue settlement is based. If the State is not the owner, the share of the produce that it takes for meeting public necessity can not be called rent. It is a tax and must be taken into account in calculating the incidence of taxation. The opium duty has to be paid to the official tax-gatherer and were it remitted it would find its way to the pockets of the agricultural and mercantile classes.

CHAPTER X.

1888.

THE SIKKIM WAR.—The complications with Tibet resulted in a small force being sent to Sikkim to expel the Tibetans from a frontier outpost. From the time of Warren Hastings the English had an eye to open up trade with China through Sikkim and Tibet but the Tibetans have always consistently refused to allow any European to put his foot beyond the high passes of the snowy range leading into Tibet. Sir George Campbell in reviewing the relations of the British Government with Tibet said in his letter to the *Times* that the Tibetans never advanced a claim of suzerainty over Sikkim but they had always civilly but firmly refused any British entry into Thibet although they allowed trade by natives. In 1886 an effort was made on a grand scale to establish commercial relations with Tibet. It was resolved to send Mr. Colman Macaulay on a mission to Lhassa. The mission was organized on an imposing scale and it was settled that Mr. Macaulay was to be accompanied with a whole host of scientific men as well as a small army. The Tibetans were convinced that this mission was not of a commercial character but was coming to invade their country and it was determined to offer resistance. They could not understand why such a large mission was necessary for the peaceful purposes which it avowed. The Tibetans are a very suspicious race and they believed that if they allowed the British to set foot on their soil, they would end by conquering and annexing it. The mission was countermanded in accordance with the terms of the treaty with China entered into by Lord Roseberry the Secretary of State for Foreign Affairs. But the Lamas feeling themselves threatened by the Macaulay mission occupied Lingtu where they built a fort across the high road and thus secured for Tibetans an advanced position from which the frontiers of their country could be watched. After the Tibetans had been in Sikkim for nearly eighteen months and after it had been clearly shown that the influence of the Chinese Government was insufficient to bring about their peaceful withdrawal the Government of India decided to take the matter into its own hands. A letter of warning was sent to the officer in command of the Tibetan troops saying that the British Government would expel him by force unless he evacuated his position at Lingtu by midnight of the 15th of March. This letter was returned unopened and several other letters sent to Tibetan frontier officers and to the Dalai Lama were also not answered, the Raja of Sikkim explaining that it was the Tibetan custom not to receive any letters. The Government then moved against them and expelled them out of Lingtu with but little resistance. But on the 2nd of May the Tibetans showed themselves in considerable numbers and attacked the British troops at Gnatong being repulsed with loss. In the meanwhile negotiations were opened but the Tibetans were not disposed to acquiesce in their defeat and they assembled in considerable numbers. General Graham was prevented by rain and mist from making any movement towards the enemy for some time but on the 24th of August he completely routed the Tibetans killing several hundreds and driving the rest over the passes. On the 26th he advanced to the Tibetan town of Chumbi, and on the 27th the British troops came back to their own border. Mr. A. W. Paul who was the political officer attached to the force made such efforts as were in his power to open negotiations and the Chinese Resident at Lhassa expressed his willingness to meet the British political officer. The Chinese had not evinced any hostility towards the British throughout this war, and it was hoped that with the intervention of China all difficulties would be settled. This war arose from the determination of the British Government to maintain its own prestige and the historian must say that it was not lightly undertaken.

OTHER EXPEDITIONS.—The tribes both on the Western

and the Eastern border gave a good deal of trouble to the British Government by a series of aggressions. The Black Mountain expedition which set out under General Macqueen from Abbotabad to punish the tribes on the Western frontier had a good deal of skirmishing but was successful in making a complete survey of the country and in exacting complete submission of the tribes in question. The Lushais on the Chittagong Hills, had a small expedition sent against them which was of a punitive nature and three expeditions had to be sent to the frontier districts of Upper Burmah to keep the unruly hilly population in order. The Burmese campaigns were of an arduous nature and General White had a difficult task before him. In these hostilities with the border tribes the British forces often resorted to the burning of villages and destruction of the standing crops. The Kashmir state sent a contingent of troops to aid the British army in the Black Mountain Expedition.

THE ADMINISTRATION OF THE MARQUIS OF DUFFERIN.—Early in the year it was unexpectedly announced that Lord Dufferin had resigned the Indian Viceroyalty and would retire at the end of the year. His Lordship in announcing this fact to the Legislative Council declared that imperative private reasons alone had made him retire from his exalted office a year earlier than the alloted term. During the last year of his Viceroyalty His Excellency had to deal with many important questions, administrative and financial. His Government had to consider the recommendations of the Public Service Commission and forward them with its own views thereon to the Sectetary of State. Lord Dufferin's despatch on the subject materially assisted in raising the age for competition in the Indian Civil Service examination, a most important reform which would tend in a great way to offer facilities to the educated natives of India, to enter the close body of the Covenanted Service and thus to take a legitimate share in the administration of their own country. In reviewing the report on the progress of public instruction in India, Lord Dufferin announced that the time had come when the Government of India would gradually retire from high education and that the people must take upon themselves the responsibility of providing for their own needs in this direction. The large expenditure in frontier defences added to the loss by the fall of silver and the large outlay in Burmah caused a deficit in the budget of nearly two crores and measures had to be adopted at once to meet this deficiency. The salt duty was raised to Rs. 2-8 per maund in British India and to one rupee per maund in Lower Burmah. An import duty was also imposed on patroleum. The raising of the salt duty excited great dissatisfaction in many parts of India, although Sir Evelyn Baring when reducing the tax had expressly reserved the right of the Government to return temporarily to the high rate should the financial position appear disheartening. The report of the Finance Committee was fully considered by the Government of Lord Dufferin during this year. The Committee had proposed the abolition of the Calcutta mint on the ground that the Bombay mint could coin monthly $1\frac{1}{4}$ crores of rupees and was alone sufficient for the necessities of the Empire. But Lord Dufferin negatived the proposal as it was a questionable measure of economy and the interests of commerce suffered thereby. The Coronership of Madras was abolished thereby effecting a saving of Rs. 9000 per annum. The stock-note scheme was abandoned. The Secretary of State thought that the Government of India in view of the unsatisfactory state of the Empire should have it in its power to revise the normal provincial contracts leaving the provincial Governments to adjust their expenditure in the best way they could. Lord Dufferin also decided that the necessities of the Empire demanded that provincial expenditure should be subordinated to the Imperial necessities and a conference was arranged under the presidency of the Hon'ble James Westland to effect some modifications of the existing system.

Lord Dufferin also paid great attention to the question of sanitary improvement. He instituted an elaborate inquiry into the question of the prevalence of leprosy in India but in dealing with the eradication of this disease he unfortunately found that medical science had not discovered any certain cure for leprosy. The death-rates in the Indian jails standing at a high figure, the Government of India directed that the task alloted to each prisoner should not be too much and such as could be gone through the day, that punishments should be sparingly inflicted in jails and that the prisoners should be properly kept that they might not get diseases through unhealthy surroundings. The Government of India also issued an elaborate scheme for the improvement of the sanitary condition of the Indian people. But the real truth is that the people are not uncleanly in India through habit but because they have not sufficient means at their command to live in an improved way after satisfying the cravings of nature. The Government scheme is also likely to do little good unless assisted by copious funds. The condition of the people in the thickly inhabited districts of Northern India where the majority of the people are agricultural labourers and whose lot is probably the hardest known to humanity, engaged Lord Dufferin's attention and he thought that emigration to the sparsely-peopled and fertile districts of Upper Burmah was the only remedy that could be adopted to relieve the pressure of population on the soil. Shortly before his departure His Excellency delivered an important speech at the St. Andrew's Dinner in which he exhaustively dwelt upon the popular movements in India. His Lordship's information as to the real character of the proposals made by the Congress, proved to be entirely wrong, and the remarks that he made to show that these proposals (which did not in fact emanate from the Congress) were utterly revolutionary in their character and inadmissible, were beside the point. But Lord Dufferin in the course of this speech made the important announcement that he had submitted proposals in accordance with the lines indicated in his Jubilee speech with reference to the expansion of the Councils of the Empire. This speech of Lord Dufferin introduced the Congress prominently to the attention of the British public, and its constitution and objects were discussed by the firesides of English homes. Lord Dufferin's persistent efforts in the matter of effecting a solution of the silver problem were placed within a measurable distance of success by the report of the Currency Commission which recommended England to secure international bimetalism.

LORD DUFFERIN'S ADMINISTRATION.—We have reviewed above the measures of Lord Dufferin's administration in detail and only a few general remarks are necessary here. His Lordship's attention had been principally engaged with foreign affairs of India and the complications on the western frontier and in Upper Burmah left him but comparatively little time to attend to the domestic affairs of the realm. His Lordship was peculiarly well-fitted by previous training to grasp foreign problems and there is no doubt that the present system of strengthening the frontier defences received its greatest impetus at his hands. Lord Dufferin took an important step in associating selected bands of the armies of Natives States in the defence of the Empire. In his speech at Patiala, he publicly recognized the loyalty of the Feudatory Chiefs and explained the practical measures which the Government of India had devised for making the Native States participate in the defence of the Empire. Those chiefs who have good soldierly material in their territories would be invited to maintain a select band of troops in a high state of efficiency, and that no native prince would be asked to keep a larger force of this description than he could afford to support. The Government of India at the same time expressed its willingness to place the services of British officers at their disposal for the training of their armies, and to provide rifles free of charge for the troops of the Imperial Service. There was a time when the native princes were regarded with suspicion and distrust, and Lord Dufferin's policy convinced them that they were integral factors of a great Empire. Before His Lordship left Calcutta in April there were several meetings of his friends and admirers to do him honor and a statue was voted to him. His Excellency in replying to the addresses presented to him entered into an elaborate vindication of the measures of his administration. The movement to do honor to His Excellency was not joined in the capital city of India, by the leading zamindars, who were greatly opposed to the Bengal Tenancy Act which his Lordship had passed and by a large section of the educated classes who thought that the reforms which they asked for had not been considered in a broad and liberal spirit by His Excellency. At some principal towns of Upper India entertainments and addresses were given in honor of Lord Dufferin. The European community were grateful to a man to Lord Dufferin for giving its members increased facilities for enterprize in Upper Burmah, and the leading European firms subscribed largely to do him honor. Lord Dufferin was acknowledged on all hands to be a statesman of great ability and tact and he always proceeded in all matters with extreme caution. On his return to England he was received with the highest civic honors and he bore emphatic testimony to the loyalty, the practical wisdom, the good sense and experience which was possessed by many natives of India. He spoke also highly of the work that is being done in India by the members of the civil and the military services who had many difficult and arduous duties to perform. Lord Dufferin was appointed Ambassador in Italy on his return to England.

GENERAL EVENTS.—Indian affairs received a good deal of attention during the year at the hands of the English people though there were but few debates on Indian questions in Parliament which was occupied with Irish affairs. Sir William Hunter drew the attention of the British public to the recent movements in India, to the changing conditions of the country and to the just claims advanced by the people in the matter of their higher employment in the public service. Sir William treated the subject with almost unsurpassed knowledge of Modern India and in a style which it is always a pleasure to read. He appealed to the English people to avoid in dealing with India those mistakes which history says was committed in Ireland where concession after concession failed to satisfy the Irish people because they came too late. The Indian cotton industry was making rapid improvement and English piece-goods were being threatened by the produce of the Indian mills. This portended the dawn of a new industrial era for India. Mr. Thornton read an important paper before the society of Arts on Canal Irrigation. He inclined to the view that the canals were the cause of improvement of the soil. But the appearance of Mr. W. C. Bonnerji, Mr. Dadabhai Naroji and Mr. Eardley Norton as delegates from India to excite the interest of the electors of Great Britain in Indian affairs, the establishment of the Indian political agency under the able guidance of Mr. William Digby and the undertaking of the responsibilities of Member for India by Mr. Charles Bradlaugh the Junior member for Northampton with the consent of his constituents, were events of great importance. The Indian delegates delivered a series of addresses on Indian topics and created a most favourable impression in many of the great towns of England. Mr. Bradlaugh who had already won a position in the House of Commons by his great abilities and his sterling independence proved a fearless champion of the Indian people and his speeches on Indian questions displayed a thorough grasp of the situation to all its aspects. Nawab Mohsin-ul-mulk who went to England in connection with the Parliamentary Committee under the Presidency of Sir Henry James to enquire into the Deccan mining scandals had an interview with Mr. Gladstone and tried to interest the Grand Old Man in all questions connected with Indian Mussulmans. The Nawab tried to obtain Mr. Gladstone's views on the National Congress and that great statesman declared that the constitutional and legitimate efforts of the Indian people to represent their own requirements commanded his warmest sympathy. The ungenerous attack of Lord Salisbury in characterizing Dadabhai Naroji the Liberal Candidate for Central Finsbury as a "black man" evoked strong criticism in the Indian press and drew forth a strong protest from Mr. Gladstone who thought it a very bad policy to use scornful epithets towards the Indian people. Mr. Slagg's motion on the Financial position of India elicited a speech of great force from Lord Randolph Churchill who thought that the situation was one of great peril that the Government of India had reached to the end of taxation and its constantly growing expenditure was a source of grave anxiety. The grievances of the uncovenanted service were ventilated in the Lower House by Mr. H. S. King and Sir Roper Lethbridge. The head and front of these were that the members of the uncovenanted service had not the privilege of having their pensions paid in sterling. Sir John Gorst pointed out in reply that up to 1863 the members of the said service could draw their pensions only in India and that when they were allowed the privilege of having their pensions paid in England, there was a distinct understanding that these pensions would be paid at the official rates of exchange. The bill that was introduced for extending the jurisdiction of the Allahabad High Court into Oudh, was greatly opposed in India and it was afterwards withdrawn. Sir Charles Aitchison retired from the Home ministership and his retirement was a great loss to India. His broad and liberal views, his ripe and wide experience and his great business capacities had made him popular both with the Government and the people and he had always exerted a beneficial influence on the counsels of the Empire. He was succeeded by Mr. (now Sir Philip) Hutchins a Madras Civilian. Sir David Barbour who took charge of the Financial portfolio was a specialist on the currency question and had served with advantage to his colleagues on the Currency Commission. He had thoroughly studied the necessity of a double standard and all the reasonable schemes for the solution of that difficulty. The Deccan mining scandals led to many revelations and a Parliamentary Committee was appointed to deal with the same. The President of the Gwalior Council Sir Gunpat Rao died being succeeded by Bapoo Sahab Jadoo, the maternal grandfather of the young chief. The Begum of Bhopal having expressed a wish for a Mahomedan minister, Munshi Imtiaz Ali from Lucknow was appointed to succeed Colonel Ward. The Mission despatched to Kurrum Valley to settle the disputes between the Turis and the Ameer's subjects reported that there was no chance of settling those complicated matters. Sir Auckland Colvin held a series of Durbars at the headquarters of the Divisions, and in addressing the assembled gentry he exhorted them to make the Local Self-Government scheme a success. Sir Auckland during the first year of his rule contented himself with carrying on the routine duties of administration but the peace of his territories was disturbed by disturbances during the Maharram at Agra, Ghazipore and Najibabad. His criticism on the report of the Madras Congress was based on the two ill-fated pamphlets that were appended to that report and he also temperately reviewed the fundamental principles of the Congress and set forth his objections to it in a long document addressed to Mr. Hume. This document was answered at great length by the Nestor of the Congress movement but it served to keep the leaders of that body always within strictly temperate and constitutional limits. The opposition to the Congress took a shape in some portions of the United Provinces under leaders who had motives of their own for joining the opposition, and the public bodies which they started vanished out of sight in a short time altogether. In Bengal the Municipal Bill excited great opposition but Sir Stuart Bayley's utterances showed that the passing of the bill was a foregone conclusion. The working of the outstill system in the districts Hooghly and Howrah, showed that the easy and cheap method of procuring liquor had increased drunkenness. The measures connected with the suppression of the mutiny in the Madras Christian College moved the Hindu community to strive towards the establishment of a Hindu Theological College. In Bombay the accusations brought against Mr. Arthur Crawford of systematic bribery were inquired into by a Commission presided over by Mr. Justice Wilson of the Calcutta High Court. The officers who had deposed as to having bought offices under promises of indemnity were declared unfit for Government Service by the Bombay High Court. The opening of the Victoria Technical Institute which was the first institution of its kind to supply a deeply felt want was an important event in the industrial annals of India. The Fourth Indian National Congress held its sittings at Allahabad under the presidency of Mr. George Yule, a merchant prince of Calcutta whose singularly able speech served to remove many misapprehensions connected with the Congress movement. The Congress was attended by 1400 delegates duly chosen and the leaders of thought in every part of the country took part in it. The delegates mixed freely with one another and thus the assembly was an important social gathering. The proceedings were marked by great enthusiasm, and were got through with marked unanimity. The Calcutta High Court received the addition of a third native Judge in the person of the Hon'ble Dr. Gurudas Banerji, whose elevation to the bench was received with great satisfaction throughout India. Sir Auckland Colvin and Sir James Lyall earned the gratitude of the native Community by appointing natives of India for the first time as District Officers. The financial aspect of Indian railways and canals was discussed at great length at the instance of Mr. Charles Bradlangh. Railways have now been constructed along the most important lines of communication and though some enthusiasts still advocate the expenditure of 100 crores more on Indian railways by the State (for the private capitalists would not invest a rupee in Indian railways without a Government guarantee) the hard fact remains that up to the end of 1888, the Indian taxpayer had to pay 75 crores, inclusive of interest for the railways. Some of the Indian canals had been undoubtedly remunerative. Lord Salisbury's remark in his famous Manchester Speech of 1875, that no canal could show a clean balance-sheet which had not for its basis the works of old native rulers, was not wide of the truth, for to the above sort we have only to add those canals which had been constructed under exceptionally favorable conditions such as the Godavery, the Kistna Canals and the Cambeyanicut. The major works in Bengal do no even earn enough to pay their working expenses. The Government admits that 10 of the 34 major canals are purely losing concerns. Sind is almost a rainless province and the canals there earn 6 to 12 per cent on the capital outlay. The irrigation by tanks and wells seems to be the better method, as irrigation by mountain waters leads to the impoverishment of the soil.

THE APATHY OF THE ENGLISH PEOPLE TOWARDS INDIAN AFFAIRS.—The strange apathy that prevails in England in relation to Indian affairs is remarkable. While the simplest question with reference to any matter of local interest in the United Kingdom excites considerable attention the affairs of a country which is as large as Europe excepting Russia are discussed only at the fag-end of the session when the House is completely empty. Lord Randolph Churchill rightly said that the loss of India would reduce England to a second-rate power in Europe and this splendid Empire while it had not cost a farthing to the British Treasury had been of immense moral and material advantage to England. The colonies of England do not pay the expenses of governing them which come entirely from the British Exchequer, but the cost of the separate department which administers India is paid entirely by the

Indian tax-payer. Some dependencies require the luxury on the part of the paramount country of having to pay dearly for them. Since 1830 France had spent 200 crores in Algeria and the only advantage that France derives is that it affords an excellent training-ground for the troops. Persistent efforts were set on foot during the year for exciting the interest of the electors of Great Britain towards their great Eastern Empire and for forming an Indian party in Parliament. Sir Charles Dilke who is one of the foremost of modern statesmen, in a thoughtful lecture pointedly drew the attention of the British public to this state of things, and boldly asserted that it is not for the good of the Indian Bureaucracy either that India should be governed in this secret and practically irresponsible way. He justly observed that should unfortunately a difficulty arise in India which would excite great public attention in England, the British public unless properly instructed in Indian affairs would probably sweep away the Indian Government in a day. England, to secure the permanence of her rule should weigh carefully both the opinions of the experienced officers, and the claims put forward by the leaders of that intellectual movement which had lately taken place in India. The National Congress movement should not be regarded as the embodiment of every thing that is bad and should not be denounced as seditious. Sir Charles Dilke thought that most right-minded people would agree with him that the time had come when the English Government ought to continue the process which it had already adopted of associating with Englishmen in an increasing degree the natives of the country in the administration of India—following the lines upon which it had travelled in the past. The close contact that is taking place between Russia and England in Central Asia should further awaken the interest of Englishmen in that dependency which is the brightest jewel in England's diadem. Sir Charles Dilke had made a special study of the N. W. Frontier question and he rightly held that it was not desirable that the frontiers of the two powers should be brought in close contact all along the line. He also cautioned the authorities in India against making English rule unpopular by grinding taxation in the face of this great military danger. Should the conscience of England awaken to her responsibilities in India, the injustice that is often done to India and her people would cease to exist.

THE MARQUIS OF LANSDOWNE.—It had been officially announced early in the year that the Marquis of Lansdowne would succeed the Marquis of Dufferin in the Indian Viceroyalty. His Lordship's selection for this important office was received with general approbation in England. His Lordship came of a family that had long played an important part in the politics of England and his grandfather, who had on one occasion delivered a most important speech on Indian affairs, was justly considered as one of the most eminent of English statesmen of his generation. His Lordship had been trained in politics from his earliest years and as Governor-General of Canada had proved a great success and displayed rare tact on all occasions. On his return from Canada he received a series of entertainments in England and it was in connection with these that he delivered his first utterances on India. As Parliamentary under secretary for India for a short period in Mr. Gladstone's second administration he had got some acquaintance with Indian affairs but his utterances in England plainly showed that it was with no light heart that he accepted the duties and responsibilities of his exalted office. In replying to the address presented to him by some Indian gentlemen at Lord Northbrook's house he laid special stress on the fact that the India of to-day was essentially different from the India of 1833 that during the last 30 years India had made great progress morally and materially and the change that had come from the spread of education, had made the supremacy of British Crown to rest more on the sympathy and good will of the people than upon the mere exhibition of physical force. Lord Lansdowne on his arrival in Bombay was warmly received and he displayed sound sense in the speeches that he delivered there. On the 10th December he assumed charge of his new office and the impressive ceremonials as well as the salute from the ramparts of Fort William announced that the 280 millions in India had passed under a new ruler. In his reply to the addresses that were presented to him in Calcutta His Lordship uttered noble sentiments although he cautiously refrained from expressing any opinions. He justly said that the Viceroy must be a hard-worked student for some time and must study all facts and figures on the spot before he could make up his mind on the important administrative problems of India. Though placed at the head of a great Empire, his Lordship did not lay aside the simplicity of a private citizen. Lord Dufferin in speaking of his successor predicted for him universal popularity and acceptance. Would that the future historian af India be in a position conscientiously to declare that that prophecy has been fulfilled to the very letter.

THE END OF THE THIRD PART.

www.ingramcontent.com/pod-product-compliance
Lightning Source LLC
Chambersburg PA
CBHW051727300426
44115CB00007B/499